SLOWHAND

Also by Philip Norman

Fiction
Slip On a Fat Lady
Plumridge
Wild Thing (short stories)
The Skaters' Waltz
Words of Love (short stories)
Everyone's Gone to the Moon
The Avocado Fool

Biography and journalism
Shout! The True Story of the Beatles
The Stones
The Road Goes On For Ever
Tilt the Hourglass and Begin Again
Your Walrus Hurt the One You Love
Awful Moments
Pieces of Hate
Sir Elton
The Life and Good Times of the Rolling Stones
Days in the Life: John Lennon Remembered
The Age of Parody
Buddy: the Biography
John Lennon: the Life
Mick Jagger
Paul McCartney: the Biography

Autobiography
Babycham Night: A Boyhood at the End of the Pier

Plays and musicals
Words of Love
The Man That Got Away
This is Elvis: Viva Las Vegas
Laughter in the Rain: the Neil Sedaka Story

SLOWHAND

The Life and Music of Eric Clapton

PHILIP NORMAN

WEIDENFELD & NICOLSON

First published in Great Britain in 2018
by Weidenfeld & Nicolson

1 3 5 7 9 10 8 6 4 2

A CIP catalogue record for this book
is available from the British Library.

ISBN 9781474606554
TPB   9781474606561

Typeset by Input Data Services Ltd, Somerset

Printed and bound by CPI Group (UK) Ltd, Croydon, CR0 4YY

Weidenfeld & Nicolson

The Orion Publishing Group Ltd
Carmelite House
50 Victoria Embankment
London, EC4Y 0DZ

An Hachette UK Company

www.orionbooks.co.uk

CONTENTS

PROLOGUE:
A CLOCKWORK STRAWBERRY

I t's December 1969, and lunchtime in a busy motorway cafeteria a few miles south of Leeds. Standing in the self-service queue are half a dozen young men whose shoulder-length hair, biblical beards and homespun clothes give them the look of nineteenth-century evangelists. Their fellow customers recognise them as rock musicians, pick up their mostly American accents and stare with curiosity or hostility, but no one yet realises that they include George Harrison.

Since the time of America's Moon landing in July, it has been clear the Beatles are headed for break-up and that, with the saddest synchronicity, they and the 1960s may come to an end together. But every press report has the fractious four battling behind closed doors in London's Mayfair. How can one of them – especially the most private, fastidious one – possibly be 170 miles to the north, in this unsympathetic environment of harsh strip-lights, clashing trays and greasy smells?

George is interrogating a female counterhand as to whether the mushroom soup of the day contains meat. 'It's mushroom soup,' she reiterates patiently, still not recognising the face behind the beard or the voice. 'It could be made with meat stock, though,' George persists. 'I'm a vegetarian, you see . . .' Meanwhile, the bushy-bearded, fur-coated figure who's next in line loads a plate with eggs, chips, bacon and baked beans and, for dessert, chooses a portion of synthetic-looking trifle in a frilled paper cup. He's the twenty-four-year-old Eric Clapton. At the cash-register, he remembers he's carrying no money – in this case not a mark of poverty but royalty. 'Can anyone lend me a pound?' he asks with a shamefaced grin at the incongruity of it.

The two choose a table in a deserted sector, where their companions respectfully leave them by themselves. George starts to eat his mushroom soup in the way taught at young ladies' 'finishing-schools', tilting the bowl away from him, plying his spoon outwards. After a few spoonfuls, he detects the presence of meat and pushes the bowl aside. By now, he's been noticed, if not yet positively identified, by a trio of women nearby, collecting dirty crockery with a trolley. After a murmured conference, their crew-boss, a formidable-looking Yorkshire matriarch, approaches and says, 'It is you, isn't it?'

'No,' George replies.

But there's no escape: the women crowd round, paper napkins are produced and, dutiful Beatle that he still is, he signs them as directed for Sharon, June and their leader's grandson, 'little Willis'. 'Why don't you ask Engelbert here for an autograph as well?' he suggests.

The trio turn to the table-companion who's quietly working his way through his outsize fry-up. In truth, the most ardent Eric Clapton fans, even those who regard him as 'God', might have difficulty in recognising him today. His Apostolic beard is newly grown, replacing the earnest Zapata moustache he previously wore in homage to his best friend George, which in turn had superseded a mushroom-cloud Afro copied from Jimi Hendrix. No one else in his profession changes their look so frequently and radically. To these three least likely aficionados of psychedelic rock, all that can be said for certain is that he isn't Engelbert Humperdinck.

'Actually,' George continues in the same flatlining tone, 'this is the world's greatest white guitarist . . . Bert Weedon.'

Another Beatly in-joke: few of Britain's modern guitar stars would be where they are today without Weedon's *Play in a Day* tuition-book. But with his lounge suits, crinkly dyed-blond hair and big white Hofner President, no one less rock 'n' roll than dear old Bert can be imagined.

The trolley-boss realises it's a wind-up, bridles with annoyance, but makes one last sally on behalf of little Willis's autograph collection. 'Are you a group as well?' she asks Clapton sternly.

'No,' he says, avoiding her eye. 'Just a hanger-on.'

Not every famous band's break-up is a world-stopping tragedy like the Beatles'. Just a year prior to this encounter, the supergroup Cream – consisting of Clapton, drummer Ginger Baker and bass-player Jack Bruce and so named because each was previously in a top group – separated after only two years together. A fusion of old-fashioned blues with embryo heavy metal and freewheeling modern jazz, Cream were largely responsible for transforming pop into louder, more male-oriented rock; in their brief career they sold 15 million albums, of which the third, *Wheels Of Fire*, was the first double one to go platinum twice over.

Clapton has a history of walking out of bands at their peak (first the Yardbirds, then John Mayall's Bluesbreakers), but this time his well-known restlessness was less a factor than the mutual, often violent hostility between Bruce and Baker in Cream's premature curdling. Anyway, these days top bands continually split and re-form in different shapes like amoeba in a psychedelic light-show. Throughout the Anglo-American rock community, musicians are resigning from ensembles where they feel misunderstood, or whose commercial success has begun to weigh on them, and joining up with kindred spirits to play the kind of stuff they've always really yearned to.

When Graham Nash quits the Hollies to team with David

Crosby from the Byrds and Steven Stills from Buffalo Springfield as Crosby, Stills and Nash, it seems that this pooling of top-level talent can't get any better. But then, seven months after the end of Cream, Clapton and Ginger Baker are revealed to have joined forces with vocalist-organist Stevie Winwood from Traffic (and before that, the Spencer Davis Group) and bass-player Rick Grech from Family. Eschewing the new fashion for baptising bands with their members' surnames like law firms, the super-supergroup will be called Blind Faith.

Though long ago credited with genius by his peers, Clapton at this moment is far from a national celebrity. In the Britain of 1969, rock music doesn't yet titillate every generation and permeate every level of life. It belongs wholly to youth; the most visible part of that long-haired, unruly nation-within-a-nation known as the underground or counterculture. The Beatles apart, its luminaries are regarded as outside normal society, appearing in the national media only in negative contexts such as promiscuity, drunkenness and drug-abuse. With his still-spotless record as regards all three, Clapton has remained largely unknown to anyone over thirty.

Lately, however, he's made a transition from the music trades to the society columns that only Mick Jagger had managed before him. The reason is his engagement to the Hon. Alice Ormsby-Gore, youngest daughter of the 5th Baron Harlech, a hereditary peer and former British Ambassador in Washington. Fleet Street loves this very Sixties romance between a member of one of Wales's noblest families and a working-class boy from Surrey, and there's little mention of the fact that when they met, the Hon. Alice had only just turned sixteen.

Blind Faith's live debut is a free concert in London's Hyde Park on 7 June in front of an estimated 120,000 people. The occasion kicks off a summer destined to be filled with epic open-air festivals marshalling rock's premier division – the Rolling Stones also in Hyde Park, Bob Dylan on the Isle of Wight, Jimi Hendrix, the Who, the Grateful Dead and Janis Joplin at Woodstock – as if the Sixties' thrice-blessed children are trying to hold on to the golden decade as long as possible and squeeze every last drop of joy from it.

Blind Faith's eponymous first album is delayed by wrangles between the different record companies to which its members are contracted, so doesn't come out until August. The cover shows an eleven-year-old girl with cloudy pre-Raphaelite hair, naked to the waist and brandishing a phallic-looking silver space ship – an image which, even in these permissive times, is notably pushing the boundaries. It immediately goes to number 1 in both Britain and the US (over there even entering the black R&B charts).

But for Clapton, Blind Faith do not live up to their hype and on their debut American tour, it becomes an increasing burden to him. He realises they're under-rehearsed and have launched before building up enough original material: onstage, they soon exhaust the supply of their own songs and have to fall back on old hits by Cream and Stevie Winwood's former band, Traffic, so that some rock critics, mortifyingly, dub them 'Supercream'.

Fatefully, among the tour's supporting acts are the American husband-and-wife country blues duo Delaney & Bonnie. Delaney Bramlett hails from Mississippi, a black-bearded, God-fearin', hell-raisin' good ol' boy. Eastern-born Bonnie is his antithesis: angel-faced, blonde and refined-looking. In the early 1960s, she became the only white woman ever recruited into Ike and Tina Turner's Ikettes, the sexiest of all backing groups. Seemingly in reaction to that, although still only twenty-five, she cultivates a grandmotherly look, pinning her golden hair haphazardly on top of her head and peering over little spectacles perched on her retroussé nose.

Clapton is immediately drawn to the Bramletts, whose soulful acoustic music seems to have all the integrity he finds lacking in Blind Faith. He starts hanging out with them, writing songs with them, even joining them onstage while giving over more and more prominence in his own band to Stevie Winwood. By the end of the tour, Blind Faith are finished and Clapton is planning to record with Delaney & Bonnie and go on the road with them. In token of his retreat from hype and over-adulation, they'll be the headliners while he merely plays in the back-up band known simply as their Friends.

The Bramletts soon feel the financial clout of that unassuming chap who never has any money on him. Their Friends are otherwise made up of high-quality sidemen brought over from America, including drummer Jim Gordon, guitarist/keyboards-player Bobby Whitlock, bass guitarist Carl Radle and saxophonist Bobby Keys. Their new Friend-in-chief pays all the troupe's air fares and hotel bills and gives them the run of his country mansion to rehearse with a set of expensive new amplifiers he's had shipped over from New York.

It's an odd moment to crave anonymity, since he's currently being interviewed for a profile in the London *Sunday Times*'s hugely prestigious and glamorous colour magazine whose readership is around 1.5 million, and his portrait is to be taken by the magazine's star photographer, the Earl of Snowdon.

That the Queen's brother-in-law (husband of her sister, Princess Margaret) should be a working photojournalist epitomises how the 1960s have sent Britain's ancient class barriers tumbling. But rock music will not touch the Royal Family for some years yet and Lord Snowdon, whose subjects are normally the elderly and impoverished, asks the profile-writer – me – to suggest how and where the portrait might be shot. I mention the graffito that appeared on a London tube-station wall in 1965 when our subject was still in John Mayall's Bluesbreakers. CLAPTON, some anonymous spraycan-artist declared, IS GOD.

The earl takes it literally, mobilising two assistants, a bank of strobe lights, an illustrated guide to the pagan deities of Norse and Germanic mythology and a smoke machine. The Delaney & Bonnie tour rehearsals are in progress at the Lyceum, a subterranean, gilt-encrusted ballroom just off London's Strand. Snowdon photographs Clapton alone on the dance-floor with a vintage black Gibson Les Paul. He's temporarily clean-shaven, revealing a face one cannot call good-looking or bad-looking, or anything really, with its wide-set eyes, pointed nose and slightly receding chin. But already, as if by some instinctive defence mechanism, the first tendrils of a new moustache have begun to sprout.

Shot from below, looming through icy clouds of dry ice with features convulsed as if in pain or ecstasy (though more likely in reaction to the smoke), he resembles a T-shirted Wotan hefting a thousand-watt spear; all that's lacking are Wagner's *Ride of the Valkyries* and a horned helmet.

On 1 December, Delaney & Bonnie and Friends appear at London's Royal Albert Hall, where Cream gave their already legendary farewell concerts almost exactly a year earlier. Ordinarily, it would be a wildly over-ambitious venue for a visiting American act with neither a hit single nor album in the UK. But the name Eric Clapton on the poster has guaranteed that it's sold out.

The troupe wait to be called onstage at the mouth of a tunnel, overlooked by a block of seats. A boy as slight and inconspicuous as Clapton spots him below and calls out, 'You're great, Eric.'

'Thanks, man,' he answers resignedly.

The evening's emcee introduces him as 'the guy who got this gig together and the band will be going to play around . . .' True to his promise, Clapton stays out of the limelight, standing on the right, well behind Delaney, identifiable only by the puffed-out sleeves of his grey silk shirt. But it soon becomes clear the audience is homing in on his guitar as if picking the best bits out of a salad. Among the songs he's written with the Bramletts is 'Comin' Home', counterpointing Delaney's near-falsetto with a bass riff like an early rough sketch for 'Layla'. Each growl of the riff receives an ovation.

He has the type of 'white' blues singing voice that many young Britons have discovered in themselves, most notably Georgie Fame and Stevie Winwood. But although he's sung in both Cream and Blind Faith, it's been little more than underscoring to Jack Bruce or Winwood. The Bramletts have told him he's far better than that, Delaney warning in Southern-preacher fire 'n' brimstone style that if he doesn't use his voice as he should, 'God will take it away.'

Unluckily, their British television debut together was on a show co-hosted by Georgie Fame and an equally bluesy-voiced Brit, Alan Price, formerly of the Animals. Seemingly intimidated by such competition (even though neither Fame nor Price performed on camera with the D&B troupe), Clapton remained a country-picking accompanist, glancing diffidently at Delaney as if to join in the vocal would have been the height of presumption.

But tonight, he sings lead on J. J. Cale's 'After Midnight' and on 'I Don't Know Why', a big-production soul number co-written with the Bramletts. Each brings the Albert Hall to its feet, rapturous that this time he's not saying goodbye but hello – and they can hear it.

The tour begins in West Germany and Scandinavia, then returns to Britain where I join its northern leg to round off my *Sunday Times Magazine* profile of Clapton. His publicist Robin Turner is on hand, but these are the days before PR people hover possessively over star clients, doling out access in half-hour portions in hotel-rooms. I ride the bus with the musicians, hang out with them between shows and watch every performance from the wings.

From this privileged vantage point, I notice an addition to the Friends: an extra guitarist in a black Stetson hat and buckskin jacket whose gaunt, bearded face noticeably lacks the good humour of his American colleagues. It's George Harrison, who has joined the tour to escape the strife among his fellow Beatles and get used to playing live again after years shut away in the recording studio. He keeps well to the back of the stage, providing chords only. Until the story gets out in *Melody Maker* – and in a motorway cafeteria near Leeds – the audiences have no idea who he is.

Here up north, 'Clapton is God' tends to be taken at face value and since the Blind Faith debacle, many have wondered when they'll see him again, if ever. His only concern is that they should appreciate his protégés and he's visibly upset when their response proves tepid. Robin Turner says the Scandinavian audiences showed even less tact: 'Eric was almost in tears because people were shouting for Delaney & Bonnie to get off the stage and for him to play on his own.'

For Turner, this whole exercise is yet further evidence of 'Eric's chameleon personality', something which goes far deeper than hair follicles. 'He has a way of turning into whoever he's with. When he was hanging out a lot with George Harrison, he bought a big house like George's and a big Mercedes . . . George gave him his Indian-painted Mini. When he was with Stevie Winwood, setting up Blind Faith, he went back to jeans and wanting to live out in the country. When he met Delaney & Bonnie, he gave up travelling first class and just climbed aboard their bus.'

Even with this colossally distinguished Friend among the Bramletts' retinue, downhome togetherness prevails. There are no star dressing-rooms: Clapton, Harrison and the Americans share communal changing areas with their British support band,

Ashton, Gardner and Dyke. Clapton's guitars lie around out of their cases, unguarded: his cherished Gibson Les Paul; a metal Dobro dating from the 1930s; a custom-made Zemaitis acoustic twelve-string, inlaid in silver, that he calls 'Ivan the Terrible'. At one point he picks it up to show George something and, looping its strap over his head, says in all seriousness, 'I'm not very good at chords.'

Perpetually circulating joints aside, there's none of the depravity associated with rock tours – at least, none visible. No move is made to trash any of the gloomy old grand hotels where they're accommodated, despite the surly staff and impossibly pretentious restaurants which refuse service to long hair, ponchos and crushed velvet trousers on principle, and close as early as nine p.m.

Nor are there groupies or orgies; quite the opposite, the Americans with their solemn beards and grave, old-fashioned speech ('I don't care for any, thank you' . . .) give the impression of a non-stop Bible meeting. In any case, Bonnie Bramlett, always the focus of things in her granny glasses, wearing a shawl, working at a piece of embroidery and sometimes breaking into a soul-smoky gospel song, would act as a powerful deterrent.

When I get Clapton alone – as I can pretty much any time between shows – he's friendly and candid, speaking in a Sixties-classless voice with a faint Surrey burr. I notice the dull teeth that are the legacy of most British boys born during or just after the Second World War. He's articulate far beyond usual rock-star level and better-read than any I've met before, save only John Lennon. At the moment, he's immersed in A.J. Cronin's *Hatter's Castle*, the story of a tyrannical Scottish hat-maker which reaches its climax with the 1879 Tay Bridge railway disaster. He already loves the 1942 film noir version, starring Robert Newton and the young James Mason.

He tells me about Robert Johnson, the blues musician who

for him surpasses all others; a figure likewise credited with genius as a very young man. It resonates hugely with him that at recording-sessions Johnson was too humble to look the engineer in the eye, but sang and played facing the wall.

He also talks about his childhood, something rock celebrities in this era seldom do. I'm the first interviewer to hear how he was brought up by his grandmother, believing that she was his mother, and how when his real mother came back into his life, he had to pretend she was his grown-up sister. This creates a bond, for there was a similar deception in my own family that blighted my existence for years afterwards. I assume the Sixties have helped him get over it just as they've helped me.

When I raise the question of his personal wealth – in reference to all that expensive equipment given to the Delaney & Bonnie band – he's neither offended nor evasive. 'I dunno how much I got, man,' he confesses.

Rock stars are granted a second childhood – for the rest of their lives if they choose – and nowhere more so than when on tour. In one of our conversations, he reminisces about his days with the Yardbirds, belting up and down Britain packed into a single van, and about musicians' roadside meeting places like the Ram Jam Inn. 'And there was a transport caff just off the M1 called the Blue Boar where you could get away with anything. Throwing plates of fried tomatoes . . . anything.'

Those memories of the old Blue Boar are clearly hard to shake. In Newcastle-on-Tyne, the hotel has unbent sufficiently to leave a cold supper laid out for the musicians after the show. It's an impressive spread but not much of it gets eaten, for Clapton starts a food-fight that leaves everyone soaked in mayonnaise and vinaigrette and picking lettuce leaves and bits of sweet-corn out of their hair and beards, helpless with laughter. 'That was great,' he says later with the exhilaration of someone fresh from a spa.

Delaney Bramlett, that black-bearded, roistering good ol' boy, has become his soulmate. During the few daylight hours that see rock musicians up and about, they disappear together for long periods, apparently perpetrating juvenile mischief in the wider world. When they return from one such expedition, Delaney has somehow lost one whole leg of his jeans up to the thigh. He continues wearing them nonetheless, even onstage.

Before the second Newcastle show, the pair sally forth again, intending to purchase water pistols. Instead they return with a quantity of little plastic fruit, oranges, lemons and pears with grotesque, leering faces that can be wound up to walk a few un-steady paces on undersized legs .That night, while the support band, Ashton, Gardner and Dyke, are playing, Clapton ducks onstage and sets a lemon toddling along the top of Tony Ashton's electric organ.

After the show, they all hold races with the clockwork fruit on the dressing-room floor. It's a scene I'll always remember: the long-haired, hippy-garbed figures cheering on their chosen miniature oranges, cherries or grapefruit; Bonnie Bramlett, gold-haired and grannyish, an island of tranquillity, working at her embroidery and softly singing 'Oh Happy Day'; her black-bearded spouse, with one leg clothed in blue denim and one bare, encouraging a scarlet strawberry: 'C'mon Big Red! You're a winner, Big Red! Go, Big Red . . . go!'

My last night with the tour is in Liverpool, a city which has raised no monument to its four most famous sons and now seemingly never will. Out of respect for George Harrison, the subject is never mentioned. Instead, the talk turns to last August's Woodstock festival and its surprise hit, an American vocal group named Sha Na Na who perform Fifties rock 'n' roll as knockabout comedy.

None of the Sixties' musical heroes, Dylan included, would

be where they are without those primordial anthems by Elvis Presley, Little Richard, Chuck Berry and the rest. Throughout the decade, they've put rock 'n' roll firmly behind them, focusing always on evolution and experimentation. But on the cusp of the Seventies – with Heaven knows what lying ahead – there's a rush of nostalgia for its exuberance, simplicity and what's recognised now as wondrous innocence.

So this evening's Delaney & Bonnie show features a bunch of golden oldies like Richard's 'Rip It Up', all so familiar that they don't need rehearsing. Despite the fine specimens all around him, Clapton's bushy beard has not returned and to get into the Fifties spirit he wets his hair and combs it into a Teddy Boy quiff that finally stamps some character on his naked face – a faint look of Gene Vincent.

The so-called rock 'n' roll 'tribute' is intended as parody – but those old three-chord chestnuts prove as potent as ever. By the end, a guitar virtuoso who normally seldom moves onstage, and never smiles, is angling his fretboard . . . going down on one knee like Cliff Gallup from Vincent's band the Blue Caps . . . actually laughing.

Even George feels the exhilaration. 'I'd forgotten what a gas playing live can be,' he says afterwards 'That Little Richard medley is in E, isn't it?'

Though the tour's live album will give Delaney & Bonnie the intended boost and Delaney will go on to produce Clapton's first solo album, his acoustic-folk-rock-Lawd A'mighty-ham 'n' grits-down-on-the-bayou interlude is nearing its end. In rock's ever-changing light-show, a new amoeba is soon to take shape.

A few months from now, Delaney & Bonnie's Friends will be no more and Clapton will have taken the nucleus to form yet another band – one giving a new twist to his relentless self-effacement. In tune with the burgeoning rock 'n' roll revival, their name will hark back to late-Fifties vocal groups whose leaders went semi-incognito (Dion and the Belmonts, Danny and the Juniors, Little Anthony and the Imperials), while wryly suggesting some clunky British contribution to the genre. They will be Derek and the Dominos, the vehicle for one of rock's greatest love songs and for their modestly pseudonymised leader to embark on the seduction of his Beatle best friend's wife.

Backstage in Liverpool, Delaney little suspects what a different place Clapton's head is already in while they and the others race their clockwork fruit over the changing-room floor. Crouched down with one leg still bare, the Satanic-looking good ol' boy cheers on his plastic strawberry, which does indeed seem to possess a turn of speed its orange, lemon and grapefruit rivals do not. 'C'mon, Big Red . . . don't let me down! You can do this! Go, Big Red, go!'

He wails in frustration – a foretaste of much more to come – as Big Red hits a bump in the carpet and topples over, its legs continuing to rotate feebly.

INTRO:
THE SUPERSURVIVOR

When I wrote *Paul McCartney: the Biography*, following on from *John Lennon: the Life* and *Shout!* the *Mail on Sunday*'s book-reviewer, Craig Brown, noted playfully that it brought the number of printed pages I'd produced about the Beatles to 2,106.* 'By contrast,' Brown wrote, 'Tolstoy's *War and Peace* weighs in at a modest, almost petite 1,273 pages.'

Even allowing that the Beatles' story, in its own way, resembles a Tolstoyan epic – and that nowadays encyclopedia-size books are devoted to individual years of the 1960s – my writing career may well look unhealthily Fab Four-fixated. In fact, I've also written biographies of the Rolling Stones, Elton John, Buddy Holly and Mick Jagger as well as novels, short stories, screenplays, television and radio drama, two produced stage musicals, an autobiography and journalism on a wide variety of subjects.

As I often protest – maybe too much – a 'rock biographer' was something I never set out to be. When I began *Shout!* in the late Seventies it was intended as a one-off, aimed at challenging the universal belief that everybody already knew everything there was to know about the Beatles. I little suspected it was the start of a chain reaction that would chain me for decades to come. After *Shout!*, I could hardly not move on to the Stones, whose story overlapped their supposed Liverpudlian arch-rivals' in

---

* Excluding paperback and foreign editions.

15

so many ways. The same was true of Elton John, who would never have dominated the post-Beatles charts and arenas without the sponsorship of their music publisher, Dick James. Those two books inevitably propelled me to Buddy Holly, whose vocal style, songwriting and backing group, the Crickets, first inspired both the Beatles and Stones, and who got Elton wearing glasses, even though his eyesight was normal.

Actually, I was writing one continuous narrative of indubitably Tolstoyan scale: how British popular music conquered the world in the second half of the twentieth century and created a seemingly everlasting template. Now and again I'd try to break free of my typecasting, only for another segment of the story and another publisher's advance to offer themselves enticingly; like Michael Corleone, struggling to break free of his Mafia crime family, just when I thought I was out, they pulled me back in again.

But after Paul McCartney, who next? A life of George or Ringo did not attract me; still less the thought of bringing my Beatles word-count closer to that of the *Encyclopaedia Britannica*. I've limited myself to writing only about music's tiny topmost echelon; names that provoke the same instant, excited reaction in every country and culture. By that measure, even behemoths like Led Zeppelin, Pink Floyd or Queen don't quite qualify; the only ones up there with the Beatles and Stones are Presley, Hendrix and Bowie (market already saturated), Dylan and Michael Jackson (each undoable for reasons too numerous to mention), and Eric Clapton.

CLAPTON IS GOD, that anonymous spraycan-artist declared more than half a century ago. Although rock stars are often treated like deities, the title has only ever been formally conferred on somebody who at first glance might seem underequipped for the topmost echelon. He writes songs, but without the fecundity of a McCartney or a Dylan; he sings, but always seemingly a bit under sufferance; as a performer, he has none of the flamboyance or daring of a Bowie or a Jackson. Such things are of no account when set against his single, immense gift, the ability to conjure magic from a slab of electrified wood.

Over the years, he has seemed less like a god than some mythic gunfighter or pool-player whom young upstarts are constantly challenging, only to retire defeated like everyone else (bar Hendrix). He's the guitar's Wyatt Earp or Minnesota Fats, peerless not only in rock but in the blues, a form which for generations was supposedly the preserve of poor black troubadours bewailing the hardship and oppression of their lives. The elite of Chicago and Memphis – the likes of Muddy Waters, B. B. King and Buddy Guy – were likewise to bow down before this white boy from the sedate English county of Surrey.

It is not merely a question of fast fingers nor even a unique 'sound', for Clapton has created so many across a spectrum from heavy metal to reggae. Like the supreme soloists in the classical sphere – the violinist Yehudi Menuhin springs most to mind – his mastery can touch the sublime, as if it comes from somewhere outside his so ordinary-seeming self. Carlos Santana, his nearest counterpart in the Latino sphere, defines such moments as 'when the Holy Ghost takes over'.

In the Sixties, when lead guitarists turned from soloists into superheroes, Clapton was the first, adorning three of the decade's most revered bands – the Yardbirds before Cream and Blind Faith – changing his appearance for each one and walking away from each when it failed to live up to his exacting standards. Uniquely, he became an ex-officio member both of the Beatles and the Rolling Stones, at the same time backing every great name of the era from Dylan to Aretha Franklin, as well as many of the American bluesmen he had worshipped since boyhood.

In the Seventies, initially with the deepest misgivings, he made the transition from team player whom no team could ever satisfy to solo recording artist and performer. It was a move that ultimately brought him record sales of 129 million, eighty gold, platinum, multi-platinum or diamond discs, eighteen Grammy awards and an unprecedented three inductions under different headings into the Rock 'n' Roll Hall of Fame. Yet his concerts were conspicuously without the spectacle and egomania rock audiences normally expect. All they ever wanted was that lone figure with the close-cut beard on which his face finally settled, usually wearing jeans like the bricklayer he almost became and crafting his matchless licks as impassively as if rinsing out a pair of socks.

Rock's greatest guitarists are not remembered for their solos but their riffs: intros and recurring phrases that define a song in half a dozen notes or less and plunge it into the listener's bloodstream before a word is sung. There's no better example than Derek and the Dominos' 'Layla' with Clapton's Fender, abetted by Duane Allman's Gibson, not gently weeping but wailing with inadmissible desire; a secret hard-on in sound.

Not the least remarkable thing about his career is how much of it he's managed to spend out of the headlines. Almost all the problems that normally go with great celebrity and longevity in the rock business seem to have passed him by. His epic addictions to drugs and alcohol never resulted in any but the slightest brushes with the law and did not reach the media until he himself was ready to confess them. Aside from a single, atypical incident in the mid-1970s, he's never been guilty of any seriously bad behaviour in public; never had to endure an embarrassing divorce-case or paternity-suit; never had children who grew up to be shiftless, damaged brats; never been pilloried for either ludicrous extravagance or meanness; never been clobbered by the Inland Revenue; never appeared on any list of offshore tax-avoiders; never had to spend fortunes on suing his management or record company or being sued by them.

Despite often considering himself the most unfortunate of mortals, he was blessed with amazing luck, leaving by the back door just before the police burst in through the front, walking away from car crashes without a bruise or a prosecution, botching serial suicide attempts, narrowly missing a helicopter crash which killed a fellow guitarist, two of his road crew and his agent, being rescued in the nick of time from drowning, and diagnosed in the nick of time not only with lethal heroin addiction and alcoholism but bleeding ulcers, epilepsy and pleurisy – all similarly on the quiet.

Only in one area was he unable to keep the covers completely on his life. From his twenties to his forties, he was a womaniser on the scale of Mick Jagger, a sex addict before the term was invented, with a jaw-dropping recklessness all his own. 'He never had to do anything,' observes a management figure who knew him in the 1980s. 'Women just stuck to him like iron filings to a magnet.'

Rock's most famous love triangle was created when he fell in love with Pattie Boyd, the wife of his best friend, George Harrison, wooing her from the concert stage and record turntable with 'Layla', the song he had written in adoration of her. As she afterwards recalled, that lovelorn, wailing riff did as much as the lyric's entreaties to wear down her resistance. A plectrum has never had more formidable pulling power.

His very nickname of Slowhand – originally not a compliment at all – was borrowed by the Pointer Sisters' 1981 hit single to signify the perfect sexual partner, endlessly patient, considerate and skilled in strumming sans guitar: I want a man with a slow hand . . . I want a lover with an easy touch . . . .*

Less alluringly, not even Jagger better illustrated the price of being a rock star's 'old lady' and living with the egotism,

* Lyrics by John Bettis and Michael Clark.

19

ruthlessness and insensibility to the feelings of others that are basic job specifications for the breed. With Clapton's old ladies (a laughable misnomer), the price could include addictions as bad as his, or worse, and permanent collateral damage while he moved on to the next one without a backward glance.

But after all those decades of getting off scot-free came a dreadful reckoning. In 1991, his child with the Italian actress Lory Del Santo, a four-year-old son named Conor, accidentally fell from the fifty-third-floor window of a New York apartment building. A man who had shrunk from the public gaze through-out his career, and whose capacity for emotion outside music had always seemed limited, now went to the uttermost oppos-ite extreme, baring his grief in a song called 'Tears In Heaven'. No old-time vagrant bluesman had ever plumbed such depths of misery as he among his mansions and Ferraris.

As he advances into his seventies, he still performs more or less continuously, seemingly unable to give up a life that once seemed intolerable past the age of thirty. And these days, he knows how much he's got, man. Concert-earnings, back royal-ties and publishing (unlike the Beatles or Stones, he controls all his own songs), a superb art collection, several lavish homes and innumerable expensive cars add up to an estimated fortune of £170 million, eleventh equal with Rod Stewart on the London *Sunday Times's* Rock Stars Rich List.

One of the most thoroughly dissolute rockers of olden times has become the most thoroughly reformed. The former drunk and druggie in excelsis is a pillar of Alcoholics Anonymous and a leading campaigner against drug-abuse who has poured mil-lions into the Crossroads treatment centre he helped to found in Antigua. If he missed out on the knighthoods given to his old friends Elton, Paul and Mick, at least his 1995 OBE (Order of the British Empire) was upgraded to CBE (Commander of the Brit-ish Empire) in 2004. And there's still time.

At the age of fifty-four, his seeming quest to seduce every female in the world came to an end when he met his second wife, a twenty-three-year-old American student named Melia McEnery. While herself maintaining a compatibly low profile, she has borne him three daughters; some restitution for the hideous tragedy of 1991. And to all appearances, she is the only woman to whom he has ever been completely faithful.

'Survivor' is a term commonly given to anyone whom rock music has not killed or sent insane or reduced to playing Golden Oldie weekends in Skegness. For Eric Clapton, as one surveys his six decades in the topmost echelon, it seems wholly inadequate. To borrow the prefix he so much hated when it was attached to groups in which he played, he is a supersurvivor.

As a journalist, I interviewed him face-to-face only that one time for the *Sunday Times Magazine* in December 1969. When we said goodbye after the Snowdon photo-shoot, he was wearing a dark blue bespoke suit with a white T-shirt saying TORONTO ROCK 'N' ROLL REVIVAL – an adventurous combination for then. 'Put it there, mate,' he said with unexpected warmth, offering me his hand.

My profile ran early in the New Year, headlined 'The Great God Clapton' with Snowdon's *Götterdämmerung* portrait as a double-page spread turned sideways (that was the old *Sunday Times Magazine* for you). I received no direct reaction from Clapton, but gathered he'd liked it: that summer, when the *New York Times* approached him for an interview about Jimi Hendrix's death, he agreed on condition I was the interviewer. I said I would do it, and was in discussions with the *Times* when my magazine bosses sent me off to America to write about the Motown organisation.

In 1972, I published *Wild Thing*, a collection of short stories thinly fictionalising my various encounters with rock, blues and country stars for the *Sunday Times*. Its title story was based on the Delaney & Bonnie tour and featured a restless, capricious guitar hero whom I named Reg Lubin. I don't know if Clapton ever read it, though his friend, and frequent saviour, Pete Townshend did and sent me a nice note, saying I had drawn him to the life.

Our only further contact came in the late 1980s when I was researching the Elton John biography and he talked to me on the phone about his occasional collaborations with Elton. I mentioned Delaney & Bonnie and the clockwork fruit races backstage, and he chuckled at the memory. It was during my American publicity tour for that book in 1991, stopping off in Atlanta, Georgia, that I first heard 'Tears In Heaven' on the radio. I'd recently become a father for the first time and the desolation in his voice had me in tears.

For someone contemplating a biography in any genre, the first task is a scan for possible competitors, past and pending. In Clapton's case, the only one of any significance is Ray Coleman's *Survivor*, an authorised life published back in 1986. There have been various unauthorised attempts since then, most recently *Motherless Child* by Paul Scott (not the author of *The Raj Quartet*) in 2015 to capitalise on Clapton's seventieth birthday. Repeated tail-gunner sweeps revealed no pre-emptive chronicler who might be reviewed ahead of me or (almost as bad) alongside me.

A formidable deterrent was his bestselling 2007 autobiography, ghost-written by Christopher Simon Sykes, which was blisteringly frank about his addictions and infidelities and fully explained the childhood confusion – growing up thinking his grandmother was his mother – which he'd first revealed to me in 1969. But it was a speed-read, sometimes condensing whole epochs into a single paragraph and, overall, withholding as much as it revealed. Also from 2007 there was Pattie Boyd's autobiography, *Wonderful Tonight*, with her account of the fifteen tempestuous years with Clapton after she left George for him.

Though wonderfully free of blame or bitterness, it illuminated Clapton's long-time inability to find any stability or contentment outside his guitar fretboard and oft-proven ability to make his own existence hellish.

In all my years of chronicling the Beatles, I'd somehow never met Pattie, who went on from being rock music's most famous muse (not only 'Layla', 'Wonderful Tonight' and 'Bell-Bottom Blues' but George Harrison's 'Something') to become a widely exhibited photographer. She turned out to be rather curious about me and accepted an invitation to lunch at The Ivy. During a highly enjoyable three hours, we hardly mentioned Eric – or George – instead ranging over diverse subjects such as Winston Churchill, British boarding schools, the Elizabeth Arden beauty salon in Bond Street where both she and my late mother once worked, and mutual friends from the Beatles' inner circle like Neil Aspinall and Derek Taylor. It was only when seeing her into a taxi afterwards that I got around to asking if she'd talk to me for a Clapton biography. 'Yes, we can do that,' she said.

Getting in, she remembered another mutual acquaintance, Derek and the Dominos' former drummer, Jim Gordon.

'Is Jim out of prison yet?' she asked.

'I didn't know he'd gone to prison. What was it for?'

'Murdering his mother.'

That alone was enough to pull me back in again.

1

RICK

Most top British rock stars of the Sixties and Seventies lost no time in putting their birthplaces far behind them. It's hard to imagine John Lennon ever showing reluctance to leave suburban Liverpool, Mick Jagger settled and content in Dartford, Kent, or Elton John irresistibly drawn back to Pinner, Middlesex. But Eric Clapton's Italianate mansion in Ewhurst, Surrey, his main home since 1968, is only twelve miles from the village where he was born and raised and to which he remains intimately connected. 'For me,' Pattie Boyd says, 'Eric will always be the boy from Ripley.'

Village Ripley may be, but it is no isolated hamlet. Situated only twenty miles south of London, it formerly lay on the A3, the main road to Portsmouth, making it less famous for its superstar son than for sclerotic traffic-jams. Drivers becalmed in their vehicles had ample leisure to study the generous sprinkling of pubs, the church of St Mary Magdalen, boasting a chancel dating back to the twelfth century, and the ivy-fronted Talbot Hotel, an old coaching inn where Lord Nelson is said to have conducted romantic trysts with Lady Emma Hamilton.

The opening of a bypass in 1976 took away the traffic-jams, leaving a main street typical of Surrey's commuter belt: upmarket coffee-houses, an orthodontist's surgery, an interior designer, the Miss Bush Bridal Boutique in a converted Methodist chapel. The low profile Clapton has always sought so assiduously was

25

never lower than here. The sole hint of 'theming' is Ripley Guitars, its small bow window all but filled by a single candy-pink Fender Stratocaster. And that might equally signify Paul Weller, formerly of the Jam and Style Council – and born in nearby Woking – whose recording studio is just down the road.

Despite such modern amenities, village life carries on very much as for generations past, deepening the sense of unreality that a great metropolis is throbbing just over the horizon. Social life revolves around the Anglican church, St Mary Magdalen, and the cricket club, said to be one of the country's oldest. Alongside the transient daily commuters there are families who go back centuries, would not think of dwelling anywhere else on earth and regard even the neighbouring village of Send, three miles away, as pitiably alien and backward. At Send, so they say in Ripley, somebody once tried to shoe a horse while it was lying down.

Any English village worthy of the name has a communal green space, usually in its centre and quite small, where the slow white ballet of cricket is staged in summer. Ripley's, however, is to be found on its easterly margin and deviates extravagantly from type. Ripley Green, where Clapton was born and grew up, comprises 67.5 acres of open grassland with an expanse of woods and undergrowth known locally as 'the Fuzzies'. As well as parochial sports and celebrations, it has always been a venue for events that attract crowds from miles around, notably Guy Fawkes Night on 5 November, featuring a mountainous bonfire, the crowning of a 'bonfire night queen', a parade and a fun fair.

Clapton's childhood home was Number 1 The Green, the corner house in a terrace of four facing directly onto that wide communal meadow. Built in the 1890s, it was a modest 'two up, two down', originally rented to local farm workers or craftsmen But the fans who journey here from all over the world will look in vain for Number 1, nor is there any commemorative plaque to help them. When his grandmother moved out in the late 1960s, numbers 1 and 2 were bought by Ripley resident Keith Best, with whom he attended both primary and secondary school. Best knocked the two houses into one, installing a bathroom – a luxury the young Eric never enjoyed – and calling the result 'Fairview'. It's also the brand-name of a home glass-engraving business run by Best's wife, Sheila. Coincidentally, 'stained-glass designer' is the only job description other than musician that Clapton ever had.

Like those of the ancient oaks at its margin, his roots in The Green run deep. His oldest friend, Guy Pullen, the cricket club's long-time president, still lives there, in the same cottage as during their childhood, and, like many older Ripleyites, refers to him not as Eric but 'Rick'. The two remainl as close as they ever were, Pullen a frequent visitor to Hurtwood Edge, Clapton's home at Ewhurst, and guest on his yacht. Behind the kitchen door hangs a parka of evidently superior downiness. 'That was from Rick. He always gives me lovely presents. A couple of Christmases ago, he gave me a new knee. I haven't had it done yet.'

He's a permanent vice-president of the cricket club, whose green and white clubhouse juts onto The Green near the Talbot Hotel. The team's score-keeper, Jennie Cliff (also Chair of the Parish Council), was at primary school with Clapton and her grandparents lived at 1 The Green before his did. For many years, he regularly played in celebrity charity matches, bringing along fellow rockbiz enthusiasts like Rolling Stone Bill Wyman. In the end security became too difficult, the club having no VIP enclosure. 'But we send him a fixture card at the start of every season,' Jennie says.

He still pays Ripley frequent incognito visits; despite not having touched alcohol for more than thirty years, he's sometimes seen at The Ship, the pub where he and his teenage friends loved to eavesdrop on the village characters as they played dominoes and told stories. 'He knows that whenever he comes back here, he can just walk around the streets or go into a pub,' says Guy Pullen. 'No one will ever bother him.'

Off The Green, his closest ties are with St Mary Magdalen Church on the High Street. He attended its 'C of E' (Church of England) primary school, which used to be next door, and its Sunday School; its vicar, the Reverend Chris Elson, conducted the funerals of Clapton's grandmother, Rose, and mother, Pat, and married him to his second wife, Melia (and baptised two of his daughters, by different mothers, at the same ceremony). Black-bearded Reverend Elson also officiated on the day in 1991 when the coffin of four-year-old Conor Clapton was lowered into the ground and Ripley suffered its first incursion by ravening paparazzi.

It's a measure of Clapton's love for the place that, after that horrific accident in New York, he couldn't conceive of his only son's being laid to rest anywhere but here. In contrast with the ancient, weathered headstones, a small, pure-white lozenge nestles close to the church, flanked by pots of flowers, with a row of decorated pebbles in front. The inscription, in letters so fine as to be barely legible, reads *Conor Clapton 1986 – 1991 Beloved Son Sweet child of infinite beauty you will live in our hearts forever.* To help out the church's groundsman, a gardener from Hurtwood Edge comes over regularly to cut the surrounding grass and keep the path tidy.

After Conor's funeral, St Mary's churchyard was closed to any further interments. But Clapton has space booked in the adjacent parish burial-ground. 'There's no real barrier between them,' the vicar says.

In 1944, Mr Jelly's blacksmith's forge stood on the corner site that one day would be occupied by Ripley Guitars. The village then seemed more like a small town, with three bakeries, a cinema, an abattoir, a telephone exchange and a police station. The traffic passing through the High Street consisted largely of military trucks whose khaki-clad personnel wore shoulder-flashes saying *Canada*. This part of Surrey was the marshalling-area for Canadian forces waiting to join the Allied invasion of Nazi-occupied Europe on 6 June.

Around the time of D-Day, fifteen-year-old Patricia Clapton from Ripley Green became pregnant by a twenty-four-year-old Canadian serviceman named Edward Fryer whom she'd met at a dance a few weeks earlier. Fryer refused to accept responsibility, there seemed no way to coerce him, and soon afterwards he faded from Pat's life, never to reappear. On 30 March 1945, she gave birth to a son in the back bedroom of her mother's house, 1 The Green, attended only by the local midwife, whose first act was to wrap the baby in brown paper to keep him warm. He was given Pat's surname and baptised Eric Patrick.

The story he would grow up with was that his father had been an airman with a wife back home in Canada, but actually Montreal-born Fryer was a soldier and unmarried. Before the war he'd been a musician, playing piano in clubs and bars, which he continued to do while on active service; hence his appeal for jazz-loving Pat. He'd also been a talented painter, though seemingly never turned it to any account. For a time, it was thought he might have joined the later waves of Canadians into France. But military records show he stayed on in Britain until 1946, receiving a dishonourable discharge for going AWOL just as his unit was about to return home.

At a time when southern England teemed with soldiery from all over the world, thousands of young women had found themselves in Pat's predicament. But to be an unmarried mother remained the ultimate social stigma, especially one so young. She and her baby continued to live with her mother, Rose, both painfully conscious of their disgrace in the village's eyes.

Although the war was over, many Canadians remained in the district and in 1947 Pat met a second soldier, Frank McDonald, who proved altogether more stable and reliable than the elusive Fryer. They fell in love and when McDonald's tour of duty ended, he asked her to return home with him and get married. As amiable as 'Mac' was, he baulked at taking on another man's child, born out of wedlock, so Pat had to choose between them. For an eighteen-year-old, offered a new life in a country with living standards far superior to grim post-war Britain's, it was not such a hard choice. She departed for Canada, leaving Eric with his grandmother.

Rose was a tiny, dark-haired, vivacious woman from one of Ripley's oldest clans, the Mitchells, one of nine sisters and two brothers. In her twenties, she had married Pat's father, Reginald – aka Rex – Clapton, the Oxford-educated son of an army officer and thus well above her in the social scale. When Rex Clapton died of tuberculosis in 1932, she had despaired of finding another husband, for a botched surgical operation on her palate when she was thirty had left a scar like a deep crease below her left cheekbone. Nonetheless in 1942 she had remarried, to a local plasterer four years her junior, with the oddly similar surname of Clapp.

Pat was assumed to have gone for good, so the couple adopted two-year-old Eric in everything but name. To spare him the knowledge of his abandonment, they decided he should grow up believing Rose was his mother. It was not so implausible for she was still only in her late thirties and many of her contemporaries in the village had children just as young.

Tall, dark, bushy-browed Jack Clapp was an old-school craftsman who seemed to live in paint-spattered overalls and smelt of sawdust, putty and the pungent 'Black Beauty' tobacco he rolled into his cigarettes. Despite appearances, he was a tender-hearted, romantic man who kissed his tiny wife in public as passionately as if they were still teenagers.

Jack had never had children and felt some initial reluctance to try parenting this late in life for fear that it might intrude on his relationship with Rose. But he couldn't have been more loving to the toddler who'd suddenly changed from his step-grandson into his stepson.

The small two-bedroom corner house which Jack rented from Ripley's Noakes family was crowded to its limits. Also in residence was Rose's other child by Rex Clapton, a teenage son named Adrian but always known as 'Sonny', who had the second bedroom to himself. Eric slept on a camp bed in Rose and Jack's room or downstairs in the sitting-room. The house had no electricity, only gas lamps, no bathroom and an outside toilet. Rose would wash him at the kitchen sink or sponge him down in a tin bath in front of the coal fire. When Jack's sister, Audrey, acquired one of the flats on the village's new estate, he would go there for a proper bath every Sunday.

A master carpenter and bricklayer as well as plasterer, Jack always earned a good steady wage, which Rose supplemented with shifts at the village telephone exchange, or by cleaning houses or working on the bottling line at Stansfields fizzy drinks factory in Newark Lane, only yards from her home. And they both spoiled Eric more like grandparents than the mum and dad they were supposed to be.

He had a huge number of toys, both shop-bought or painstakingly home-made by Jack. Rose got him all the weekly comic books he wanted and – sugar still being rationed – gave him her weekly sweets-allowance, even spreading granulated sugar on his bread and butter. She bought him special delicacies, for example canned mock turtle soup, costing considerably more than regular tomato or vegetable. She humoured the pernicketiness he showed even as a toddler, when he'd refuse to eat his breakfast cereal unless the milk was poured over it from a certain angle.

Everything had been set up to give him the happy childhood

his unwanted, inconvenient birth had never promised. Unfortunately, no one had bargained for his being unusually sensitive and observant. From the age of six or seven, he felt he was different from other children and that his pampering represented some kind of atonement for it. The house was always full of relatives, for Rose was famously hospitable, especially at the Sunday high teas she served in her tiny living-room. When the grown-ups talked, Rick was often the subject; the question 'Have you heard from his mum lately?' would float down to him as he played on the floor and sometimes he overheard his supposed big brother Adrian jocularly refer to him as 'a little bastard'.

Finally, he wormed the truth out of Rose; that his real mother had left him, gone to Canada and married a man with whom she'd since had two more children. That shattering discovery revealed his whole world to be full of deceptions: not only was Rose his grandmother, but Adrian was really his uncle, his aunts were his great-aunts and Rose's father – living round the corner in Newark Lane – wasn't his grandfather but great-grandfather. Pattie Boyd believes that moment determined his character until his mid-forties:

'He became the wounded child. From then on, everybody around him seemed to feel an obligation to take care of him and prop him up . . . his family . . . then managers . . . other musicians, like Pete Townshend . . . girlfriends like poor Alice Ormsby-Gore, who had to drive up to London and score his heroin for him. There was always someone to shield him from anything unpleasant, like taking a driving test or getting rid of a musician in the band that he didn't like. When we got married in America and he had to take a blood-test, he didn't even have to do that. One of the roadies took it for him.

'He never hit the ground, never grazed his knees, never bumped into life.'

*

'As little kids, Rick and I virtually lived in each other's houses,' Guy Pullen recalls. They were only six doors apart and Guy's mother, Marguerite – known as Peg – was a friend of Rose's and equally small and busy. The two boys started at Ripley Church of England Primary School at the same time and were seated next to each other. 'The thing I remember about Rick was the brown ring he always seemed to have around his mouth. It was from that mock turtle soup Rose used to buy for him.'

Guy was impressed by all his toys: fleets of metal Dinky cars, numerous board games, a Hornby clockwork train set, a spectacular medieval knight's sword and shield Jack Clapp had beaten out of metal. Like other local children, Guy had always thought the paint-spattered, beetle-browed plasterer rather scary, but at home Clapp was 'very docile', happy to let Rose stuff their charge with sugar and buy him whatever new plaything took his fancy.

Like most small boys of that era, Guy knew to expect 'a wallop' from his father if he misbehaved. No such sanctions applied at 1 The Green. 'Jack was a hard man, very firm, but I never once saw him lay a finger on Rick.'

At school, he was for the most part a shy, retiring character, adept at none of the sports at the centre of village life, as Guy was. 'I was always into my football and cricket, but Rick was no good at either of them, though he loved watching. Whenever we'd pick up sides for a game, he was always the last one to get chosen.'

He has since recalled how much he disliked competing and always sought to be anonymous. 'I hated anything which would single me out and get me unwanted attention,' he was to write in his autobiography. Even so, he and Guy Pullen were often in trouble with the headmaster, Mr Dickson – whose hearing-aid emitted a piercing whistle – for giggling and making jokes behind their teachers' backs. 'We had the same silly sense of humour,' Pullen says. 'Still do today.'

In the music class, taken by Mr Dickson's sister, Mrs Lewis, he got no further than playing tinny tunes on a recorder, once winning a prize for his rendering of 'Greensleeves'. The only definite talent he seemed to possess (emulating the Canadian father he'd never known) was for drawing and painting.

Outside school he and Guy went around in a big group of boys, mostly from houses along The Green, including the slightly younger Stuart Shoesmith and Gordon Perrin – both likewise destined to remain his friends for life.

In those days in a place like Ripley, children could disappear for hours without causing their families a moment's anxiety. Their main haunt was 'the Fuzzies', the belt of woodland beyond The Green, where they could climb trees, construct dens and play cowboys and Indians, 'English and Germans' or 'English and Japs', perpetuating the hostilities of the recent world war, all blissfully free from adult interference.

On the nearby River Wey, under the tutelage of an older boy named Ivor Powell, Rick discovered what would be an enduring passion for fishing. When he returned home excitedly after their first outing, Rose immediately ordered him his own rod from a catalogue.

The Green determined the village calendar, from summertime cricket to the huge Guy Fawkes celebration on 5 November. Guy Pullen's father, Fred, a psychiatric nurse, had helped to originate the event and been responsible for bringing Tom Benson's fun fair to add to its parade and the crowning of its Bonfire Night Queen. Benson's formidable wife personally controlled the bumper cars, directing customers to just-vacated vehicles with a shout of 'One more car, one more rider!' One day, when Rick was a superstar beyond measure, he would nostalgically title a double live album after Mrs Benson's catchphrase.

Ripley's de facto lord of the manor was the insurance magnate and pioneer aviator Charles Hughesdon, whose Georgian mansion, Dunsborough Park, adjoined The Green where he was often to be seen riding on a white horse until he was well into his eighties.

Hughesdon was married to the film and stage actress Florence Desmond and their legendary 'helicopter parties' flew in celebrities from the Duke of Edinburgh and the ballerina Margot Fonteyn to Marlene Dietrich and Elizabeth Taylor. As president of the cricket club, Hughesdon often brought his guests to watch matches, sometimes even to take part. One day, Guy and Rick spotted Tyrone Power, a huge Hollywood star from films like *King of the Khyber Rifles*, and they both managed to get his autograph.

The pair cemented their friendship as comprehensively incompetent members of the 1st Ripley Boy Scouts. 'We were terrible scouts,' Pullen recalls. 'The absolute despair of our scoutmaster, Stu Paice. I can still picture him, when we were trying and failing to put our tent up, gritting his teeth and going "Stone the *crows!*" Once we were supposed to read a map to get to his house about four miles away. It took us four and a half hours – and that included thumbing a lift part of the way. Then we camped in his garden, where he had a real Native American totem pole. We nicknamed it "Jeffrey".'

The scouting ethos of honour and fair play had little effect; as they grew older, they and their little gang became, in Pullen's words, 'the rogues of the village'. Much of their time was spent at Ripley's cinema – converted from the old village hall and popularly known as 'the Bughutch' – watching British black-and-white war films starring Jack Hawkins and Michael Redgrave and American comedy shorts with the Three Stooges or the Bowery Boys. The projectionist would set the main film running, then retire to The Anchor pub across the road, from which he'd have to be fetched if it broke down, as it often did. 'You got in by buying a card which had no name or serial number on it. Two of us would buy cards, then go into the loo and pass them out to our friends through the window. You could do that any number of times.'

There was also petty larceny from the village sweetshop, kept by an elderly and short-sighted woman named Miss Farr. They would crowd into Miss Farr's, ask for something that made her turn her back, then grab handfuls of sherbet lemons or flying saucers and bolt. Rick usually went for Ovaltine or Horlicks tablets, solid versions of the bedtime drinks which he'd later identify as his very first addiction.

Ripley's police station had a permanent strength of three or four under the popular Sergeant Lock, whose son also attended St Mary's C of E Primary. For minor juvenile offences, like 'scrumping' apples from Dunsborough Park's orchards or illegal entry of the Bughutch, the penalty from Lockie and his fellow officers was often no more than 'a clip round the ear' with the full approval of the offender's parents. But, setting a lifelong pattern, Rick was never in trouble for anything.

Sometimes he and his friends would just sit inside the bus-shelter in the High Street, watching the traffic to and from Portsmouth endlessly crawl by, hoping to spot something flash like a Ferrari. Little did he dream that one day he'd own fleets of them.

He felt no qualms about singing in those days. At the Christmas family gathering, when everyone was expected to do some kind of 'turn', Rose would stand him in the sitting-room's bay window, pull the curtains behind him and he'd give them 'I Belong To Glasgow', Will Fyffe's music hall song about a Scottish drunk:

I belong to Glasgow,
Dear old Glasgow town.
But there's something the matter wi' Glasgow
'Cause it's going round and round . . .

Rose had a strong musical streak; in his early years, the furniture at 1 The Green included a harmonium, on which she'd pump out hymns and sentimental songs like Gracie Fields' 'Now Is The Hour' and Josef Locke's 'Bless This House'. Her son Adrian, Rick's former stepbrother, now uncle, played chromatic harmonica, owned the best record collection in Ripley and danced the jitterbug with an abandon that set his Brylcreem-flattened hair flying. Adrian possessed what would later emerge as the Clapton addictive gene though in his case he was hooked only on vinegar, which he sloshed over everything he ate, puddings included. 'I used to tell him, "Every bottle of Sarson's ought to have your name on it,"' his widow, Sylvia, recalls.

The nearest to a 'real' musician in the family was Rose's father, Jack Mitchell, a huge man who'd formerly been a threshing contractor to local corn farmers and owned a traction engine that always featured prominently in Ripley festivities. Mitchell played accordion and violin and at summer fetes on The Green would perform with a local busker named Jack Townshend on guitar, violin and spoons.

Rick thought he'd like to play the violin like his new great-grandfather, so Rose immediately got him one. But the curmudgeonly Mitchell (who was 'usually quite drunk') offered no help or encouragement and his attempts to learn simply by copying soon petered out.

As he grew older, Ripley seemed to be full of music, albeit largely confined to pubs whose thresholds he and his friends were forbidden to cross. At the ex-servicemen's British Legion club, in particular, Saturday nights always featured a succession of amateur vocalists like the ebullient Sid Perrin, uncle of his friend Gordon, who specialised in Mario Lanza songs like 'Because You're Mine' and 'Cara Mia'. Rose herself took a leading part in the entertainments that the 'ladies' section put on, assuming the roles of gipsies or moustachioed pirates with gusto.

Three doors along from Jack and Rose's lived a man named Buller Collier who liked to play his piano accordion outside his front door on summer evenings. Rick would eavesdrop on the recital, more fascinated by Buller's accordion than any music it made. 'It was red and black,' he would recall, 'and it shimmered.'

At home, music poured more or less continuously from the family's one and only radio, then known as 'the wireless', provided solely by the BBC's Light Programme and mostly performed live by an immense range of in-house orchestras and bands.

One of the very few concessions to recorded music was *Children's Favourites*, a request programme broadcast on Saturday mornings and hosted by 'Uncle Mac' (in reality the BBC's head of children's broadcasting, a one-legged Great War veteran named Derek McCulloch). Every week, Rick would sit waiting for the nine o'clock pips, presaging an hour of seemly infantile choices like 'The Runaway Train' or 'Nellie the Elephant'.

Then one Saturday, some little clever-dick sent in a request for 'Whoopin' The Blues' by Sonny Terry and Brownie McGhee. The BBC had a long list of banned songs and strictures about 'good taste', which kept just about the whole blues catalogue from the adult airwaves. But Uncle Mac, thinking this was a comedy number, played it without demur. So the boy in Ripley was introduced to the blues through one of its most captivating duets, a madcap mixture of chugging harmonica and exuberant falsetto whoops. 'It cut through me like a knife,' he would remember. 'After that, I never missed *Children's Favourites* just in case it came on again.'

As would soon become apparent, his was the last generation of Britain's young to grow up in a Garden of Eden. The notion that children should receive sex education before reaching puberty was still far in the future. The only sexual titillation he and his friends experienced were the well-covered 'bathing beauties' in *Reveille* or *Tit-Bits* magazine; their only glimpse of nudity was in the naturists' journal *Health & Efficiency* (whose seemingly clinical name carried a massive erotic charge). One day, playing alone on The Green, he came upon a piece of real pornography, a home-made book whose stapled-together pages had drawings of male and female genitalia. It was his first inkling there was any difference between them.

He had recently discovered that 'shag' could mean something other than the coarse tobacco smoked by workmen like Jack Clapp. So when a new girl joined his school class and was put at a desk in front of him, he casually asked her, 'Do you feel like a shag?' An almighty row resulted: he was made to apologise to the victim and, by his later account, given 'six of the best' by the headmaster, Mr Dickson (though Guy Pullen has no recollection of Dickson ever using corporal punishment). 'From that point on,' the future rock god would claim in his memoirs, 'I tended to associate sex with punishment, shame and embarrassment – feelings which coloured my sexual life for years.'

In June 1953, twenty-seven-year-old Queen Elizabeth the Second was crowned and Ripley celebrated with its usual gusto. An amateur colour film records the procession of decorated floats along the High Street on Coronation Day, with toddlers dressed as beefeaters and big strong men dressed as hula-hula girls, and the multiple festivities on The Green.

Eight-year-old Rick is there somewhere with Guy, Stuart and Gordon in their short flannel trousers and porous cotton shirts. On the open-air stage, Mrs Lewis, the primary school's music teacher, clad in an old raincoat, her wisps of grey hair floating in the breeze, thumps an upright piano as her pupils perform traditional country dances, bowing and curtsying to each other, and skip around a maypole. Never again would English childhood have such innocence.

2
PAT

I n 1954, when Rick was nine, his mother suddenly re-entered his life, thereby doing infinitely more damage than she ever had by walking out of it.

After seven years in Canada, the woman now called Pat McDonald felt an urge to see the toddler she'd left behind in Ripley in 1947. Her husband Frank, who was still serving in the Canadian military, did not accompany her but she brought along the two children they'd since had together, six-year-old Brian and one-year-old Cheryl.

Transatlantic air travel then was only for the very rich, and Pat and the children made the journey by sea. When her ship arrived at Southampton, Rick was waiting on the dockside with Rose and Jack. He had no clear memory of her from his babyhood, so for him it was a twenty-five-year-old stranger who came down the gangway. He later recalled that she seemed 'glamorous and charismatic, with her auburn hair piled up high in the fashion of the day'. But he presciently felt 'a coldness in her looks, a sharpness'.

By now, he was well aware that she was his mother. However, to forestall any resurgence of gossip about his birth out of wedlock, his family had reverted to the story that she was his grown-up sister. He went along with it for the moment, certain in his own mind that at long last she'd returned to claim him. He imagined her gathering him into an embrace that would blow away the clouds of mystery, shame and deception and lead to some indeterminate golden future together.

But nothing of the sort happened when he met her off the boat, nor at the grand family reunion back in Ripley. The occasion was all about the gifts Frank McDonald had sent following a recent tour of duty in Korea – lacquered boxes and silk dressing-gowns embroidered with dragons, somewhat incongruous in a house with no bathroom and a toilet in the garden.

Finally plucking up his courage, he went up to Pat and asked, 'Can I call you Mummy now?' She replied that after all Rose and Jack had done for him, he'd better go on calling them Mum and Dad and pretending she was his sister. The coolness in her manner shocked even her own mother, as it did her new sister-in-law, Adrian's wife Sylvia. 'I couldn't believe anyone could be so nasty to a child,' Sylvia would recall.

To make matters worse, he found he'd lost his accustomed place as the centre of attention. Now, everybody was all over his stepbrother Brian and stepsister Cheryl; indeed, the whole of Ripley regarded them as stars with their Canadian accents and exotic-looking clothes. And all the time he had to listen to both of them calling Pat 'Mommy'. At one heartbreaking moment, she heard him tell Brian (whom he'd also been told not to call his brother), 'You see the lady over there in that bed? She's my mummy, too.'

Any child psychologist, had there been one in mid-1950s rural Surrey – and had that era's working-class Britons held with such things – could have predicted the outcome. He became moody and fractious, even turning on his beloved Rose. His revenge on Pat was refusing to make a playmate of six-year-old Brian, who had been temporarily enrolled at his school. Among his relations, only Jack Clapp's sister, Audrey, seemed able to get through to him and came to the house every week especially to see him, bringing him sweets – and still more toys.

In the end, Pat stayed for the best part of a year, every day bringing her son reminders of the new distance she had put between them and his obligation to lie about their relationship.

She was highly gregarious, fond of music, especially the big bands of Benny Goodman and Harry James, and of what the polite phraseology of that time called 'a tipple'; as the months passed, she seemed less absorbed with her family than reconnecting with the friends she'd had as a teenager and drinking with them in one or other of Ripley's five pubs. In particular, she saw a lot of Sid Perrin, the bachelor uncle of Rick's friend Gordon Perrin, with whom she'd had a teenage romance. Local opinion was that the extrovert Sid, with his Saturday-night Mario Lanza impressions at the British Legion club, might have been the man for her all along.

Towards the end of her visit, the rows between her and her disappointed son became increasingly bitter. She had decided he was 'a loner', a serious flaw in her book. One day, after an extended screaming-match, he stormed out of the house onto The Green, shouting, 'I wish you'd never come here! I wish you'd go away!'

This emotional turmoil could not have come at a worse moment. Soon after Pat's return to Canada, he took his 11-Plus, the state examination that sorted children into successes or failures at the age of eleven, sending the brightest to high-quality grammar schools and the others to avowedly inferior 'secondary modern' ones. Distracted and destabilised as he was, he failed the exam miserably and so, instead of Woking or Guildford Grammar School, was relegated to St Bede's Secondary Modern in Ripley's 'twin' village of Send. The only consolation was that Guy Pullen and several more of his cronies from The Green accompanied him there.

Despite its monastic sound, St Bede's was a tough co-ed establishment whose headmaster, Bill Short, kept order through the liberal use of corporal punishment. 'He was a Geordie, one-time captain of Gateshead football club, a real hard man,' Pullen remembers. 'He always wore shoes with steel caps. Anyone who got sent out of class and heard Short's steel-capped shoes on the stone floor knew they were in for a slippering. You got hit with a gymshoe that he sent you to the changing-room to fetch. And you got in more trouble if you didn't bring one that was big enough.'

Under the stimulus of St Bede's, he and Eric and their fellow Ripley 'rogues' became borderline juvenile delinquents. From pilfering Horlicks tablets at old Miss Farr's sweetshop, they graduated to more ambitious shoplifting in Woking or Cobham. A favourite pastime was vandalising the trains that chugged slowly around Surrey's numerous branch lines. The carriages had no corridors, allowing upholstery to be ripped up and mirrors smashed without fear of interruption. Now they were risking penalties far graver than 'a thick ear' from a Ripley village bobby – yet still Rick always got away with it.

At other times, he retreated into himself, wanting no company but the family dog, a black Labrador named Prince. The artistic streak he'd inherited from his vanished father grew stronger: he took to drawing obsessively – eye-catchingly skilled cowboys or spacemen, copied from his many comic books, or the curly-crusted wares of the hot pie vendor who periodically visited The Green.

Like many children who find the adult world unreliable, he created imaginary companions he could count on never to betray him: a pony named Bushbranch and an alter-ego called Johnny Malingo who was part-Wild West outlaw, part-gangster. In those days, such reckless, raffish role-models were usually Johnnys, but never Erics.

He was a couple of years too young for Britain's first wave of guitar mania, in 1956, when Elvis Presley employed one in the sexiest vocal act ever known and transformed the character of an instrument that had previously never raised its voice above a murmur.

The rock 'n' roll fan at 1 The Green was his Uncle Adrian, now converted from big band jazz to Presley, Bill Haley, Little Richard and Fats Domino, and from tweed jackets and baggy flannel trousers to drape suits, string ties and sideburns. To Rick, it was just something else weird from America which, all the newspapers insisted, would be forgotten six months from now.

At St Bede's he'd got to know a boy named John Constantine whose well-to-do parents lived on the outskirts of Ripley. The Constantines possessed a radiogram, a bulky wooden cabinet combining the functions of radio and gramophone. It was on this domestic showpiece that Rick first heard 'Hound Dog', its electric solo by Presley's guitarist Scotty Moore – a masterclass in 'less is more' for every player who came after – all but smothered by lacquered walnut.

Surprisingly, he was also untouched by the concurrent craze for skiffle, folk music harking back to America's Depression years when people could afford no instruments beyond cheap guitars, kazoos and box-and-broomstick 'basses' and the only percussion came from serrated washboards swept up and down by thimbleshod fingers.

Whereas rock 'n' roll, played by professional session musicians like Sun Records' Scotty Moore, was impossible to deconstruct, skiffle was made up of simple one- and two-finger chords which any beginner could instantly master. In the heyday of its only national star, Lonnie Donegan, from 1957–9, hundreds of British boys who'd never played or sung a note of music formed skiffle groups in imitation of Donegan's, received their first taste of performing in public – and discovered the guitar's magical effect on the female sex. But somehow all of it passed Rick Clapton by.

Among the other disruptive voices now blowing across the

Atlantic, he responded most strongly to Buddy Holly, who recorded both as a soloist and with the Crickets, the prototype rock band. Holly's songs were excitingly guitar-driven yet almost as easy to play as skiffle while his geekish spectacles made him seem normal and comprehensible where Presley was exotic and remote.

The teenage Rick continued to have better toys than any of his friends. On his thirteenth birthday in 1958, Rose and Jack gave him a portable record-player, a Dansette 'Cub', costing nine guineas (about £9.45). The first single he bought was 'When' by the Kalin Twins, the first album was *The Chirping Crickets*, fully revealing the vocal, instrumental and songwriting talents of Buddy Holly.

That year, Holly and the Crickets made their only British tour, culminating in an appearance on ATV's *Sunday Night at the London Palladium* show. Rose and Jack didn't own a television set, so he had to watch it at the home of the affluent Constantine family. Holly was revealed playing a strange, flat object with a lever and a streamlined tuning-head – the first Fender Stratocaster ever seen in Britain. To Rick, it was like 'an instrument from outer space . . . I thought to myself "That's the future. That's what I want."'

Then in February 1959, Holly died in a plane crash while touring the snowbound American Midwest. For the many young British guitar-learners whom he'd helped make the transition from skiffle to rock (John Lennon, Paul McCartney and George Harrison in Liverpool, to name but three) it felt like the loss of a personal friend. Though Rick wasn't part of that fraternity, he still shared in the general shock and disbelief at the news.

He had expected nothing from his secondary education. But, to his surprise, the St Bede's art teacher, Mr Swain, praised his work and encouraged him to develop in new directions, like calligraphy. Those who'd failed the 11-Plus had now been given a second chance to rise in the state-education system by sitting a new exam called the 13-Plus. Largely to repay Mr Swain, Rick worked hard, passed his 13-Plus and won a place at Hollyfield School in Surbiton, twelve miles away.

Hollyfield was a conventional secondary modern but unusual in having a large visual arts department encompassing subjects like glass-engraving and graphics as well as drawing, painting and sculpture. Rick was enrolled on a three-year course with art as its main subject.

Surbiton and its neighbouring towns of Kingston, Richmond and Twickenham make up the most prosperous stretch of the River Thames; a waterside conurbation of expensive homes, posh restaurants, upmarket shops and department stores, its broad flowing highway crossed by stately stone bridges and lined with luxurious cabin cruisers. In the late Fifties, it was still redolent of Victorian straw hats, parasols and Jerome K. Jerome's *Three Men in a Boat*; at the same time, the many colleges and schools in the area gave it a buzzy, youthful atmosphere.

After countrified, insular Ripley, Rick found it all dizzyingly glamorous and grown-up. Though he still had to wear a school uniform (maroon blazers for juniors, black ones for seniors), Hollyfield's arts pupils worked in a separate building from the purely academic ones and were given a much-envied extra measure of freedom. On Saturdays, they attended classes at Kingston Art College, to which it was assumed many of them would eventually graduate.

In response to his new, sophisticated milieu, he dropped the pet name by which he'd been known since babyhood and introduced himself to everyone at Hollyfield as Eric. It was how he signed his contribution to the next edition of the school's classily designed magazine – a poem called 'Battle Cry', giving some hint of the turbulence and confusion inside him.

'Forward into battle, men'
The cry rings loud and clear,
And on the field a thousandfold
Are armed with sword and spear.
The Foe approach with cunning eye
The blood of men to seek.
But underneath the bright breastplate
A heart beats humble and meek.
The sword is drawn, the spirit roused
The charge is swift and harsh.
Cold steel and iron clash one on one
As men die upon the marsh.
And now the fight is really on
And death is everywhere,
But men who fight for glory's sake
Have neither fear nor care.
The dark black marsh is stained with red
The men are growing few,
The blades strike home, the spears are launched,
The arrows swift and true.
At last the fight is over,
The enemy have fled.
But many of the warriors
Lie on their black Death Bed.

Eric Clapton 3rd Art

By now, rock 'n' roll seemed to have burnt itself out, as the media had predicted and the older generation fervently hoped. Buddy Holly was dead, Elvis Presley had been shorn of his sideburns and joined the army; a series of scandals involving major American artistes and bribe-taking disc jockeys apparently confirmed the power of the rogue beat to incite depravity and corruption.

As a reaction against sleazy rockers, the fashion was for bland boy crooners, mostly named Bobby, marketed on looks rather than talent and aimed squarely at pubescent girls. The notion of musical heroes for young men seemed to have vanished.

But not for Eric; not since hearing Sonny Terry and Brownie McGhee perform 'Whoopin' The Blues' on Uncle Mac's BBC radio show. 'I [had] recognised it immediately,' he would recall. 'It was as if I was being reintroduced to something I already knew, maybe from another, earlier life . . . for me there [was] something primitively soothing about this music . . . it went straight through to my nervous system, making me feel 10 feet tall.'

Its name could be found throughout popular music, when the mood was melancholy. Traditional jazz had 'St Louis Blues', 'Jelly Roll Blues', 'Yellow Dog Blues', 'Basin Street Blues' and 'West End Blues', balladry had 'The Birth Of The Blues', 'Learning The Blues' and 'Blues In The Night'. Rock had appropriated its immemorial twelve-bar, three-chord structure; Britain's first rock 'n' roll star Tommy Steele reached number 1 with 'Singing The Blues', followed by 'Knee-Deep In The Blues'. Skiffle above all had ransacked its repertoire, most notably that of Huddie Ledbetter, aka Leadbelly, while the 'King of Skiffle', Lonnie Donegan, had changed his first name from Anthony in homage to the bluesman Lonnie Johnson.

Its creators were rather more elusive. They had been active mainly in the American South of the 1920s and '30s and comparatively few had ever become famous outside it. For some, music had been a sideline to menial work of various kinds; others had been little more than beggars, performing for small change on street corners. It was out of their hard lives but uncrushable spirit that the blues had been born – a cry of despair which at the same time was comforting and life-affirming. As a consequence of endemic childhood disease and malnutrition, many had been blind; indeed, the likes of Blind Lemon Jefferson, Blind Blake,

Blind Boy Fuller and Blind Willlie Johnson constituted a kind of elite with their special understanding of suffering unbowed.

Those fortunate enough to record commercially had done so for a segregated market known demeaningly as 'race music', seldom receiving anything like proper recompense. Some of the greatest might have been lost to posterity altogether but for an enlightened white man named Alan Lomax who in the 1940s travelled thousands of miles through the South, recording them in their homes, in work-gangs, sometimes even prisons, like a naturalist conserving some threatened species of fauna.

In late-1950s Britain they were to be found only in the loneliest aisles of specialist record shops, most often lumped together in cheaply packaged compilations. Brilliant instinctive musicians who in their own time had not been known as African Americans but 'negroes' – or worse – were dimly outlined in sepia in their dusty suits or dungarees, holding ancient acoustic guitars that looked as malnourished as they did.

Yet collectively they had reached out to a diffident, insecure white schoolboy in Ripley, Surrey. 'I felt through most of my youth that my back was against the wall,' he would one day reflect. 'I felt the only way to survive that was with dignity, courage and with pride. I heard that in certain forms of music; I heard it most of all in the blues. Because it was always one man with his guitar versus the world – he had no option but to sing and play to ease his pain.'

Instead of cowboys and spacemen, he began to draw blues musicians, skilled pen-portraits with as much care lavished on their instruments as on their faces. He also read everything he could about them, learning how many had come from a region not shown in his school geography book, the 7,000-square-mile Delta region between the Mississippi and Yazoo rivers, the deepest Deep South.

From his cold-weather world of neatly trimmed hedges, red

telephone kiosks and Green Line buses, he envied their heat-soaked one of cotton fields, wood cabins, juke-joints and antique Coca-Cola signs. Knowing nothing of the poverty and persecution from which only a lucky few had escaped, 'that seemed like Paradise to me'.

Each morning, on the long uphill walk to Hollyfield School's art annexe, he passed – and increasingly lingered outside – Bell's music shop. Bell's had formerly specialised in piano accordions but, with the skiffle craze, had gone over to the instrument almost every British boy suddenly lusted after. Now, two years behind the pack, Eric found himself lusting after one, too.

The guitar he'd picked out in Bell's window was far from the most expensive there: a German-made Hoyer, like an acoustic Spanish model but with steel strings instead of gut or nylon ones, priced at only £2. As ever, his wish was Rose's command.

But after he brought the Hoyer home, it became progressively less thrilling. It was too large to hold comfortably in a standing position and had a gap between its fretboard and strings, making them hard to press down and painful as their steel bit into his virgin fingertips. He broke a string almost immediately and, not knowing how to change it, had to carry on with only five.

He never had a formal teacher, even though Ripley's guitar-playing busker, Jack Townshend, could have shown him the basics. Instead, he sat listening to records and trying to copy their guitar-playing by ear. The first was Harry Belafonte's quasi-spiritual 'Scarlet Ribbons', which he'd encountered in a more bluesy version by Josh White. The ever-indulgent Rose and Jack also bought him a small Grundig tape-recorder on which he could hear himself playing along with his models and judge how close to them he sounded.

Initially, he fantasised that his ungainly, steel-strung instrument might metamorphose him into an American-style rock 'n' roll wild man, much as it went against his innate dislike of attracting attention. One day, alone at home, he was kneeling on the sitting-room floor in front of a mirror, miming to a Gene Vincent record on his Dansette 'Cub', when one of his mates passed the house, looked in through the bay window and saw him. The incredulous grin that spread over the mate's face and his own churning embarrassment almost made him give up there and then.

Not every bluesman of the old school had fallen victim to blindness, disease, racism, alcoholism and mendacious record companies, but in a few cases had lived to a reasonable age and earned a decent living from their music. The most notable example was Big Bill Broonzy, who enjoyed a substantial following in Britain and throughout Europe and gave periodic concerts at London's Royal Albert Hall under the sponsorship of the traditional jazz band leader Humphrey Lyttelton.

Broonzy died from throat cancer in 1958, before Eric could see him onstage. But a film clip of him shown later on grainy black-and-white TV proved as instructive as any one-to-one masterclass.

The 'Big Bill' had suggested some mountainous, ebullient character but Broonzy, while admittedly very tall, was delicate of feature and wonderfully light of touch. He was playing a blues instrumental called 'Hey Hey' without a plectrum, his thumb beating a rhythm on the bass strings while his fingers flicked the treble ones in an ever-changing descant. With no means of visually recording it, Eric had to learn the technique in just a couple of minutes.

'Broonzy was his main man after that,' his childhood friend Guy Pullen remembers. 'He'd listen to the riffs over and over again ... copy and copy ... Then he'd sit me down on The Green, play them on that old guitar and ask, "Do I sound like the record?" The answer was always "Yes".'

3

TROUBADOUR

At Hollyfield, he'd expected to be an outsider for prizing ancient sepia bluesmen so far beyond shiny new pop sensations like Cliff Richard and the Shadows (even though they used a Fender Stratocaster imported by Richard directly from its American makers). Instead he found classmates who not only shared his passion but were often considerably more knowledgeable on the subject.

One to whom he would owe a particular debt was Clive Blewchamp, in later years a well-known designer of stained glass and record album-covers. Blewchamp set him off on a musical voyage of discovery that had as much to do with modern American history and continuing racial prejudice and social justice.

He learned how some Delta bluesmen had joined the post-war mass migration of black people from the impoverished rural South to northern cities where work was more plentiful and racism less naked; how, under the stimulus of urban life, especially in Chicago, they had exchanged plaintive acoustic guitars for strident amplified ones, inventing rock 'n' roll in all but name; how electric blues had still been stigmatised as 'race' music and fenced off from white ears until the astute Chuck Berry changed its subject-matter from sex to high schools and hot rods (though Berry was already past thirty), so creating a formula acceptable across the racial divide.

It was now that he first encountered three electrifying new

names suggesting, respectively, a pirate, a cut of meat and the villain of Walt Disney's *Three Little Pigs* – John Lee Hooker, T-Bone Walker and Howlin' Wolf – whose voices were steeped in sex as rock 'n' roll never dared and who didn't finger a guitar fretboard respectfully, like he did, but reduced it to shivers with a sliding metal bar or broken bottle-neck.

He also discovered the undisputed 'King of the Chicago Electric Blues', Muddy Waters, raised in Mississippi as McKinley Morganfield, a supreme stylist whose versions of Willie Dixon's 'Hoochie-Coochie Man' and Preston Foster's 'Got My Mojo Working' had no trace of mud, still less angst, but, rather, twinkled with benevolent self-mockery. Another milestone moment for Eric was reproducing Muddy's 'Honey Bee' with its treble three-string riff like a glimpse of Hawaiian grass skirts and leis.

At the opposite extreme was Jimmy Reed, a sometime worker at the Armour meat-packing plant, whose voice held a built-in sneer where Muddy's did a chuckle and whose lion's share of life's misfortunes included periods of epilepsy. Eric listened to Reed's 'Bright Lights, Big City' and 'Big Boss Man', played along with them and finally played them so many times that '[They] became part of my metabolism.'

And now this wasn't just boys' stuff. Many of Hollyfield's female students sported the beatnik look that had just arrived simultaneously from America and super-chic France. As well as shapeless black clothes, long hair, heavy eye-makeup and sombre talk of Sartre and Existentialism, being a beatnikette demanded a contrarian approach to everything, music above all. So here were girls who didn't scream for Cliff but hearkened to Muddy or Howlin' Wolf just as reverentially as he did.

In such surroundings, a passably good-looking thirteen-year-old with a guitar ought to have had the time of his life. But the business with Pat had left him horribly uncomfortable with any woman outside his family circle, bereft of self-confidence and

terrified of suffering another such rejection. Though he had con-
tinual wild crushes on girls, he shrank from getting too close to
any particular one; though his libido was healthily hyperactive,
he found the thought of actual sex terrifying.

In his first term, he began dating a fellow-pupil named Diane
Coleman, who lived in Kingston. He later described it as 'a short
but intense little fling', for all that their dates usually consisted of
playing records in the sitting-room of Diane's house.

He saw himself now as a troubadour or wandering minstrel,
as so many Delta bluesmen had been (to say nothing of his unknown father, Edward Fryer, playing piano around Montreal
clubs and bars before the Second World War.) His debut, he
decided, would be at a coffee bar named L'Auberge, a popular
student hangout at the bottom of Richmond Hill. Rather than
fix it with the management in advance, he planned just to turn
up with an admiring beatnik girl – Diane – in tow, then suddenly
get to his feet and start playing. To take the weight of the Hoyer,
he threaded a string around it and, in a vaguely medieval touch,
printed LORD ERIC in ballpoint pen on its face.

Three times he and Diane acted out their entrance into L'Auberge but always at the moment he was supposed to burst into
minstrelsy, his nerve failed and he stayed rooted to his seat.

The relationship with Diane ended, as he would later put it,
'when sex reared its head' and he began a less demanding one
with Sue Cullen, another Hollyfielder, a year his junior. Sue was
a beatnik with ribbons, often adding a black Tarantella skirt,
purloined from her mother, to her regulation black duffel coat,
sloppy jumper, tights and pixie boots.

She lived in Richmond and, again for Eric, a typical date
would be going to the girl's home to listen to records, usually
with her mother in earshot. Sue was seriously into the blues and
had managed to find a record of Blind Lemon Jefferson's 'Black

Snake Moan', a piece of blatant sexual imagery dating from the 1920s. 'Both of us would lie on the floor, but not for anything naughty,' she recalls. 'We were trying to get as close as possible to the record-player to catch all the words.'

He also took her home to Ripley to meet Rose, whom she found 'very welcoming but a bit formal . . . I remember Eric telling me what had happened with his mother, how she'd gone away when he was nine, then come back and gone away again. He was obviously still very pained about it.'

Despite his new bohemian life, he still followed the Ripley calendar, which in winter meant regularly joining the beaters on local pheasant-shoots. 'He often said he was going out beating next weekend, but I had no idea what he meant.'

Blues music may have been his obsession but it was by no means the only one. Anything that caught his interest tended to become an obsession.

Clothes had been one since he was eleven or twelve, the time when British adolescents first took to wearing jeans. While his friends had been content with regular blue denim, he insisted on black with three rows of green stitching down the side seams. There had to be three and only green would do.

At Hollyfield, as Sue Cullen recalls, he became a beatnik but one as meticulous over his khaki combat jacket, 'Ban the Bomb' T-shirts and slip-on moccasins as a Guardsman over a dress uniform. At the same time, he was infatuated with the traditional English bespoke tailoring of London's Savile Row which only the very wealthy, like Ripley's squire Charlie Hughesdon and his helicopter-borne houseguests, could afford.

If he couldn't yet aspire to a 'City Gent' suit, he could at least simulate the shirts, which had stiff white collars but were otherwise dark-coloured or striped. 'Every new shirt he bought, I had to take its collar off and sew on a white one,' Rose would recall.

David Holt lived in Clandon, a small village a couple of miles from Ripley. He'd been in the class below Eric at St Bede's and arrived at Hollyfield a year after him. Having previously been not that friendly, they now discovered a bond. 'Eric and I were the same clothes size – medium – so he'd borrow mine and I'd borrow his. Not things like suits; I don't think either of us possessed such a thing in those days. Mainly jumpers and cardigans.'

As modest as Eric's home was, it seemed luxurious compared with David's. 'His place had a toilet in the back garden but at least it was one you could flush. At our house we just had an Elsan [chemical toilet] that a truck came and emptied every Tuesday.

'I remember him being totally spoilt by his grandmother. She was working at the soft drinks factory behind the house, so their little kitchen was always full of lemonade, cream soda, and cola in cans which was still quite a rarity. Eric was never made to do anything he didn't want to – even basic things like cleaning his teeth. He had quite black teeth in those days.'

David, too, was infatuated with guitars but at the time possessed only a plastic toy one, a souvenir of Tommy Steele mania in 1957–8, whose shaming existence he kept secret from Eric. He was hugely impressed by the problematic Hoyer, which he recalls as having ERIC CLAPTON TROUBADOUR printed around it in large black letters.

Eric had by now inherited the house's second bedroom after his Uncle Adrian left home to get married. Here, David Holt watched various other obsessions come and go. 'We'd seen the film *The Magnificent Seven* and Eric loved the scene when James Coburn throws the knife. So he bought himself a knife and used to practise throwing it in his room, using the door as a target. And he'd put on clothes as close as he could to the ones Coburn had worn.

'He also got heavily into cycling. There was a special racing bike called a Gerrard you could get by mail order which came in a kit and you had to assemble yourself. Eric had one of those and he got cycling shorts and all the other proper kit. He even shaved his legs because that was what cycling champions did.'

By the age of fifteen, Eric had long been seeking a better guitar, but nothing else in Bell's window display was in his – or, rather, his grandmother's – price-range. Then one Saturday in a Kingston flea market, he happened on a treasure.

It was another Spanish-style acoustic model but with a narrow rosewood body, like something a medieval troubadour might actually have used. In fact it was American, made by the George Washburn company of Chicago in the 1930s or '40s. Possibly it had been left behind by some wartime GI, which might explain the image of a nude woman pasted on its back. All that mattered was that after the Hoyer, it was a dream to play.

Eric bought it by selling the Hoyer to David Holt for almost £5, more than twice what Rose had paid. The flaws which had so irked him mattered little to David. 'It was way better than a plastic guitar with a picture of Tommy Steele.'

In the year below David's at Hollyfield were two other blues-lovers and tyro guitarists, Anthony Topham – known as Top – and Chris Dreja. Now properly equipped, he started practising with Topham and Dreja. 'Often I'd be in Ripley, watching Eric, then I'd cycle over to meet Top and Chris and show them what I'd learned from him.'

Though both David's new classmates were two years Eric's junior, he soon realised they were worth knowing. Top, in particular, was the son of a well-known painter, John Topham, a rare instance in their circle of an older person who appreciated the blues. Wartime service with the Royal Navy had taken Topham senior to the American South and he'd visited New Orleans where jazz and blues are all but inseparable. He'd passed on the interest to his son, who owned an impressive collection of records by Slim Harpo, Tampa Red, Lonnie Johnson and others, many on ancient, breakable shellac discs with labels like Vocalion and Okeh.

'Eric often used to come to our house in Norbiton on Saturdays,' Top recalls. 'We'd listen to records, then my mum would make him lunch. He wasn't an easy person. On some days he could be absolutely charming and on others absolutely foul – moody, with an unkindness about him. My grandmother had bought me an acoustic guitar and Eric was always incredibly rude about it, even though his wasn't much better.

'But you could see what an extraordinary connection he had with the blues. It seemed to go directly to his soul because of some pain that was in him.'

In his final year at Hollyfield, Clive Blewchamp lent him an album which sparked the greatest obsession of all. It was titled *King Of The Delta Blues Singers* and contained sixteen tracks by Robert Johnson.

Johnson is the most mysterious and mythologised figure in blues or any other music. When that album appeared, he had been dead for twenty-three years and no images or film footage of him were known to exist; since then, only two still photographs have come to light. Other Delta bluesmen seem to have been born old and careworn, but Johnson is young, good-looking, brimming with vitality. One photo shows him in a snazzy three-piece suit and a hat worn at a rakish slant; in the other, he's in close-up, wearing a white shirt or sweater with a modern-looking roll-collar, smoking a cigarette so fat that it could be a spliff.

His fragmentary life story has him born in Hazlehurst, Mississippi, in 1911 and raised around cotton plantations still only a few steps beyond slavery. The dazzling virtuosity on guitar he suddenly attained at an early age – having initially struggled with it every bit as much as his future disciple in Surrey – gave rise to popular music's darkest legend. The story goes that he was told to go to a certain crossroads at midnight. There he found the

Devil who offered a Faustian bargain: genius as a bluesman in exchange for his soul.

Most of his short life was spent as an itinerant musician – a troubadour – around Mississippi, Tennessee and Arkansas. The only recordings he ever made were in Dallas, Texas, in 1936 and '37, not even in a regular studio but an hotel bedroom fitted with recording-equipment. During the sessions he sometimes preferred to face the wall – seeming evidence of his shyness and humility, though possibly the acoustics were better that way.

He died in 1938, aged twenty-seven, after drinking whisky poisoned by the jealous husband of a woman he'd flirted with. In the future, similar musical prodigies such as Jimi Hendrix, Janis Joplin and Jim Morrison would be killed off at the same age by alcohol or drugs, making death at twenty-seven almost a prerequisite of immortality.

The *King Of The Delta Blues Singers* album resurrected a revolutionary talent for which a soul mightn't have been so bad a trade. The voice had a raw intensity which plumbed the blues to its depths while still retaining the buoyancy and impudence of youth. The lone unamplified guitar had a modern electric sound, switching back and forth from complex treble riffs to a bass beat that was rock twenty years too soon. Where other blues singers in the recording studio simply regurgitated their street repertoire, Johnson's songs were structured and tailored to the three-minute length of an old '78' single. He had been a superstar stillborn.

Like some Tibetan monk poring over an ancient scroll, Eric dedicated himself to the study of Johnson's technique on tracks like 'Kind-Hearted Woman Blues', 'Terraplane Blues', 'Walkin' Blues', 'Milkcow's Calf Blues', and especially 'Cross Road Blues', a seeming reference to that diabolic midnight tryst. For him, their vocals were, and would always remain, 'the most powerful cry . . . you can find in the human voice'. With hindsight, a trainee lama was very much what he considered himself: 'I realised that, on some level, I had found the Master,' he would write in his autobiography, 'and that following this man's example would be my life's work.'

He shared the revelation with everyone he knew – and also, inadvertently, with a complete stranger. The next time he visited Top Topham's house, he decided to take the album with him. Waiting for the Norbiton bus, he put it down on the pavement, then absent-mindedly boarded the bus without it. Before he'd gone very far, he realised what he'd done and raced back, but it had gone.

Those three years at Hollyfield School proved transformative in other directions, too. In 1961, aged sixteen, he passed the state GCE examination in art at advanced level and English at ordinary level (the latter with a distinction) and was reward-ed with a place at Kingston Art College for a probationary one year.

There is scarcely a major British rock star of the 1960s and '70s who did not spend some time at an art school or college, from John Lennon, Keith Richards, Pete Townshend, Ray Davies, Syd Barrett and Jimmy Page to David Bowie, Bryan Ferry, Ian Dury and Freddie Mercury. All were broadly the same kind of working-class boy, in whom obsession with guitars and rock 'n' roll coexisted with strong aesthetic impulses (one day to come out in album cover- and stage-design) and a rebellious spirit that resisted formal learning of any kind.

For others, art college was the place where they met vital future collaborators and honed their craft at student hops and in empty lecture-rooms. But this was to be Eric's experience only in a roundabout way.

At Kingston, the first musician he met had the dual distinction of being American and a woman. She was a folk singer named

Gina Glaser who did occasional nude modelling for the life-drawing class. She was as skilled an instrumentalist as any man he'd seen, playing finger-style guitar, five-stringed banjo or dulcimer while performing American Civil War songs Iike 'Pretty Peggy-o' and 'Marble Town' in 'a beautiful clear voice'.

A single mother with a young child, Gina said little about her impressive musical pedigree back in the States. She'd been a part of the Greenwich Village folk revival that later fostered Bob Dylan, and had made field trips to the Appalachian mountains, collecting folk songs much as earlier aural conservationists had collected the blues.

Eric was 'smitten' – always to be his word for his instantaneous crushes – by Gina's gamine crop-haired look while her willingness to take off her clothes, even if only for artistic purposes, had an exciting whiff of 'nude mags' like *Razzle* and *Health & Efficiency*. He thought she might be attracted to him, too, but her much greater age – she was in her late twenties – inhibited him from trying anything.

He became everything he thought an artist should be, wearing a stripy scarf, cultivating the requisite italic handwriting, developing an interest in Continental and Japanese cinema, reading authors like Baudelaire and Kerouac. But, rather than in college, he practised his growing guitar skills around Kingston, at its main student pub, the Crown, in coffee-bars where stage-fright no longer paralysed him, and occasionally, just like a real troubadour, in the open air.

He never joined any kind of band, preferring to play on his own or else jam with kindred spirits he met on Saturday nights at the Crown's open-mic sessions. One whom he'd have special cause to remember – and not just for music – was Dutch Mills, a fellow Hollyfield alumnus who'd gone on to become an apprentice toolmaker but remained a passionate performer on the blues harmonica.

'There was no compromise with Eric,' Mills recalls. 'He didn't want to learn to play the guitar – he wanted to own it, to be the best of the best. He'd worked out that he could fingerpick to the old blues classic "Nobody Knows You When You're Down And Out", which was a favourite of Bessie Smith. And I'll never forget the night I egged him on to play it on the wall outside All Saints Church, where a group of us often sat.'

When he played at the Crown, it was always alone with his George Washburn acoustic, tucked away in a corner next to the bar-billiards table. From there, he always noticed a certain superior-looking little clique, the boys in black leather jackets and the new elastic-sided Chelsea boots, the girls in tight slit skirts and black stockings with headscarves pushed back on their bouffant hair and knotted high on their chins. He thought the latter seemed 'very exotic, very fast, very well educated', but assumed they'd never want anything to do with a working-class boy like him.

Then one night during his set, he realised the group had stopped talking among themselves to listen – the chin-knotted headscarf girls especially – and realised what a social equaliser he held in his hands. 'It was the first sign I'd had of anything that was in my being that could garner some respect,' he would remember, 'that made people stop and got their attention and admiration.'

Just over the threshold to the Sixties, there was little sign of what was to come. In Britain, the hottest commercial sound was Trad, a homogenised version of traditional or Dixieland jazz, its stars the beery jazzmen that rock 'n' roll had once threatened to obliterate. Now they enjoyed the sweetest revenge in their fancy dress of faux-Victorian bowler hats and waistcoats or Confederate army uniforms. The guitar was driven into exile and the bleating banjo ruled.

Trad found a special home on that stretch of the River Thames that was now Eric's main habitat. A few yards from the Twickenham shore lay the privately owned Eel Pie Island, accessed by a footbridge and dominated by an old hotel whose cavernous ballroom had been popular with fashionable boating folk during the Twenties. Latterly, this had been used for weekly jazz sessions featuring top bands like Kenny Ball's and Acker Bilk's. On Friday nights, it seemed the whole juvenile population of the Thames Valley crossed the footbridge, paying a toll of four old pennies per head, not just to listen but also dance the prancing, half-ironic beatnik step known as the Stomp.

Eric and Sue Cullen were no longer seeing each other. The cautious Sue decided he was becoming altogether too important to her when they were reading a fashion magazine one day and he couldn't stop looking at one of the models. 'It was Pattie Boyd,' she recalls. 'He kept admiring her and I felt this surge of jealousy.'

With a vague idea of hedging her bets, Sue allowed herself to be chatted up by another member of their circle at L'Auberge coffee bar. Though it never got as far as an actual date, Eric found out about it when he and the chatter-up separately arrived at L'Auberge when Sue was there. 'Afterwards, he was very upset and hurt,' she remembers. '"No point, is there?" he said.'

Casual though their relationship had been, the experience of 'chucking' somebody was a revelation. For it showed that in his dealings with women he needn't be the same passive victim who had borne his mother's rejection and neglect. 'I realised I was capable of doing exactly the same to the opposite sex – and worse – than she ever did to me.'

He'd grown up in a village where life revolved around pubs and popularity and personal charisma were synonymous with the consumption of alcohol (Ripley's celebrated Sid Perrin being the paramount example). So now he viewed drink – or, rather, drunkenness – as an essential part of courtship, either to impress girls to whom he was attracted or dull the pain or shame of being chucked.

At college, he developed a mad crush on a 'stunning' girl named Gail, the daughter of a local politician, who was both 'high class' and 'pretty wild', a combination that increasingly fascinated him. He decided the way to win her was to get blind drunk, alternating ten pints of beer with gin and tonic, gin and orange and rum and blackcurrant juice and stopping just short of passing out.

That summer, with three friends including a potential girlfriend, he went to the annual jazz festival in the grounds of Beaulieu Abbey in Hampshire. (At that time, only jazz inspired festivals.) On the way, they stopped off at a pub where Eric got blind drunk in the way he believed made him irresistible to females and, at some point later, he passed out completely.

When he awoke, he was lying in the woods where he and his friends were to have camped and found that they'd abandoned him. While unconscious he had vomited over himself – which might have killed him if he'd ingested any – and both urinated and defecated in his underpants. He had no money for his return train fare and got home only by persuading a kindly railway official to accept an IOU. 'The really insane thing,' he would recall, 'was that I couldn't wait to do it all again.'

There's no telling how long he might have continued to guard his virginity but for Dutch Mills. To reward Dutch for having become an industrial apprentice rather than a blues musician, his parents allowed him to have regular parties at the family home in Kingston after the Crown closed. A large, tipsy crowd always pitched up and some time after midnight, the lights went out and a sexual free-for-all would begin.

At one such moment, Eric found himself paired with a girl named Lucy whose regular boyfriend was out of town, and found himself going all the way. As he would recall, he was 'terrified and fumbly'.

He hadn't thought to use contraception so, in case the experience should recur, hastened to equip himself with what in those days were not called condoms but Durex, their most visible brand-name, Johnnies or FLs (French letters). Since they were available only from barber shops or chemist's, whose counter staff were often female, their purchase was an ordeal for any seventeen-year-old, none more so than this one.

Not long afterwards, he returned to the house with Dutch and two girls for a more private afternoon session. This time as he fumbled, the sheath broke.

His companion reacted with fury and disgust and, a couple of weeks later, told him she thought she was pregnant and demanded money for an abortion. He could be forgiven for wondering if there was any more to sex than this cycle of embarrassment, humiliation and guilt.

4

ROOSTER TO ENGINEER

By 1962, Trad was passé and blues music was spreading through London's south-western suburbs as if the Thames had developed its own Delta region, albeit one with cotton fields replaced by privet hedges, alligator-infested swamps by duck ponds and juke-joints by ancient, low-ceilinged pubs which no jukebox had yet defiled.

The surge began in March when Britain's only dedicated blues club opened in hitherto rather dull and stuffy Ealing. Its founder, Alexis Korner, had started out as a jazz banjo-player but during the late 1950s had converted to the guitar and formed the country's first dedicated blues band, Blues Incorporated. However, London jazz clubs still refused to acknowledge the music's legitimacy and considered Korner a 'traitor'. Disillusioned by repeated rejections from key venues like the Marquee in Oxford Street, he had turned to Ealing in search of more open minds.

The new club, situated under an ABC bakery, attracted a huge membership that was by no means limited to Ealing and adjoining river towns like Richmond, Kingston and Surbiton. It included two friends who were struggling to launch a band called Little Boy Blue and the Blue Boys in far-off Dartford, Kent. One was a student at the London School of Economics, Mick Jagger; the other a habitual malingerer at Sidcup Art College, Keith Richards.

At the Ealing club, they met Brian Jones from even further-off

Cheltenham, Gloucestershire, a multi-talented musician who could play slide guitar like Elmore James. Alexis Korner saw something in the non-guitarist of the trio and Jagger became Blues Incorporated's first featured vocalist, singing in a way that no blues artiste ever had before.

Korner was a generous-spirited man and, over the following weeks, gave a similar chance to several other aspiring performers among his clientele. Blues Incorporated's fluid line-up came to include a pink-faced blond beanpole known as Long John Baldry; an Oxford University undergraduate named Paul Pond, later Paul Jones of Manfred Mann; a former child skiffler named Jimmy Page, later of Led Zeppelin; a diminutive Scot who played upright bass named Jack Bruce, and an unruly red-haired drummer named Ginger Baker, both later of Cream.

But for the present, Cream's future third member stayed in the audience, studying the technique of whichever guitarist was onstage. His capacious memory now stored the intros of dozens of blues songs and he could tell which was coming from the very first note or chord.

News of Korner's Ealing coup soon leaked back to Soho and showed the anti-blues Marquee club what a revenue stream it was missing. As a result, Blues Incorporated began appearing regularly at the Marquee and, in July 1962, were booked to appear on BBC Radio's *Jazz Club* programme. However, the BBC's fee would not stretch to a vocalist, so to console Mick Jagger, Korner arranged for him to appear at the Marquee on the same night, fronting an ad-hoc band including Richards and Brian Jones during the intermission between Long John Baldry sets. They named themselves the Rollin' Stones, after the Muddy Waters song 'Rollin' Stone', and played material by Waters, Jimmy Reed, Elmore James and Robert Johnson.

Eric, meanwhile, was coming up for assessment at the end of his probationary year at Kingston Art College. Because of his skill at drawing, he'd been put on the graphics course, which he soon came to hate, for while fine arts students were painting or sculpting he spent his time designing packaging or ad-campaigns for things like soap and cornflakes. The one part he enjoyed was a spell in the stained-glass department alongside his blues-savvy friend Clive Blewchamp.

As the guitar increasingly took over his life, he'd taken to cutting classes and leaving many exercises undone or half-finished. His portfolio was consequently rather meagre but still, he felt, of sufficient quality to get him into the full three-year course. It thus came as a great shock to learn he was one of only two probationers among fifty whose courses were to be terminated. When he called at the college to pick up the various pieces of work he'd left there, he found they'd all been thrown away. Rejection seemed set to be the theme of his life.

He delayed breaking the news to Rose and Jack, remembering how often they'd seen him supposedly set off for college when his only objective was to lounge in pubs and play guitar on All Saints Church's wall. When he finally found the courage to tell them, he later recalled, 'They were bitterly disappointed because they'd found out that I was a liar as well as a failure.'

Jack Clapp, usually so taciturn and indulgent, took an unwontedly firm line. 'You've had your chance, Rick,' his step-grandfather told him, 'and you've chucked it away.' If he wanted to go on living at home, he'd have to start contributing to the household expenses, which meant getting a 'proper' job, nothing whatever to do with art – nor, it went without saying, music.

Such a job was readily available and, in the circumstances, impossible to refuse: he would go to work alongside Jack as a plasterer and bricklayer's mate.

Despite Rose's disappointment, he still knew how to get round her. At Bell's music shop in Surbiton he had found a guitar to replace his George Washburn – and raise him to a new level of playing altogether. It was an American-made Kay, thin-bodied with a double cutaway, that could be played electrically or acoustically. Though clearly a knock-off of the hugely expensive and prestigious Gibson ES355, its blues pedigree couldn't be faulted. Kay guitars were favoured by one of his greatest idols, Jimmy Reed, while Alexis Korner used this same model and endorsed the brand in advertisements in the music press.

The price-tag of £99 was far more than Rose could afford, but it seemed the only thing capable of filling the void in his life at present, so she put down a deposit and contracted to pay off the balance in instalments.

But once the Kay was his, just like his first guitar from Bell's, it revealed faults he'd brushed aside in his eagerness to possess it. The 'sunburst' finish, normally gold shading to mahogany at the edges, was yellowish, shading to pink. As with his old Hoyer, the strings were too high off the fretboard, so an effort to hold down; it also had a weak neck which soon began to bend under the pressure he put on it.

It was still an impressive-looking instrument – but something that he'd thought he couldn't live without seemed to lose all attraction now it was actually his. In the future, other such objects of obsessive desire would leave him with the same feeling.

Surprisingly, the former indolent art student took naturally to being a builder's labourer – he even recalled later that he'd 'loved it'. C. Neal & Sons, the West Horsley firm for which Jack worked, had several major construction projects in the area, including a school in Camberley. Eric received what was then a generous wage of £15 per week. No skill was required of him, just physical strength and a head for heights, his main duty to carry buckets of semi-liquid mortar or hods of bricks up ladders to feed to Jack.

As a result, he became more physically fit than he ever would be again in his life. For the first time, he came to appreciate Jack's multifarious skills in building work and to see that plastering a wall in a few deft strokes or laying bricks in a perfect line could be every bit as creative in its own way as music or art. He would always say it was from Jack that he learned the importance of always trying to do one's best and finishing what one started.

Yet he never regarded his job as anything other than a temporary stopgap and was ready to abandon it without a qualm when something else came along, as he was sure something would.

The winter of 1962–3 is remembered in Britain for two events above all: the first outbreaks of Beatlemania and arctic blizzards which snowed up the whole country for almost four months, bringing chaos to road and rail transport and, among other things, paralysing the construction industry. With all Neal's outdoor sites frozen solid, Eric found himself spending days as idle as any at art college.

One of the Thames Delta's less compelling music venues was the Station Hotel, a rather characterless pub across the road from Richmond Underground station. The pub had a spacious back room with a professional-size canopied stage, but its resident attraction, the Dave Hunt Group, were an uneasy mixture of Trad jazz and Louis Jordan 'jump' band music.

Here, one icy Sunday night in January 1963, Eric ran into an acquaintance from Kingston Art College, a fashion student named Jennifer Dolan. With her was her boyfriend, Tom McGuinness, a bespectacled twenty-one-year-old from Wimbledon whose Jesuit education and day job with the Norwich Union insurance company had not stopped him turning into a passionate blues fan and guitarist. McGuinness, in fact, had brought along his guitar and amplifier with a view to joining the Dave Hunt line-up.

'But one look at their trombones told me they weren't for me. Then Eric and I started talking about the blues in the usual name-dropping way. I said, "John Lee Hooker", he said, "Muddy Waters", I said, "Howlin' Wolf . . ."'

McGuinness longed to be in a blues band, but was beginning to despair of finding the right companions. The previous year he'd managed to connect with two in the Oxford area: sometime undergraduate vocalist Paul Pond (later Jones) and a woodcarver-cum-pianist named Robin Benwell Palmer. But as they'd been unable to find any further kindred spirits, the project had stalled.

Now Eric agreed to join up with McGuinness, enabling him to lure 'Ben' Palmer back from woodcarving in Oxford. Two further recruits quickly materialised: a Barclays Bank employee named Robin Mason to play drums and a painter and decorator named Terry Brennan to handle vocals. 'There were no auditions,' McGuinness recalls. 'The fact that we all loved the music was qualification enough.'

They called themselves the Roosters and their first rehearsal took place on a March Saturday morning in a room above a pub in New Malden. Eric's clothes-sharing arrangement with his friend David Holt still continued and he was currently borrowing one of David's sweaters – jumpers, as the British cosily call them – which its owner was due to reclaim from Ripley the following Wednesday. But a surprise follow-up rehearsal obliged Eric to cancel their meeting and hold on to David's jumper for a little longer. In an apologetic note, he reported that the rehearsal 'went like a bomb'.

The quintet were woefully under-powered, with only Tom McGuinness's little 20-watt amplifier for two guitars and the vocalist's microphone. Now for the first time, Eric's Kay spoke in an electrified voice, and the result impressed no one. 'Its tone was terrible,' McGuinness recalls. Then in the adjoining room they discovered a set of far superior amps belonging to another band that rehearsed at the pub at different times from themselves. 'So we started using those until one day the other band came in unexpectedly and caught us. Quite a lot of diplomacy was needed to get out of a very awkward situation.'

The Roosters were to develop none of the internal tensions that bedevilled Eric's later bands. From day one he was punctilious about rehearsing, sometimes coming straight from construction-sites in clothes spattered with paint or plaster.

Though he always got along with Tom McGuinness, he was initially uncertain about the vocalist, Terry Brennan, who sported an elaborate Teddy Boy cockade and sideburns, suggesting archaic rock 'n' roll tendencies. For all that, Brennan was a blues connoisseur whom he had to thank for pointing him to another glorious original. This was Freddie King, one of the so-called 'Three Kings' of electric blues, along with B. B. and Albert, and the most youthful and extrovert of the triumvirate. His 'I Love The Woman' and finger-picked instrumental 'Hide Away' were two more tracks that Eric would never stop loving.

A powerful stabilising influence was Ben Palmer, the woodcarver-turned-pianist, who was eight years older than Eric. 'It seems a bit obvious to say that Ben became a father-figure to Eric,' McGuinness says. 'But he did – and to me and a lot of other people, too.'

While the Roosters huddled around one feeble amp in New Malden, the Beatles were becoming a national talking-point in the wake of their first number 1 single, 'Please Please Me'. British newspapers, which hitherto had scarcely noticed pop music, gave ever-increasing coverage to their bizarre fringed haircuts, round-collared suits and the juvenile female hysteria at their live shows, which all but obliterated every song they played.

Eric at this stage saw the Beatles as no more than an extreme version of the generally mindless commercial pop for which all true blues musicians felt nothing but disdain. To him, it seemed monstrous that they could earn this vast adulation with such apparent ease when so many of his sepia heroes had spent their lives in obscurity and died penniless. He could not know that the Beatles were huge fans of R&B, electric blues' modern off-spring, and it had formed a large part of their stage act before John Lennon and Paul McCartney's songwriting became their energy source and the screams took over.

As the media surrendered to Beatlemania and other pro pop bands hurriedly ceased imitating Cliff Richard's Shadows and took to fringes, round-collared suits, chirpy smiles and winsome harmonies, continuing to like the blues, let alone *play* it, felt to Eric like a form of insurrection, which was even more reason to give it his undying loyalty.

London's Marquee club, so long the blues' sworn enemy, had become a safe haven where the names John, Paul, George and Ringo were anathema and the smoky air was guaranteed un-polluted by adolescent shrieks. He never missed the Marquee's Thursday blues nights even though they ended long after the last train back to Surrey and, knowing no one who lived in the city, he often ended up wandering its streets until dawn.

Among the performers to whom the Marquee had latterly opened its doors were three who would later play an important part in his career, as he would in theirs. The first was John Mayall, who had only just quit a job as a commercial artist to form a pro blues band – giving himself a year to make it before he went back to regular employment. The other two, who had appeared with Alexis Korner in Ealing before teaming with keyboard-player Graham Bond, were Ginger Baker and Jack Bruce.

Eric regularly encountered the Rolling Stones, by this time a sextet consisting of Mick Jagger, Keith Richards and Brian Jones, plus bass-player Bill Wyman, drummer Charlie Watts and pia-nist Ian Stewart. Following their debut at the club almost a year earlier, not too much had happened for the Stones and Jagger; Richards and Jones were living together in squalor in Chelsea, dependent on the charity of their bandmates, the only ones with regular jobs.

Over the following months, Eric felt he became 'quite close' to Mick Jagger, who in those days seemed a comparable blues zealot, dedicated solely to preserving and spreading the music. However, a possible other agenda was hinted at by the personal hand microphone he always carried in his pocket.

Eric still did the occasional troubadoury gig outside the Roosters and for one of these, back in Richmond, he was allowed to borrow Mick's mic. He knew he'd be unable to cope with it at the same time as playing, but presumed the venue would have a stand he could clip it to. This turned out not to be the case, so he had to improvise by piling up two chairs and taping the microphone to the top one.

The Roosters stayed together only from the early spring to the summer of 1963. Eric would later say they rehearsed more than they performed, but Tom McGuinness contradicts this. 'We did about a dozen gigs and took it very seriously. We even advertised in the *Melody Maker* with the slogan "Can't Be Beat".'

They started in a modest way with appearances at the Kingston Jazz Cellar (actually located up two flights of stairs), the Wooden Bridge Hotel, Guildford, and the St John Ambulance Hall, Reading, but eventually made it into a hot new London club, The Scene in Ham Yard, just off Great Windmill Street. On their first visit, they found themselves sharing the bill with Bo Diddley, an R&B artiste distinct from all others for creating a totally new rhythm, then writing a song to launch it named after himself.

A couple of times, they played the Marquee as support to the Man-Hugg Blues Brothers, featuring Paul Jones on vocals and harmonica, who were soon to rename themselves after their chin-bearded South African-born leader, Manfred Mann. 'The fee was £5 for the four of us, which I told Paul was hardly enough to pay for Ben Palmer's petrol from Oxford and back,' Tom McGuinness recalls. 'But Manfred said, "Don't you realise some people would pay *us* for this opportunity?"'

'Looking back, it all seems incredibly innocent. We didn't take drugs, we hardly drank. The greatest self-indulgence I can remember was a doughnut-eating contest Eric and I once had on Brighton pier.'

McGuinness remains unsure just why the Roosters broke up, though an appearance at Uncle Bonnie's Chinese Jazz Club in Brighton, immediately after the doughnut-eating contest, may have been a factor. 'The place was full of French students, all looking incredibly chic, and from the first moment it was obvious that they hated us. They all crowded to the front of the stage and started chanting "Le jazz 'ot! Le jazz 'ot!"'

However, the Roosters had made enough of an impression for both Eric and McGuinness to be offered jobs in a professional band named Casey Jones and the Engineers. Its leader, Brian Casser, had fronted a leading Liverpool band, Cass and the Cassanovas, when the Beatles were still barely known in the city, and had given them many tips about presentation and stagecraft. He'd subsequently moved to London to manage a nightclub, the Blue Gardenia, and score a solo recording contract with the Columbia label.

Being one of Casey Jones's Engineers gave Eric his first real experience of Britain outside the Home Counties, for the gigs he played with them were mostly in the north, beginning with the Civic Hall in Macclesfield, then moving on to Manchester's Oasis club and Belle Vue open-air amusement-park. 'One of the guys had a girlfriend who was a prostitute,' Tom McGuinness recalls. 'The van used to start out from her flat in Westbourne Grove and sometimes while we were waiting there, one of her clients would turn up and we'd all have to go outside and wait for twenty minutes.'

The Engineers wore matching black uniforms, topped off by 'confederate caps' according to Eric, though McGuinness has no memory of any such headgear. They played some R&B but the main fare was pop cover versions including Casey's own current single, 'One Way Ticket'. At the two Manchester gigs, they also had to back a cabaret singer named Polly Perkins.

Though Eric liked Casey, and later said he gained much valuable experience with the Engineers, he soon developed the itchy feet for which he would become so famous. When the band were booked to appear at The Scene in London, he failed to turn up and they never saw him again. McGuinness quit a day later, soon afterwards switching from guitar to playing bass in Manfred Mann.

Unlike some other musicians who have worked with Eric over the years, he has only positive memories of their partnership. 'Did I think he was a great guitarist? Not at the time. And I was never aware of the demons he's supposed to have had. What comes back to me is the amount of time we spent laughing. I remember the two of us walking away from that pub in New Malden after a rehearsal. Both of us were still holding our guitars because we didn't have carrying-cases, and Eric started playing the Beatles' song "Misery".

'Even in a darkened, crowded cinema, I could always instantly recognise that laugh of his.'

5

YARDBIRD

'Like Bluto with an Italian accent' was how Eric would remember Giorgio Gomelsky. His first manager's black beard, stocky build and excitable temperament undeniably had something of the cartoon heavy who always loses out to Popeye the Sailor. And the music world had not seen such a loser since Sam Phillips had sold Elvis Presley's contract for $40,000.

There were many sides to Gomelsky, perhaps too many for his own good. He was born in the old Soviet Russian state of Georgia, brought up in Switzerland by way of Syria and Egypt and educated in Italy. Though not yet thirty when Eric first met him, he spoke in the effusive yet distracted style of some elderly Italian movie mogul, addressing all the boy musicians in his care indiscriminately as 'Baby'.

He had arrived in London in 1955 as a journalist and would-be film-maker but soon diversified into launching one of the city's first espresso bars, the Olympic in Chelsea's King's Road, and publicising, then organising jazz concerts and festivals. This brought him into contact with Chris Barber, one of the few jazz celebrities to value the blues and bring its surviving pioneers across the Atlantic as honoured co-performers. Gomelsky became as passionate an advocate for the music as Barber and their mutual friend Alexis Korner while still pursuing a career as a film director and editor and also attending classes in Method acting.

He had opened an R&B club named the Piccadilly in London's West End – booking the Rolling Stones for an early, unimpressive appearance – but, like Korner, had been frozen out by the jazz community and gone seeking a new young audience in the suburbs. As Korner had found his Ealing bakery basement, so Gomelsky lit on Richmond's Station Hotel, whose large rear 'function room' he rented as a Sunday-night R&B club with the last £5 he had in the world.

Rather than book a rota of groups he had the idea of keeping one on a retainer and building a rapport between them and their audience. His first incumbents were the Dave Hunt Group but then one day during the arctic winter of 1962–3 Hunt's band got snowed in and, having nowhere else to turn, Gomelsky reluctantly gave a second chance to the Rolling Stones.

After a shaky start (in part thanks to posters misprinting their category of music as 'Rhythm and Bulse'), the Station Hotel became to the Stones what Liverpool's Cavern Club had been to the Beatles.

Indeed, the Beatles themselves were seen there after Gomelsky managed to contact their manager, Brian Epstein, and arrange for them to drop in one Sunday after a TV appearance in nearby Teddington. Eric was among the audience when they arrived, all four in identical long black leather overcoats; amid the resulting kerfuffle, he little suspected the presence of a future best friend. 'They appeared to be wearing their stage outfits and for some reason that bothered me,' he would recall. 'There was obviously a mutual admiration thing going on between the Stones and them, so I suppose it was only natural that I would be jealous and think of them as a bunch of wankers.'

Gomelsky was the Rolling Stones' manager in every way but on paper when in April 1963 he was summoned back to his family home in Switzerland by the death of his father. During his absence, a nineteen-year-old freelance PR man named Andrew

Loog Oldham, who'd been working for Brian Epstein, caught the Stones' performance after a tip-off from a music journalist. Oldham cared nothing for the blues but in this group of its missionaries, especially the lead singer, he saw an instant appeal to young record-buyers for whom the Beatles were becoming a bit too tuneful, a bit too attractive to older people, altogether a bit too *safe*.

When Gomelsky returned from Switzerland, he found the Stones had signed a management deal with Oldham and were on their way to releasing their first single, a cover of Chuck Berry's 'Come On'. Having no written contract with them, he received nothing from what would be the second biggest band of all time.

His immediate concern was finding a new resident attraction for his Sunday nightclub at its new venue. Although the Stones' Station Hotel performances were entirely free of bad behaviour (unlike their later ones), the brewery that owned the pub had become alarmed by the size of the crowds they attracted and banned any further R&B on its premises. Gomelsky was forced to transfer operations across the road to the Richmond Athletic Ground, which had a spacious bar and meeting room in the lee of its grandstand. This now became the Craw Daddy club, after the Deep Southern nickname for crayfish and Bo Diddley's song 'Doing The Craw-Daddy'.

The band given the task of following the Rolling Stones had come out of Eric's secondary school, Hollyfield, and the Crown, the pub where he used to busk while at Kingston Art College. Lead guitarist Anthony Topham, known as Top, and rhythm-player Chris Dreja had both been two years behind him at Hollyfield and he'd spent long hours listening to blues records at the Topham family home in Norbiton. The vocalist and harmonica-player, Keith Relf, had been a contemporary of his at college. The only unfamiliar faces were bass-player Paul

Samwell-Smith, who'd played with Relf in a previous band, the Metropolitan Blues Quartet, and drummer Jim McCarty, who'd attended Hampton Grammar School with Samwell-Smith.

The name the five had chosen was a Depression-era term for hoboes who haunted train-yards to catch free rides, and the full nickname of the bebop genius usually known as Charlie 'Bird' Parker. They were the Yardbirds.

In a few months, they had become the most talked-about local blues band, winning the approval of the great harmonica-player Cyril Davies (co-founder of Blues Incorporated with Alexis Korner) after serving as Davies's interval-act on Eel Pie Island. They had come to Gomelsky's notice just before the Rolling Stones' defection and it was some comfort now to pour his energies into them, this time with the safeguard of a proper contract.

When he assured his Craw Daddy membership the Yard-birds were as good as the Stones he seemed – for once – not to be exaggerating. The singer and harmonica-player, Keith Relf, blond-haired and wide-lipped, was like a cross between Mick Jagger and Brian Jones. Lead guitarist 'Top' Topham, though still only fifteen, was more than a match for either Jones or Keith Richards. Where the Stones had roused their Sunday-night audiences to stomping frenzy with Bo Diddley's 'Doing The Craw-Daddy', the Yardbirds ended their sets with long instru-mental 'rave-ups', to equally potent effect.

But then, a couple of months into their residency, they gave Gomelsky a headache of a different kind. Top Topham, a preco-ciously gifted artist, was about to leave school and go to Epsom Art College. For his father, John – whose renown as a painter had never brought any great affluence – it was to be the culmination of years of preparation and sacrifice. Now Top was starting to think that playing guitar in the Yardbirds offered an altogether more attractive future. But John Topham, huge blues enthusiast though he was, vetoed the idea and fifteen-year-old Top had to accept the paternal edict.

The issue was still unresolved when Eric bumped into Keith Relf, his old Kingston student acquaintance, at a party and Relf sounded him out about taking Top Topham's place. He was far from certain he wanted to be in another band after his Casey Jones experience, but was won over by the quality of the Yardbirds' playing; still more so by an assurance that 'their entire reason for existence was to honour the tradition of the blues'.

Top at the time was away on holiday with his family, and returned to find himself ousted from the band he felt he'd created. It came as a particular blow, remembering all the educative hours Eric had spent listening to his and his father's blues record collection. 'I was very badly affected,' he recalls. 'For about six months afterwards, I couldn't even pick up a guitar.'

To make matters even more awkward, the far-from-wealthy John Topham had recently bought the Yardbirds an expensive amplifier, for which he was still paying in instalments and which the band had turned over to Eric. After a month of fruitless requests, the Tophams had to resort to a lawyer's letter to get it back.

Eric was only just eighteen so he, too, needed parental permission for a step that few British parents in 1963 would have welcomed. However, in his case only Rose's consent had to be obtained and, as always, whatever he wanted was all right with her. Jack Clapp, he recalled, was 'quietly amused', evidently feeling it would be just a matter of time before he returned to plastering and bricklaying. But even Jack was impressed that he'd be receiving a weekly wage of £20.

In October 1963 there was a meeting of the group and their respective guardians at Keith Relf's home at which Rose countersigned the contract that turned Eric into a professional musician (later admitting that she'd had no idea what she was signing).

Its provisions were the same as for the other Yardbirds save in one particular: he had to be given a week's holiday that following Christmas. Why was not explained and his new bandmates thought it rather odd since Christmas would be a specially busy time and only two months after his arrival they'd need to hire a temporary stand-in.

The answer was that, in her usual sudden and disruptive way, his real mother had again re-entered his life.

Pat by now was no longer living in Canada but West Germany, where her soldier husband, Frank McDonald, had been posted with NATO's Canadian contingent. Although Ripley was within comparatively easy reach, she made no ceremonial homecoming this time; instead, she'd asked Rose to bring Eric to spend Christmas on the base near Bremerhaven where McDonald was stationed.

Otherwise, the new Yardbird seemed an effortless fit. He made his debut on 20 October 1963 at the Studio 51 Club in Soho, playing a set that included Howlin' Wolf's 'Smokestack Lightning', John Lee Hooker's 'Boom Boom', Chuck Berry's 'Little Queenie' and Bo Diddley's 'You Can't Judge A Book By The Cover'. 'He seemed reserved, quiet, slightly nervous,' bass-player Paul Samwell-Smith remembers. 'His stance was very contained, upright and precise.' Though the nerves would improve, the stance would always stay much the same.

From then on, he found himself working almost every night. Gomelsky by this time operated a circuit of Craw Daddys, with another at the Star Hotel in Croydon and another at Edwina's Club in Finsbury Park. Like Richmond, these new territories were deluged with press advertisements, flyposters and handbills in typically brash Giorgio style, offering free admission to anyone who brought along two friends. Often, crowds of Richmond members would be ferried in by bus to pump up the enthusiasm of the locals.

For Eric, having a manager brought one immediate major benefit. A few days after he'd signed his contract, Gomelsky gave him the use of a red Fender Telecaster, a single cutaway version of the two-horned Stratocaster that had so thrilled him in Buddy Holly's hands. It was goodbye to the old, unsatisfactory Kay, which Rose was still paying for in instalments.

Conscious of the financial burden on her, Eric had tried to contribute by signing up as a temporary postman during the snowbound Christmas season of 1962. But this only other attempt at a normal job in his whole life had not gone well and been prematurely terminated. Rose would not take the £3 he'd earned, so he'd spent it on a bottle of perfume for her.

When he got his Telecaster, the Kay was taken over by Roger Pearce, his soon-to-be Christmas substitute in the Yardbirds – as were the remaining payments on it. Each week, Pearce would go to Ripley and hand another instalment in cash to Rose, who entered it punctiliously in a notebook.

At the end of 1963, the growing passion for electric blues among young people across Europe brought several hallowed names across the Atlantic to take part in West Germany's American Folk and Blues Festival, then make individual appearances in France, the Netherlands and Britain. Among them was Sonny Boy Williamson, whom Giorgio Gomelsky had met and be-friended during his jazz-promoting days.

As a means of raising the Yardbirds another notch, he arranged for them to back Sonny Boy in an appearance on the Craw Daddy circuit, during which they would make a live album together.

This was not, however, the Sonny Boy Williamson who'd been a pioneer of the blues harmonica and written 'Good Morning Little Schoolgirl' (originally just 'Good Morning Schoolgirl'). He had been murdered during a Chicago street-crime in 1948 and his name had been appropriated by another 'harp'-player, born Aleck or Alex Miller and also known professionally as Little Boy Blue and Rice Miller.

In contrast with elegant blues masters like Big Bill Broonzy and Muddy Waters, Sonny Boy Williamson the Second was chunky and crop-headed, with a straggly goatee beard. Years on from his identity-theft, he remained extremely touchy on the subject, as the Yardbirds discovered at their very first encounter. Seeking to impress as the blues historian of the band, Eric asked him, 'Isn't your real name Rice Miller?' At this, Sonny Boy II 'pulled out a small penknife and glared at me. It went downhill from there.'

His consumption of alcohol was far beyond any the English boys had ever seen. 'He always carried a briefcase with him,' drummer Jim McCarty recalls. 'But all he ever had in it were his harmonicas and a bottle of Johnnie Walker.' As he couldn't be trusted in an hotel-room (having recently set one alight while trying to cook a rabbit on the hotplate of a coffee-percolator), Gomelsky heroically invited him home for a stay that ended up lasting three months.

His performances with the Yardbirds, portions of which were taped for their projected live album, took place between 7 and 9 December at the Richmond and Croydon Craw Daddys. Sonny Boy clone or not, he was still a harp virtuoso who'd played with the likes of Elmore James and Arthur 'Big Boy' Crudup, and both venues were crammed to the rafters.

But what was supposed to be a career-enhancing honour for his young sidemen instead proved something of a trial. Onstage, Sonny Boy wore a garish pink and green suit he'd bought specially for the tour, one leg of which was pink, the other green. The show included a bizarre moment when they had to kneel while he did a Chuck Berry-style duck-walk around them. 'We'd gone through the whole set that afternoon, but when we got onstage, he was so drunk that he did completely different things from what we'd rehearsed,' Jim McCarty recalls. 'He didn't even tell us which key they were in, so we could only try to follow him as best we could.'

In time, blues masters would rhapsodise about the experience of playing with Eric, but about the Yardbirds Sonny Boy Williamson the Second was scathing. 'These English boys want to play the blues so bad,' he said. 'And they play 'em *so* bad.'

Between 23 December and New Year, as Eric's contract had stipulated, he was on the NATO military base just outside Bremerhaven visiting his mother.

This reunion did not go any more smoothly than the earlier one when he was nine. By now, Pat had had three children with Frank McDonald: Brian and Cheryl, to whom Eric had been introduced on the previous occasion, and a second daughter, Heather. So someone else was entitled to call her 'Mummy' as he never had been.

Living with Rose and Jack, he'd grown accustomed to doing exactly what he liked with never a breath of criticism. But with Pat and his stepfather, in their rigidly conventional service life, things were very different. His beatnik phase was long past – his turn-out these days as immaculate as any soldier's – but his hair committed the serious military offence of partially covering his ears. The usually affable McDonald told him bluntly that he wouldn't be allowed to join the family in the officers' mess unless he had it cut.

His older half-siblings, Brian and Cheryl, to whom he appealed for support, both took their father's side and even Rose, usually his staunch defender, pleaded with him not to make a fuss. He had no choice but to submit to the base barber, emerging with the same drastic crewcut that was given to new recruits. Having rejected him as a baby, Pat had now rejected who he was. His first look at himself in the mirror made him cry.

Worse was to come. He'd been allowed to bring his still much-loved George Washburn acoustic guitar with him and, two days later, Brian accidentally sat on it and snapped its slender neck in half. Though he forgave the contrite Brian (whom he thought 'a sweet kid') the incident plunged him into one of the moods that had made his mother mark him down as 'a loner'.

'There and then,' he would recall, 'I vowed internally that [she] and her family could go to hell. I didn't lose my temper; I just withdrew. Not only had my identity been ripped away but my most treasured possession had been destroyed. I went inside of myself and decided that from there on, I would trust nobody.'

As many another aggrieved child will know, it's easy to say one washes one's hands of a parent, but not so easy to do.

He returned to the Yardbirds with his shaming crewcut to find he hadn't been particularly missed; indeed, Roger Pearce had done so well in his place, playing his old, troublesome Kay, that the others were half-wondering if they wanted him back at all.

And now even the gorgeous Fender Telecaster Gomelsky had provided him with began to reveal flaws as he got used to it. In particular, the lighter-gauge strings he preferred were quite unsuitable for the band's extended instrumental 'rave-ups'; repeatedly bending them, as the blues demanded, often caused one to break and the music had to grind to a stop while he changed it.

When Eric changed a guitar string, it was with the same care and deliberation that his step-grandfather, Jack Clapp, laid a line of bricks. He seemed so oblivious of the Craw Daddy stompers, waiting in suspended animation, that some would break into an impatient slow handclap. After this happened several times, Gomelsky dubbed him 'Slow-handclapton'.

As it stood, it was not a nickname any musician would want.

But Eric's luck would even extend to etymology: its last two syllables soon fell away, leaving 'Slowhand', the former jibe now a tribute to leisurely virtuosity in more ways than one. The memory of that maddeningly deliberate teenager was superseded by the Pointer Sisters' vision of 'a lover with an easy touch', as skilled at finding G-spots as G7s.

We shall discover other such differences between the public's vision of his life and its actuality.

6

JOURNEYMAN

Despite the very different characters in their line-up, the Yardbirds were remarkably free of internal personality problems when Eric arrived. The most pressing concern was the health of their vocalist/harmonica-player, Keith Relf, a sufferer from acute asthma who nonetheless smoked forty cigarettes or more per day.

For much of the time, this lethal combination seemed not to affect his singing nor the breath-control demanded by his instrument. And the frail-looking Relf was nothing if not a trouper: in his worst paroxyms of coughing and wheezing, Giorgio Gomelsky would always manage to urge him onstage with a bellow of 'You can do it, baby!'

Then, suddenly, he would develop pulmonary complications that put him in hospital for days, even weeks at a time and a stand-in would have to be used. There was quite a pool of these, including a Kingston art student who usually fronted an ensemble known as Hogsnort Rupert's Famous Porkestra.

Although the Yardbirds had recently turned professional, they were still in music primarily for fun, whereas Eric had already been in one pro band and was utterly serious about the job. 'He was a journeyman,' recalls rhythm-guitarist Dreja, using the centuries-old word for a craftsman who's completed his apprenticeship but hires out to others rather than being in business for himself. 'He worked at every aspect of his performance – not just his solos but his posture onstage and his whole look.'

The Yardbirds' look hitherto had not greatly bothered its two principals, Relf and bass-player Paul Samwell-Smith, both of whom considered the most appropriate garb for celebrating the blues a lived-in denim jacket. Eric by contrast was heavily into the Ivy League style of square-cut, high-buttoned jackets, thin ties and round shirt-collars, fastened with a pin. Topped off by the Canadian military crewcut he'd decided to keep, it fitted him perfectly into the Mod movement, whose members were dedicated to fastidious tailoring, R&B music and making war on their stylistic opposites, the black leather-clad, rock 'n' roll-loving Rockers.

'With Eric, it was more than a question of just liking clothes,' says Samwell-Smith. 'Clothes were an essential part of his being.'

The drummer, Jim McCarty, disliked him at first for being 'too cocksure of himself', but warmed to his sense of humour. 'He'd put on all kinds of funny voices, then pull faces to match them, which we'd all copy. He'd usually hitch-hike from Ripley to Richmond, where our van started from, and he'd tell us all these stories about being picked up by gay guys who'd tried to seduce him.'

His strongest rapport was with Chris Dreja, a gentle character who'd been feeling somewhat lost since the departure of his old schoolfriend, Top Topham. 'Eric got me into being a Mod just like him,' Dreja says. 'We'd go up to London on shopping trips and he'd take me to a place in Shaftesbury Avenue that imported American clothes. He seemed to know people all over the West End, which really used to impress me.'

Paradoxically, as Eric later recalled, what he liked about Dreja was his only very moderate guitar skills, his lack of ambition and his ability to enjoy the moment. 'He was quiet, shy and kind and I trusted him completely – a rare thing for me.'

But with Paul Samwell-Smith he found no empathy whatsoever. 'The two of us just never clicked,' Samwell-Smith admits.

British pop musicians in that era were not immune from the country's deep-rooted class system – the Beatles and Rolling Stones included – and it seems that the bass-player's double-barrelled name was part of the problem.

'Paul's mother's maiden name had been Samwell, but she'd married a man named Smith,' Jim McCarty remembers. 'She didn't want to be "Mrs Smith" so she'd hyphenated the two. They weren't at all posh: Paul's dad was an electrician and they lived in an ordinary semi [-detached house]. But Eric didn't like the hyphen because in those days he always aligned himself with the workers.'

Another factor may have been that Samwell-Smith owned a Fender Stratocaster with three electrical pickups rather than the two on a Telecaster. 'Any nice guitar Eric saw, he wanted,' Chris Dreja recalls. 'And the more out of his reach it was, the more he wanted it.'

In February 1964, the Beatles arrived in New York, ending America's immemorial resistance to British popular music and opening the door to an 'invasion' of this massive new market by their main rivals back home. But Britain had already been invaded by American musicians of an earlier generation, some corporeally, others only in spirit.

While pop was at an unparalleled shrieking zenith, the sound of cool was the blues in its electric form, the names to conjure with not John, Paul, George and Ringo but Muddy, Bo, John Lee, T-Bone and Howlin'. Whereas it had formerly seemed to belong only to the sophisticated south, authentic yet highly distinctive blues bands were emerging from the Midlands and the north, such as Birmingham's Spencer Davis Group and the Animals from Newcastle-on-Tyne. The music that had for so long been segregated and disparaged in its own country had received the freedom of the British Isles.

The Yardbirds seemed made for the moment. As well as the Craw Daddy circuit and the blues clubs proliferating throughout the Thames Delta, they had a regular spot at the Marquee in its new Wardour Street premises and at the nearby Flamingo Club. Keith Relf's father, Bill, gave up his plumbing business to act as their driver/roadie.

On 28 February, Relf was back in hospital with a collapsed lung, but he recovered sufficiently to appear with the others in an R&B festival at Birmingham Town Hall also featuring Long John Baldry, the Spencer Davis Group and Sonny Boy Williamson. There they rejoined Sonny Boy to live-record further material for the projected album they'd begun at the Craw Daddy before Christmas. It proved an easier experience this time around – though the album wasn't to see the light of day until 1966, by which time Eric's name rather than Sonny Boy's would be its main selling-point. The night ended with an all-star jam session in which the Spencer Davis Group's fifteen-year-old singer/guitarist, Stevie Winwood, demonstrated his astonishingly mature talent.

To save time lost in commuting between their Richmond base and their various family homes, Gomelsky rented a small top-floor flat in Kew, near the famous botanical gardens, where Eric, Keith Relf and Chris Dreja took up residence and Samwell-Smith and McCarty could crash when they needed to. Dreja was waiting for his American girlfriend to join him there and in the meantime he and Eric shared a room.

This first experience of living away from home, and from Rose's coddling care, had one great advantage: he could have sex with girls in a bed rather than in the back of a van or in still more uncomfortable alfresco situations. Chris Dreja's presence in the other bed a few feet away did not inhibit this; Dreja grew accustomed to eavesdropping on Eric's favourite seduction-line invoking the Cuban Missile Crisis which had almost started a

Third World War in 1962. 'I heard it so many times: "Oh, come on . . . we could all be blown up by Cuba tomorrow."'

Like most new-school British blues bands, the Yardbirds stuck to the old pop formula of a singer who claimed most of the audience's attention and gave way to the lead guitarist usually in only one spot per song. Keith Relf was doubly prominent since the harmonica he played with such brio, for all his fragile respiration, was as much a lead instrument as Eric's guitar.

Yet at gigs where the spectators massed in front of the stage, it became increasingly noticeable that separate little crowds were collecting to watch Eric and that, unprecedentedly, they consisted of boys more than girls – 'Clapton's clique', Chris Dreja took to calling them.

Relf might have been expected to resent this, as might his closest friend in the line-up. But Paul Samwell-Smith says it never crossed either of their minds. 'We never had that kind of jealousy in the Yardbirds. We just looked on it as another good thing for the band.'

Gomelsky's urgent priority in his campaign to prove them every bit as good as the Rolling Stones was to secure them a recording contract. And here, luck seemed to have returned to him. The Richmond Craw Daddy had recently begun to sell a new fanzine named *R&B Monthly*, one of whose founders, eighteen-year-old Mike Vernon, had recently become a trainee producer at Decca Records, the label which had signed the stolen Stones. Such was his enthusiasm for the Yardbirds that *R&B Monthly* devoted a whole issue to each of them in turn – significantly, beginning with Eric rather than Keith Relf.

Vernon agreed to try to help get the Yardbirds signed to Decca and, as a first step, suggested helping them make an audition tape at the independent RG Jones Studio in Morden. It was a step not wholeheartedly welcomed by Eric; purist that he was, he thought the blues should only be played live and that any connection with buying and selling must taint it irrevocably. ('A ridiculously pompous attitude,' his adult self would admit, 'considering that all the music I was learning from was on record.')

At RG Jones's studio, with Mike Vernon as producer, the Yardbirds cut two tracks, Jimmy Reed's 'Baby What's Wrong?' and 'Honey In Your Hips', written by Keith Relf. Though Vernon loved the performance overall, Eric's contribution didn't particularly impress him. 'There wasn't a solo in either track, just the odd riff that sounded like Jimmy Reed or Billy Boy Arnold. They were competent and in the groove, but nothing that took your breath away.'

As always, no one could think less of Eric than Eric did. 'I was just embarrassed because in the studio my inadequacy was there for all to see,' he would recall. 'But it wasn't just me . . . as exciting as it was to be actually making a record, when we listened to it back and compared it to the stuff we were supposedly modelling ourselves on, it seemed pretty lame. We just sounded young and white.'

Despite Vernon's enthusiastic endorsement, his bosses at Decca rejected the tape. 'I was never told why. I gathered that they felt they'd already got the Stones and Keith didn't have the same power as a frontman that Mick Jagger did.' He stayed on good terms with the Yardbirds nonetheless, even joining the pool of ad-hoc vocalists they could call on when Keith Relf was ill.

The obvious next target was Decca's arch-rival, the huge multi-label EMI corporation, which had had the incalculable good fortune to sign the Beatles after Decca turned them down. This time, Gomelsky made the pitch in person, taking care to drop the name of Brian Epstein at every opportunity; as a result, the Yardbirds were offered a contract with EMI's Columbia label.

Their debut single, released in May 1964, was a cover of Billy Boy Arnold's 'I Wish You Would', heavy on echo and with no guitar solo by Eric. Columbia's promotional campaign focused on Keith Relf's omnipresent harmonica: 'Do you suffer from an incredible urge to let loose and shake away all your frustrations? Then listen to the Yardbirds' most blueswailing record – I Wish You Would.'

It managed to climb only to number 26 in the *New Musical Express* chart and was rejected by EMI's American affiliate, Capitol. The best US deal that could be found was with the small Epic label, under a contract paying only half the (already minuscule) standard royalty-rate. On its release by Epic, mistakenly titled 'I Wish You Could', it received no measurable radio play and did not appear on any chart.

The best thing that Columbia did for the Yardbirds was let them make an album before achieving a hit single and also to recognise how much energy their 'blueswailing' might lose in a sterile recording studio. The album, therefore, was recorded in front of a live audience at the Marquee, where their following had become as ardent as back in Richmond. Released later in the year as *Five Live Yardbirds*, it 'honoured the tradition of the blues' as devotedly as Eric could wish, with tracks including Bo Diddley's 'Pretty Girl', Slim Harpo's 'I Got Love If You Want It' and the first Sonny Boy Williamson's 'Good Morning Little Schoolgirl'.

Gomelsky assumed the title of producer, assisted by Bill Relf, who held a boom microphone over the spectators' heads to catch as much of the cheering and whooping as possible.

While more and more of the world fell in love with the Beatles, so in Britain revulsion mounted against the Rolling Stones, those formerly blameless blues purists whom Andrew Loog Oldham had brilliantly marketed as tangle-haired, sneering, disrespectful anti-Beatles. The Yardbirds came to national notice as something midway between the two.

They could do so mainly thanks to a major expansion in British television coverage of popular music. The BBC's new 'arty' second channel, BBC2, was the first to take it seriously in all its forms, jazz, folk and blues, and transmit live performances in shadowy settings as intimate as clubs. At the opposite extreme, on the sole commercial network, *Ready, Steady Go!* was a nonstop revue in an undisguised hangar of a studio, mixing top British acts with visiting American ones, many from the blues and soul sphere like James Brown and the Famous Flames, Little Stevie Wonder, the Miracles and Martha and the Vandellas.

The Yardbirds were highly telegenic, offering a touch of the Stones' edginess without the slightest offensiveness; a later era might have termed them Rolling Stones Lite. This was overwhelmingly down to Keith Relf, whose hyperactive harmonica and brooding poetic air gave no clue to his terrible health. Eric – apart from arraying himself in some crisp new high-collared, buttondown shirt – made no attempt to play to the camera, and studio audiences as yet contained no Clapton cliques. *Ready Steady Go!*'s legendary producer Vicki Wickham, who chose the band to be the first to play live on her programme, retains no memory of him whatsoever from that occasion.

The lack of a hit single remained a serious handicap and Gomelsky had to work hard to maintain their profile in an ever more crowded and competitive field. Over-extended as he now was as their producer as well as manager, he took on a young PR man named Greg Teller, who quickly proved to be in the Andrew Loog Oldham mould.

In May 1964, the Labour peer Lord Willis (who as Ted Willis had scripted the long-running TV police drama *Dixon of Dock Green*) made a speech in the House of Lords, condemning the music of the Beatles and the Rolling Stones as 'a cheap candy floss substitute for culture'. Though the Yardbirds had not been included in the attack, Teller conceived the idea of a staged

confrontation between them and Willis at his home in Chisle-
hurst, Kent, with the press in attendance.

They, Gomelsky and several Fleet Street photographers arrived to find the peer on a sun-lounger in his garden and at first
not at all keen to receive them. His daughter, Sally, having persuaded him, the Yardbirds performed Big Bill Broonzy's 'Louise'
standing on a low garden wall. Willis offered them beer and con-
ceded that what he'd heard wasn't candyfloss but 'real folk music
in the modern idiom'. The next day's coverage was everything
that could be desired, even if the *Daily Mirror*'s expansive spread
referred to them throughout as the Yardsticks.

Sally Willis later remembered that, unsurprisingly, Gomelsky
had done most of the talking and that of all the band, Eric had
said least, though he was the only one to request a tour of her
father's extremely large and luxurious house.

At moments like this Gomelsky was brilliant, but in the prac-
ticalities of running a band, he was shambolic. His haphazard
scheduling of the Yardbirds' out-of-London gigs (as far to the west
as Redruth, Cornwall and to the north as Liverpool's famous
Cavern Club) meant frequent round trips of hundreds of miles,
crammed into their single van. 'It was awful,' Paul Samwell-
Smith recalls. 'Like being married.'

Life on the road bore little resemblance to what it would soon
become, especially not with Keith Relf's father as the driver/
roadie. 'I don't remember any drugs – not of any kind,' Samwell-
Smith says. 'It was just alcohol.' In that regard, the addictive one
was not Eric but Keith, who smoked, coughed, wheezed and
drank beer more or less continuously; for hour after hour, the
others would hear the alternate puffing of his asthma inhaler
and the hiss of a fresh can being opened.

There was always much griping about Gomelsky and how
it could be that after ten months of virtually non-stop gigs at

ever-rising rates, so little money was coming through to them. 'We were in a logistical nightmare,' Samwell-Smith says. 'Soon to turn into a financial nightmare.'

On 9 August, they were due to appear in what had formerly been the Richmond Jazz Festival but was now the National Jazz and Blues Festival, with the Rolling Stones making their last appearance as hometown boys at the head of a massive bill from both camps including Memphis Slim, Jimmy Witherspoon, Mose Allison, Chris Barber, Humphrey Lyttelton, Long John Baldry, Georgie Fame and the Graham Bond Organisation.

The day before, during the recording of a spot for BBC2, Keith Relf again suffered a collapsed lung and had to be rushed to hospital. He almost died, underwent the removal of the fallible lung and was told he would never sing again. Although this proved too pessimistic a forecast, he was to be out of circulation for six weeks.

The Yardbirds closed the festival with Mike Vernon standing in for Relf, after which they were joined onstage for a jam session by Georgie Fame and Graham Bond's rhythm section. So for the first time, Eric shared a stage with Ginger Baker and Jack Bruce.

After this, the Yardbirds' 136th gig of the year, Gomelsky announced that they needed a rest and so he was giving them a two-week, all-expenses-paid holiday at a luxury hotel in Lugano, Switzerland, where he had grown up.

On 10 August, they set off in their van, followed by a second vehicle carrying a number of their female supporters from the Craw Daddy – a detail that aroused no one's suspicions at the time. 'We should have known,' says Jim McCarty, 'because Giorgio was always bussing our fans from gig to gig.'

After a hair-raising journey across the Alps, they arrived in Lugano to find the hotel was only half-built and that they'd been allocated one room between them. Gomelsky then informed them that, far from it being a holiday, Bill Relf was following behind with their equipment and that in exchange for room and board they would be expected to perform every evening beside the hotel pool. They were also booked to appear at the jazz festival he'd founded in nearby Ascona and at the opening of a record store in Lugano's town centre.

Any other manager who exploited his musicians so shamelessly would have faced wholesale mutiny but Gomelsky managed to persuade the Yardbirds, Eric included, that it was all for their own good, and they put in the full two weeks at the half-finished hotel, playing to an audience largely consisting of their own portable fan club.

Another Gomelsky deal from which they seemed to derive no income came from his determination that they should emulate the Rolling Stones in everything. The Stones had just made a television commercial for Rice Krispies, so he contracted the Yardbirds to make one for Rael-Brook drip-dry shirts.

Again, the band fell into line – albeit one of them this time with visible ill-grace. The ad showed Relf, Samwell-Smith, McCarty and Dreja in Rael-Brook 'Toplin' shirts no different from what they wore every day and looking dapperly at ease. But Eric, usually the biggest shirt-enthusiast of them all, wore a sweater, setting off a fresh-mown crewcut, and glowered like a skinhead before his time.

The second Yardbirds single was 'Good Morning Little Schoolgirl', a title no more questionable in October 1964 than when the original Sonny Boy Williamson had recorded it in 1937. This version, however, followed a recent pop-oriented one by the Chicago R&B duo Don and Bob, mentioning innocent trysts with the schoolgirl concerned in a soda-shop and modern dance crazes like the Twist and the Stroll.

It had double-tracked vocals, a cutesy 'oh-oh-oh' harmony, even an outbreak of Beatle-like whooping. It also contained the first guitar solo by Eric to reveal a distinctive voice – in this case a note-bending swoop and slide, totally at odds with the rest of the production and very clearly intended to be so. The single fared no better than its predecessor, 'I Wish You Would', reaching only number 45 in the UK and failing to secure an American release.

That October, the Yardbirds joined a national package tour headlined by Billy J. Kramer and the Dakotas (another hugely successful Brian Epstein discovery) which also mustered Cliff Bennett and the Rebel Rousers, the Nashville Teens and the Kinks. Such tours usually combined British artistes with imported American ones and played a different city or large town every night, usually at cinemas in the Odeon or ABC chains whose sound-systems were rudimentary or non-existent. Even for the biggest names, performances were seldom longer than twenty minutes.

Since the Beatles, every act, whether or not they had a hit record behind them, was greeted by demented shrieks. Eric would later recall his bewilderment the first time it happened to the Yardbirds. 'I mean, at one moment you were at school and you were pimply and no one wanted to know you. And then suddenly there you were onstage with thousands of girls screaming their heads off.'

Second on the bill to Kramer were the Ronettes, whose 'Be My Baby', produced by the famously neurotic Phil Spector with his Wall of Sound technique, had brought a new sexiness to female African American vocal groups. During the tour, Eric developed one of his all-consuming crushes on their lead singer, Ronnie, aka Veronica Bennett, after what he interpreted as encouraging signals from her.

Too shy to attempt anything on the road, he hung around outside the Ronettes' London hotel, hoping for a word with her alone. His hopes were dashed when Ronnie came out on the arm of Mick Jagger, followed by another Ronette with Keith Richards.

The Yardbirds had acquitted themselves so well on the Billy J. Kramer tour that Brian Epstein booked them for the Beatles' Christmas Show alongside Freddie and the Dreamers and Sounds Incorporated at the 3,500-seat Hammersmith Odeon in west London, from Christmas Eve through to 16 January 1965.

The experience was a thankless one since the audiences were there solely to see the headliners, who appeared in comedy sketches and routines as well as playing music, and everyone else on the programme had their performances blotted out by impatient, warring screams of 'John!' 'Paul!' 'George!' or 'Ringo!'

The Yardbirds' name appeared at the bottom of the poster, lumped together with Elkie Brooks, Michael Haslam and the Mike Cotton Sound. In a group photograph taken on the stage during rehearsals, Eric is barely visible.

However, the Beatles at close quarters proved not to be the 'wankers' he'd thought when they came to see the Stones at the Craw Daddy. Huge as they were, they treated even this least important of their support bands as equals. Paul McCartney was especially friendly, playing the Surrey boys a new song he was working on with the working title 'Scrambled Eggs', later changed to 'Yesterday'.

John Lennon was generally amiable but could be devastatingly rude, sometimes to those least able to retaliate. One evening, en route to Hammersmith by tube, Eric fell into conversation with an American woman and mentioned he was appearing in the Beatles' show. She got so excited that he took her with him to the Odeon and smuggled her into their dressing-room. They were all impressively polite to her except John, who 'made a face of mock boredom and started doing wanking movements under his coat'.

Eric naturally had most in common with George Harrison as the Beatles' lead guitarist – though his role had less of its usual importance in the face of Lennon and McCartney's phenomenal creative axis. The pair had already written dozens of songs together as against George's handful, and monopolised the attention of their producer, George Martin, in the recording studio. Few people in those days suspected to what extent one of the four most adored young men in history felt overshadowed and underappreciated.

Talking shop about their common instrument broke down George's usual shyness and reserve. He showed Eric his collection of Gretsch guitars; Eric introduced him to lighter-gauge strings and told him where to buy them. So one of rock's strangest friendships was born.

At the end of 1964, the British blues boom reached its zenith when the Rolling Stones' cover version of Willie Dixon's 'Little Red Rooster' (featuring the most sexually charged lyric since Blind Lemon Jefferson's 'Black Snake Moan') became the first blues song to reach number 1 in the UK singles charts. Yet in truth it was now no longer a blues number so much as a Stones one, whose performance on television first revealed, to the horror of all British parents with young daughters, the size and suggestiveness of Mick Jagger's lips.

Despite the Yardbirds' reputation as a live band, Giorgio Gomelsky had been unable to bring them anywhere near the Stones in record-sales. Neither of their singles had made the Top 20 and their album, *Five Live Yardbirds*, despite generally positive reviews, had not sold much better. So early in 1965, Gomelsky told them they had to stop being such blues purists and try to reach the mainstream pop audience.

Two major British bands had already gone the same way, with spectacular rewards. The formerly cerebral Manfred Mann had released 'Do Wah Diddy Diddy', originally by an American vocal group called the Exciters, while the Animals had transformed an ancient folk song, 'The House of the Rising Sun', with a blisteringly modern rock arrangement. Both singles had shot to number 1 in both Britain and America.

The idea of selling out his cherished blues for commercial gain could not have been more repugnant to Eric – but, according to bass-player Paul Samwell-Smith, he wasn't alone. 'None of us felt comfortable about being pushed towards becoming a pop group. We were all equally pissed off about it.'

As Gomelsky pointed out, America still held a vast store of blues and soul that could be turned into comparably rewarding cover versions. Each Yardbird, therefore, was to pick a candidate and then a vote would be taken on the most promising one. This air of a competition only added insult to injury where Eric was concerned. Yet he not only went along with it but did his best to win. 'I was still afraid of fucking everything up,' he later recalled, 'and finding myself back plastering walls with my grandfather.'

Coincidentally a fellow EMI signing, Manfred Mann – the person not the band – had expressed interest in producing records with the Yardbirds, so was gratefully co-opted as a proven expert in crossing over from blues to pop. He made two demos with them: 'Sweet Music', a Major Lance B-side, with backing vocals by his own band's lead singer, Paul Jones, and the Shirelles' 'Putty (In Your Hands)'. But neither had the instant, mindless magic of 'Do Wah Diddy Diddy'.

Eric, meanwhile, looked around for something commercial yet not ruinously compromising and found an Otis Redding track, 'Your One And Only Man'. When the others didn't care for it, he went to the opposite extreme and suggested 'Hang On Sloopy', then only a minor hit on the American R&B charts for the Vibrations. That, too, was voted down and, a few months afterwards, became an American number 1 (and all-time dance-floor favourite) by the McCoys.

He hardly needed to have bothered. His least favourite band-mate, Paul Samwell-Smith, had developed ambitions to become a record producer and was seen by Gomelsky as the Yardbirds' de facto musical director. Samwell-Smith therefore chose the make-or-break next single over the others' heads.

It was not after all an American import but 'For Your Love', an angst-ridden ballad by an unknown songwriter from Man-chester named Graham Gouldman (later one of the influential Seventies band 10cc). Samwell-Smith produced it in his own arrangement, which bore no resemblance to the band's usual 'blueswailing' style and, whether by accident or design, reduced the guitar to a minimum.

The lead instrument was a harpsichord, played by an outside session musician, Brian Auger, supported by Keith Relf's bongo drums. Apart from a subdued bass riff in the middle eight, Eric was inaudible. By way of a consolation prize he was given the B-side, an instrumental entitled 'Got To Hurry', somewhat like Booker T and the MGs' 'Green Onions'. Gomelsky had hummed its basic structure to him and so claimed the composer's credit under the name Oscar Rasputin.

To compensate for his burial on the A-side, 'Got To Hurry' was credited to the Yardbirds 'featuring Eric "Slowhand" Clap-ton'. Nonetheless, the 'For Your Love' session was the beginning of the end for him and the band: henceforward, he became 'a grizzled and discontented individual' who deliberately made himself as unpopular as possible. His attitude hardened still fur-ther after the biggest sell-out of the blues to date. In February, the Rolling Stones released 'The Last Time' by Mick Jagger and Keith Richards, a piece of pure pop that further enlarged Jagger's terrifying mouthiness and ignited a writing partnership that ul-timately would be second only to Lennon and McCartney's.

'There was a horrible atmosphere,' drummer Jim McCarty recalls. 'At band-meetings, it was always Eric against the four of us. On the way to and from gigs, he'd sit in the van with a long face, lost in his own little world.' He himself readily concedes: 'I was a nasty piece of work in those days. I was unreliable . . . dogmatic . . . anti-social for a lot of the time.'

Finally, Gomelsky told him that if he wanted to leave the Yardbirds, nobody would stand in his way. Sure enough, nobody did. Less than a month after his departure, 'For Your Love' reached number 1 in the *New Musical Express* Top 30.

7

BLUESBREAKER

All this and what soon followed may look like a supremely arrogant twenty-year-old using a so-called matter of principle as an excuse for bad behaviour, as twenty-year-olds are apt to do, then strolling into a new band without a backward glance. In reality, finding himself out of the Yardbirds hit Eric as hard as being forced to leave Kingston Art College had two years earlier. Thanks to the childhood trauma with his mother, rejection always devastated him and always would, however much he'd seemed to ask for it.

His immediate response was to head home to Ripley, to Rose and Jack, the little corner house with the outside toilet and his ever-dependable old schoolfriends around The Green. He was 'totally disillusioned,' he would recall, and 'ready to quit the music business altogether'.

It hardly helped his mood to hear what little trouble the Yardbirds had had in replacing him. Their first choice was the baby-faced Jimmy Page, a friend since Ealing Blues Club days who'd since become one of London's top session musicians. But Page, unwilling to give up that steady income, steered them to Jeff Beck, formerly of Wimbledon College of Arts, now lead guitar in the Tridents. (Later, Page would cease session work and join Beck in the Yardbirds en route to Led Zeppelin. Eric had therefore unwittingly opened the way to two of his strongest future competitors.)

Now he could only sit beside Rose and Jack in the tiny living-room at 1 The Green, watching the new Yardbirds on television with 'For Your Love' at the top of the charts: Keith Relf, seeming-ly the healthiest of mortals with his shades and bongo drums; the provokingly hyphenated Paul Samwell-Smith, so triumphantly right in his unilateral song-choice; and the snakily handsome Jeff Beck, looking as if he'd always been there. Jack Clapp's words after the art college disgrace seemed doubly applicable now: 'You've had your chance, Rick, and you've chucked it away.'

After the Roosters fell apart in 1963, he had stayed in touch with Ben Palmer, the piano-player whose day job was furniture-restorer and woodcarver. Palmer, eight years his senior, was 'an incredibly charismatic man, very funny, very intelligent and very worldly-wise, with strong aristocratic features that made him look as if he came from the eighteenth century. He was a creative man of great depth who could turn his skill in any direction.' In other words, a father-figure tailor-made for this particular father-seeker.

At a loose end as he now was, Eric thought the two of them might make a guitar-and-piano blues record together and he got a friend named June Child – later the wife of Marc Bolan – to drive him to Oxford, where Palmer worked and lived alone above some old stables.

Palmer couldn't be tempted to abandon his workbench for music again – at least, not at present. But Eric ended up staying for several weeks in what amounted to a convalescence from the Yardbirds. Palmer looked after him almost like a second Rose, cooking him appetising meals, listening to his troubles and dis-pensing advice as solidly trustworthy as good oak or teak. For additional therapy, his host introduced him to a fantasy epic by an Oxford professor of Anglo-Saxon, as yet still little known out-side American college campuses, J. R. R. Tolkien's *The Lord of the Rings*.

It was while he was immersed in the adventures of Bilbo Baggins, Frodo and Gollum, still unsure whether he had a future in music, that out of the blue he was invited to join John Mayall's Bluesbreakers. Mayall had long been watching his development at the Marquee and been impressed by his playing on 'Got To Hurry', the instrumental B-side of 'For Your Love'. So that hated harpsichord-fest hadn't been such a waste of time after all.

Coincidentally, Mayall wanted to lose the Bluesbreakers' present lead guitarist, Roger Dean, for not being bluesy enough. Hearing that Eric was available, he contacted June Child, who gave him Ben Palmer's telephone number.

John Mayall is the daddy of British blues or, at least, those many blues musicians nurtured by art colleges. He was born in Macclesfield, Cheshire in 1933 and at age fourteen went to Manchester Junior Art School, where he combined his studies with learning piano, guitar and harmonica. Unlike the great majority who were to follow the same path, he built a successful career in commercial art, working as an illustrator and photographer before forming the Bluesbreakers and turning fully professional in 1963.

Eric was first in a long line of younger instrumentalists he recruited who would go on to form or join major rock bands, among them Peter Green and Mick Fleetwood, later of Fleetwood Mac, Mick Taylor, later of the Rolling Stones, Aynsley Dunbar, later of the Mothers of Invention, Jefferson Starship and Whitesnake, and Andy Fraser, later of Free. Mayall became renowned for giving his protégés room to develop – and for firing almost as many as left him to go on to greater things.

Offstage, he bore little resemblance to the stereotypical hard-drinking, tobacco-addicted, feckless, footloose bluesman: he was a teetotaller, non-smoker, vegetarian and health nut, married with three children and living in a substantial Victorian house in Lee Green, south-east London.

Eric had not much cared for the Bluesbreakers' only album to date and briefly wondered how he might fare in a band with a leader twelve years his senior. What mattered more was that, while others were selling out the blues on every hand, Mayall's band remained incorruptible, sticking to the sacred Muddy/John Lee/Howlin' songbook and regarding the stage as its true home – everything in fact that Eric had expected from the Yardbirds.

He joined the Bluesbreakers in April 1965 on a salary of £35 per week, with no formal audition or even rehearsal. Mayall had played 'Got To Hurry' to his other two sidemen, bass-player John McVie (later of Fleetwood Mac) and drummer Hughie Flint (later of McGuinness Flint), both of whom accepted it as a more than sufficient entrance exam. 'We just got into the van and went off to the gig,' Flint recalls.

Mayall and the Bluesbreakers were managed by Rik Gunnell, a former boxer who ran both an artistes agency and Soho's Flamingo Club, best known as the home of Georgie Fame and the Blue Flames. It differed from the nearby Marquee in having a large black clientele, drawn from American air force bases and west London's Caribbean community. The 1963 Profumo scandal which toppled Harold Macmillan's Conservative government had started with the two West Indian boyfriends of a topless dancer named Christine Keeler fighting over her at the Flamingo.

Gunnell and his scarfaced younger brother, Johnny, who acted as his assistant, had fearsome reputations as tough guys both in the club and with their agency clients. When Georgie Fame became nationally popular and wanted to change managers, Rik looked thoughtfully at Fame's hands and said, 'Clive [his real first name], you *do* want to go on playing the piano, don't you?'

The Gunnells kept Mayall on a work schedule that made the

Yardbirds' under Gomelsky seem leisurely. 'If there had been eight nights a week, we would have played them,' Eric recalls. 'With two shows on a Sunday.'

The Bluesbreakers travelled in a single van fitted with a bed for their leader's exclusive use; the others shared a mattress on the floor. 'We'd leave Newcastle some time after midnight,' their drummer, Hughie Flint, recalls, 'and John would be snoring by the time we reached Gateshead [just across the River Tyne].'

London gigs like their regular one at a pub-club named Klooks Kleek in West Hampstead would be followed by an all-nighter back at the Flamingo amid wreathing clouds of marijuana smoke. 'There were notices all round the place saying "Anyone smoking reefers will be prosecuted,"' Flint says, 'but you could buy the stuff from the office.'

Eric's impact on the Bluesbreakers was immediate, nowhere more noticeably than with the Flamingo crowd whose racial make-up made it particularly demanding. 'Before that, we'd always felt a bit overshadowed by people like Georgie Fame and Zoot Money. We'd been accepted, but not in a great way. As soon as Eric came in, everybody dug us.'

Even the Gunnells' punishing work rate could not satiate his hunger to perform and he made numerous one-off appearances at other Soho venues like The Scene. One night he accepted a gig at a Mayfair club named Esmeralda's Barn, unaware that it belonged to the East End's notorious twin crime bosses Ronnie and Reggie Kray. He fronted the house musicians and the only audience were the lethal twins themselves, seated at a table at the back as if conducting an audition.

He also made an auspicious start as a session musician, although hardly conscious of it at the time. A month after taking him on, Mayall seconded him to record some tracks with Bob Dylan, who was currently in Britain on the tour chronicled in D. A. Pennebaker's classic documentary *Dont Look Back*.

Dylan at that point was still the unignorable voice of America's Civil Rights movement through quasi-religious anthems like 'Blowin' In The Wind' and 'A Hard Rain's Gonna Fall' – so, in Eric's book, just a 'folkie'. His main bugbear in the Yardbirds, Paul Samwell-Smith, had been a passionate early Dylan fan and Eric on principle hated everything that Samwell-Smith liked.

Dylan on this tour made friends with many young British blues musicians, as the Pennebaker film shows. Eric wasn't among them, although one scene shows Dylan watching the Bluesbreakers on television, asking who their young lead guitarist is, then going 'Wow!' Even so, recording with him proved a severe letdown. Ever unpredictable, he barely spoke to anyone in the studio; then, with the tracks only half-finished, he flew to Madrid, never to return. Not until the advent of 'electric' Dylan and albums like *Blonde On Blonde* would Eric realise he'd been in the presence of greatness.

Despite the splash he was making with John Mayall, the music press knew him mainly for having been unlucky or foolish enough to leave a band just when it rocketed into the charts. His first substantial interview, in the trade paper *Disc and Music Echo*, was headlined THE YARDBIRD WHO GOT LEFT BEHIND and portrayed a dejected, pessimistic figure, although the writer, Dawn James, was struck by his 'super eyes'.

He said he still thought nostalgically about nights with the Yardbirds at the Marquee – even found himself worrying about Keith Relf's asthma. By contrast, the future seemed to hold little promise. 'I don't expect I'll be a great success. I'm not that sort of a bloke. I never expect good things to happen to me.'

A twenty-year-old earning £35 per week in 1965 could easily afford a luxurious flat in one of the choicest areas of newly identified 'Swinging' London. But throughout his career in the Bluesbreakers, Eric would continue to billet himself with other

111

people in the same way he had at Ben Palmer's. It was sometimes whispered that he was a bit of a freeloader, but he never had any trouble in finding people willing to take him in.

The next such 'crash' was offered by a friend of Mayall's named Charles Radcliffe, a radical political activist and magazine editor with the looks of a pop star. Meeting Radcliffe and his girlfriend, Diana, at a Bluesbreakers gig, Eric happened to mention he currently had nowhere to live. They immediately offered him a room at their flat in the Fulham Road.

These months with Radcliffe expanded his literary horizons far beyond Tolkien; he read American beat poets like Allen Ginsberg and Lawrence Ferlinghetti, even esoteric tracts like Kenneth Patchen's *The Journal of Albion Moonlight*, which he loved, despite not understanding a word of it. From Radcliffe, too, he learned about Dadaism, the use of absurdity to make a satirical or political point, which culminated in Marcel Duchamp's solemn exhibition of a plain white toilet-bowl.

'I remember him telling an interviewer from *Rave* magazine that he was in a Dada kind of mood,' Radcliffe says. 'But we never had any serious discussions about politics. He made it clear that he wasn't interested. 'He was a very good guest, although it never occurred to him to make any contribution to the household expenses. Finally, Diana said something to him about it and he brought us a strawberry gateau and some Mateus rosé.'

Fulham was a great deal more central than Ripley, yet still Eric often had problems in getting to John Mayall's house in Lee Green, south-east London, in time to board the van for the night's gig. So, for the sake of efficiency, Mayall invited him to stay for as long as he liked.

This being a more formal boarding arrangement, he could not accept until Mayall's wife, Pamela, had been down to Ripley to meet Rose. 'She was definitely checking us out,' Pamela recalls. 'I took along my little daughter, Tracey, and while we were there, Tracey needed to go to the loo. Out in the garden there was a fairy path to this little shed, and I remember her hopping and skipping all the way down it. Anyway, the upshot was that his grandma agreed to let him go.'

Eric spent almost the next year living with the Mayalls and their three children, occupying an attic room little wider than its single bed. Pamela remembers him as 'a sweetheart . . . very young, very naive. Once, I even had to sign a paper as his legal guardian.'

It might have become an imposition as Pamela, too, was an art school graduate, now teaching at Goldsmiths College. But she recalls, 'He was never any trouble. He ate everything that was put in front of him. He was always very thoughtful, too. Whenever he went away with the band, he always brought Tracey back a little gift. Once, he bought her a dress, which was an unusual thing for a young boy to do.'

The main attraction of the house for Eric was Mayall's huge and catholic record collection, ranging from field recordings of Delta bluesmen in the 1930s to avant-garde jazz by the likes of Ornette Coleman. The two would spend hours playing tracks and discussing their suitability for the Bluesbreakers, then Eric would take the record up to his garret and stay there with his guitar until he could reproduce it. 'When I'd leave for Goldsmiths in the mornings, he'd already be playing,' Pamela remembers. 'And when I came home at night, he'd still be up there.'

In many ways, the age gap between his bandleader and himself counted for little. Mayall shared his literary bent, in particular his current side-obsession with Harold Pinter's play *The Caretaker*, recently filmed with Donald Pleasence as the down-and-out Davies. Eric had seen the film numerous times and even bought a copy of the script, so could recite whole scenes by heart. It has a cast of only three and he, Mayall and bass-player John McVie would act it out, rotating the roles of Davies, Aston and Mick and convulsing with hysterical laughter the playwright never intended.

Relationships within the Bluesbreakers were generally amicable, even though Mayall could sometimes resemble a schoolteacher with his class mocking him behind his back. The reward of his clean-living ways was an impressive physique which he liked to show off by performing stripped to the waist – a spectacle that always reduced Eric and McVie to ill-suppressed giggles. 'He was tolerant up to a point,' Eric recalls, 'but we knew there was a limit and we did our best to push him to it . . . We liked to see just how far we could go before he lost his temper.'

'The worst argument Eric and I ever had was about jazz, which I loved and he didn't,' Hughie Flint recalls. 'He said it was just a three-minute melody, followed by long, meandering solos. I reminded him about that later when he was in Cream.'

Eric naturally gravitated towards John McVie, who'd come to bass-playing after training as an income tax inspector (and was currently dating Pamela Mayall's much younger sister). 'John was very funny, very bright and very hard to control,' says Flint. 'I think he was fired from the band three times altogether.'

Mayall, the total abstainer, disapproved of drinking at gigs, but McVie always managed a large surreptitious intake. 'Lovable though he was, there were times when his drinking made him aggressive,' Eric recalls. 'He would either be left behind . . . or sometimes turfed out of the van on to the side of the road.'

During performances, McVie kept a large glass of Scotch and Coke at the side of the stage, from which he would gulp when Mayall wasn't looking. 'One night, when he went to take a drink, the level in the glass was much less than he'd left it the last time,' Hughie Flint recalls. 'Someone in the audience was helping himself to it. So he took the glass away, peed into it and put it back.

The next time he looked, the level had gone down even more, so whoever it was was drinking his pee.'

With Eric at that time, the over-indulgence was not yet in alcohol. He has admitted how, almost every night, he would chat up some pretty young blues enthusiast before the show, have a fully clothed quickie with her somewhere backstage in the thirty-minute interval between the Bluesbreakers' two sets, then go back on again 'with the knees of my jeans covered in dust from the floor . . . It wasn't a girl in every port but a girl at every gig.'

These were months in which young heterosexual Britons were adopting clothes and coiffures which a few years earlier would have stigmatised them as 'pansies' or 'poofs'. And, as always, Eric reflected every twist and turn in fashion, however radical. He now had sidewhiskers of a length not seen since the age of the Victorian paterfamilias and a thin moustache like a pantomime villain's which came and went as if responding to in-audible boos. 'Once, he turned up for a gig in a fur coat,' Hughie Flint remembers. 'Another time, his fingernails were painted.'

John Mayall's bare torso might be fair game for mockery, but Eric's fashion choices never. 'McVie and I giggled among our-selves,' Flint says, 'but we didn't let him see. He was someone you didn't take the piss out of.'

The autumn of 1965 brought a bizarre episode showing both the irresponsibility of which Eric was capable and the quixotic loyal-ty and selflessness.

Oxford University had been in the vanguard of the British blues revival and through Ben Palmer he had met a trio of recent graduates, now living in London, for whom it remained a con-suming passion. John Baily was an anthropologist and aspiring vocalist who'd once booked the Roosters for a college dance; Bernie Greenwood was a newly qualified doctor who worked at a Notting Hill clinic by day and played sax with Chris Farlowe and the Thunderbirds at the Flamingo after dark; Ted Milton was an aspiring poet who'd been at (Quaker) school with Baily.

Milton's girlfriend, Clarissa, also recently down from Oxford, rented a flat in Long Acre, above a fruit wholesaler's serving the nearby Covent Garden produce market, still in full swing with porters carrying piles of empty baskets on their heads like ambulatory Towers of Pisa. In the adjacent flat lived two Cambridge graduates, Peter Jenner and Andrew King, soon to begin managing a new (and entirely ex-art school) band named Pink Floyd.

While still officially lodging with John and Pamela Mayall, Eric took to spending long periods with Milton, Greenwood and Baily – and, often, Ben Palmer – at the Long Acre flat, finally even renting a room there. For someone whose education had stopped at age sixteen, it was intoxicating to be around these 'clever' people who nonetheless spoke the same musical language he did, drinking newly fashionable Mateus rosé and smoking cannabis.

He developed a particular admiration for the poet Ted Milton who, rather than singing or playing the blues, expressed it in mime. Never a good mover himself, he was fascinated by the way Milton could physically interpret a Howlin' Wolf song, 'dancing and employing facial gestures . . . I understood for the first time how you could listen to music and bring it completely to life.'

That summer, Baily and Greenwood decided to form a band and drive overland to Australia, paying their way with performances en route. Ben Palmer signed up as pianist and Milton as drummer. For Eric, this was troubadouring on a grand scale and, with Palmer's presence an added inducement, he agreed to join them.

It seemed bafflingly perverse, just as he was beginning to make a name for himself with the Bluesbreakers. It was also gross ingratitude to John Mayall, who had rescued him from despair, housed and fed him for months – and could expect a steep decline in bookings without him. But Mayall, showing extraordinary forbearance, put no obstacle in his way and promised to keep his job open.

As the late September departure date neared, Ted Milton dropped out and Eric, with even less consideration for John Mayall, asked the Bluesbreakers' drummer, Hughie Flint, to take his place. However, Flint was then newly married (to the Mayalls' former au-pair girl), so Milton's student brother, Jake, was enrolled instead, along with trumpet-player Bob Rae. Their name, chosen by Bernie Greenwood in a nod to his daytime medical practice, was the Glands.

The original plan had been to make the journey in a red double-decker London bus, converted to allow one side to open out as a stage. This proving impracticable, Greenwood bought an American station-wagon, a 1953 model Ford Fairline Country Sedan – like a battleship with fins.

John Baily went ahead by air to Athens, a city he knew well, to try to arrange some gigs. The other five drove through France, Belgium and West Germany, stopping off for Munich's Oktoberfest, the annual two weeks devoted to mass beer-swilling. The party duly got roaring drunk, all but Eric. 'He was very abstemious,' Bernie Greenwood recalls. 'He didn't drink too much and didn't smoke at all.'

Tensions within the Glands were already starting to develop, particularly between Greenwood and the trumpeter, Bob Rae. At the Oktoberfest, the two came to blows after Greenwood objected to Rae ostentatiously lighting a cigarette with a £5 note. The others voted to abandon the trip then and there, and all the gear was unloaded so that those who wished to do so could take homeward trains.

The combatants having sobered up and made up, it was agreed to keep going. But from that point, mishaps occurred on an almost

Marx Brothers level. At a stop for fuel, Greenwood had his hand badly bitten by a dog he tried to stroke. In their haste to drive him to hospital, the others forgot that all their passports and travel documents had been spread out on the Country Sedan's roof and now were lying in a page-fluttering trail behind them.

In Yugoslavia, the cobbled road between Zagreb and Belgrade jolted the Country Sedan so severely that its bodywork parted company with its chassis. With no garage to hand, they could only tie it back on with rope and pray that it held. When they reached Thessaloniki, they were so broke and hungry that they bought meat from a butcher's and ate it raw in the street. One of them was so desperate to be rid of his companions that he went to the beach and began collecting driftwood to build a raft on which to sail back to England, *Kon-Tiki*-style.

Amid all the bickering and backbiting, only Eric – normally that least tolerant and self-sufficient of beings – never lost his temper or seemed downhearted. 'He was nice and sweet the whole time,' Bernie Greenwood recalls.

With the Country Sedan's bodywork still miraculously holding on to its chassis, the Glands arrived in Athens to find that John Baily had successfully pitched them to a club named the Igloo. However, the manager, George Karamousalis, whom Baily had not informed of their lead guitarist's identity, insisted that they audition first. Changing their name to the Faces – this was years before Rod Stewart's band of the same name – they gave him Chuck Berry's 'Johnny B. Goode' and were pleased to learn that they'd passed.

For the late boy wonder of John Mayall's Bluesbreakers, this was a comedown indeed. The Faces would merely be a support to the Igloo's Greek house band, the Juniors, who specialised in Beatles and Kinks cover versions. They would appear six nights a week for no pay, only board and lodging at a nearby hotel.

Just before opening night, Jake Milton dropped out to return to his college studies in Britain and they had to use a Greek drummer named Makis Saliaris who was also an airline pilot and, consequently, sometimes delayed by bad weather. Saliaris later remembered Eric as 'a shy, sober, serious guy, even if he was the leader of the band'.

The Faces went over well enough at the Igloo, though never to the extent of their Greek headliners, the Juniors. They soon discovered that the club's waiters controlled its music in the same way as its air-conditioning, shouting at them to 'Play faster' or 'Play slower'. They developed their own ways of teasing their wealthy and rather dim-witted audience; for example, at a single rimshot from the drummer, usually during the Kinks' 'You Really Got Me', they would repeat the same phrase over and over like a record stuck on a turntable.

Then, just three days into the engagement, the Juniors were involved in an horrific car crash that killed their leader and keyboard-player, Sougioul Thanos, and his eighteen-year-old fiancée and seriously injured their lead guitarist, Alekos Karakantos. The Igloo's manager, George Karamousalis, who had been secretly in love with Thanos, went berserk with grief and trashed the place.

Eric had grown to like the Juniors, and now showed a solidarity with them that few of his British bandmates would ever know. He volunteered to fill the injured Karakantos's spot while continuing to play with the Faces, which meant he was onstage for around six hours every night.

Meantime, his companions were growing anxious to be on the move again. A rival club had discovered they were working without the necessary permits and had informed the police, while their hotel had received no payment for their accommodation from Karamousalis and was threatening to evict them.

But Karamousalis had finally realised he was employing one

of the Yardbirds whose 'For Your Love' had topped the Greek charts, and was determined to capitalise on it. He insisted on giving Eric a room in his own home – house-arrest masquerading as Hellenic hospitality – and impounded the Faces' equipment at the Igloo. The Juniors' drummer tipped Eric the wink that, like Rik Gunnell back in Soho, Karamousalis had underworld connections; if he tried to leave, nasty people might come after him and cut off his hands.

It was decided to do a runner after a two-concert memorial for the Juniors' dead leader, in which Eric had volunteered to perform with the band's survivors. This took place at a cinema in Piraeus and attracted an audience of 10,000 – by far his largest to date. It ended in a near riot which almost capsized the escape plan as the police would not allow him to leave the premises until they'd restored order and he was temporarily locked in an office.

The group then split up, with Eric, Ben Palmer and Bob Rae returning to London by train while the others valiantly drove the Country Sedan onward towards Australia. (Miraculously, it would get as far as Karachi, Pakistan.) Eric had managed to keep hold of his precious Telecaster guitar, although his amplifier had to be left behind at the Igloo. Terrified that Karamousalis's heavies or the police might appear at any moment, he and his co-fugitives hid in the station toilets until their train left.

On arrival back at Victoria, he borrowed some money from Palmer, went into a phone box and rang John Mayall to say he was home and wanted to resume his old job in the Bluesbreakers.

'It just struck him as perfectly natural – he was back in England and should be back in the band,' Palmer recalled. 'It never crossed his mind that Mayall might have said no . . . He got into a taxi round to John's and left me there.'

Eric with toy guitar
– already a refuge for
'the wounded child'.

Eric's mother Pat, who
left him when he was aged
two but came back into
his life during his thirties.
Their relationship was
never to be easy.

(Pattie Boyd)

With his first band, the short-lived Roosters.
Tom McGuinness, later of Manfred Mann, is in the back row (right).

(Tom McGuinness)

The 'blueswailing' Yardbirds, 1964

(Getty Images)

With Giorgio Gomelsky (left), who managed the Yardbirds
after the Rolling Stones had slipped through his fingers.
Eric was to do the same.

(Getty Images)

Afro Eric and Cream bandmates Jack Bruce and (sitting) Ginger Baker,
the matchless rhythm-section who, unfortunately, couldn't stand each other.

Robert Stigwood, Cream's first manager – and later a hugely successful producer of films and Broadway shows. When band-meetings were convened at his office, Eric was the only one to be driven there in 'Stiggy's' Rolls-Royce.

(Rex/Shutterstock)

George Harrison and Pattie Boyd at the time of their marriage in 1966.

(Alamy)

Eric and Charlotte Martin, with whom he lived at
The Pheasantry on Chelsea's King's Road.

(Rolls Press / Popperfoto / Getty Images)

8
JUST LIKE FREDDIE

I t wasn't as if Mayall had been stuck for a suitable replacement. In the process of trying out various other lead guitarists, he'd chanced on Peter Green from Bethnal Green, east London, who, at twenty, was already a player of fluid mastery. But a promise was a promise. After appearing with the Bluesbreakers only three times, Green found himself elbowed aside by Eric. He would be back sooner than he knew.

Nor was this the only personnel-change during Eric's Greek adventure. John McVie had been fired as bass-player yet again and been replaced by Jack Bruce, formerly of the Graham Bond Organisation.

Bruce was one of the uncommon breed who came to rock from a classical music background. Born in Lanarkshire, Scotland, in 1943, he had studied cello, piano and musical composition at the Royal Scottish Academy of Music before switching to stand-up bass and traditional jazz. That milieu first brought him together with south London-born Peter 'Ginger' Baker, four years his senior, whose hair was flaming red and who played drums, one early bandmate noted, 'like a wild animal'.

Bruce and Baker were both in Alexis Korner's Blues Incorporated, the seminary for young British bluesmen underneath a teashop in Ealing. Their graduation was to team with Korner's pudgy keyboard-player Graham Bond in what became the Graham Bond Organisation. Augmented by a fourth Korner

121

alumnus, saxophonist Dick Heckstall-Smith, the GBO played a jazz-blues fusion that never scored commercially but was highly regarded within the profession. In particular, Bruce, now on bass guitar, and Baker were regarded as a rhythm section without peer. The trouble was that they detested each other.

That one was a truculent pocket-size Scot, the other an Irish Cockney with a hair-trigger temper had guaranteed conflict from the start. In all rhythm sections before, save the Beatles', the drummer had been the focus of attention, the bass-player simply a vague background thud. But Bruce, to whom a bass guitar was a doddle after the stand-up variety, never mind the cello, showed an increasing tendency to play it as if it were a lead instrument.

Open warfare frequently broke out onstage, with Baker firing off drumsticks like guided missiles at the back of Bruce's head and Bruce hurling his bass – not just the guitar but the stand-up one – at Baker. The worst eruption came one night in Golders Green, north London, during the climactic Baker drum solo that closed the GBO's set. According to Baker, Bruce kept playing along with his bass drum, then screamed into the mike: '"You're playing too fuckin' loud, man!" So I offloaded a right-hander on him and he goes down on the ground and I'm kicking him and going "Get up, you little cunt!" I just let go, and I was going to kick him to death.'

Bruce at the time was newly married and his wife, Janet – who ran the Graham Bond Organisation's fan club, so attended most gigs – doughtily took her husband's part. The battles in the band-room often rivalled those witnessed by the audience.

Baker, along with Graham Bond himself, had become a heroin addict at a time when few British musicians had yet ventured beyond marijuana. He took to carrying a knife and, in the grip of the drug, was apt not only to pull it during altercations with Bruce but actually to throw it. 'I got the same thing once,' Janet Bruce recalls. 'In the band-room one night, I said "hello" to him in the wrong way and suddenly there was a knife sticking in the wall behind my head.'

Bond had by now lost control of his own band, thanks to massive drug-use and an equally mind-addling fixation on the occult. (Despite his pioneering talent on the organ and Mellotron, he would never achieve success and would die under the wheels of a London tube train in 1974.) Baker became de facto leader and lost no time in firing Bruce at the point of his knife.

Bruce's presence gave Eric's return to the Bluesbreakers an extra fillip. 'Jack was a jazz musician and a very very avant-garde jazz musician, into people like Charlie Mingus and Miles Davis. He tore up the rule-book and he took me along with him.'

He found an equal rapport with drummer Hughie Flint, who shared his passion for jazz and had none of Ginger Baker's terrifying touchiness. Often, indeed, Clapton, Bruce and Flint seemed like a self-contained trio ahead of its time. 'We did a lot of improvising,' Flint recalls. 'Jack and I would be playing in 6-8 or 12-8 and then suddenly double the tempo. Eric loved all that.'

But after about a month, Bruce found he couldn't survive on Bluesbreaker wages and left to join the by now hugely successful Manfred Mann (whose leader, rather embarrassingly, lived just up the street from Mayall). A fellow musician commented that using him to play the elementary bass riffs the Manfreds required was 'like doing your shopping at Sainsbury's in a Lamborghini'.

It is related of Eric's hero of heroes, Robert Johnson, that at the start of his career he showed only modest talent on the guitar and had little about him that compelled attention. At a certain point, he dropped out of sight for a period of time, then reappeared in full possession of his astonishing brilliance. The same was true of Eric when he returned to John Mayall's Bluesbreakers, also after having dropped out of sight for a while. At one moment, it seemed, he was just really good; at the next, he was great.

With Johnson, there was at least some explanation – he had bartered his soul. But in Eric's case, the gift seemed to come with no strings attached: not after a midnight tryst with Satan at a Mississippi crossroads but somewhere between a woodworker's shop near Oxford, the attic of a suburban house in south-east London and an obscure club in Athens.

Nor had Satan figured in the transaction apparently, for it was around now that CLAPTON IS GOD appeared on a corrugated iron fence in Islington, north London, spray-painted by an anonymous (but inevitably male) disciple. In the London of 1965, graffiti were still relatively rare, especially as a medium of exaltation rather than execration, and this one achieved the aerosol equivalent of going viral.

Not even the Beatles had been elevated to such a level – at least, not yet – and it left Eric characteristically conflicted. On the one hand, he could not have received a bigger boost after being edged out of the Yardbirds and seeing them go on to glory without him. Those splattery black letters were worth more than the most rapturous trade review because they came from the street and, as he reflected, 'There's something about word of mouth you cannot undo.'

At the same time, he could reel off a long list of guitarists, British and American, whom he thought capable of outplaying him: Reggie Young from the Bill Black Combo that had backed the Ronettes, or James Burton, who'd contributed dazzling solos to early Ricky Nelson singles, or Bernie Watson from Screaming Lord Sutch's Savages, or even Jeff Beck and Jimmy Page, his present and future successors in the Yardbirds.

Half of him felt triumph that the music he'd championed for so long was receiving recognition beyond anything he could have imagined. The other half felt guilty because people like the anonymous worshipper on that north London wall seemed to regard him as its Creator.

*

If anyone deserved credit for spreading the gospel, it was Mike Vernon, the Decca Records producer who had made some early demos with the Yardbirds and been among their occasional stand-in vocalists.

Vernon had since lost touch with Eric but had followed the drama of his departure from the Yardbirds and recruitment by John Mayall from a sympathetic distance. Then one day in March 1966 he saw that Mayall and the Bluesbreakers were to play a one-nighter at Klooks Kleek, the West Hampstead pub-club located right next door to Decca Records' studio complex. On an impulse he decided to drop in at the club after work.

It was a pure Robert Johnson moment: Vernon hardly recognised the capable but not-so-far-above-average lead guitarist with whom he'd once shared a stage. 'Eric had a Gibson Les Paul and a huge stack of an amp. He was playing in this really strong, aggressive style like Freddie King. In fact, he might have *been* Freddie King.'

Decca had already released a John Mayall album without much success, but Vernon urged his superiors to give Mayall another shot, augmented by Eric's volcanic new talent. 'In the end, I was grudgingly told to go ahead. But I only had a few days and if it didn't work out, my arse would be on the line.'

The initial plan was for a live album and one was duly recorded in its entirety at the Flamingo Club just before Jack Bruce's departure to Manfred Mann. Unfortunately, the sound quality was so poor that it had to be redone at Decca's West Hampstead studios with John McVie back on bass.

As Vernon soon discovered, the parallels between Robert Johnson and Eric went only so far. For here was no prodigy so humble and overawed by the mysteries of recording that he kept his face turned to the wall. Whatever the deal struck for his talent, a new self-assertiveness seemed to have been thrown in.

The transfixing new sound derived from the marriage of his vintage Gibson Les Paul with one of the whopping Marshall amplifiers that had been specially developed for the Who, then acknowledged to be the world's loudest band. At all recording-sessions, it was standard practice for producers to reduce the decibel level in the interests of giving the finished disc a 'pro-fessional' sheen. However, Eric wanted to be heard at the same volume on the album as he was onstage.

Sympathetic old chum that Vernon was, he agreed to this unprecedented demand. But his young engineer, Gus Dudgeon – later a distinguished producer for Elton John and David Bowie – was totally unprepared for the result. 'The first time Gus went onto the studio floor and Eric hit a chord, a kind of cockeyed look came over Gus's face. After that, he always went out there wearing headphones with the lead hanging loose. He looked like one of those people you see on airport tarmac, directing planes to their parking-stands.'

To protect the ears of everyone else, a special booth was built to house Eric's mighty Marshall with extra insulation provided by a grand piano-cover, sound-softening wooden baffles, blan-kets and pillows. 'Even then, his playing made everything in the studio rattle,' Vernon recalls. 'It had two double-insulated doors with several feet of space between them, but still people in other parts of the building started complaining about the noise.'

The album was titled *Blues Breakers*, with John Mayall's name in large red letters and Eric's in smaller white-on-grey ones. Mayall played piano, Hammond organ and harmonica, per-formed all but one of the vocals and scattered four of his own compositions through the twelve-song tracklist. But everyone, Mayall included, knew whose showcase it really was.

In truth, despite its obeisance to Otis Rush, Freddie King, Mose Allison and even Ray Charles, *Blues Breakers* counted as only half a blues album. There was scarcely a track where Eric's serious little sunburst Les Paul and mighty-mouthed Marshall didn't seduce him into playing the rawest rock yet to be caught on vinyl. It also contained his first recorded lead vocal, a Robert Johnson song with an unwitting warning to Mayall: 'Ramblin' On My Mind'.

The cover image was a straightforward portrait of Mayall, Eric, Hughie Flint and John McVie seated side by side on a low wall in London's Old Kent Road. Eric was pretending to be engrossed in a copy of the *Beano*, one of the weekly comics with which his grandmother, Rose, had deluged his childhood. He later said he'd wanted to be 'totally uncooperative' with the photographer, although such faux-naïveté was common among British pop musicians in the later Sixties.

Ramblin' certainly was on his mind, albeit with no firm destination yet. In an interview with *Melody Maker*'s Nick Jones, he let drop that he was thinking of emigrating to America because 'forming a blues band in England is like banging your head against a brick wall'. He also made the first of many efforts to deal with the hair-shirt burden of 'Clapton is God': 'I think I have a power and my guitar is a medium for expressing that power. I don't need people to say how good I am. I've worked it out by myself. It's nothing to do with technique and rehearsing. It has to do with the person behind that guitar . . . [it's] a medium through which I can make contact to myself. It's pretty lonely.'

A more suspicious man than John Mayall might have felt unease over the amount of session work Eric was managing to do outside the Bluesbreakers. At times, indeed, he seemed more drawn to the life of an anonymous studio musician on whom no one could pin a God tag.

The bookings coming his way nowadays were a definite improvement on that aborted collaboration with Bob Dylan a year earlier. Among Mike Vernon's other current projects was an album with the American blues pianist Otis Spann. After *Blues Breakers*, Vernon asked Eric to play on a session with Spann that was to include one of his own earliest musical gods, Muddy Waters. 'He was very sheepish about it,' Vernon recalls. '"Are you sure you really want *me*?" he kept saying.'

For contractual reasons, Waters appeared on the album under a pseudonym ('Brother') and the master of Chicago electric blues furnished only rhythm to Eric's lead. 'Muddy and Otis both loved his playing and they liked him,' Vernon says. 'In my experience, he was never other than completely likeable.'

He was also approached by the American producer Joe Boyd to join a London-based studio band for the new Elektra label, largely recruited from Manfred Mann and the Spencer Davis Group and known as the Powerhouse. What resulted was a supergroup in all but name, with Paul Jones on vocals, Stevie Winwood on guitar, Pete York on drums, Ben Palmer on piano and Jack Bruce on bass. Though the project came to nothing, it deepened Eric's respect for Bruce's musicianship and they found the same easy rapport they had as colleagues under John Mayall.

While all this – and more – was going on, Mayall continued to believe Eric's wanderlust had been satisfied by his Greek adventure and to treat him almost like a son. The birth of a fourth child had obliged the Mayalls to take back the attic room at their house that he'd been occupying for almost a year. Yet, with continuing open-heartedness, they threw a party there for his twenty-first birthday on 30 March. Such an enormous crowd turned up that when Pamela Mayall returned from teaching her evening class she was unable to get in via the front door and had to climb through a downstairs window.

Among the leavening of Eric's 'intellectual' friends was a rising young poet named Pete Brown, who'd recently found himself sharing a bill with the Bluesbreakers at an arts festival at Southampton University. 'It also included a beauty contest, which John Mayall, Eric and I were asked to judge,' Brown recalls. 'Eric may have thought there could be some sexual perks involved but at the end the winner made a quick exit, unscathed.'

The party was in fancy dress, fulfilling a fantasy of Eric's since he used to stare into the windows of Berman's theatrical costumiers in his dawn wanderings around the West End after the Marquee closed. 'He wore a gorilla-suit,' Pete Brown says. 'I think it was partly to dodge a certain female singer who was after him but he wasn't keen on. I'd better not say who because she's still around.'

John Mayall's costume, ironically, was that of a Cyclops, the mythical being with a single eye in the centre of its forehead. Yet the trusting Mayall still did not think to keep even one eye on Eric.

Until then he had barely smoked but to mark his coming of age he opened a packet of twenty Benson & Hedges Gold cigarettes, crammed every one into his mouth and lit them simultaneously. It was the start of a thirty-year addiction that would eventually reach sixty per day.

Eric had been in Oxford when John Mayall recruited him and it was in Oxford that Mayall lost him. One May night in 1966, when the Bluesbreakers were appearing at the city's town hall, Ginger Baker unexpectedly dropped by.

Like most people who came into Baker's orbit, Eric had always been a little afraid of him. Although only twenty-six, he seemed preternaturally aged or, rather, ageless, his long frame emaciated, his cheeks hollow, his eyes glaring through a constellation of freckles, his flaming hair tied back in an undersized bun like a small detonation on its own. All in all, Nature had constructed so perfect an image of a heroin addict that it hardly seemed worth the trouble of actually becoming one.

He sat in with the Bluesbreakers for a single number that

brought Hughie Flint's drumkit to the brink of destruction, then offered Eric a lift back to London in his rather impressive Rover 3000. After his display on the skins, it was no surprise to his passenger that he drove 'like a maniac'.

While beating up the A40, he explained how, owing to the disintegration of Graham Bond, it had fallen to him as the lesser of the Bond Organisation's two junkies to take the reins of leadership. Now, after three years of running someone else's band, he'd decided to form one of his own – and the first name he'd thought of was Eric's.

'He saw something in me that I never saw before,' Eric would recall. 'Ginger was pretty dismissive and antisocial . . . seriously antisocial. But he had the gift, the spark, the flair, the panache. He had it in spades.'

As it happened, Eric had recently watched one of his younger blues heroes, the effervescent Buddy Guy, give a memorable performance at the Marquee. In place of the usual three- or four-strong backing band, Guy worked only with a drummer and bass-player, yet still generated such showmanship, and sheer volume, that no spectator could feel short-changed.

He'd also seen Baker and Jack Bruce play together in the Graham Bond Organisation 'like a well-oiled machine' on nights when Bruce chanced not to be throwing his double bass at Baker nor Baker trying to kick Bruce to death. To him, they seemed the ideal partners in a Buddy Guy-style trio – a configuration until then almost unknown in commercial rock or pop. He therefore agreed to join up with Baker on condition that Bruce was also invited. Merely the mention of the name, he recalls, made Baker 'almost crash the car'.

It was a measure of Eric's potential value that Baker agreed to go away and think about it. A few days later, he reluctantly acquiesced, muttering 'It'll never work' and providing Eric with a lengthy inventory of Jack Bruce's character defects.

A man not best known for his diplomatic skills then had to woo the bandmate he'd recently fired from the Graham Bond Organisation at knifepoint. Astonishingly, Bruce did not dismiss the idea out of hand: he had already become disillusioned with Manfred Mann and was delighted by the prospect of working with Eric once again.

'They met on neutral ground – my parents' flat in St John's Wood,' Janet Bruce says. 'In my memory, Eric and Jack both said they'd only work with Ginger if he came off the smack. Which, being Ginger, he did in about a week.'

With the line-up complete, Baker contacted the *Melody Maker* journalist Chris Welch to impart what he expected to be a front-page story in *MM*'s imminent next issue. Much to his annoyance, the front page had already gone to press, but a small inside piece announced Eric's defection from the Bluesbreakers and Jack Bruce's from Manfred Mann to join him in a 'sensational groups' group', as yet unnamed. That was the first John Mayall heard of it.

The ensuing confrontation with Mayall, Eric would later say with some understatement, was 'not a happy experience'. Leaving aside questions of ingratitude and underhandedness, an album was soon to come out by John Mayall and the Bluesbreakers 'with Eric Clapton' which now would be out of date before it hit the turntables. The only consolation was that a successor, the brilliant Peter Green, was already waiting in the wings.

In June 1966, the trio had a first, acoustic-only rehearsal at Ginger Baker's home – not a cave on some wild moor, as might possibly have been expected, but a maisonette on Braemar Avenue in the crushingly ordinary London suburb of Neasden, where he lived with his totally calm and normal wife, Liz. Beyond his back garden lay the huge Brent Reservoir, known as 'the Welsh Harp', on whose raised grass embankment children from the neighbourhood were playing in the sun.

The arguing started almost immediately. Like Eric, Bruce had had no chance to inform his present band he was quitting, and was furious with Baker for rushing the story into *Melody Maker* without consulting him. At intervals, like parents warring in front of a child, each of them called on Eric to bear witness to the truth of their grim forewarnings about the other: 'That's *typical* of him . . .' and 'You see . . . he *always* does that . . .'

Then they began to play together. Baker and Bruce both stopped looking daggers and broke into smiles. And through the window, on the Welsh Harp's grass embankment, the neighbourhood children could be seen boogieing along.

9

STIGGY

Another dispute quickly blew up about the management of the still-unnamed trio. Ginger Baker wanted to give the job to the Graham Bond Organisation's Australian manager, Robert Stigwood – 'Stigboot', as Baker called him. Bruce resisted the idea, saying that a good booking agent was all they needed, so Eric in effect had the casting vote.

Stigwood, then aged thirty-two, had barely started on the road to becoming pop music's first multi-media showman. Born in Adelaide, reputedly Australia's most straitlaced city, he had felt an early vocation for the Catholic priesthood but had instead chosen training as an advertising copywriter. In 1955, he'd made his way to Britain overland via India, arriving with a severe dose of dysentery, and just £3 in his pocket. To begin with, the only work he could find was as a supervisor in an institution for what were then termed 'backward teen-age boys'. More useful preparation for his future can hardly be imagined.

By 1961, he was a partner in a small theatrical agency which, not entirely coincidentally, specialised in good-looking young male actors. One of them, John Leyton, possessed a singing voice of sorts and Stigwood paid for him to cut a single, 'Johnny Remember Me', with the independent producer Joe Meek. The record made no impression until Stigwood fixed for Leyton to perform it in a TV soap opera, whereupon it went to number 1.

It was the first example of the cross-media marketing of pop at which he would later excel.

As a manager and promoter, 'Stiggy' grew famous for constantly teetering on the edge of insolvency – which somehow never inhibited his opulent lifestyle – and for the hefty cut he took from his artistes. After a Rolling Stones UK tour he organised, the musicians ended up with so little that an enraged Keith Richards beat him up in a club full of people. 'He got the knee for every grand he owed us,' Richards later recalled. 'Sixteen of 'em.'

Still more extreme physical retribution followed his attempt to entice the Small Faces away from their manager, Don Arden, a terrifying figure justifiably nicknamed 'the Al Capone of Pop'. Turning up unannounced at Stigwood's office accompanied by four heavies, Arden scooped him from behind his desk and dangled him out of the fourth-floor window by his ankles.

Stigwood's real skill lay not in spotting and developing new talent but diversifying into areas that managers normally left to others, such as music publishing, concert promotion and record production. In March 1966 he set up his own record company, Reaction, quickly scoring a huge British hit with 'Substitute' by the Who, whom he'd lured away from Brunswick by dint of already being their booking agent.

Like many of the first generation of British pop managers including its two best-known figures, Larry Parnes and Brian Epstein, Stigwood was gay. At a time when homosexuality was still illegal, the fact had to be carefully concealed, nowhere more so than in a business whose raw material overwhelmingly consisted of pretty young men.

Even now that male fashions were becoming increasingly feminised, nothing in Stiggy's appearance or manner gave the slightest hint of his perilous secret. What Eric saw at their first meeting was a seemingly conventional executive type in a flared suit and platform-heeled boots, his hair clouding his ears, his eyes slightly protruding, his Australian accent determinedly low-key, his expansive smile a little too full of teeth to seem quite trustworthy.

They talked in Stigwood's office at his luxurious flat in New Cavendish Street, Marylebone. As he sat behind his ornate desk, expatiating on his plans for the new threesome, Eric thought it mostly 'a lot of flannel'. But he was impressed that Stigwood seemed to understand and utterly sympathise with their musical mission. In fact, it was *all* a lot of flannel: Stigwood had little interest in the blues and how it might be refashioned, but a great deal of interest in Eric.

For a time, it looked as if the threesome would take the superlatively embarrassing name Sweet and Sour Rock 'n' Roll. Then Eric thought of calling themselves Cream, 'for the very simple reason that we were the cream of the crop, the elite in our respective domains'. It was also a nod to the new hedonism which the Swinging Sixties had brought to Britain, epitomised by the lavish use of double cream by fashionable cooks like Robert Carrier and in recipes in the glossy Sunday colour supplements. Plain Cream without a 'the' was as radical a step as being only three, not four or five.

In fact, Eric's former keenness on the guitar/bass/drums format was giving way to anxiety that it might be altogether too nonconformist and, in particular, that he'd be unable to cope with playing both rhythm and lead.

His anxiety increased at Cream's first full electric rehearsal, in a church hall in Kensal Rise where a troop of Brownies also happened to be convening. Without a fourth member, preferably on keyboards, he thought they sounded too 'thin', and proposed getting Stevie Winwood from the Spencer Davis Group as reinforcement. But neither Baker nor Bruce would hear of it.

The only journalist invited to the rehearsals was Chris Welch from *Melody Maker*. Welch found Baker and Bruce somewhat at cross-purposes with Eric in viewing Cream as a new medium for the jazz they both still loved. In another surprising show of harmony, Bruce characterised the two of them as 'fugitives from Ornette Coleman' for whom the blues was unfamiliar, even unsympathetic, terrain. However, Eric defined the band's objective firmly as 'Blues ancient and modern. I'd say jazz is definitely out and sweet and sour rock 'n' roll is in.'

The erstwhile art student came to the fore as he outlined some of his Dadaesque ideas for stage presentation. 'We want to have turkeys onstage while we're playing. We all like turkeys and it's nice to have them around. Another Dada thing – I was going to have this hat made from a brim with a cage and a live frog inside. It would be very nice to have stuffed bears onstage, too.'

Robert Stigwood was hovering in the background, clearly at a loss as to what to make of all this and wondering whether his new acquisition stood any chance of commercial success. 'Are they any good?' he asked Chris Welch anxiously. Welch reassured him fervently that they were.

July saw the release of John Mayall's *Blues Breakers* album 'with Eric Clapton' a billing now almost three months out of date. It gave Mayall the biggest commercial success of his career, reaching number 6 in the UK chart and staying in the Top 20 for seventeen weeks, despite the pressure of heavyweight pop albums like the Beach Boys' *Pet Sounds* and the Beatles' *Revolver*.

The reviews all paid tribute to Mayall's dedication to the blues but, in truth, his thankless surrogate son had hijacked the whole thing, even down to its unofficial title, the Beano Album.

Among Eric's professional rivals there was awed discussion of the 'Clapton sound', that Freddie King fieriness shading into rock with a Marshall amp at full throttle. Many believed a first step to replicating it was to equip themselves similarly with sunburst

Gibson Les Pauls – no easy matter as Eric's particular model, henceforward dubbed the Beano guitar, had ceased production in 1960. Such was the clamour for second-hand instruments that Gibson eventually had to reintroduce it. In the future, vintage specimens would fetch as much as £250,000.

John Mayall and the Bluesbreakers *without* Eric Clapton would go on, giving a first platform to many other brilliant young players, though none ever surpassing him. The seemingly inde-structible Mayall would still be gigging in his eighties, just as Eric still would be in his seventies.

Cream were to make their official debut at the Windsor Jazz and Blues Festival (which was the old Richmond Jazz and Blues Festi-val, transferred to Windsor's 'royal' racecourse) on 31 July 1966. The night before, they did a warm-up gig at the Twisted Wheel club in Manchester – a familiar venue to Eric since his days with the Roosters – deputising at the last minute for the American soul singer Joe Tex.

They made the journey not in the usual cramped van but an Austin Westminster saloon car, just a couple of notches below a limo, purchased by Stigwood for their exclusive use. At the wheel was Eric's friend and fellow Rooster Ben Palmer, acting as their chauffeur just this once, as he naively thought, and looking forward to watching the performance at his leisure.

Only after delivering them did the kindly woodcarver find he was also expected to carry in their equipment and set up the stage, despite possessing barely enough technical expertise to stick a jackplug into an amp. He realised he'd been appointed Cream's roadie and, as always, found it impossible to say no to Eric.

The timing of this sneak preview could hardly have been worse. A few hours earlier, England had won the soccer World Cup after a thrilling final against West Germany amid national jubilation – tinged by memories of the recent Second World War – which would still be resonating half a century on. Even the most besotted Mancunian music fans that night were more pre-occupied with the make-up of a football eleven than a rock trio. Eric, Bruce and Baker played blues covers to an almost-empty club, treating it as little more than an extra rehearsal.

But when the Windsor Jazz and Blues Festival kicked off the next day, World Cup euphoria turned into an advantage. A 15,000-strong crowd cheerfully braved the squally weather for the Who, the Spencer Davis Group, the Move, the ever-decreasing sprinkle of jazz combos and a struggling band named Bluesology whose podgy organ-player, Reggie Dwight, was not yet remotely recognisable as the future Elton John.

The three-day programme should also have included the Yardbirds, now with two further hit singles, 'Shape of Things' and 'Over Under Sideways Down', to their credit since Eric's departure. However, they pulled out because of illness: not Keith Relf's for once, Jeff Beck had tonsillitis. A backstage encounter might have been awkward as Eric, still bitter, had told a music paper they habitually used Relf's bad health as an excuse to welsh on bookings.

The festival's undisputed headliners were the Who, who concluded their set by smashing their equipment to pieces – a ritual characterised by their former art student/guitarist Pete Townshend as an 'auto-destructive art event' but regarded by most of the audience as straightforward, joyous vandalism – while their joint managers, Kit Lambert and Chris Stamp, tossed smoke bombs among the broken guitar-necks and kicked-in amps.

Cream's name having been decided on too late to appear in the programme, they were billed simply as 'Eric Clapton, Jack Bruce and Ginger Baker', a running-order that would become as unchangeable as John, Paul, George and Ringo. Theirs was hardly a star spot, halfway through the concluding Sunday evening with the Harry South Big Band standing by to follow them. It had already been raining intermittently but before they were announced, a heavy shower began. They elected to go on nevertheless.

Despite all the rehearsing, they had only about four songs which they thought ready to unveil to a live audience. At one point, Ginger Baker found himself in the unusual position of apologising because they were playing everything twice over. Still, the crowd stayed put amid the downpour, sustained by something more than post-World Cup good spirits. 'Eric's incredible guitar induced the audience to shout and scream for more,' wrote *Melody Maker*'s Chris Welch, 'even while he *was* playing more.'

Apart from riding to gigs in an Austin Westminster, Eric at first found life under Robert Stigwood's management little different from before. Stigwood was booking Cream into much the same club, pub and college venues they were long accustomed to playing with their respective previous bands, and charging only £5 more for them than he did for the Graham Bond Organisation. It was several weeks before the various promoters could be dissuaded from billing them as *the* Cream.

Then, in a seeming ill omen for the new regime, Eric's cherished Gibson Les Paul was stolen from a rehearsal-room. The *Record Mirror* published a description as detailed as a missing-person bulletin – 'cigarette-burns on the front . . . shoulder-strap carved with the names of Buddy Guy, Big Maceo and Otis Rush on the inside' – but it never came back. A week later at Klooks Kleek, its carrying-case was also stolen, evidently by the same faithful fan.

Actually, Stigwood was investing heavily in a band that hadn't yet released a hit single or even entered a recording studio together. If they didn't have much extra cash to spend, they were now represented by a West End PR firm, Mayfair Public Relations, which operated out of a mews house in Bruton Place and sounded as if it had been there for ever.

Mayfair was in fact a brand-new company whose youngest partner, Ray Williams, in true Swinging London style, was only nineteen. Golden-haired and angelically handsome enough to have been a pop star himself – a fact that did not escape Stigwood's attention – Williams took on the Cream account.

He already knew Eric vaguely from his early days as an unpaid dancing extra on the *Ready Steady Go!* television show. 'Whenever the Yardbirds appeared, I always noticed him as the most friendly one, even though they were the big stars and I was nobody.'

Cream proved anything but a tough sell for their teenage PR man. 'When Stiggy gave Mayfair the account, there was already a tremendous buzz about them,' Williams recalls. 'At the sound of those three names, every pop journalist in Fleet Street took notice.'

Many went along expecting the onstage slugging-matches for which Bruce and Baker had been famous in the Graham Bond Organisation. But after their opening exchange of volleys, they observed an unspoken armistice. 'The conflict between them didn't go away, but it was shelved, at least for a time,' recalls Pete Brown, the poet who was soon to become an indispensable element in Cream's rise. 'They just settled down and got on with it.'

There was, however, one pressing problem that threatened to scupper the supergroup before it had begun. Fleet Street's grubbiest Sunday scandal sheet, the *News of the World*, had discovered Ginger Baker's history as a heroin addict and was about to splash a story that still could do great harm even though Baker was now clean.

This was averted in a manner unimaginable today: Williams and Mayfair co-director Simon Hayes met the journalist concerned in a pub and managed to persuade him the story was untrue and should be killed.

A lesser but vexing problem for a publicist was Cream's seemingly contradictory ingredients of rock, blues and jazz. Jack Bruce, more articulate than most journalists ever bothered to discover, offered the clearest mission-statement: 'We want to be ourselves and take the fabulous language of the blues and apply it to rock music.'

But for Eric, whose only motivation had once been 'to honour the tradition of the blues', the very word now seemed almost a stigma. 'A year ago, I used to listen to all blues bands, but I wouldn't now because they are just playing blues, not developing their own style,' he told *Record Mirror*'s Richard Green. '[Chris] Farlowe and [Zoot] Money are just churning out Tamla [Motown] and stuff . . . I'm no longer trying to play like anything but a white man. The time is overdue when people should play like they are and what colour they are.'

At the time, the only other sole guitarist in a prominent band was the Who's windmill-armed, guitar-smashing Pete Townshend. And for a brief space, Eric seemed to be heading in Townshend's direction. During an appearance at Leeds University, in another scene unimaginable today, he brought an outsize firework onstage, announcing that it was a bomb capable of blowing up the whole band and if anyone cared to light it, they could.

Cream were nonconformist, above all, in their lead vocals which – save on the few occasions when Eric could be persuaded – would be Jack Bruce's department. For the truculent little Scot with the delicate poet's face possessed a pure, clear tenor which soared high above the guitar and drums, devoid of rock's obligatory raunch yet nonetheless suffused with ardour or angst. At that time, the only remotely comparable voice belonged to Brian Wilson of the Beach Boys; in the Seventies, the same air of a fallen angel or ruined choirboy would be manifested by Freddie Mercury of Queen.

Undaunted by all these diverse elements, Ray Williams came up with a tag-line of almost biblical portentousness: 'The first is last and the last is first but the first, the second and the last are Cream.'

Trios currently dominated Eric's life, as he was living with three young women in a flat in Ladbroke Square, Notting Hill Gate. They were Americans, part of the transatlantic pilgrimage to what *Time* magazine that summer had dubbed 'the Style Capital of Europe'. He had met them after a show, at a moment when he was once again temporarily homeless, and, true to form, had immediately been offered lodging with them.

Despite their foggy-eyed adulation, his relationship with all three was purely platonic. The experience of simply being friends with attractive females, he later recalled, made him feel 'very grown-up', though it would seldom recur in his life. Given the demands of his sex-life away from the flat, it was also rather a relief.

The Style Capital of Europe's latest trend – the ubiquitous word of the moment – was to look back with irony on the Victorian age still enshrined by its palaces, monuments and monarchical pageantry. Young men who preached the ideals of 'love and peace' and railed against American colonial oppression in Vietnam saw no contradiction in sporting antique military tunics of the same bully red with which the British Empire used to colour the globe.

The zeitgeist was perfectly caught in a new shop on the Portobello Road called I Was Lord Kitchener's Valet, pastiching the moustachioed commander-in-chief whose pointing finger had summoned millions to slaughter in the Great War. Eric was among its best customers and his collection of braided and buttoned scarlet tunics – like all his crazes, bordering on the obsessive – was renowned.

For his numerous shopping-expeditions, he discovered a sympathetic companion in Jack Bruce's wife, Janet. 'We were in the tube one day, coming up the escalator,' she recalls. 'Suddenly, some people on the down escalator recognised him and shouted "Look, there's God!" Eric didn't know where to put himself.'

He had also acquired a car, despite being still unable to drive and unequal to the exertion of learning and taking a test. It was a bulbous 1938 Cadillac with running-boards and white-walled tyres that he'd seen on a used car lot on the Seven Sisters Road and impulsively purchased for £750. The dealer drove it to Ladbroke Square where it remained, like an abandoned getaway vehicle in a pre-war gangster film, gradually obscured by a carapace of leaves from the plane trees above.

Having a homosexual manager, albeit one so discreet as Robert Stigwood, was something to which Eric had quickly adjusted. Tolerance had little to do with it: the word 'gay' was still barely used outside the theatrical profession and working-class boys like himself and his bandmates spoke of 'queers', 'poofs', 'nances' or 'fruits' without an iota of understanding. They regarded Stigwood's sexuality as an occupational hazard, each fervently hoping he'd never be put in the position of having to thump the man who'd promised to make their fortune.

At the outset, Stigwood had had designs on Eric and, to a lesser degree, Jack Bruce. 'There was a certain amount of pursuit of both of them,' says Pete Brown. 'Eric was very pretty in those days. He was the sex-interest. But, as Robert discovered, you couldn't have found two more heterosexual guys.'

Eric's fending off of Stigwood had no adverse effects on their professional relationship, as it might easily have done. (When the American teen star Fabian rejected his manager's advances, his career ended in that moment.) 'There was never any doubt about his favourite member of Cream,' recalls Neville Chesters, who'd recently quit as the Who's roadie to become Stigwood's driver/ PA. 'Ginger was a great drummer, but he frightened everyone and Jack was very quiet. Robert recognised Eric had something special that he could build on.'

Proof of this most favoured status was that while Bruce and Baker were expected to make their own way to Stigwood's office-apartment in De Walden Court, New Cavendish Street, Chesters would be sent to fetch Eric in the manager's white Bentley Continental. 'I think it was the first time he'd played the part of a rock star, being chauffeur-driven around town,' Chester recalls. 'He used to sit in the back and count the number of stares he got.'

Stigwood at the time was seeing a great deal of Brian Epstein, whose gay life was far less under control. As it happened, Cream's publicists, Mayfair Public Relations, also represented the Saville Theatre in Shaftesbury Avenue, which Epstein owned and had latterly turned into a venue for top American rock and soul acts. 'Simon [Hayes], my business partner, and I lived above our office in Bruton Place,' Ray Williams recalls. 'Late one night, there's a ring at the door and it's Stiggy, Brian – and Eric. They'd been out to dinner, drunk a lot of wine and were very giggly.

'In my office, I had a record turntable and a stack of records, the little vinyl 45s. Stiggy picked one up and threw it across the room and in no time we were having a 45s fight. It was all great fun until I threw one at Stiggy, which hit him on the forehead, opened a cut and blood started pouring out.'

On 1 October 1966 Cream were playing another rather small-scale college gig, at the Central London Polytechnic on Great Titchfield Street. In the adjacent pub, Jack Bruce ran into a fellow bass-player, Chas Chandler, formerly of the Animals, a podgy Paul McCartney lookalike who had lately branched out into management. With Chandler was a discovery he'd just signed in New York: a young black singer/guitarist of extraordinary beauty, wearing a many-buttoned military tunic and the first Afro haircut Eric had ever seen. His name was Jimi Hendrix.

In the way familiar in jazz and blues, but not yet in rock, Chandler asked if his protégé could sit in with Cream for a number. Both Eric and Bruce were amenable, having already heard rumours that the protégé was rather good. Baker muttered, but was overruled.

By an unlucky coincidence, the number was Howlin' Wolf's 'Killing Floor', which Eric had recently succeeded in mastering after some little effort. Now he had to watch the gorgeous stranger in British Empire scarlet perform it with nonchalant ease, alternately singing and playing lead as seamlessly as Muddy Waters or B. B. King but otherwise owing them nothing. For here was a black musician refusing to be contained by the ghetto of blues and R&B, and doing white acid rock. But doing it as no white man ever had, with a left-handed guitar of dazzling ingenuity and a low-pitched voice steeped in soul and sex, yet with no trace of 'colour' and imbued with a paradoxical gentleness.

These were still early days and Hendrix's stage-act had none of the eye-popping gimmicks for which he would become notorious. Thus far, his impact had been confined to other guitarists with whom he had shared a stage: black and white alike capitulated at once like Victorian howitzers faced by an atom bomb.

So it happened now even with 'God'.

'Halfway through the song, Eric stopped playing,' Chas Chandler would recall. 'Both his hands dropped down to his sides, then he walked offstage. I ran back to the dressing-room and he was standing there, trying to light a cigarette with his hand shaking. He said, "You never told me he was *that* fuckin' good."'

10

NSU

A week later, Cream's first single, 'Wrapping Paper', was released on Robert Stigwood's Reaction label, to widespread disappointment and puzzlement. Expecting a thunderbolt, the music press instead got a sleepy lullaby with Jack Bruce singing in an unaccustomed low, whispery tone as well as playing honky-tonk piano and 'bowing' a cello with a sound like whales distantly calling to each other. Little was heard from Eric and Ginger Baker but background harmonies vaguely reminiscent of a barbershop quartet.

After the instrumental tracks were recorded, Bruce had summoned the beat poet Pete Brown to Rayrik studios in Chalk Farm to improvise some lyrics about 'wrapping paper in the gutter' awakening memories of lost love in 'a house by the shore'.

The reviewers bent over backwards to be charitable, *Melody Maker*'s influential columnist 'The Raver' almost apologising that 'it's too weird for us'. It managed to reach only number 34 in the UK chart and did not find an American release. Stigwood sought to save face by claiming that 10,000 copies had had to be withdrawn from sale because of 'pressing problems'.

Baker loathed 'Wrapping Paper', ever afterwards calling it 'the most appalling piece of shit I ever heard in my life'. By his account, Eric felt the same, but the two of them had been outmanoeuvred by the entity that henceforward he would refer to with increasing rancour as 'Bruce–Brown'. 'Eric and I hated it, but they went and formed their little club and got it released.'

Eric, however, expressed himself perfectly happy with 'Wrapping Paper' and firmly stamped on the idea that it – or anything else – had caused dissent within Cream. 'It's the only group where we all work to knock each other out as well as the audience. It's true we do have rows – rows you wouldn't believe – but they're followed by big embraces. If a row is really big, then afterwards it's almost like falling in love again . . .'

The notion of a rock band employing the services of an outside lyricist was novel enough, but Pete Brown was already a poet of considerable reputation. In 1965, he had taken part in the International Poetry Incarnation, marking the birth of Britain's counterculture, at the Royal Albert Hall alongside American's foremost beat poets, Allen Ginsberg, Lawrence Ferlinghetti and Gregory Corso. Like few of his profession in any era, he would actually earn a living from publishing and reading his work.

Brown had originally been introduced to Cream by Ginger Baker, who'd seen him reading his work to a jazz backing and marked him down as a potential songwriting partner. 'Ginger had great song ideas,' he recalls, 'but they were mostly related to jazz and world music. Then Jack and I found we had a natural chemistry.'

Bruce also wrote alone and in partnership with his wife, Janet; their 'Sleepy Time Time' was one of Cream's earliest original stage numbers. Then, in an ironic twist, Janet found herself creatively paired with her husband's bête-noire. 'Ginger came round to our flat in Hampstead one night, moaning about how he couldn't work with Pete Brown,' she recalls. 'I happened to have some words scribbled down that fitted the music he had, and it became "Sweet Wine".'

Eric, for the moment, was not part of this busy composing collective. But he instantly warmed to the black-bearded Brown, a fellow Surrey boy (born in Ashtead) whom he already knew slightly through the poet/mime Ted Milton. The two shared a lasting addiction to the *Goon Show*, which had brought surreal anarchy to BBC radio comedy during their otherwise monotone Fifties childhoods. Like Eric, Brown could quote whole episodes in the deranged accents of Bluebottle, Eccles and Major Bloodnok. 'Behind the craziness of the Goons, there was always real subversiveness,' he recalls. 'Eric and I agreed that was the quality Cream ought to have.'

Hearteningly, Stigwood wrote off 'Wrapping Paper' as merely an unfortunate false start and sent them back for another go, this time at the Ryemuse studio, located above a chemist's shop in South Molton Street, Mayfair. He designated himself as the producer, but effectively left them alone to get on with it.

The result was another Bruce–Brown collaboration, 'I Feel Free'. It was like nothing Cream would ever record again – nothing, indeed, that any rock band had done before or has since. After a muffled 'bomp bomp bomp ba-bomp-bomp' vocal intro with Eric, Bruce hit a register not so much falsetto as hermaphroditic. It was not rock nor blues nor jazz nor any approximation thereof; if anything, it suggested some exotic Thirties Hollywood musical full of white dinner-jackets, hibiscus flowers and frilly-sleeved Cuban orchestras.

The B-side was a Bruce-only composition entitled 'NSU', which for everyday Britons was a German-made brand of motor scooter but to pop musicians stood for non-specific urethritis, the low-level infection which in those days was the severest penalty for heterosexual hyperactivity. Bruce later said the title referred to a bandmate whom he declined to identify.

Released on 1 December, 'I Feel Free' reached number 11 by Christmas. Pop video was just starting to come in, albeit of a very basic black-and-white kind, and Cream's first showed them in the ain't-life-wonderful mode laid down by the Beatles, and latterly the Monkees, disporting themselves on the swings and seesaw of a children's playground. The curious difference was that they wore long, dark robes with cowls, like Benedictine monks, which at the end they threw off to gambol down a hillside together, seemingly the jolliest of best friends.

Their debut album, released just eight days after 'I Feel Free', the first to appear on Stigwood's Reaction label, offered a different though not much more revealing image. Its cover was a shadowy photograph of Eric and Bruce wearing outsize goggles like old-fashioned aviators or racing-drivers while Baker sported a military tunic in blue rather than the usual scarlet, lined with its former owner's campaign-ribbons. The title, *Fresh Cream*, was drop-shaped as if poised to fall into a goblet of Irish coffee.

The ten tracks, which did not include 'I Feel Free' or 'Wrapping Paper', were divided between regular blues from their stage act – Willie Dixon's 'Spoonful', Muddy Waters' 'Rollin' and Tumblin'', Skip James's 'I'm So Glad' – and original songs from their various hands which did not easily fit into any category: 'Dreaming', 'NSU', 'Sleepy Time Time', 'Sweet Wine', 'Toad'. The collection was above all a showcase for Jack Bruce's lead voice, its purity, agility and passion. Eric's only solo lead vocal amounted to a musical comfort-blanket: Robert Johnson's 'Four Until Late'.

Fresh Cream received unanimous praise in the British trades, *Melody Maker* typifying a general note of relief that they'd finally come good. 'These, then, are the men of Cream, the group they said would never work,' wrote Chris Welch. 'Three exceptional and confident young musicians, successful and free to play what they want. It couldn't happen a few years ago. It's happening now. It augurs well for 1967 and music.' By January, the album was at number 6.

It was no less a breakthrough for Ray Williams, the gold-topped young PR who'd handled Cream's press. Two years later, as head of Liberty Records' London office, he would be responsible for bringing together another songwriting team of performer and poet/lyricist in the Bruce–Brown mode: Elton John and Bernie Taupin.

Robert Stigwood had promised to reward Williams with an all-expenses-paid foreign jaunt if Cream became a hit. Accordingly, he now found himself spirited away to Antibes in the South of France, where Stigwood had been lent a yacht belonging to his financial backer, David Shaw.

'We had dinner on shore, then I very firmly said "Goodnight, Robert" and went to my cabin,' Williams recalls. 'About three minutes later, there's a knock at the door. It's Stiggy, saying he loves me.'

The most important dividend of the album's success was to send Cream to the country from which all their eclectic musical inspiration derived. In March 1967, Stigwood negotiated a deal for *Fresh Cream* to come out on New York's Atco label, a subsidiary of Atlantic Records. For once, a managerial decision provoked no argument in the ranks, Baker being just as 'chuffed' as the other two.

Atlantic was in large part the creation of Ahmet Ertegun, son of a former Turkish ambassador to the US, who had abandoned his college studies in medieval philosophy to pursue his passion for blues and soul music. With his brother, Nesuhi, and producer Jerry Wexler, he had built up a matchless catalogue that included Ray Charles, Otis Redding, Aretha Franklin, Wilson Pickett, Percy Sledge, Sam and Dave, Solomon Burke and the Drifters. Implausible as it seemed, the bald, bearded, immaculately-blazered Turkish-American was also the composer of numerous classic R&B songs.

Ertegun had had his eye on Eric as a potential signing since seeing him jam with Wilson Pickett's band at London's Scotch of St James club a few months earlier. On the evidence of *Fresh Cream*, other Atlantic executives thought Jack Bruce the star of the band, but their boss knew better. 'I always knew what I had – and what I had was Eric Clapton,' he would remember. 'The trio was great, but the soul part was Eric Clapton.'

Ertegun was insistent that Cream should visit New York with all speed to promote the album and begin recording a follow-up one in Atlantic's own studios, which the canny Stigwood found a means of financing through his role as the Who's booking agent. On 25 March, the guitar-batterers were scheduled to begin a ten-day appearance in a live show at Manhattan's RKO Theater, presented by the famous deejay Murray the K and co-starring Wilson Pickett, Simon and Garfunkel, Smokey Robinson, Mitch Ryder, Blues Project and the Young Rascals. Stigwood popped Cream in at the bottom of the bill.

The trip to New York brought a radical new look, dictated by their most fashion-conscious member. At Eric's impetus, out went military tunics and Amy Johnson goggles; in came brocaded waistcoats, crushed velvet flared trousers, snakeskin boots, peach-coloured satin shirts with leg o'mutton sleeves and collars reaching down to nipple-level, all embellished with scarves, cummerbunds, necklaces, bracelets and amulets.

The makeover extended to their instruments. Through their PRs, they had met a Dutch couple named Simon Posthuma and Marijke Kroger who were currently designing Art Nouveau-inspired posters for Brian Epstein's Saville Theatre. Later, under the pseudonym of 'The Fool', they would decorate the exterior of the Beatles' ill-fated Apple boutique in Baker Street.

Posthuma and Kroger's first commission as court artists to Britain's rock aristocracy was to paint psychedelic designs on Eric's Gibson SG guitar and Bruce's Fender bass and around the sides of Baker's drums. The image they chose for Eric was a naked cherub figure with wild, flowing hair, a starry sky above it and Hell flames beneath.

The cherub's hirsuteness had a real-life model, for his hair had been sculpted into the Afro style he'd seen on Jimi Hendrix: a tightly curled aureole whose volume was a tribute to the ongoing health of his scalp. It gave him a rather top-heavy look, accentuating his pointed features and habitual expression of wary anxiety.

During Eric's grey post-war childhood, America had been a paradise by proxy that flaunted its colour and energy and luxury and enormity on cinema-screens while remaining as unreachable as the Moon. Before setting off, in his methodical way, he made a to-do list of everything he'd once fantasised about in the darkness of Ripley's single picture-house: he would buy a pair of cowboy boots and a fringed buckskin jacket and visit a diner for a hamburger and milkshake that would be nothing like their feeble British counterfeits.

Stigwood did not feel it worth his while to be present at this crucial moment in Cream's career, and organised the journey as much on the cheap as possible. With them to New York went an entourage of only three: Eric's faithful Ben Palmer acted as tour manager, supported by two roadies, Mike Turner and Bert Schrader. Janet Bruce also went along. Baker could have claimed the same prerogative, but his wife, Liz, preferred to be at home with their small daughter.

Times had certainly changed since the Beatles' historic landing at John F. Kennedy Airport in February 1964. Since then, America had become satiated with British-accented music and fallen entirely out of love with British long hair, no longer a signifier of charm and decorous wit but drugs, promiscuity, protest against US foreign policy in south-east Asia, and 'faggots'. 'Some

people looked at Eric, Jack and Ginger as if they were wild animals,' Janet Bruce recalls. 'Eric's Afro, in particular, got a lot of
very hostile stares.'

Kindred spirits were not far away for in Central Park, that
Easter Sunday, 10,000 hippies were holding a 'Be-in' in protest
against the Vietnam War. Despite their jetlag, the British visitors could not resist a stroll among the multitudes lying about
the greensward in a haze of marijuana smoke. 'We only smoked
dope,' Janet Bruce says. 'But then Jack was given some popcorn
spiked with LSD. He was freaking out in case he wouldn't be
able to play afterwards.'

Whereas the Beatles had stayed at the luxurious Plaza on
Central Park, Cream were accommodated at the grim-looking
Gorham Hotel on West 55th Street. 'Cockroaches ran out of
every cupboard or drawer you opened. Next door, a building
was being demolished, so explosions were going on all the time.
We still thought it was all *so* exciting.'

But the show on which they were booked at the RKO Theater, three blocks away, proved a severe letdown. The promoter,
Murray 'the K' Kaufman, had found fame by latching on to
the Beatles as a radio WINS disc jockey in 1964, and had since
pursued an entrepreneurial career as a self-styled 'Fifth Beatle'.
Although grandiosely titled Music in the Fifth Dimension, it was
a hangover from the package shows at the old Paramount which
used to run continuously from mid-morning to early evening.
Cream were contracted to give four performances a day, between 10.30 a.m. and 8.30 p.m., and were forbidden to leave the
theatre between shows.

Murray the K, whom they had expected to be full of wise-
cracking bonhomie, proved to be a neurotic character in an
ill-fitting toupee, obsessed with the box-office and haunted by
fears of misbehaviour among his artistes. The two top American acts, Smokey Robinson and Simon and Garfunkel, both

pulled out at the last minute. In a nod to Swinging London, the programme included a cheesy dance routine by the promoter's wife, Jackie, and a troupe of go-go dancers, known as 'Jackie and the K Girls' Wild Fashion Show'.

As the bottom of the bill, Cream were allotted time enough for only three songs. Since the Who and other headliners all began wildly overrunning, this was cut to only one, 'I'm So Glad', then Murray the K told them to hurry through even that. Nonetheless, in a telephone interview with *Melody Maker*'s Chris Welch, Eric said everything was 'great . . . too much'.

On the first day of the run, seventeen-year-old Catherine James managed to sneak into the theatre between shows with her friend, Emeretta, hoping for a glimpse of Smokey Robinson. As they hid out in the stalls, watching the rehearsal in progress, they realised Eric was sitting a few rows away.

According to his autobiography, Catherine approached him 'and, sensing my shyness with women, did her best to put me at my ease'; according to her, he was the one who did the approaching. 'He looked so cute in his Grannys [velvet trousers from Chelsea's Granny Takes A Trip boutique] and his Afro.'

Catherine had packed a lot into her seventeen years. Born in California to an alcoholic, transsexual father and a sadistically cruel mother, she had run away at fourteen and since then survived alone on her eye-popping beauty, golden hair and an infallible homing instinct for British rock stars. When she met Eric, she had just returned from London after an affair with Denny Laine from the Moody Blues. She was currently borrowing a friend's apartment in New York and, after only a few minutes' conversation, invited Eric to stay with her there. The gods who always found him cosy billets had smiled again.

Catherine showed him around the city and helped him tick the various items off his wish-list, 'the music shops . . . the clothes shops . . . the boot shops. He was very generous. He bought me a Guild guitar for my birthday and a Native American necklace. He was incredibly sweet, though he could be moody, too – so deep in his own thoughts. I have to admit that was a big part of his attraction.'

The only consolation in Cream's daily house-arrest at the RKO Theater was the camaraderie with their fellow musicians, especially the Who, whose drummer, Keith Moon, aka 'Moon the Loon', gave even Ginger Baker lessons in anarchy, both on and off the kit.

Eric developed a special friendship with Al Kooper, who played keyboards in Blues Project and had been a key session musician in Bob Dylan's controversial transition from folk to rock. Kooper was in the process of forming a new band named Blood, Sweat and Tears, and took Eric to the Cafe Au Go Go in Greenwich Village to see one of their first performances.

Another night at the Cafe Au Go Go, he caught B. B. King, the stateliest and most dapper of old-school bluesmen who played only one note where others would have played three on the cherry-red guitar he called 'Lucille'. Afterwards, they were introduced, and spent a couple of hours jamming together. B. B. noticed how 'Eric put the music together so carefully, like the pieces of a puzzle. In the blues, you have to have a story to tell, and he told me quite a few.'

While *Fresh Cream* had reached only number 29 in the US charts, it had received admiring airplay on FM radio stations across the nation and Ahmet Ertegun was still just as keen for them to make a follow-up at Atlantic's own studios in the footsteps of Ray Charles, Otis Redding and Aretha Franklin.

Ertegun had assigned them Atlantic's most talented engineer, a collegiate-looking young man named Tom Dowd. Like other studio people before him, Dowd's first experience of their volume-level was traumatic. 'They had two of everything other

bands only had one of,' he would recall. But once he'd adopted their British engineers' practice of wearing headphones at
all times, things went swimmingly. With their short-stay work
visas about to expire, there was time to lay down only one track,
'Lawdy Mama', which Eric had pulled off Buddy Guy and Junior
Wells's album *Hoodoo Man Blues*. It was agreed they would return
to make the bulk of the album the following month.

Back at the RKO Theater, Murray the K was growing increasingly paranoid about the show's poor receipts and the behaviour
of its British cast. 'How's he gonna *play?*' the Fifth Beatle was
heard to wail on finding Ginger Baker under a table, insensible
after downing a whole bottle of Bacardi. Most provoking was
their ill-concealed mockery of his wife, Jackie, and her go-go
dancers in the 'wild fashion show' whose length had seemed to
increase as Cream's stage-time shrank.

By way of farewell, the Who and Cream between them had
planned to give the show an unscheduled finale by pelting Jackie
and the K Girls' Wild Fashion Show with flour and eggs. The
plot was discovered and foiled by Murray the K, but the flour and
eggs did not go to waste. They were emptied into the backstage
showers to form a glutinous cream-coloured pudding, then Pete
Townshend was thrown into it.

Even for lords of misrule like Baker and Keith Moon, it went
without saying that one did not try such things with Eric.

In 1967, anyone who was anyone in London's rock community
hung out at the Speakeasy club in Margaret Street. This echo of
gangster-operated drinking dens in Prohibition-era America had
an added frisson as its co-manager, Laurie O'Leary, had previously run Esmeralda's Barn for the Kray Twins.

Entry was down a narrow staircase with murals of mob wars
in Twenties Chicago and through a mirror-glass door into Sty-
gian gloom where the alabaster face of a Beatle, a Rolling Stone

or some lesser chart-deity was often dimly visible. Mixing celebs with non-celebs in this way, 'The Speak' seemed to embody the egalitarianism and classlessness so dear to Sixties youth culture. In reality, it was as classbound as any Victorian 'gentlemen's club' in Pall Mall or St James's; its management kept the most secluded booths for VIPs and ensured that no ordinary mortals bothered them.

There, one spring night, Cream's PR man Ray Williams introduced Eric to his girlfriend of the moment, an eighteen-year-old French fashion model named Charlotte Martin, often to be seen in glossy magazines like *Vogue*, *Nova* and *19*. Eric, in his usual instant, apocalyptic way, was 'totally smitten' with Charlotte. 'She was very beautiful in an austere way, classically French with long legs and an incredible figure,' he would recall, 'but it was her eyes that got me. They were slightly oriental with a downward slant, and a little bit sad.'

Williams obligingly stood aside; Eric and Charlotte began an affair and before long were living together. Eric's former semi-squatting domestic arrangements now clearly would not do, but the task of finding a flat was as far beyond him as taking a driving test. Robert Stigwood therefore arranged for him to borrow one in Regent's Park, owned by Stigwood's business associate, David Shaw.

It was at the Speakeasy that he first took one of the 'mind-expanding' or 'consciousness-altering' synthetic drugs now flooding into London, mostly from America's West Coast and only recently made illegal. That particular night, all four Beatles were in the club, having just finished their next album, *Sgt. Pepper's Lonely Hearts Club Band*. Somebody started handing round tablets warranted to be STP (standing for Serenity, Tranquillity, Peace), a particularly potent hallucinogen whose effects could last for days.

When everyone had freely partaken, George Harrison gave

the club deejay a first rough pressing of *Sgt. Pepper* and asked him to play it. The tiny dance floor filled with stoned people, Eric among them, blissfully dancing to the most blissfully stoned music ever caught on vinyl.

At dawn, everyone spilled outside to find a large contingent of police waiting on the other side of the street in a weird state of paralysis. A few weeks earlier, the Law had decided to make an example of the disorderly Rolling Stones by arraigning Mick Jagger and Keith Richards on drugs charges and sending them to trial. But busting a sacred Beatle, never mind all four at once, remained unthinkable. John Lennon simply gave the massed constabulary the finger, then got into his psychedelic Rolls-Royce and was driven away.

As can so easily happen with hallucinogens, Eric's initially beatific first trip turned into a nightmare. For the next three days he was unable to sleep and saw everything as if through a thick pane of glass covered with mathematical equations and hieroglyphics. He couldn't eat meat because it seemed to turn into the living animal it had once been. But this drug, at least, was never to become a serious problem.

The Speakeasy helped break the block he had seemingly felt about joining Cream's songwriting circle. For some time he'd been toying with a chord sequence based on the Lovin' Spoonful's 1966 hit 'Summer in the City'. Then one night he found himself sharing a table with an acquaintance of Charlotte's named Martin Sharp, an Australian graphic designer and cartoonist who had been part of the recent antipodean influx into London's media. Sharp was co-founder of a satirical magazine named *Oz*, which had already been prosecuted for obscenity in its home country and whose newly launched British edition was to meet a similar fate.

Learning that Eric was a rock musician, he said he'd written a poem which might make suitable lyrics for a song. It was inspired by Homer's epic *The Odyssey* about the siege of Troy and the eventful ten-year homeward voyage of its Greek hero, Odysseus or Ulysses. Eric asked to see it and Sharp jotted it on a paper napkin. It began:

You thought the leaden winter would bring you down for ever . . .
*And you touch the distant beaches with tales of brave Ulysses . . .**

Like all the girls who'd ever meant anything to him, Charlotte was soon taken to Ripley to meet Rose, travelling by the Green Line suburban bus service he still used more frequently than chauffeur-driven cars.

For all his growing fame and sophistication, he was drawn back as strongly as ever to the village where almost everyone still knew him as 'Rick', whose pubs were still as alluring in their own way as any Speakeasy and whose eternal cribbage- or dominoes-players still treated him as if he was about twelve. Though they no longer mocked his hair and clothes, he still received the same greeting from Charlie Cumberland, a local farm worker who was said to have walked to Surrey all the way from Cumberland during the Depression: 'Still playin' that ol' banjo, boy?'

Charlotte found his grandparents 'a lovely couple. Rose was besotted with Eric and Jack was the gentle giant, quieter but as solid as a rock. I remember a warm, modest home with cakes and tea and everything English.' The only awkward moment came when she innocently repeated some swear-words picked up from Ginger Baker and Eric had to kick her under the table. And to a Frenchwoman, the toilet at the end of the garden presented no problem at all.

Early in May, Cream returned to New York to resume their interrupted second-album sessions for Atlantic. This time, as

* Eric Clapton and Martin Sharp.

protégés of Ahmet Ertegun – one of them at least – they were-n't quartered at the Gorham Hotel but at the luxurious Drake on Park Avenue. At Atlantic's hallowed studios they were treat-ed like VIPs – one of them at least – with label-mates like Otis Redding and Booker T continually dropping by their sessions to listen.

As well as the empathetic engineer Tom Dowd, Ertegun had assigned them a producer, twenty-eight-year-old Felix Pappalar-di, who was also a performer and multi-talented instrumentalist. It was a partnership as fortunate, though not as long-lasting, as the Beatles' with George Martin. 'Felix was the first person to produce Cream imaginatively,' Pete Brown recalls. 'Before then, they'd just blasted things out in the studio as if it was a live performance.'

Like Dowd, Pappalardi had instructions to establish Eric as their leader beyond any doubt, principally by giving him a greater share of lead vocals, hitherto Jack Bruce's near-monopoly. While they were briefly back in London, the producer had found their version of Buddy Guy and Junior Wells's 'Lawdy Mama', taken the tapes home and, helped by his songwriter wife, Gail Col-lins (who, some years later, would shoot him dead for infidelity), revamped it as a weird, somnambulistic chant called 'Strange Brew'. This he now cajoled Eric not merely into singing but ven-turing out of his Brit-blues comfort-zone into a near-falsetto.

Eric agreed only on condition he was allowed to play a solo sounding like another Atlantic stalwart, Albert King. Back in his normal register, he also sang Blind Joe Reynolds' 'Outside Woman Blues' dating from 1928.

The whole album was recorded between a Thursday and a Sunday. Jack Bruce was puzzled and resentful at having been so obviously downgraded, but still gave his full-throated all to 'Tales of Brave Ulysses', which matched Martin Sharp's rather good words with Eric's 'Summer in the City' chords. From the

'Bruce–Brown' axis came Cream's first and perhaps greatest classic, 'Sunshine of Your Love', built around a bass riff Bruce had extemporised after seeing Jimi Hendrix onstage at Brian Epstein's Saville Theatre.

The trio left New York, exhilarated by what Felix Pappalardi had helped them achieve and eager to share it with their peers, maybe at the Speakeasy like *Sgt. Pepper*. But their homecoming brought a severe letdown. The debut album by the (similarly three-man) Jimi Hendrix Experience had just been released in Britain, containing incendiary tracks like 'Foxy Lady', 'Manic Depression' and 'Red House'. *Are You Experienced?* was already on its way to spending sixteen weeks in the UK album charts, peaking at number 2. In the music press, even Cream's great supporter Chris Welch seemed to write about nothing but this 'Black Elvis' and the brazen lasciviousness his stage-act had acquired since his arrival in Britain – how he would play his guitar with his teeth as if fellating it or lie it flat and kneel over it in simulated dry-humping, all without fluffing a note. As Eric gloomily remarked, Jimi wasn't just 'flavour of the month' but 'flavour of the year'.

And after communing with the giants of soul in New York, Cream were back to small-scale British gigs like the May Ball at Pembroke College, Oxford, which now came in for some of the same misconduct recently visited on Murray the K. During the evening, Jack Bruce found a bucket full of vomit, which he took great satisfaction in leaving in a professor's study, and Ginger Baker purloined a bicycle and rode it through the bar. 'The students were amazed at the amount of food Ginger ate,' Pete Brown recalls. 'They asked him if he wanted more and he kept roaring "Yeah!" They looked at him as if he was some mythical beast.'

In June, 'Strange Brew' was released as a UK single, coupled with 'Tales of Brave Ulysses'. It was the first test of the 'Eric-first'

Cream prescribed by Ahmet Ertegun but, disappointingly, reached only number 17. Although waves of brilliant music were ushering in this so-called Summer of Love, to Eric the radio still seemed like 'wall-to-wall Jimi'.

Nor could he count any longer on Robert Stigwood's undivided attention. In January, Stigwood's company had merged with Brian Epstein's NEMS organisation, a move initiated by an increasingly exhausted and unstable Epstein. When first mooted, the idea had outraged NEMS' four original and pre-eminent clients, on whom Epstein had always lavished uniquely personal attention and who unanimously disliked and distrusted Stigwood. Paul McCartney had threatened that if he were given any sway over them, they would record nothing further except 'God Save the Queen' out of tune.

The Beatles had therefore been left out of the merger deal to remain under Epstein's personal care. Stigwood had still come into an impressive new client-list, not only comprising NEMS' other Liverpool acts but easy-listening attractions like Petula Clark and Matt Monro.

Additionally, he had just signed up a band consisting of three brothers, Barry, Robin and Maurice Gibb, born in Britain but raised in Australia, whose name, the Bee Gees, seemed rashly similar to 'Beatles'. He was now spending large amounts on advertising them in the music press, as Ginger Baker fulminated, 'when we get a two-line mention on the next page'.

Little did Baker or Bruce suspect it was to the despised Gibb brothers that Cream owed their Atlantic Records contract. 'At the beginning, Ahmet Ertegun only wanted to sign up Eric,' a former Stigwood associate recalls. 'But he also really wanted the Bee Gees. Stiggy said he couldn't have them unless he took Jack and Ginger, too.'

11

THE PHEASANTRY

Australians, traditionally derided by the British as muscle-bound, beer-swilling philistines, were suddenly cool and in Martin Sharp, Eric had met one of the coolest. Sharp seemed to know everyone in Swinging London's top drawer and most of them seemed to find their way through the psychedelic-blue door of his studio at 152 King's Road, Chelsea.

This coolest of addresses on London's swingingest boulevard was better known as The Pheasantry, a faux-Louis XV mansion with a walled front courtyard and grandiose entrance-arch, on whose site during the eighteenth century pheasants had been bred for the royal household.

In 1967, The Pheasantry was one of Chelsea's last refuges for impecunious artists and bohemians. It had been divided into studios that still rented cheaply and imposed few, if any, restrictions on their tenants. The basement was a nightclub of legendary loucheness whose clientele, past and present, included Augustus John, Francis Bacon and Humphrey Bogart.

Sharp's top-floor studio-cum-apartment had a large spare room and, following his debut as a rock lyricist with 'Tales of Brave Ulysses', he invited Eric and Charlotte to move in. It was an irresistible offer to the one-time failed art student; hardly less so to one who'd spent so many winter afternoons of his boyhood as a beater for pheasant-shoots around Ripley.

In addition to Sharp, designing scurrilous but graphically

brilliant covers for *Oz* magazine, The Pheasantry pulsed with creative endeavour and wild eccentricity. On the ground floor, portrait-painter Timothy Whidborne was at work on a life-size study of the Queen reviewing troops, unironically scarlet-coated and mounted on a horse named Doctor. Whidborne's neighbour was another new arrival from Down Under, Germaine Greer, typing what would be feminism's defining manifesto, *The Female Eunuch*. The middle floors harboured a resident with a pet rabbit painted green which he fed with LSD until it apparently committed suicide by jumping off the roof.

One of the few journalists to visit the Sharp apartment, *Melody Maker*'s Chris Welch, found himself ascending a dark Dickensian staircase through 'clouds of chicken feathers'. Beyond the psychedelic-blue door he found 'a state of indescribable clutter ... vast, eye-assaulting paintings, old copies of *Beano*, a rubber statue of Mickey Mouse and postcards of Victorian nudes were some of the objets d'junk that hit me'.

Soon after Eric and Charlotte's arrival, the other spare room was taken over by Philippe Mora, an aspiring young film-maker whose French-Australian parents were friends of Sharp's family back in Melbourne. Eighteen-year-old Mora was in awe of the handsome, charming Martin – and was surprised to find Eric somewhat the same. 'Eric was the rock star, but we both said the same thing about Martin: "How does he get *all* the girls?"'

Mora remembers that, despite Eric's growing celebrity with Cream and Sharp's dominant presence in *Oz* and other underground magazines, the household was permanently impoverished. 'We seemed to live mainly on Bird's Custard. I'd go out early in the morning and steal bottles of milk from people's doorsteps to make it.

'In fact, the only person with any money was Charlotte, who earned a good living from modelling. But she didn't have much idea about cooking. Once, I remember, she heated up a tin of baked beans without opening it first. The tin exploded and the beans went all over the ceiling. The stain's probably still there.'

Although both Sharp and Mora were devout rock fans, it formed no part of their conversations with Eric. 'All we ever talked about was art,' Mora recalls, 'and we talked about it for hours. Art in music . . . art in film . . . art in the theatre . . . Martin was heavily into Van Gogh and we spent hours discussing madness in art and the fine line between it and genius.'

As well as an aspiring film-maker, Mora was an artist – like both his parents – and helped Sharp on *Oz* projects, notably its all-illustrated Magic Theatre issue. The atmosphere soon affected Eric, who began to sketch again for the first time since leaving Kingston Art College, and to paint and decorate again, as he'd learned from Jack Clapp, refurbishing his and Charlotte's room in dark red and gilt yellow.

He even thought of making art his career after all when rock blew over, as even its most celebrated performers still expected. 'I'll pack [the guitar] in when I start to go downhill,' he confided to *Melody Maker.* I don't know when it'll come, maybe tomorrow, maybe when I'm thirty. I'll do something that's not so much in the public eye, maybe painting.'

The blue door that Sharp left permanently ajar admitted a constant stream of visitors. 'It seemed like everyone interesting who came to London ended up at The Pheasantry,' Philippe Mora says. 'Artists like Eduardo Paolozzi and Malcolm Morley, the poet Heathcote Williams, the art critic Robert Hughes, the model Amanda Lear, the jazz singer George Melly, *Oz*'s editor Richard Neville . . . Martin would be cartooning, I'd be painting, Eric would be there with his guitar. It was a *salon.*

'Once, we had the whole American Living Theatre group there, and several slept over. Another time, someone brought R. D. Laing, the psychologist who said there was no such thing as crazy because the whole world was insane anyway. He sat there, making notes of everything we said and did . . . even "Eric Clapton just went to the loo." The journalist Anthony Haden-Guest brought Brigitte Bardot once, but it was one of the few times when Martin had locked the door. He never did again.'

Their most frequent visitor – so much so as to seem like an extra tenant – was a gay Russian-Jewish East Ender of thirty-nine named David Litvinoff whose slightly old-fashioned Italian suits stood out among the satin shirts and crushed velvet flares and whose hawkish face bore a livid white scar stretching from ear to ear.

A sometime *Daily Express* gossip columnist, Litvinoff had connections stretching from London's *haute bohème* to the darkest recesses of its criminal underworld. He was at the same time a crony of painters such as Lucien Freud and Francis Bacon and a factotum of the Kray Twins, reputedly tasked with picking up boys for the psychotic pederast Ronnie Kray. The terrible scar across his face, he would say without rancour, indeed with pride, was 'a little present from the Krays'. Freud had done his portrait in oils, titling it 'The Procurer'.

Latterly, his social circle had extended to the Rolling Stones, who liked having real hard men around to bolster their synthetic bad-boy image. Mick Jagger and Keith Richards, who both lived in Chelsea, were still trying to unmask the informer who had precipitated their drugs-bust at Richards' Sussex cottage the previous February.

The chief suspect was a King's Road hippy named Nicky Cramer, also well-known at The Pheasantry, who had been among Richards' house-guests that weekend. Litvinoff was deputed to beat up Cramer systematically until he confessed his guilt. When he did not, even after being battered to a pulp, he was pronounced in the clear.

'David never mentioned his underworld connections around

us,' Philippe Mora recalls. 'And, though he was gay and we were all young boys, he never tried to lay a hand on any of us. The crucial thing was that he loved blues music and just about worshipped Eric.'

Litvinoff was incredulous that Eric came nowhere near worshipping Eric and still felt positively hounded by the 'Clapton is God' graffito that, to Litvinoff, was an incontrovertible statement of fact. Appointing himself Eric's unofficial PR man, he enlisted a squad of graffitists to revive the sentiment on walls throughout central London – though he was too much of an aesthete to include The Pheasantry's entrance arch and orange-and-white façade in the campaign.

His claim to know everyone and be able to fix anything proved no idle one. During one of their frequent long talks at the nearby Picasso coffee bar, he learned of Eric's fascination with Harold Pinter's play *The Caretaker* and, in particular, the charismatic, manipulative tramp known simply as Davies who dominates the action.

A few days later, he came through the blue door accompanied by Pinter's supposed model for the Davies character, a cadaverous, toothless Welshman named John Ivor Golding. Clad in a decaying outfit of pinstripe trousers and old-fashioned frock coat, Golding was not just a down-and-out like his fictional counterpart, but a psychiatric patient, currently on the run from the institution that had been treating him.

In that era before destitution became commonplace in Britain, there was a romantic view of tramps as men of intellect deserving respect, even envy for having resigned from the rat-race. And Golding's sonorous, cryptic monologues did seem to suggest a weird wisdom and insight. 'Eric loved listening to him,' Philippe Mora says, 'as we all did.'

The Pheasantry salon was some consolation to Eric for missing out on much of the Summer of Love which, by June 1967, was in full flower in Britain and America – in both, often conspicuously failing to live up to its name.

If the Beatles' *Sgt. Pepper* album had been its aural starting-point, its physical one was a three-day pop festival in Monterey, California, whose extensive bill included the Grateful Dead, Jefferson Airplane, the Who, Otis Redding, Ravi Shankar, Big Brother and the Holding Company with Janis Joplin, the Mamas & the Papas and the Jimi Hendrix Experience. In the hippy spirit of togetherness and altruism, everyone (Shankar excepted) performed for free and the money they would have earned was given to charity.

Cream had been invited to take part, but Stigwood would not let them, arguing that they might get lost amid such heavyweight competition and should relaunch their American performing career in a less high-risk fashion.

Reading the ecstatic press reports of Jimi Hendrix's performance at Monterey, Eric could only wonder if the crown that was such a burden to him hadn't slipped a little further. After a rendition of the Troggs' 'Wild Thing' amounting to an act of public indecency with a guitar, Hendrix had doused it in lighter-fuel, put a match to it and tossed its burning carcass into the crowd.

The initiative switched back to Britain on 25 June when the first international satellite television broadcast, beamed to a world-wide audience of between 40 and 70 million, climaxed with the Beatles performing 'All You Need Is Love' in a flower-bedecked studio, filled with fellow musicians and friends. Inconspicuously among them was Eric, seated with Charlotte a few places from George Harrison's wife, Pattie.

Otherwise, he remained invisible throughout that brilliantly sunny season when pop stars seemed to monopolise Britain's headlines, often in a far from loving context: the conviction of

Mick Jagger and Keith Richards on microscopic drugs charges and committal to prison in handcuffs . . . the hotly clashing arguments of those who held long-haired musicians responsible for turning young people to drugs and those protesting the harmlessness of cannabis and calling for its decriminalisation . . . the huge 'legalise pot' rally in Hyde Park and the open letter to the same effect in *The Times*, signed by leading figures in the arts and media including Brian Epstein and the martyred Stones' good friends and tacit supporters, the Beatles.

The job of Cream's tour manager was way beyond the gentle Ben Palmer, as their first American visit had shown, and to take over Stigwood hired Bob Adcock, a Liverpudlian who had previously worked with two bands from his home city, the Road Runners and the Merseys. 'I didn't want the job, but Robert kept phoning me and saying "I'm desperate", so I agreed to do it for two weeks. I ended up being with them for the rest of their career.'

Adcock had heard tales of the Bruce–Baker wars but in his experience most bands had internal conflicts of some kind and compared with his previous charges, the Merseys, Cream were 'like travelling with the London Philharmonic Orchestra'.

'Jack and Ginger could have their moments, but I never had a word out of place with Eric. He'd sit in the front seat of the car with a shoebox on his lap that was full of singles versions of blues songs. I carried a portable record-player around and all he wanted was to listen to that music.' As Eric still couldn't drive, Adcock would take him down to Ripley for his regular visits to Rose. 'She was such a lovely lady. I knew she was his grandma but she could have been his mum, the way she fawned over him.'

The album Cream had made in New York the previous May was not scheduled for release until November. Since July was almost empty of live gigs, their new producer, Felix Pappalardi, came over from New York to work on new material for the one to follow, including Albert King's 'Born Under A Bad Sign' and a new Bruce–Brown composition, 'White Room'.

They also recorded a radio commercial for Falstaff beer, a sell-out that they swallowed for the sake of the free publicity it would give them in America. Jack Bruce's voice lost none of its passion in extolling 'the beer you reach for first . . . when you want to quench your thirst' and Eric put just as much into a riff with an echo of 'White Room'.

Working at IBC Studios with Pappalardi exposed Stigwood's pretensions to be a record-producer to an often embarrassing degree. 'He had absolutely cloth ears,' Pete Brown recalls, 'but he kept turning up and trying to interfere with what Felix was doing. In the end, when he was there, Ginger just poured Coca-Cola all over the recording-desk.'

August would find the band back at the Windsor Blues and Jazz Festival, where they had launched exactly a year earlier, yet with no sense of major accomplishments behind them – on the contrary, a nagging fear of having already fallen behind musical fashion.

For a couple of years already, the guitar's barometer-shaped Eastern cousin, the sitar, had been infiltrating Western pop. First employed by the post-Eric Yardbirds in 'Heart Full of Soul', then successively taken up by the Kinks ('See My Friends'), the Stones ('Mother's Little Helper') and the Beatles ('Norwegian Wood'), a classical instrument dating back to the Mughal Empire lost its 'i' and became a star.

The hippies, with their hunger for the mystical and meaningful, had not only embraced the sitar but the whole culture, multitheistic religion and ancient philosophies of India behind it. From George Harrison's 'Within You Without You' on *Sgt. Pepper* to Scott McKenzie's 'San Francisco', its wiry voice was as essential to the Summer of Love as kaftans, joss-sticks and the raindrop-sparkle of good acid trips. If it could be mixed with

Alice in Wonderland faux-naïveté, as on Traffic's 'Hole In My Shoe', the effect was doubly potent.

Eric had been a fan of the Indian musician Bismillah Khan since John Mayall days – often trying to make his guitar mimic Khan's oboe-like shehnai – and Jack Bruce was currently mastering the sitar as rapidly as all Western stringed instruments, yet not the slightest suspicion of a raga would ever be heard on a Cream track.

In August, the Beatles took the Indian vogue to the next level by becoming followers of the Maharishi Mahesh Yogi and his Transcendental Meditation movement. The instigator was George Harrison's wife, Pattie, who had become interested in meditation during a trip to Bombay the previous year. Hearing that the Maharishi was scheduled to give a lecture in London, she made George round up the others to attend.

The following August Bank Holiday weekend, while they were receiving further instruction from their new guru at a teacher-training college in north Wales, Brian Epstein was found dead of an alcohol- and barbiturates-overdose at his London home.

Epstein's death was an immeasurable catastrophe for the Beatles but good for his lately-acquired business partner. The ensuing reorganisation of the NEMS company saw Robert Stigwood swiftly axed as managing director and replaced by Epstein's younger brother, Clive. Stigwood received a substantial sum in compensation and walked away with the choicer names on NEMS' roster, including Cream and the Bee Gees.

Eric hadn't missed the Summer of Love after all, though he didn't catch up with it until the leaves were starting to turn. Late in August, Cream returned to America for a seven-week tour, starting out at Bill Graham's Fillmore auditorium in San Francisco.

Graham, born Wulf Wolodia Grajonca, the child of Jewish

refugees from Nazi Germany, was that rarity, an entrepreneur with a soul. Under his management, the Fillmore had given a home to the Californian bands who created psychedelic rock as well as to theatre and poetry-readings by San Francisco's earlier beat-makers, Michael McLure, Gregory Corso and Lawrence Ferlinghetti. He had chanced to hear Cream on the radio and, on the strength of it, had booked them for eleven straight nights.

They set out on 20 August, their entourage as modest as it had been on the much smaller-scale trip to New York the previous May. With the new tour-manager, Bob Adcock, were just the two roadies, Mike Turner to handle Baker's drums, and Bert Schrader to handle the guitars. In defiance of the rock world's most sacred rule, 'no wives or girlfriends on tour', Janet Bruce was also along, and Eric's girlfriend, Charlotte, and Baker's wife, Liz, were to join up for short periods at various points along the route. At that point, it all seemed very civilised and homely.

Despite the number of brilliantly inventive, polysyllabic bands San Francisco had produced and was still producing, Cream had built a sizeable following there and its welcome put cold-shouldering New York to shame. 'When we woke up on the first morning at the Sausalito Inn, there was a big crowd of hippies on the grass in front,' Janet Bruce recalls. 'And all the cars were covered in flowers.'

Nor was Bill Graham another Murray the K, measuring out their stage-time like a miser. At the Fillmore, they and their co-attraction, the Paul Butterfield Blues Band, were each allotted two forty-five-minute sets; their second technically ended the night's proceedings, but no one would be standing by with a stop-watch. 'Stretch out,' Graham urged them. 'If you want to play "Spoonful" [their new American single] from night till dawn, do it.'

So Cream stretched out songs whose recorded versions lasted only two or three minutes into half an hour or more, largely by means of extended solos having more in common with bebop than rock. By that time of night, the Fillmore's 2,000 $3-per-ticket patrons were a heaving, amorphous mass, drenched in colour or flickering black-and-white in the light-show projected from the bandstand, many under the influence of acid or grass and so with all critical faculties suspended. No matter how long the number thundered on, it was never long enough.

Eric would always remember the perfect cohesion of Bruce, Baker and himself when times were good. 'We had no other interest. There was nothing else going on. There was no family, there was no desire for success, no commerciality. There was no responsibility other than to that unique moment in time. And for a short period, it was unfettered and extreme and beautiful.'

More often than not, he was on an acid trip himself, in a world of his own bounded by his giant twin Marshall stacks. 'Sometimes I didn't know if my hands were working, what the guitar was that I was playing or even what it was made of,' he would recall. 'On one trip, it was in my head that I could turn the audience into angels or devils according to which note I played.'

Between shows, there was ample time to explore the hinterland of the two streets named Haight and Ashbury that were the hippies' Mecca or hang out in Sausalito, the houseboat community where Otis Redding had written 'Dock of the Bay'.

Here, usually over a joint or a tab, Eric acquired a new circle of friends including David Crosby from the Byrds, Mike Bloomfield, the Paul Butterfield band's brilliant guitarist/pianist, Terry the Tramp, the 6ft 2in leader of the Oakland Hell's Angels (one of whose number would fatally stab a spectator at a Rolling Stones concert two years later), and Owsley Stanley III, who financed the Grateful Dead by selling high-grade LSD he cooked in a laboratory that he convinced the police was used for scientific experiments on rats.

'Owsley came to the Sausalito Inn,' Janet Bruce remembers.

'There was a clanking noise outside because he was carrying a big canister of laughing gas, which he took a big puff from, then passed around.'

'Stigwood had hired a yacht to take them on a sail around San Francisco Bay and before they set off, Owsley and David Crosby turned up with a bunch of the most enormous spliffs,' says Bob Adcock. 'Ginger climbed the mast and then accidentally lost all the money out of his pocket, a big sum that went fluttering down into the sea. He was screaming "Stop! Stop!" to the skipper. The single dollar-bills were near the boat and easy to get back but the hundred-dollar ones were floating just out of reach.'

As an impresario, Bill Graham combined the ego-massaging skills of a geisha with volcanic ferocity when the occasion demanded. 'To me, he looked like another Hell's Angel,' Adcock recalls. 'Later, after he'd opened the Fillmore East in New York, I once saw him take on twenty thugs who were trying to wreck the place. He took off his belt and whirled it around his head like a maniac and they all ran.'

General good vibes notwithstanding, there was a dispute with Graham over Cream's fee, which had been fixed before anyone expected them to be a sell-out. It ended in a confrontation with Bruce and Baker so acrimonious that Graham later made a peace-offering of antique gold watches.

But Eric took no part in the fracas – nor any other one, ever.' [He] kept away from all the flash-points and stayed in his room a great deal,' Ben Palmer remembered. 'Nobody picked on him. He was completely safe.'

After the Fillmore, Cream had weeks on the road, travelling on domestic flights or by hire-car and greeted with rapture by anyone of either sex in sandals or a headband, with suspicion by police and hotel desk-clerks, and blank disbelief by huge men in white short-sleeved shirts with cigarette-packs shadowing their breast-pockets and hair cropped to the scalp-bone. Yet all of it still seemed the greatest fun.

In Los Angeles, they played three nights at the Whisky A Go Go on Sunset Strip, where people were still talking about Jimi Hendrix's appearance months previously. Charlotte took a break from modelling to join the party, staying with Eric at the glamorous Beverly Hills Hotel. 'We saw Joni Mitchell perform in a very small club,' Janet Bruce says. 'There was a plane trip over the Grand Canyon but it didn't have enough seats for everyone, so only the boys went.'

America's Summer of Love had been belied by race-riots in several major cities, one of the worst in Detroit where Cream were booked for three nights at the Grande Ballroom. 'The streets were still empty except for the police and National Guard,' Bob Adcock recalls, 'with tanks on every corner.'

Yet despite the tense inter-racial atmosphere – and Detroit's natural bias towards black soul music, as apotheosised by its Motown label – Cream broke all attendance-records at the Grande. In contrast, at Boston's Psychedelic Supermarket and at the Action House in Long Beach, New York, only a few dozen people turned up.

New York City this time around kept them downtown, at the Village Theater (which Bill Graham was soon to turn into an East Coast Fillmore) and then the Cafe Au Go Go, supported by Ritchie Havens, who did not sing so much as weep nor play a guitar so much as try to scrub it into extinction.

Some nights, their opener was Tiny Tim, the furthest pop music would ever go from Elvis Presley, singing 'Tiptoe Through the Tulips' in a camp falsetto to his own ukulele accompaniment. One of his sets goaded a Cream fan into throwing a heavy metal padlock at his head but Graham, who happened to be present, caught it before it could make contact.

The New York stopover allowed further recording-time at

Atlantic Records and brought further evidence that in Ahmet Ertegun's eyes they were not all equal. One night, he called Eric to the studio where Aretha Franklin, until then Atlantic's greatest asset, was working on her album *Lady Soul*.

He found the famously temperamental and insecure Franklin with her clergyman father and sisters, and a crowd of top session musicians with five guitarists among whom he recognised the brilliant Joe South, Jimmy Johnson and Bobby Womack. Ertegun dismissed them all and sent him in alone.

'Aretha was at the piano,' Ertegun would recall. 'When Eric walked in with his Afro hair and pink trousers, she started to laugh. But as soon as he played, Aretha stopped laughing.'

12

'FUCK! I'M RICH!'

Cream's second album was released in November 1967, with a cover, designed by Martin Sharp, on which their three sombre faces loomed from a firmament of Day-Glo red, pink, green and blue like a phantasmagorical Mount Rushmore.

Its title was inspired by the van driver with John Mayall's Bluesbreakers, an Irishman named Tony Shakespeare whose malapropisms had entertained Eric and Jack Bruce during many monotonous all-night journeys. One of his best had come in a discussion about cycling (still a passion with Eric) when he awarded Derailleur three-speed gears the name of Queen Victoria's favourite prime minister. 'You can't beat those Disraeli gears,' he declared.

The Mount Rushmore-esque group photograph at the centre of Sharp's design was by Robert Whitaker, who had set up the Beatles' infamous 'butcher' album-cover and whose studio was at The Pheasantry. There was a connection between these rock faces and actual geological ones: Whitaker had accompanied Cream's summer 1967 Scottish tour and, prompted by Bruce, had shot them at the summit of Ben Nevis, the highest mountain in the British Isles.

Needless to say, the decision to climb to an elevation of 1,345 metres was not taken with their full wits about them. 'We were all on an LSD trip,' Janet Bruce remembers. 'It was the only time I ever took it with Eric. 'We went up by the supposedly easy route, but it seemed pretty difficult to us and at one point we met some climbers in full gear, who asked Eric for his autograph. About three-quarters of the way up, there's a kind of plateau and I sat down and began to cry because I was thinking "I'm never going to get off this mountain."

'After the photo-shoot, we decided the only way to get down was to run all the way. I remember us going through this gully of broken rocks – do they call it a scree? – sliding and slithering in the mud.'

Disraeli Gears was the fruit of those three-and-a-half days at Atlantic Studios back in May when producer Felix Pappalardi and engineer Tom Dowd had honed the new 'less is more' approach with 'Strange Brew', 'Tales of Brave Ulysses' and 'Sunshine Of Your Love'. True to Eric's promise of a Dada/Goons element, the Bruce–Brown partnership satirised mystical lyrics with 'SWLABR' (She Walks Like A Bearded Rainbow), a Bruce vocal as charmingly playful as the title was heavy-handed. Side two ended with 'Mother's Lament', a faux-music hall ballad (better known as 'Your Baby Has Gone Down The Plug-'ole') sung by all three in a rare instance of Cream publicly having fun together.

'Tales of Brave Ulysses', in particular, demonstrated how far Eric's technique had developed beyond the basic syntax of blues and rock. Thanks to Jimi Hendrix, he had discovered the wah-wah pedal, a device that allowed the guitar a vastly greater range of moods and emotions and – in hands such as Hendrix's and his – gave it an almost human quality, as if breath were being exhaled and inhaled rather than strings being struck. He had subsequently developed his own softer, blurrier sound that he named 'womantone' with no feminist objection as yet from his Pheasantry neighbour, Germaine Greer.

Disraeli Gears was Cream's breakthrough in America, receiving saturation-play not only on specialist rock FM radio stations but AM Top 40 ones, reaching number 4 on every album chart (as against 5 in the UK) and ultimately becoming *Cash Box*'s top album of 1968.

'I was with Eric at The Pheasantry one day when he got a phone call from Robert Stigwood,' his co-tenant Philippe Mora remembers. 'I heard him say "Fuck" and then, a moment later, *"Fuck!"* and then "FUCK!" He hung up, turned to me and said, "I'm rich!"'

'The first big amount of money he was owed, from records or touring, had just come through. And – this was so Eric – one of the first things he said to me after he found out was, "Didn't you want to make a film?" 'That same day, he took me to Stigwood's office in the chauffeur-driven car that had been sent for him. He walked in and said to Stigwood, "Philippe needs £5,000 to make a film." Stigwood said, "Hold on . . . what's the deal?"

'Eric said, "There's no deal. Just give him £5,000 to make his film." It spoilt me for the rest of my film-making career.'

Despite his new wealth, Eric showed no desire to move from the top-floor flat at The Pheasantry, where so many interesting people were always coming and going and the talk was always more about art than music. The balance changed slightly when he arranged with Martin Sharp for Pete Brown to move in also. Brown's writing duties for Cream took up only a small portion of his time and he was developing as a performer in his own right with bands more overtly fusing rock, poetry and jazz.

'I was just starting the First Real Poetry Band with this fantastic young guitarist named John McLaughlin [later a contender for Eric's crown through his work with the Mahavishnu Orchestra and Miles Davis]. Martin Sharp didn't like me rehearsing them in my room – and didn't like me much. So I didn't last very long.'

Being under the same roof as Cream's main lyricist, however briefly, might have been expected to stimulate Eric's still-negligible songwriting. 'We did work together on a song that became "Anyone For Tennis",' Brown says. 'But the chemistry just didn't seem to be there.'

From early 1968, another musician began slipping through the flat's blue door with a reticence unusual among its *saloniers*. Since meeting George Harrison when the Yardbirds played on the Beatles' Christmas Show, Eric had stayed on friendly terms with him but their paths had crossed only seldom. Now, in what was an increasingly fraught time for George inside the Beatles, he began dropping in frequently to see Eric, encouraged by the fact that one could park a Rolls-Royce or psychedelic Mini without restriction on the King's Road right outside The Pheasantry.

'George was always very sweet and very shy,' Philippe Mora remembers. 'He and Eric didn't seem to do much guitar-playing together: they'd talk for hours in Eric's room, then go off somewhere, just the two of them.' Eric himself would recall how 'being with George felt like basking in this golden light. Walking with him into a restaurant or anywhere, everything that I might have thought I was just shrivelled to nothing.'

Hanging out with George had the inevitable result of wanting to look like him. So Eric let his hair fall to his shoulders the way George's had since discovering transcendental meditation, and grew a bushy moustache exactly replicating the one that latterly seemed to have swept all humour from the Beatle's face.

Yet he still barely knew George's wife, Pattie, who, like all Beatle spouses, was seldom seen in public with her husband. He had met her after a Cream performance at the Saville Theatre, thought her the most beautiful woman he'd ever seen and – his inferiority complex instantly kicking in – assumed her to be immeasurably above and beyond him.

'She belonged to a powerful man who seemed to have everything I wanted,' he would recall, once again not for the ears of Germaine Greer. 'Amazing cars, an incredible career and a beautiful wife . . . They were like Camelot. I was Lancelot.'

In February 1968, George's path and his diverged again. The Beatles – and their wives – travelled to Rishikesh in India to meditate with Maharishi Mahesh Yogi. Cream set out on a five-month American tour that would simultaneously take them to their zenith and blow them apart.

Disraeli Gears had contained two unwitting advance warnings. Jack Bruce's stand-out lead vocal was a keening lament, written by him without Pete Brown, called 'We're Going Wrong'. And in Eric's rendition of Blind Joe Reynolds's 'Outside Woman Blues', the line 'Great God, don't lose your mind' had a faint vinyl whisper of King Lear's 'Let me not be mad, sweet Heaven'.

Even in the best cases, a rock band is an unnatural entity whose members, more often than not, have only music in common and are otherwise totally incompatible, yet must live in close confinement together for weeks and months on end like hostages with room service. Internal personality problems, exhaustion, boredom, the awful millstone of mega-fame, finish all of them in the end. But historically, even the most strife-torn have managed to keep going longer than Cream's two years.

'Our last tour was two years and two months,' says Lars Ulrich, the drummer with Metallica, one of numerous modern heavy metal bands who regard themselves as Cream's heirs. 'We've had *parties* that lasted longer than two years.'

Rather than the fisticuffs and knife-waving of the Graham Bond era, Ginger Baker and Jack Bruce had settled into perpetual nagging like an old married couple who know all each other's weak points and scratch away at them remorselessly. 'They focused on each other all the time, for their aggressions and their frustration – and it wore me out,' Eric recalls. 'From time to time, I'd break down and go, "I can't stand this any longer."' More than once it reduced him literally to tears.

Yet musically they were the power that drove him, even while driving him half-mad. 'They both had an energy and determination that jazz musicians don't usually – and that Eric certainly didn't at the beginning,' Pete Brown says. 'Between them, they got more out of him than he can ever have known was in him. That was the basic difference between Cream and the Jimi Hendrix Experience: Jimi was always challenging his rhythm section and Eric was always being pushed by his.'

Matters might have been helped by increasing the trio to a quartet, as was often suggested, thereby lightening the musical load on each of them and giving Eric a bulwark against the bickering. But Stigwood would not hear of it because of the extra expense involved. For the same reason, Brown did not travel around with them as Elton John's lyricist, Bernie Taupin, later would with Elton. Stigwood had never liked the tousled, bearded poet and considered him an unnecessary appendage. 'If they could have written more songs on the road with Pete,' Janet Bruce says, 'they might not have got as bored with their repertoire as they did by the end.'

External pressures contributed almost as much to the rapidity of their disintegration; even now, with America supposedly at their feet, they travelled with none of the luxury and ceremony and protection that even minor rock bands nowadays take for granted.

Their road crew still numbered only three: tour manager Bob Adcock and one 'tech' each for the drums and the guitars. In those pre-oil crisis days, aircraft seldom took off more than half-full, so Adcock would simply check in their equipment as excess baggage. 'Cream were the last major band to go on the road without their own sound-system,' he says. 'So in every city where they played, they had to use a new PA. There usually wasn't time for them to do soundchecks and there were no monitors, so they couldn't hear themselves onstage.'

Chauffeured limos, the norm for other bands, were rarely deployed for Cream. 'When they played Santa Monica Auditorium, the support band were Deep Purple, who had a limo each, plus another one for the management – six in all. We had one Ford Mercury station wagon, driven by me.'

Although Stigwood was often in America, he rarely attended their tour gigs. 'He might as well have been on another planet,' Adcock says. 'He never felt comfortable around Cream, specially not after he took on the Bee Gees as well. They all hated the Bee Gees and thought he gave more time to them than to Cream. And they used to take the piss out of him something rotten.'

For those five months, Adcock was effectively their manager, carrying a lump sum in US dollars (few Brits used credit cards then) and noting down their seldom excessive on-the-road expenses by hand in a Woolworth's notebook: 'London–LAX $30.25. Hotel Bill $308.46 Jack amp. rental $15.75 beers & Cokes $5.00'.

As it happened, the summer of 1968 was the worst possible time to be on the road in America. In April, the great Civil Rights leader, Martin Luther King, was assassinated, unleashing further traumatic race-riots. In June, Robert Kennedy met the same fate as he campaigned for the Presidency in succession to his brother, John F. Kennedy, who had been cut down in Dallas five years earlier.

The night after Dr King's murder, Cream played at Boston's Back Bay Theater with James Brown, 'the Godfather of Soul', appearing on the opposite side of the street. They had to be smuggled off the premises when Brown's audience went on the rampage, looting and beating up white bystanders. 'At every airport we landed,' Adcock recalls, 'there were cops . . . National Guard . . . tanks . . . helicopter gunships.'

In the Deep South, the length of their hair stigmatised them as freaks or 'faggots' at best, at worst a menace to public health.

'We woke up one morning, pulled back the curtains, and the mayor of the town had paid for a billboard right opposite our hotel, saying "Keep America Clean. Get A Haircut."'

As the tour wore on, Eric became increasingly depressed by what to him was the stagnation of Cream's music. Like the Beatles in concert, as his friend George had bitterly recounted, they soon realised it wasn't worth trying. However bad the sound-system, however ragged their playing, the ovations never slackened. 'It became impossible to keep the music afloat and we began to drown,' he would recall. 'I began to be quite ashamed of being in Cream because I thought it was a con.'

Both his bandmates were equally unhappy. Jack Bruce chafed at being downgraded in the recording-sessions that were crammed between the live shows, and longed for a normal married life with Janet. Ginger Baker chafed at receiving no royalty-share from Bruce–Brown songs which had benefited from his perfect time, 'like the 5-4 bolero in "White Room" that *makes* it'.

Besides, the cadaverous, ponytailed, freckle-spotted, wolfishly-grinning wild red man who nightly battered the living daylights out of twin bass drums, double-stacked cymbals and high and low tom-toms – and whose twenty-minute solos with supersized sticks doubling as missiles enthralled young men and made martyrs of their girlfriends all over the continent – had begun to accuse his bandmates of playing too loud.

'When we started in 1966, Eric and Jack had one Marshall each. Then it became a stack, then a double stack, finally a triple stack,' Baker would recall. 'I was just the poor bastard stuck in the middle of these incredible noise-making things. Once, Eric and I stopped playing for two choruses. Jack didn't even notice.'

The hooliganism of British rock bands touring Middle America in the late Sixties has passed into legend – the post-gig drunkenness, orgies with groupies and trashing of hotel and motel rooms. Such behaviour demanded a degree of sociability among the musicians but after every show, Eric, Bruce and Baker always firmly went their separate ways.

'There was never any of that hotel-wrecking nonsense with them,' Bob Adcock says. 'Big cities like LA were sensible places where they could have bought their way out of trouble, the way people like the Rolling Stones did. But in some of the Southern shit-holes where they played, it could have got them lynched.'

Not that individually they were models of puritanical decorum. During the LA leg, Adcock drove Jack and Janet Bruce and the two roadies over the Mexican border to Tijuana, where Jack got wasted on mescal, the brain-blasting liquor that has a live worm in every bottle. Back on the Californian side, during a stop for gas, he got into an altercation with some police which ended in him shouting 'Fuck America!' and being carted off to jail.

The incident got into the local media, and hippies picketed the police-station, demanding Bruce's release. 'He was in really serious trouble,' Adcock recalls. 'Stigwood had to bring in a heavyweight lawyer to sort it out.'

Ginger Baker was the groupie-magnet even though they shrieked in mock terror at his approach like children on Hallowe'en. Nor did the line of brazen would-be bedmates dwindle when his wife, Liz, was visiting from England. 'Once there was a knock at our hotel-room door,' she recalls. 'I opened it and there were three of them standing there.'

And despite Eric's knack for avoiding trouble, the tour brought what was to be his one and only brush with the law over drugs.

In Los Angeles, his main escape from the tensions within Cream was spending time with Steven Stills from the short-lived but brilliant Buffalo Springfield. One evening, he was invited to watch Springfield rehearse at the Topanga Canyon home of Stills's girlfriend. With him he took Mary Hughes, a blonde actress best known for 'bikini beach movies' who had recently starred opposite Elvis Presley in *Double Trouble*.

A neighbour complained about the noise to the police, who arrived to find the place swimming in pot smoke. Eric was among a random group hauled off to Malibu police headquarters and, since it was Friday night, held in the LA County Gaol over the weekend to be dealt with on Monday morning. He found himself sharing a cell 'with a group of black guys who I immediately concluded must be Black Panthers. As I was wearing pink boots from Mr Gohill in Chelsea and had hair down to my waist, I thought "I'm in trouble here."'

Although soon let out on bail, arranged by Ahmet Ertegun, he faced possible imprisonment, at best instant deportation from America and a criminal record that would have given him endless problems if ever he tried to return. But when he came to court a few weeks later, it was merely on a charge of 'being in a place where marijuana [was] suspected of being smoked'.

He swore on the Bible that he didn't know what marijuana was and walked free without a stain on his character. There never was a better instance of the Clapton Luck.

Cream's boredom with themselves showed all too plainly in an appearance on the Smothers Brothers' television show to promote their new American single, 'Anyone For Tennis'. The song that Eric was unable to write with Pete Brown he had finished with Martin Sharp and it had been chosen for the soundtrack of a biker film, *The Savage Seven*, although played by another band, the American Revolution.

The show's bizarre staging hardly helped. After a close-up of live toads appearing to croak 'Cream . . . Cream . . .', they were shown standing in a weary-faced row, Ginger Baker merely patting a pair of fortunate conga-drums with a cigarette the size of a generously made spliff drooping from his lips. In an inserted film clip, they executed a half-hearted Pied Piper dance, wearing black uniforms with peaked caps which made them look like bus-drivers and strumming tennis-rackets for guitars. Eric did little more than mumble the prissy lyric through his new George Harrison moustache:

> *Twice upon a time in the valley of the tears*
> *The auctioneer is bidding for a box of fading years*
> *And the elephants are dancing on the graves of squealing mice.*
> *Anyone for tennis? Wouldn't that be nice?*

At intervals, they had returned to New York to work on the album begun at IBC Studios in London the previous summer. But neither these rests from the fatigue and tedium of the road nor the transformative input of their producer, Felix Pappalardi, and engineer, Tom Dowd, seemed able to lighten the atmosphere. 'There were times,' Dowd remembered, 'when I thought they were going to kill each other.'

The album, *Wheels Of Fire*, was in the new double-disc format that normally contained around twenty-four tracks and required months of concentrated work in the studio. Since Cream's piece-meal sessions would not nearly fill such a yawning space, the first disc consisted of studio productions, the second of live recordings made during the tour. It was released in July 1968, with a cover once again designed by Martin Sharp, this one a whirling collage of silver and black that could have fronted any audacious issue of *Oz* magazine.

In live performance, their individual isolation and apathy were painfully obvious even to the most myopically devoted Cream fans. The most glaring example occurred in a show at the old Wembley Empire Pool, an arena normally devoted to ice-skating spectaculars which retained its sharp chill when converted to rock concerts, forcing many bands to go onstage in winter clothes whatever the weather outside. Wearying of trying to play bass in an overcoat and woollen muffler, Jack Bruce walked offstage in mid-performance, got into his car and drove home. The other two played for a further hour or more without realising he had gone.

Yet on *Wheels Of Fire*, the trio's disharmony had never been less evident. Never less so than in 'White Room', Pete Brown's SOS from his padded cell as 'an alcoholic speed freak', with its never-more-perfect synthesis of Jack Bruce's vocal passion, Eric's furry 'womantone' and Ginger Baker's bolero 5-4 time. Never less so than in the searing blues covers: of the Mississippi Sheiks' 'Sitting On Top Of The World' and a version of 'Born Under A Bad Sign' that would forever rank alongside Albert King's original.

They could hardly bear to be in a room together but in the studio, with the extra instrumentation Pappalardi had provided – and sometimes played – they had made one another masters of every modish rock style, from the atonal, raga-like 'As You Said' and 'Passing The Time' to 'Politician', about the 1963 Profumo scandal (which had kicked off at Soho's Flamingo Club), and Baker's whimsical Cockney monologue 'Pressed Rat and Warthog'.

The highlight of the live disc had been recorded at Winterland, Bill Graham's new and much larger San Francisco venue, back in March. This was 'Crossroads', Eric's interpretation of Robert Johnson's 'Cross Road Blues', a supposed direct reference to Johnson's soul-bartering midnight tryst with Satan.

Now, the acoustic blueswail in a 1936 hotel-room was hard rock for 5,000 hippies with every Marshall turned up to the max. Yet Johnson's shade seemed to be at Eric's shoulder that night, imbuing his voice with a power and abandon aeons away from the embarrassed mumbler of 'Anyone For Tennis'.

Wheels Of Fire went to number 1 in America and 3 in the UK and became the first double album to go platinum with sales of two million copies. Surely, no one in their right mind would want to walk away from this kind of success.

★

A few weeks previously, Eric had taken his Pheasantry flatmate Philippe Mora into his room to hear a new American album, *Music From Big Pink*, by the Band. This part-Canadian quintet whose artless name conveyed the same unassailable superiority as Cream's – not just a band: *the* band – had been sidemen to Bob Dylan when Dylan controversially 'went electric'. They had since turned their backs on contemporary rock to explore the roots of American country and folk music with a love and respect that were particularly striking at a time of profound national self-doubt.

'Eric sat me down with the headphones on and made me listen to every track, commenting on each one very seriously, almost like a schoolmaster,' Mora recalls. 'It was a side of him I'd never really seen before.'

With their Civil War songs and acoustic mandolins and dulcimers, the Band were as intricate and subtle as Cream were brash and thunderous. And *Music From Big Pink* spoiled any triumph Eric had felt over *Wheels Of Fire*. 'Listening to that album made me feel we were stuck,' he would recall. 'And I wanted out.'

The critics seemed to be feeling the same disenchantment. On Cream's most recent American tour, Eric had received the accolade of an interview in San Francisco's new, 'serious' rock paper, *Rolling Stone*, with his George Harrisonised face on the cover. But in the same issue, reviewer Jon Landau had described him as 'a virtuoso performing other people's ideas' and 'a master of the blues cliché'.

'When I read it, I was in a restaurant and I fainted,' he recalls. 'When I woke up, I immediately decided it was the end of the band.' He made repeated phone calls to Robert Stigwood in London, pleading, 'I can't do this any more . . . I want to go home . . . Get me out of here.' But Stigwood always managed to persuade him to do 'just one more week'.

On 6 July 1968, 'Sunshine Of Your Love' from *Disraeli Gears*, which had previously performed poorly as a single, was rereleased in the US to begin a rapid ascent to number 6 in the *Billboard* chart. A week later, *Melody Maker* announced Cream's break-up. Eric had told Chris Welch in May but asked him to hold off on the story until 'business problems had been sorted out'.

The explanation he now gave was 'a change of attitude among ourselves . . . We've been on the road a long time before Cream started. That was a big hang-up. I went off in a lot of different directions, but I find I have floated back to straight blues playing. I was not being true to myself. I am and will always be a blues guitarist.'

It was, in fact, what Stigwood, and Ahmet Ertegun, had always wanted: an unencumbered Eric who could now be developed to the full limit of his potential as a solo artist. With only a token show of regret, Stigwood busied himself with wringing every last drop of profit from Cream, persuading them to put out a final album and squeeze in yet another tour: nineteen American cities in five weeks, followed by two farewell concerts at London's Royal Albert Hall.

Actually, Eric's thoughts were fixed on anything but solo stardom. 'I am rather off the virtuoso kick,' he told Welch. 'It was over-exposed. I want to be in a band where I can control the music, but I want to be at the back.'

In October and early November, Cream went through the five weeks and nineteen cities of their American farewell tour like schoolboys counting down the days until the end of term. There were no brushes with the law, no mishaps, barely so much as a raised eyebrow between Bruce and Baker. 'What I remember mainly is the overwhelming feeling of relief,' says Bob Adcock. 'Especially from Eric.'

In New York, where they played to a capacity 22,000 crowd

at the newly rebuilt Madison Square Garden, Ahmet Ertegun presented them with their platinum disc for *Wheels Of Fire*. 'That was one gig Stigwood didn't miss,' Bob Adcock remembers.

The two Royal Albert Hall concerts, on 25 and 26 November, were filmed by the BBC with a hyperbolic introduction such as even the Beatles had never received. Cream, the sonorous (and, naturally, male) voice-over declared, had given rock 'a musical authority which only the deaf cannot acknowledge and only the ignorant cannot hear. Their records have sold more copies in the last twenty-four months than the Bible has sold in the past twenty-four years. They earn more per year than the annual British government subsidy to the arts. They are admired by Leonard Bernstein and Igor Stravinsky . . .

'[Eric Clapton] a twenty-three-year-old former stained glass-designer, is acknowledged the finest instrumentalist of his kind in the world . . . his guitar straining and soaring against the entire dark ages of music which still, in spite of Stravinsky, be-lieves in 4-4 and the common chord.'

Both concerts sold out months in advance and were attended by the cream of rock's new aristocracy. Eric, wearing a fancy red cowboy shirt and using a Gibson Firebird (borrowed at the last moment from Billy Kinsley of the Merseys), had never been more lionised and never looked more uncomfortable. As he played, the people in the front seats repeatedly showered him with confetti. But gone for ever was the tripartite power that at its best, in Chris Welch's words, had generated 'the exhilaration of a Lightning jet, screaming past at street-level'.

That Eric had already moved on at his own customary subson-ic speed was obvious from his appearance. The George Harrison moustache had faded to almost nothing and the shoulder-length hair was much shorter and shaped, just like the boys' in the Band.

13

INTO THE WOODS

A few weeks earlier, George had driven Eric to Abbey Road
studios where the Beatles were at work on the follow-up to
Sgt. Pepper's Lonely Hearts Club Band that had the plain title *The
Beatles* but would become known as the White Album. It was
supposed to have been just a social call, but on the way George
suddenly suggested Eric should play on a song he'd written for
the album and was about to record.

Eric had already been on a single produced by George, Jackie
Lomax's 'Sour Milk Sea', to which Paul McCartney and Ringo
Starr had both lent a hand. But this was temporarily *joining*
the Beatles, something no outsider had ever been invited to do
before. The accolade was so unexpected that he hadn't thought
to bring a guitar with him, so had to borrow one of George's.

It became clear that he was needed for moral support as
much as musicianship. The White Album sessions were making
George feel more crushed than ever by the Lennon-McCartney
songwriting juggernaut, which had always limited him to only
a couple of tracks per album. The one on which he wanted Eric
had already been tried out by his bandmates, but in a grudging,
half-hearted fashion.

Entitled 'While My Guitar Gently Weeps', it found George
expressing more emotion than he ever had before in a song
– tenderness, sadness, above all the feelings of exclusion and be-
littlement to which he felt he could fully give voice only through

his instrument like a ventriloquist throwing his voice into a doll. Yet when it came to it, he wanted that voice to be Eric's. This was probably the closest moment in their friendship.

But being the friend of someone so monstrously famous, and so famously private and hypersensitive, had its pitfalls. Before Eric left on Cream's farewell American tour, George gave him an acetate, or rough pressing, of the White Album which he played to various musician friends in Los Angeles, believing he could only be thanked for spreading word of its brilliance. Instead, George regarded it as a grave breach of confidence and gave him a furious dressing-down by phone. This, he recalled, 'hurt like hell' and made him draw back from the relationship for a while.

The honorary Beatle was also co-opted as a Rolling Stone, at least by association. That December of '68, the Stones staged their *Rock and Roll Circus*, a belated answer to the Beatles' *Magical Mystery Tour*, filmed in a mocked-up circus tent with a live audience and support acts including the Who, Jethro Tull and bluesman Taj Mahal, interspersed with amusingly third-rate acrobats, jugglers and clowns.

Eric appeared in a one-night-only supergroup with John Lennon, Keith Richards and drummer Mitch Mitchell from the Jimi Hendrix Experience, playing Lennon's 'Yer Blues' under the Lennon-bestowed name Winston Legthigh and the Dirty Mac. Though it was Lennon's song and Richards' film, there was no contest as to the Dirty Mac's lead guitarist.

The band represented a show of support for Lennon amid the ferocious, often racist outcry that had greeted his new romance. So Eric and Richards also backed a vocal performance by Yoko Ono modelled on the shrieks of female domestics in labour she'd overheard during her privileged Tokyo childhood. Thanks to the caprice of Mick Jagger, the film would not be released until 1996.

Jagger was concurrently making *Performance*, a cinema feature about an encounter between a rock star and an East End heavy with links to a pederastic crime boss overtly based on Ronnie Kray. David Litvinoff, who had lived such a role with Eric, albeit without any sexual overtones, was employed as the film's technical adviser and its director, Donald Cammell, visited The Pheasantry several times to get set-decorating ideas for the weird old house in which it was meant to take place.

Performance, in turn, gave impetus to the film Eric's flatmate, Philippe Mora, was making with the £5,000 that Eric had extracted from Robert Stigwood. The Jagger project's co-producer, Sandy Lieberson – another regular at Martin Sharp's soirées – gave Mora a quantity of unused film stock, which enabled him to begin shooting at various locations around Chelsea with a cast including the editor of *Oz*, Richard Neville, and Germaine Greer in the decidedly unfeminist role of a dance-hall chanteuse.

The film, for which Eric would receive a producer's credit, was entitled *Trouble In Molopolis* and starred John Ivor Golding, the enigmatic tramp whom David Litvinoff had sold to him as Harold Pinter's model for Davies in *The Caretaker*. On the first day, in a scene Pinter would never have dared, Golding publicly defecated on the set.

Cream's final album appeared in February 1969, titled simply *Goodbye*. It was meant to have been a double LP like *Wheels Of Fire*, but barely enough material could be scraped together for a single disc; the only two new studio tracks, 'What A Bringdown' and 'Doing That Scrapyard Thing', were bulked out by lengthy live versions of 'I'm So Glad', 'Sitting On Top Of The World' and 'Politician', recorded at the Los Angeles Forum during their American farewell tour.

There was also a song written by George Harrison as an Eric vocal, with George playing rhythm guitar under the alias L'Angelo Misterioso. It was listed as 'Badge' despite having nothing discernible to do with badges. George's handwriting was notoriously indecipherable and Eric had misread the word 'bridge' on his lyric-sheet.

The cover showed Bruce, Baker and himself as in the finale of a Hollywood musical, dressed in shiny silver tailsuits and doffing matching top hats. One commentator wrote that it was the first time in their career he'd seen all three smiling. Despite giving vastly shorter weight, *Goodbye* did a smidgen better than *Wheels Of Fire*, reaching number 1 in Britain and 2 in America.

For Eric, it was also goodbye to The Pheasantry. Since the Jagger–Richards trial, the police had been cracking down on rock stars for the drug-use that few bothered to conceal – and some positively flaunted. Nor did the Beatles' status as national treasures any longer guarantee them immunity.

One officer in the Metropolitan Police's drug squad, Detective Inspector Norman ('Nobby') Pilcher, was celebrated for the famous scalps he had accumulated, among them John and Yoko in October 1968, and George on the day of Paul McCartney's wedding to Linda Eastman in March 1969. Now Ginger Baker came to see Eric and warned him he was next on 'Pilcher's List'.

His response was to run, so intent on self-preservation he didn't think to warn his flatmates, and fellow pot-enthusiasts, Martin Sharp and Philippe Mora, that a police raid was imminent. For the next few days he and Charlotte hid out at Robert Stigwood's baronial country home, The Old Barn in Stanmore, enjoying amenities that included a private go-kart track, while Stigwood looked into finding him a new address well outside the danger-zone.

Pilcher and his squad swooped early in the morning. 'I woke up to find a bloke in a raincoat standing at the end of my bed,' Mora recalls. 'There were about seven of them, with a dog. They'd got into the house by telling Martin over the entryphone that it was a telegram-delivery.'

Nothing incriminating was found in Mora's room and only a small amount of pot in Sharp's. Nonetheless, both were added to Inspector Pilcher's bag, along with the photographer Bob Seidemann, who turned up while the raid was in progress and unsuccessfully tried to do a runner down the King's Road. 'The cops were very disappointed,' Mora recalls. 'It was obviously Eric they were after.'

To make some amends to Mora and Sharp for being left in the lurch, Stigwood provided a lawyer to defend them. 'All the charges against me were dropped,' Mora says. 'And Martin was told he'd only have to pay a £5 fine if he told the judge he was sorry. Instead, he made a speech about how great pot was and how the judge and all other judges ought to smoke it. So he got done for £50.'

Eric never thought of owning a country house anywhere but in Surrey and as close to Ripley as possible. Equally, being a rock star who did none of life's mundane chores for himself, he never thought he'd be the one to find the perfect place.

Initially, the search was left to Robert Stigwood's office, which came up with several properties in the Box Hill area for him to view, but none caught his fancy. Then one day, while leafing through *Country Life* magazine, he saw an oddball six-bedroom house for sale in the village of Ewhurst, just ten miles from Ripley. It was called Hurtwood Edge, a forbidding image belied by mellow sandstone walls, tiled roofs and colourfully paved front terrace, all suggesting some towered villa or small palazzo in Tuscany.

Built in 1910 by the architect A. G. Bolton, it was so named for its commanding position on the edge of the Hurtwood, a 3,000-acre expanse of pine forest and heath, of which its tower provided magnificent views away to the South Coast and the sea. In its extensive gardens, poplars, palm trees and several giant redwoods added to the Mediterranean feel. The surrounding woodland made its approach road into a green tunnel and imposed a silence one could hear.

When Eric drove down to view the house, it had been empty for about two years and visitors came so rarely that in summer the estate agent responsible for selling it was in the habit of sunbathing nude with his girlfriend on its terrace. The advertisement did not mention one particular item of interest only to this potential buyer. During the Second World War, Hurtwood Edge had been used to accommodate officers from the Canadian army formations in which his long-lost father, Edward Fryer, had served. Close to its front gate stood Ewhurst's village pub, The Windmill, and Fryer might well have drunk there or even played the piano for singsongs in the bar parlour.

The house was anything but welcoming with its cavernous rooms, abandoned odds and ends of furniture and dusty curtains. Yet as he stepped inside, the boy who'd grown up with a toilet in the garden – who'd never considered owning property while there were couches to be borrowed in friends' flats and who normally agonised over the smallest decisions, except about clothes – instantly made up his mind. 'I had the most incredible feeling of coming home,' he was to recall. 'I decided it would be the place where I would live for the rest of my life.'

The asking price was £30,000. 'It seemed like millions to us,' recalls Guy Pullen whose father, not long previously, had purchased the freehold of their family home on Ripley Green, a few yards from Eric's birthplace, for £250. However, Stigwood seemed to think it not extortionate and the earnings of which Eric had by now lost count – and never sought to check on – were debited accordingly.

He decided to move in immediately despite having little to put into his woodland palazzo beyond a couple of armchairs, a bed and a sound-system he upgraded with a pair of six-foot-high cinema loudspeakers (despite there being no one for miles around to object to the noise). Aside from guitars and clothes, his only other significant possession was a vintage 1912 Douglas motorcycle that he'd never managed to start and now positioned like an art object in the centre of the main living-room.

After acquiring a few pieces of furniture off his own bat from Chelsea and Fulham antique markets, and being thoroughly ripped off, he found professional help through his connection with the Rolling Stones. The fashionable young interior designer David Mlinaric, who had recently decorated Mick Jagger's Cheyne Walk home – installing, among other things, a chandelier whose £6,000 cost caused the parsimonious Jagger actual physical agony – agreed to give Hurtwood Edge the 'Spanish or Italian feel' Eric desired. Mlinaric in turn enlisted the antiques-dealer Christopher Gibbs, who'd been innocently caught up in the Jagger–Richards drugs bust, and, more recently, designed the sets for *Performance* with more than a nod to The Pheasantry.

A house of such size would have been impossible for any single occupant to keep up, never mind a rock musician who in twenty-four years had never had to do anything for himself. So it was that, after a few baptismal parties at Hurtwood for his musician friends, a card advertisement appeared in a local newsagent's window. 'Cleaner required,' it said. 'Urgently.'

The card was spotted by a local man named Arthur Eggby, an ex-soldier whose wife, Iris, happened to be looking for work. 'When I phoned the number on the card, a man's voice said, "Can you get over right away? The place is in a bit of a mess,"' he recalls. 'I didn't have a car, so the man said, "That's OK, I'll send one for you tomorrow." Next day, Iris said, "Eggy, come and look, there's a Rolls-Royce outside." It was a vintage 1924 Rolls-Royce that had come to fetch her.'

'A bit of a mess' proved something of an understatement. 'Iris said that in the kitchen there were about four sinks full of washing-up and every surface was covered with dirty dishes, plates and knives and forks that had been standing there for a very long time.' It was only now that the Eggbys discovered the deficient washer-upper's identity. 'I remember the first time I met this person who our neighbours said was a marvellous guitarist. He was wearing a yellow shirt and platform-heeled boots and I noticed he was a bit wobbly on them.'

The gardens at Hurtwood also needed work, having been neglected for many years, so Eric offered live-in jobs to both Iris and Arthur Eggby, she as cleaner, he as gardener/handyman, and they took up residence in the flat above the gatehouse with their schoolboy son, Kevin.

Now that he'd found a dream home for himself, Eric wanted to do the same for the person who meant most to him – the little woman with the crease in her cheek who'd been both his mother and grandmother. Since becoming rich, he'd spoiled Rose every bit as much as she used to spoil him with mock turtle soup and sugar-coated bread and butter; after a lifetime's self-effacement and -denial, she had a wardrobe full of designer clothes and an elaborate bouffant hair-do.

'Whenever she came to his concerts, she was treated like royalty,' Guy Pullen recalls. 'All Eric's fans knew who she was; they'd give her a round of applause and she'd stand up and take a bow.'

Rose would usually be alone, or accompanied by her son, Adrian, and his wife, Sylvia, but never her husband, Eric's step-grandfather Jack Clapp. Jack remained mystified by the profession he had chosen in preference to bricklaying and plastering and was a little resentful of Rose's delight in it. Eric could never rekindle the rapport they had once enjoyed working together on building sites and, as time passed, found it harder to think of anything to say to Jack.

It was no easy job persuading Rose to leave Ripley, where her family had lived for generations, and the little house at 1 The Green, where Eric had been born, along with the fiction that she was his mother. Eventually, he found a postcard-perfect cottage in Shamley Green, on the other side of Woking, that melted her resistance. Sadly, only a couple of weeks after taking up residence, Jack suffered a major stroke and remained bed-ridden, lovingly cared for by Rose, for the last two years of his life.

Ewhurst was only eight miles from Esher, where George and Pattie Harrison lived in a psychedelically-painted bungalow named Kinfauns. After Eric moved into Hurtwood Edge, he began calling regularly on the Harrisons, and they on him.

Since the White Album, George's unhappiness with the Beatles had intensified still further. In January 1969, collectively influenced by the Band, they had begun recording a 'back-to-roots' album on a freezing sound-stage at Twickenham film studios. During the increasingly uncomfortable and aimless sessions, George had temporarily walked out, with gallingly little effect. 'If [he] doesn't come back by Monday or Tuesday,' John had shrugged, 'get Eric Clapton.'

Now, the four had abandoned the 'roots' project and were back in the studio, trying to recapture their old cohesion in the album that would become *Abbey Road*. One day, as George and Eric walked round Hurtwood's garden with their guitars – something Eric would never have thought of doing with anyone else – the spring sunlight filtering down through the ancient redwoods started George strumming a new song of atypical lightness and optimism: 'Here Comes The Sun'.

Eric by now had ended his two-year relationship with Charlotte Martin. It had broadened his horizons immeasurably; without her, he would never have known Martin Sharp and Philippe Mora, nor lived in The Pheasantry, nor hung out with

David Litvinoff, R. D. Laing, George Melly and Germaine Greer, nor met the model for Davies in *The Caretaker*.

Those two years had seen Eric metamorphose from cult blues guitarist to international star and, though he was not in the least egotistical – the very opposite in fact – Charlotte felt their relationship to be increasingly under strain.

'I was in love with Eric but now the whole world was, too,' she recalls. 'And with the tours and recording, there was less and less time to be together. The guitar was there, too, all the time. Sometimes when I said something, I'd just get a riff back. I'd always felt he was running away from something, but we couldn't talk about feelings. He'd just never go there.'

Unknown to Charlotte, 'someone else was commanding my every thought', with whose beauty went a turn-on he'd previously felt only from guitars. She seemed utterly out of his reach.

If the Sixties had allowed Eric to blot out the insecurities of his childhood, it was even truer of Pattie Boyd, later Harrison – though in her case, they were to return with a vengeance.

Born in Somerset in 1944, Pattie spent her early years in Kenya at the tail-end of British colonial rule. Her father, Jock, a former RAF officer, had suffered disfiguring burns from a wartime runway accident and in consequence was moody and withdrawn. Her mother, Diana, was a beautiful socialite with little interest in children. Pattie spent long periods away from her younger siblings, Jenny and Colin, boarded out with relations or crying herself to sleep at a succession of bleak boarding schools.

After the birth of a third daughter, Paula, in 1951, Diana divorced Jock and married Bobbie Gaymer-Jones, an ex-Guards officer employed by the Dunlop rubber company. Bobbie was a domestic tyrant, given to physically abusing his three oldest stepchildren with a streak of inventive sadism. He also began an open affair with the wife of a neighbour to which Diana turned a blind eye, even when the other woman scratched an erotic message on his car windscreen with her diamond ring.

Pattie's salvation was to grow up gorgeous, with a gap in her front teeth and a snub nose that wrinkled when she laughed, as she often did – a secondary salvation in years to come.

She arrived in London just as the swinging was getting started, and it gobbled her up. After a brief period as a trainee beautician for Elizabeth Arden, she joined the new breed of long-haired, doe-eyed, knock-kneed 'dolly-bird' fashion models invading the pages of *Vogue*, *Honey* and French *Elle*. She acquired a boyfriend named Eric, in this case the photographer Eric Swayne, who first aroused her interest in getting behind a camera as well as pouting in front of one.

When she was nineteen, she did a television commercial for Smith's crisps whose director, Richard Lester, was about to start shooting the Beatles' first feature film, *A Hard Day's Night*. Lester recruited her as an extra for the sequence on the train that rescues them from a mob of screaming fans. She and a companion were dressed as schoolgirls – which in 1964 did not raise a single eyebrow – and Pattie spoke a one-word line, 'Prisoners?' In the lunch-break, she sat next to George, who jokily asked her to marry him.

Their first date revealed what a protective bubble Brian Epstein had created around his cherished 'boys'. It was dinner at London's super-stuffy Garrick Club; Epstein went, too, and chose their food and wine for them. When George proposed for real two years later, he had to clear it with Epstein and be instructed when the wedding should take place.

Initially, the romance had to be kept secret for fear of alienating George's fans. Pattie grew accustomed to being a shameful secret, allowed to appear with him only in protected environments like the Ad Lib club, on one occasion – in company with

John's wife, Cynthia – being smuggled past the press in a pair of outsize laundry baskets.

Once unmasked, she faced verbal abuse, sometimes even physical assault, from frenzied adolescent females who regarded George as their personal property. And like all royal consorts, she had to stay one step behind the monarch. 'When we'd go to an hotel,' she recalls, 'they'd hold open the door for George, then let it slam in my face.'

She was the silent witness to formative events in the Beatles' later career, from their first LSD trip (administered at a dinner party by their dentist) to the moment they learned of Brian Epstein's death and their sojourn with Maharishi Mahesh Yogi in Rishikesh. Her younger sister, Jenny, who'd followed her into modelling, also joined this inner circle, running the short-lived Apple boutique, joining the expedition to Rishikesh and inspiring Donovan's song 'Jennifer Juniper'. Jenny was an eyewitness to the awful moment when Cynthia Lennon returned from holiday to find John had installed Yoko in their home. Seemingly unconcerned, he wiggled his bare toes at her and did a squeaky voice as if they were saying 'Hello, Jenny'.

For their first two years of marriage, Pattie recalls, George was 'divine . . . sweet and kind' and adored by her whole family. She was his inspiration for 'Something', a love song of a tenderness he had never touched before, destined to be covered by the likes of Frank Sinatra, Elvis Presley, Ray Charles and Shirley Bassey (and a victim of Lennon–McCartney blockage as it was written long before being included on the *Abbey Road* album).

Things changed after their return from the Maharishi's ashram. If the experience had given George a fulfilment he no longer found with the Beatles, she felt it also had 'taken some of the lightness out of his soul'. Far from granting the inner peace his guru had promised, his obsessive meditating and chanting and spinning of a prayer-wheel seemed to make him depressed and moody in a way he never had been before.

'He was angry because he couldn't achieve the level of spirituality he wanted,' Pattie recalls. 'He wanted to reach Nirvana. Derek Taylor [the Beatles' press officer] told the story of being with him on a flight from New York to London. The stewardess asked if he wanted anything to eat or drink and George said, "Fuck off, can't you see I'm meditating?"'

On a less spiritual level, he was fascinated by images of Krishna, the love god, surrounded by nubile handmaidens, and overtly aspired to a similar role. Pattie knew only too well that the supply of nubile handmaidens available to a Beatle would have made even Krishna's jaw drop. Left at home while George was in London, recording or at the Apple offices, she took refuge in her diary and in designing the perfect suicide for herself: a leap from the top of Beachy Head, wearing an Ossie Clark dress.

In the frequent get-togethers with Eric and Charlotte Martin, she took little notice of Eric, beyond thinking him 'rather nice', totally unaware of his infatuation with her. However, in her solitary, insecure state, she became extremely friendly with his girlfriend. When Eric broke up with Charlotte at the end of 1968, it seemed natural for Pattie to offer sympathy and invite her to stay at Kinfauns while she considered her future.

In the aftermath of a New Year's Eve party at Cilla Black's, she recalls, 'everything went swiftly downhill . . . Charlotte didn't seem remotely upset about Eric and was uncomfortably close to George'. He denied there was anything going on and accused Pattie of paranoia, whereupon she fled from the house and went to London to stay with friends.

'On about day three, Eric rang me, saying, "I know you're on your own. Would you like to come out for dinner?"' She refused the invitation. 'I was actually quite annoyed that he had done that while George was with his girlfriend, as if the whole thing was a plot. It felt like a set-up.'

After six days, George phoned to say that Charlotte had gone. She moved to Paris and subsequently began a relationship with Jimmy Page, one of Eric's successors in the Yardbirds, by now with Led Zeppelin and one of his principal rivals.

Pattie agreed to return home, little imagining how the triangle of George, Eric and herself was to develop or how bizarre would be its outcome.

Cream's break-up had left Eric feeling like the survivor of a particularly brutal war and the best person he could think of to help him recuperate was Stevie Winwood. They'd been friends since Winwood was the fifteen-year-old wunderkind of the Spencer Davis Group, playing keyboards and guitar and singing in a voice that stood comparison with Ray Charles. Eric had several times unsuccessfully tried to bring him into Cream as a calming influence. Now he, too, happened to be at a loose end, having recently walked out on Traffic.

He was living in a cottage near the Berkshire village of Aston Tirrold and for some weeks the two of them hung there, smoking pot and jamming for the sheer, pointless pleasure of it. Winwood received a preview of the first real song Eric had written, prompted by moving into Hurtwood Edge. It was called 'Presence Of The Lord' and was literally a hymn of praise: 'I have finally found a place to live/just like I never could before . . .'

Then one night at the cottage there was an unexpected knock at the door. Winwood opened it to reveal a flaming-red head and a pair of staring, triumphant eyes. Ginger Baker had somehow got wind of their activities and found his way to this remote niche in the Berkshire Downs to participate. Eric's immediate thought, he would recall, was 'Oh, no. Whatever's going to happen, I know it's all going to go wrong.'

The presence of the lord had an extra meaning now that he was romantically involved with the Hon. Alice Magdalen Sarah Ormsby-Gore, youngest daughter of the 5th Baron Harlech.

Alice came from an unusual mixture of aristocracy, wealth and brains. Her father's title was among the most ancient in Wales, enshrined in 'Men Of Harlech', an anthem well-known to every British schoolchild of Eric's generation. Prior to inheriting it, he had been Sir David Ormsby-Gore, a Conservative government minister and then British Ambassador in Washington from 1961–3. Alice, born in 1952, was one of Ormsby-Gore's five children with his first wife, Sylvia.

She grew up on the family's extensive estates in Wales and Shropshire with a two-year break at the British Embassy in Washington, where Ormsby-Gore enjoyed a close relationship with President John F. Kennedy. In 1962, while Yardbird Eric was using the Cuban Missile Crisis to lure girls into bed ('What does it matter? We could all be blown up tomorrow'), Alice's father had been an essential link between Kennedy and the British government in staving off a potential Third World War.

She was beautiful in the ethereal style of her Lewis Carroll namesake and the camera discovered her early. When she was nine, she posed for America's mighty *Life* magazine before Thomas Gainsborough's portrait of her great-great grandmother.

In 1967, her mother was killed in a car crash, leaving Ormsby-Gore with five children to parent. London's society columns announced that fifteen-year-old Alice had been placed in the care of her grandmother, the Dowager Lady Harlech, and would be attending New York's exclusive Dalton School under the chaperonage of a former US Ambassador to London, John Hay Whitney. After a decent interval, her father proposed marriage to the widowed Jackie Kennedy but was turned down in favour of the shipping billionaire Aristotle Onassis.

Her two older sisters, Jane and Victoria, were among the aristocratic hippies who gravitated to Chelsea in the mid-Sixties, many of them to employ their titles in business ventures like interior designers or model-agencies. Jane was said to have had an affair with Mick Jagger and inspired the Rolling Stones' song 'Lady Jane', while her husband, Michael Rainey, opened the Hung On You boutique, Eric's favourite purveyor of flowered shirts and kipper ties.

Alice herself inclined towards fashion-modelling, a career now as open to Chelsea posh girls as to East End Cockney ones. Her 'in-Wonderland' look made her perfect for the floaty, bangly, Moroccan-influenced fashions of the late Sixties; she was photographed by the likes of Clive Arrowsmith and Patrick Lichfield, appeared in two consecutive issues of British *Vogue* and had a walk-on role in Andy Warhol's short film *Pre-Raphaelite Dream*.

Instead, just after turning sixteen, she took a job with the interior designer David Mlinaric, whose current projects included doing up Hurtwood Edge. Meeting her was a weird moment for Eric. As a small boy, his favourite game with his bosom friend Guy Pullen had been to dance around, chanting the double-barrelled names of posh people they had read in newspapers or heard on the radio and cackling hysterically. And the one that always had them most in fits was Ormsby-Gore.

He was immediately taken by Alice's 'enigmatic smile and wonderfully infectious giggle', but thought no further than that. She took the initiative by asking him to a party in London; then when he turned up, she ignored him for the entire evening. It was his first taste of British upper-class cool, against which rock 'n' roll cool stands no chance.

One of the more interesting non-musical friends he had made

in Chelsea was an actor and television director named Ian Dallas whose family owned a large estate in Ayr, Scotland. A few years later, Dallas would convert to Islam, take the name Abdalqadir-al-Sufi and become an early Muslim radical preacher, founding the Marabitun sect whose followers eventually ran into the hundred-thousands.

Around the time that Eric met Alice Ormsby-Gore, Dallas read him the twelfth-century Persian tale of a young man named Majnun who falls hopelessly in love with a high-born maiden named Layla. Her father will not hear of the match and marries her off to someone more suitable, reducing Majnun to despair and madness.

Alice's father, Lord Harlech, looked easily capable of such despotism. He was an archetypal toff, tall and lanky with a languid drawl and a great beak of a nose that seemed made to be in the air. Among many public posts, he was president of the British Board of Film Censors, meaning that every film Eric had seen for several years past had borne the signature 'Harlech' on its certification.

However, he was not in the least censorious of his daughter for going with a working-class rock star, not even when Alice moved into Hurtwood Edge. In fact, Eric and he had more in common than they knew: Harlech was a passionate music fan who in younger days, especially during his Washington posting, had known many jazz stars about whom he loved to reminisce. He was always to treat Eric with sympathy and understanding – almost miraculously so as time went on – and Eric would always regard him with 'love and respect'.

Outwardly, countercultural high society seemed to have gained a perfect couple in the landed gentleman rocker and his exquisite blue-blooded wild child. But, as was so often the case with Eric, his life was a good deal less enviable than it seemed.

Although, in that permissive era, no finger was ever pointed at him for cohabiting with Alice, he was uncomfortably aware of and deeply dismayed when she informed him she was still a virgin. With this element of guilt on his part, sex played little part in their affair. They were more like brother and sister or platonic classmates at Hollyfield School; when not out at gigs or clubs, they spent most of their time smoking dope and listening to records.

Alice was not his Layla. He embarked on the relationship still helplessly infatuated with George Harrison's wife, Pattie, and remained so throughout its unexpected length until its terrible end.

Since Ginger Baker had materialised out of the West Country darkness, a new group with the dread word 'super' attached to it was exponentially taking shape like a car airbag that can't be stopped from inflating.

That first jam at Stevie Winwood's cottage, unfortunately, had been too good, with Baker and Winwood finding an instant empathy. Baker exercised his considerable charm on the boy wonder, who decided that all the stories about him must be exaggeration and it would be crazy for the three of them not to team up properly. So keen was Eric to work with Winwood that he did a U-turn straight back into everything he'd been running from.

The new entity – for this time no name suggested itself as naturally as Cream, save perhaps Double Cream – was born amid managerial complications that set the tone for its brief, unstable existence. Robert Stigwood could not scoop it up, as was his wont, because Stevie Winwood had a powerful and prestigious manager in Chris Blackwell, the founder of Island Records. There was no alternative but for Stigwood and Blackwell jointly to manage the Clapton/Baker/Winwood project. And, unluckily, the gentrified Australian and the laid-back English public school-boy could not stand each other.

When jamming turned into proper rehearsals at Hurtwood Edge, Eric and Winwood realised that the latter playing bass lines on his electric organ was not enough and they needed a bass-player whose main qualifications would be negative ones, i.e. not being small and Scottish and truculent and called Jack Bruce. These were all present in Leicester-born Rick Grech, whom Eric had known since Blues Boom days when he was with John Mayall and Grech was with the Farinas. Grech would add another line to the supergroup tag as he was now in Family, an aggressively mystical ensemble whose every show began with a dedication 'to Krishna'.

In February 1969, the still-unnamed quartet went into Morgan Studios in Willesden, north-west London, to start work on their first (and, it would prove, only) album. However, music journalists who picked up the story were told to forget any idea of Eric's being involved in further supergroupery; he was simply making a solo album with Stevie Winwood's help.

The sessions began under the supervision of Chris Blackwell, who was as noted a producer as he was an entrepreneur. Work had not proceeded far before Baker was screaming at Blackwell with a savagery that made several of the women present flee in terror. For the good of the project, Blackwell turned over the control-room to Traffic's (and, later, the Rolling Stones') producer, Jimmy Miller.

By May, when work transferred to Olympic Studios in Barnes, the story could no longer be contained. Rock fans knew they had a new supergroup potentially surpassing all others – one indeed whose line-up made the term seem almost an understatement, even though it still didn't have a name.

As to its aims, Eric had no very clear idea beyond a British version of the Band, cohesive and interdependent and in every way different from the clash of individual egos that had been Cream. His own role sounded so modest as scarcely to put him onstage at all – a subordinate and nurturer of Stevie Winwood. 'Stevie is the focal point. He needs a lot of encouragement. I think a lot of his energies have been wasted.'

By now, the album was at the design and marketing stage, yet still its makers had not come up with a name for it – or themselves. The cover was to be by the American photographer Bob Seidemann, whose portfolio included the Grateful Dead and Janis Joplin and who'd been caught in the Pheasantry drug-swoop after Eric had beat his hasty retreat.

In a few weeks' time, America was to make the first attempt to put a man on the Moon. Seidemann's idea was to juxtapose such modern scientific marvels with the innocence of 'a girl as young as Juliet' (Shakespeare's star-cross'd heroine is said to have been around fourteen) but not wearing Elizabethan hoops and ruffs. In fact, not wearing anything.

On a tube journey to Stigwood's office, he encountered the perfect model, aged thirteen and dressed in a school uniform of blazer and ankle socks. She proved willing to model nude for a record cover and her parents, a wealthy couple named Goschen, made no objection; these were the Sixties after all. Then she had second thoughts and her eleven-year-old sister, Mariora, volunteered to take her place.

Seidemann's picture showed Mariora topless and holding a silver ornament resembling the hood of an American Chevrolet Bel Air, made by Eric's celebrity jeweller friend Micko Mulligan. Mulligan's creation, the photographer explained, symbolised 'the fruit of the tree of knowledge' and the pre-Raphaelite-looking schoolchild 'the fruit of the tree of life'. To express youthful trust in science's benefit to humankind, he captioned it 'Blind Faith'. The phrase was instantly seized on to name both the album and the band.

In 1969, no one worried too much about the manifold ways in which the rock business made use of very young girls, then known as 'nymphets', whether as groupies, subjects for leering lyrics ('Good mornin', little schoolgirl') or titillating images for records and concert posters.

But a naked eleven-year-old brandishing what resembled a metal phallus was a first, and caused panic at Polydor, the label that was to release the album in the UK. Eric insisted that the picture was beautiful and tasteful and refused to change it, further demanding it shouldn't be defaced by any typography and the album title appear only on an outer wrapper.

That summer, the endemic shape-shifting among top rock bands reached even the Rolling Stones. Their lead guitarist, Brian Jones – who had both created and named them – had become too much of a liability thanks to drug and psychiatric problems and so was summarily fired. To replace him, Mick Jagger made approaches to Eric, though no definite offer ever resulted and Eric, in any case, was hardly in a position to consider it.

Instead, the job went to twenty-year-old Mick Taylor, one of his many fellow graduates from John Mayall's Bluesbreakers who was already shaping up as a contender for his title.

14

MILLION-DOLLAR TIMEBOMB

B lind Faith made their performing debut on 7 June at a free concert in London's Hyde Park attended by 120,000 people, the first in a series of huge alfresco musical happenings that would try to hold back the end of the Sixties – and almost seem to have succeeded.

Among the backstage VIPs on that gloriously sunny afternoon were Mick Jagger and his girlfriend, Marianne Faithfull. It would be no coincidence that, a month later, the Rolling Stones gave their own free concert in the park, to introduce Mick Taylor and as a memorial to Brian Jones, who'd been found dead in his swimming-pool a few days earlier.

That day in June should have been a moment of supreme triumph for Eric, topping an impressive supporting bill of Donovan, Richie Havens, Edgar Broughton and the Third Ear Band; surveying a huge, basking, pot-hazed multitude agog to see his new beyond-supergroup and hear how they might evoke an unclothed young girl holding a silver motor-accessory.

But his day had been poisoned when the band met at Robert Stigwood's office before going to Hyde Park. He looked into Ginger Baker's eyes and – expert drug-diagnostician that he had become – realised that Baker was back on heroin. He would later recall that 'I felt . . . I was stepping back into the nightmare that had been part of Cream.'

In truth, Cream cast a shadow over the whole performance,

for the Marshall amplifiers still bore their white-stencilled name and spasmodic cries of 'Bring back Cream!' and 'Where's Jack?' floated through the warm, multi-scented air.

Though Blind Faith were all seasoned performers, none of them had ever faced an audience on this scale, stretching to the westward horizon, standing on car roofs, overloading rowboats on the Serpentine and perched in trees like schools of spaced-out monkeys. It was as if even the mighty Marshalls were suffering from stage-fright and unable to give out their accustomed roar.

But the real problem was one that Jimmy Miller had already faced with *Blind Faith* the album. In the headlong rush to launch, they had not written enough new songs to differentiate them either from Cream or Traffic. Stevie Winwood had made the largest contribution with 'Sea of Joy', 'Can't Find My Way Home' and 'Had To Cry Today'. Eric had offered only 'Presence Of The Lord' and a radically new arrangement of Buddy Holly's 'Well . . . All Right'.

Winwood was, as Eric had promised, the focal point, taking lead vocal even for 'Presence Of The Lord'. As a result, the predominant tone was not of rock but somewhat meandering jazz-funk. Eric, using a Fender Telecaster, chose the least visible place, behind Ginger Baker's drums, and remained unsmiling and motionless but for the occasional girlish shake of his hair off his forehead. 'He'd been doing amazing stuff in rehearsal and recording,' Baker recalls. 'But in Hyde Park, I kept wondering when he was going to start playing.'

In the retreat from Cream's improvisational style, every song had a set arrangement from which no one departed; even Baker's solos lasted nothing like as long as their former hundred years. Much as the music press longed to be captivated, there was a decided faintness to the praise, as to the applause. 'They played together tastefully, almost gently, in contrast to the violence of Cream,' noted *Melody Maker*, 'with arranged passages well together.'

'I wasn't really there. I had zoned out,' Eric would admit. Then, after a third encore that stretched the band's repertoire to the limit, a typical reaction set in. 'I came offstage shaking like a leaf because, once again, I felt I'd let people down.'

Straight after Hyde Park came a four-concert appearance in Scandinavia, then a seven-week stadium tour of America lasting until the end of August. Box-office advances added to record sales and film and TV rights, negotiated by Stigwood in uneasy harness with Chris Blackwell, added up to more money than any rock act had ever made off the back of one album.

Yet amid the whirl of interviews and photo-calls, no time had been set aside to reflect on the lessons of that debut performance or to write desperately needed new material. As Stevie Winwood would observe in bruised hindsight, Blind Faith were not so much a band as 'a million-dollar timebomb'.

In America, advance sales of 250,000 guaranteed the album its number 1 spot even faster than in Britain. There was a nasty wobble when US record retailers first beheld Bob Seidemann's cover and around 70 per cent refused to stock it. Atlantic Records' president, Ahmet Ertegun – who himself saw nothing offensive in the image – came up with a brilliant strategy that appeased the retailers' moral outrage, yet avoided the kind of contretemps Eric had had with British Polydor.

Seidemann's image was replaced by a straightforward shot of the musicians in the main living-room at Hurtwood Edge. However, a note inside each album said that purchasers could write to Atlantic Records and have the censored cover sent to them. This hugely alluring suggestion of the dirty book trade was enhanced by widespread rumours that the unidentified model was

Ginger Baker's daughter, or was a groupie kept as a slave to service the whole band.

Most American music critics commented on the album's combined virtuosity and insubstantiality. *Rolling Stone*, reviewing it three times in the same issue, called it 'phenomenal in places, weak in others' but praised Eric's 'Presence Of The Lord' with a paraphrase of Winston Churchill on the Battle of Britain: 'Never has a guitarist said so much so beautifully in such a short time.' For the *New York Times*, Blind Faith were 'more versatile and precise than either Cream or Traffic, but unfortunately not as exciting as either'.

America's welcome was very different from the languorous crowds and good vibes in Hyde Park. The opening show before 20,000 people at Madison Square Garden ended in a riot and invasion of the stage that took half an hour to bring under control. As would repeatedly happen throughout the tour, police and security personnel behaved worse than the spectators. A young boy who tried to pick up one of Ginger Baker's cast-off drumsticks was clubbed to the ground by a security man, bringing Baker leaping to the attack, just like in days of old with Jack Bruce.

All these audiences wanted to hear were the greatest hits of Eric's and Stevie Winwood's former bands and, with so little original material, there was no choice but to oblige them. At one moment, Blind Faith would sound like Cream, at the next like Traffic. What they never remotely sounded, looked or felt like was Eric's ideal, a British version of the Band.

It had been at his personal request that the husband and wife duo of Delaney and Bonnie Bramlett were booked on the tour. He'd heard their album, *The Original Delaney & Bonnie* (also known by its subtitle, *Accept No Substitute*), at the same time that he became enamoured of the Band, and had found the same relief from roaring Marshall amps in their largely acoustic blend of country, blues and gospel. Also along, for diplomatic reasons, were Free, a young British hard-rock band lately signed to Chris Blackwell's Island label.

Eric was immediately drawn to the black-bearded, roistering Delaney Bramlett, the blonde, cherub-faced Bonnie, and the highly accomplished backing band known simply as their Friends. 'He adopted us right off,' Bonnie recalls. 'We didn't know what to make of this British guy who'd come over to the States playing music that we felt belonged to us. I was ready to be a little tough on him . . . But the moment he started to play, I knew he was one of the anointed. And, let me tell you, no one could ever be as tough on him as he was on himself.'

The couple were not quite as they appeared. Although Delaney seemed saturated in country blues, his career until this point had been largely in mainstream pop, playing bass in the *Shindig* TV show's house band. The refined-looking Bonnie, by contrast, had been raised in East St Louis, the city's vibrant blues quarter, learning her 'chops' from the great Albert King, who regarded her as an unofficial goddaughter, and later working almost exclusively with black groups like Sly and the Family Stone and Ike and Tina Turner.

'But Delaney told Eric he'd been to the crossroads, just like Robert Johnson,' she says. 'From there on, Eric loved him.'

He took to jamming with the Bramletts in their dressing-room, then sitting in with them onstage until he had all but forsaken Blind Faith for them. While his bandmates travelled between shows by air, he 'scrambled onto Delaney and Bonnie's bus,' his friend Ben Palmer remembered, 'with all the enthusiasm of someone climbing into their first Dormobile and going off to the Ricky Tick Club'.

It was on these journeys that he saw a way out of his prison of hype and over-adulation. Delaney and Bonnie must come to Europe on tour and he would join them as just another of their Friends. The couple were, of course, delighted and a date was set for the end of the year. No escapee in his favourite war film, *The Colditz Story*, ever looked forward more yearningly to going 'under the wire'.

But with the transfiguring new friendship came an uncomfortable revelation. Delaney Bramlett was physically abusive to his wife, often beating her up so badly that she went onstage with her eyes blackened and face bruised. The trigger tended not to be domestic disputes so much as their professional partnership, in which Delaney seemed to feel an illogical resentment of Bonnie's honeyed vocals and impeccable blues pedigree. His violence therefore usually erupted in front of other people, as she recalls, 'like he was giving them some kind of entertainment'.

These were days when wife-battering was still widely regarded as a husband's prerogative, and nobody else's business, so like all their musical collaborators Eric could only stand sheepishly looking on.

Stevie Winwood, very naturally, felt hurt at being dropped by his once-appreciative jamming partner and resentful to find almost the whole burden of Blind Faith shifted onto him. The young support band, Free, had spent their first two weeks on the road without even being introduced to their headliners. Then one night, to their astonishment, Winwood came into their dressing-room to hang out, and he spent much of the time telling them how he envied their being at the start of their career, without the burdens of supergroupdom and super-hype – in a word, free.

Now, too, Winwood realised why Eric had been so reluctant to go back on the road with Ginger Baker. For Baker, in his own recollection, was 'flying all the time', fuelled by the heroin which Eric still resolutely refused. There was, at least, a harmony in Blind Faith's rhythm section that Cream's had never had, Rick Grech being a drug-abuser almost on the same scale: at his farewell concert with Family, the previous April, he had been so stoned that he could barely pluck a note.

Baker was 'as happy as a pig in shit' and the happier he got, the more Eric and Winwood feared consequences from the battalions of over-zealous cops at every gig. He remembers 'driving a Shelby Cobra with three gorgeous girls in the car [when] suddenly, the radio stops the music with the news that Ginger Baker, Blind Faith's drummer, has been found dead in his hotel-room of a heroin overdose. I thought to myself, Fucking hell. I must be in Heaven.'

The concert at the Los Angeles Forum took place on the same weekend as the giant Woodstock festival in upstate New York where Jimi Hendrix delighted an audience of close to 400,000 with a solo rendition of 'The Star-Spangled Banner' riven with contempt for America's laying waste of Vietnam. As if in reprisal against rock-lovers everywhere, the Forum show was stopped twice as police dragged dozens of fans outside and worked them over.

Rumours were already circulating that Blind Faith couldn't last much longer and, significantly, only Grech was put up to deny them. 'We'll be together as long as things are good,' he said, 'and tonight they were way up there.' News had just come in that their eponymous album had gone gold.

Delaney & Bonnie and Friends' last date on the tour, the Memorial Coliseum in Phoenix, Arizona, was the most chaotic yet. When Eric tried to join the duo onstage, his path was blocked by crash-helmeted cops. 'I'd never seen him so angry,' Ginger Baker remembers.

Bonnie suffered injuries for once not at her husband's hands when, blinded by the lights, she fell off the stage and plunged ten feet onto concrete. The police treated her like another troublemaker, locking her in an office and refusing all access to her. When Delaney finally brought her out in his arms he accidentally dropped her onto more concrete and she had to be hospitalised with a broken vertebra.

After the tour ended, in Honolulu on 24 August, Eric flew back to Britain to see Bob Dylan headline at the Isle of Wight pop festival. Deciding it was time to get clean of heroin again – a task even harder in Hawaii than LA – Baker moved on to Jamaica, sending for his wife and children and having his car brought from the UK at phenomenal cost.

'When I finally came back home I went to see Stevie, taking him a big bag of grass as a present. He told me Blind Faith was over and Eric was off with Delaney and Bonnie.'

On 7 September 1969, Eric and Alice Ormsby-Gore announced their engagement. A widely syndicated photograph showed them seated on a kerbside, she in her *haute-bohème* maxiskirt and boots, he giving a double peace sign and wearing the kind of short, sculpted beard known as a 'balbo' favoured by Delaney Bramlett.

It would be two months before the arrival of Delaney & Bonnie for the British and European tour on which he'd volunteered to join them. In the meantime, one Beatle helped to keep him occupied and another kept him deeply preoccupied.

The following Saturday morning, according to his autobiography, he received a phone call from John Lennon, asking if he was doing anything that evening. He said he wasn't, expecting an invitation to some party or club. 'Then how would you fancy playing at a rock 'n' roll festival with the Plastic Ono Band in Toronto?' Lennon asked.

The Plastic Ono Band were the latest step in Lennon's repudiation of the Beatles and promotion of Yoko – by now his wife – as his musical equal. As much art installation as band, its only permanent fixtures were a set of perspex columns, but a shifting cast of sympathetic superstar friends were to augment it as and when required. This Toronto Rock and Roll Revival festival would be its first live appearance. Eric's show of support of Yoko in the Rolling Stones' Rock and Roll Circus had put him on automatic call.

The idea of flying 3,500 miles for a one-night gig was irresistible and a few hours later he was Toronto-bound with the Lennons, their entourage and two fellow recruits, bass-player Klaus Voormann and drummer Alan White. They rehearsed en route, playing acoustic guitars in their seats in the first-class cabin. Yes, air travel really once was that relaxed.

Togetherness proved to have a limit, however, when the plane touched down in heavy rain. An enormous limo was waiting for John and Yoko but none had been provided for the three sidemen who'd dropped everything to accompany them: Eric, Voormann and White could only hitch a ride in the baggage truck.

The troupe were accommodated at the home of one of Canada's richest men, the financier Cyrus Eaton. The house was besieged by journalists but John and Yoko, atypically, refused to come out and talk to them. Eric took their place and, despite being severely jet-lagged – and lagged by a few other things, too – won praise for his articulacy and good humour.

It was Lennon's first appearance in front of a large audience since the Beatles' farewell tour three years earlier. He was almost paralysed with stage-fright that increased still further when the Plastic Ono Band were programmed to appear between Chuck Berry and Little Richard. Toronto's eagerness to see him produced the first recorded instance of what would become a rock-concert ritual – a flickering forest of candles and lighted matches. Backstage, he and Eric did so much cocaine together that he threw up and Eric had to lie on the floor.

Going on after midnight, they performed eight songs, the rehearsed-inflight rock 'n' roll standards first, then John and Yoko compositions, the climax a Yoko vocal, 'John, John, Let's

Hope For Peace'. Eric and Voormann leaned their instruments against amps turned to the maximum to create a complementary howl of feedback.

This successful solo foray gave Lennon the nerve to do what he had long been postponing. On the homeward flight, he admitted to British journalist Ray Connolly that he was leaving the Beatles, but asked Connolly to sit on the story for the present. Eric was paid for his services with some Lennon drawings, which he subsequently mislaid.

Of all the Plastic Ono's Band elite auxiliaries, he was the only one whom Lennon asked to join a more permanent line-up. Nothing ever came of this, but he did play on 'Cold Turkey', Lennon's harrowing evocation of heroin withdrawal-symptoms with which he himself would become all too familiar.

He was also back working with George (who, unbeknown to him, had been Lennon's first choice for the Toronto trip but had dismissed it as laughable). The two played together on Leon Russell's debut album, then George in producer mode enlisted Eric's help to plan a solo album for Blind Faith's bass-player, Rick Grech.

Getting engaged to Alice had been a perverse impulse, for Eric remained totally infatuated with Pattie Harrison yet constrained by his friendship with George from giving the slightest sign of it. He could only watch from the most uncomfortable of front seats as the Harrisons' marriage staled, and reflect how differently he would act in George's place. As he would later write in a song-lyric, he 'tried to give [Pattie] consolation' by small attentions that George no longer bothered with, admiring her clothes or extravagantly praising her cooking on the many occasions when he went for meals at their house.

With the stoicism of her mother's generation, Pattie had come to terms with George's coldness, the meditation-mania that often made her feel invisible to him, the infidelities he no longer tried to hide. Left at home in their psychedelic bungalow in Esher, she tried to manufacture a life of her own by learning to fly, attending art classes, running an antiques stall with her sister Jenny, taking photographs with a professional camera George bought for her.

Pattie knew Alice, as she did the whole Harlech family, and had visited their Welsh ancestral home, Glyn Cywarch. Her youngest sister Paula, like Alice, was seventeen, and the two were friends. 'Alice was a wonderful girl,' she recalls. 'So young and innocent.'

Delaney & Bonnie and Friends arrived in Britain several weeks ahead of their UK and European tour. Their new Friend wanted plenty of time to rehearse and had invited them to stay at Hurtwood Edge before they took to the road together. He had done up a whole floor of the house to accommodate them and paid for a set of expensive new amplifiers to be sent from New York for their use. As several of the other Friends wore bushy beards, he grew an identical one, rather in the spirit of a welcome-mat.

Being under Eric's roof did not inhibit Delaney's physical violence against Bonnie. Indeed, one of the worst assaults she suffered was at Hurtwood, with the tranquil Surrey woods all around. The troupe's British concert debut at the Royal Albert Hall had to be postponed until the swellings on her face had gone down.

'None of the band made any move to stop it, although they were right outside the door,' she recalls. 'The only one who tried to help me was the guy from Polydor Records. He told Delaney that if he wanted to fight someone, he ought to fight a man.'

Eric's live-in couple, Arthur and Iris Eggby, saw what was going on and went out of their way to be kind to Bonnie, but didn't feel they could intervene. She also found 'two wonderful girlfriends' in Pattie Harrison and young Paula Boyd, while letting neither of them into her humiliating secret.

But Eric didn't get involved, perhaps for fear of jeopardising the musical plans he had with Delaney – and because such was always his policy. 'I knew he felt bad about it,' Bonnie recalls. 'When we met, I told him jokingly that I'd wanted to be a singer so I could earn enough to buy myself a purty red dress. So he got me a red dress.'

Pattie attended the Albert Hall concert with George, who was keen to sign Delaney & Bonnie to the Beatles' Apple label. Then, backstage, he too volunteered to join their Friends and go on the rest of the tour as a mere sideman. 'Or are there too many guitars?' he asked, showing the depths to which his self-esteem as a musician had sunk.

Afterwards, there was a party at the Speakeasy, where Pattie hardly saw Eric. Her main memory of the evening was Denny Laine, formerly of the Moody Blues, singing his old band's greatest hit, 'Go Now'. And receiving what she thought was a sisterly kiss from Laine's girlfriend only to feel a tongue thrust into her mouth.

Going on the road with Eric and a group of sympathetic musicians was perfect therapy for George after the turmoil and anger within the Beatles. In their shared conspicuous anonymity, Eric reintroduced him to the exhilaration of playing to live audiences – something which, like John, he'd thought he could never feel again.

There would also be positive reverberations on the debut solo album he was currently assembling. He became fascinated by Delaney Bramlett's slide-guitar style and, with Delaney's help, worked out the swooning riff for its keynote track, 'My Sweet Lord'. The song itself emerged spontaneously in a backstage jam with Billy Preston and Bonnie.

By the time the troupe reached Liverpool George had lightened up so much that Pattie was allowed to come and see the show for a second time, accompanied by her youngest sister, now turned eighteen.

As the baby of the Boyd family, Paula had received the affection withheld from her three older siblings by their mother, Diana, and escaped the physical abuse inflicted on them by their stepfather. Consequently, while just as beautiful as Jenny and Pattie – whom she resembled the more – she had none of their insecurity, caution and self-restraint.

Too short, at five-foot-five, to follow her sisters into modelling, she had gone to drama school and subsequently landed a couple of parts in children's television series. At sixteen, she accompanied Pattie when the Beatles and their consorts cruised around the Greek islands, looking for one to buy and turn into a refuge from their ravening fans. From that moment, she had wanted Pattie's rock 'n' roll life and resisted all her and their mother's efforts to keep her on the rails.

'She was totally enamoured with the idea of fame and glamour and at seventeen was hanging round with people of my generation, all of whom took drugs,' Pattie recalls. 'But she'd always wanted to grow up quickly and be like Jenny and me.'

George had already shown more than a brother-in-law's interest in Paula, not bothering to hide it from Pattie. Quite the opposite: one day as the two of them were walking around George's precious garden together, he deliberately put an arm round Paula when he saw her sister watching from a window.

Now in Liverpool, he'd decided to seduce Paula, but needed to get Pattie out of the way first. He therefore offered her to Eric for the night to keep her occupied while he himself went to work on Paula.

Pattie herself knew nothing of the proposed arrangement at the time and, half a century on, is more amused than anything by this 'minxy' behaviour on George's part, which Eric would later surpass many times over. 'Because they'd been famous from a youngish age without growing up first and having any experience of normal life . . . they'd had too many toys too quickly . . . they thought they could do whatever they wanted.'

However, the plan misfired: it was not George but Eric who ended up with Paula, unable to resist her because of her resemblance to Pattie.

In January 1970, George purchased Friar Park, an immense redbrick Gothic mansion near Henley-on-Thames, Oxfordshire, that was half-stately home, half-early theme park. Built by an eccentric Victorian horticulturalist named Sir Frank Crisp, the house had twenty-five bedrooms, a ballroom and a library; its twelve-acre gardens contained such novelties as a maze, a replica of Capri's Blue Grotto, caves walled with distorting mirrors and a lake with stepping stones just below the surface to give an illusion of walking on water.

Pattie loved Friar Park and its multitudinous peculiarities as much as George did, and hoped the two of them might rediscover some of their old togetherness in planning the major renovation that was needed, inside and out.

It had been some time since she'd seen Eric who, she understood, was in Los Angeles, making his first solo album. Then, one day in March, a letter arrived at Friar Park, addressed to her and marked 'Express' and 'Urgent'. Inside was a single-page letter in the italic script used by anyone who'd ever been at art college, with the Greek 'e' but no capital letters save in the name of its addressee, 'Dearest L . . .':

> *i am writing this note to you with the*
> *main purpose of ascertaining your*
> *feelings toward a subject well known*
> *to both of us . . . as you have probably*
> *gathered, my own home affairs are a*

galloping farce, which is rapidly dete-
riorating day by intolerable day . . . it
seems like an eternity since i last saw
or spoke to you! however, all of this
is not the point . . . what i want to
ask you is if you still love your hus-
band, or if you have another lover? all
these questions are very important, i
know, but if there is still a feeling in
your heart for me . . . you must let me
know! in fact, you must let me know
whatever your feelings are . . . don't
telephone! send a letter . . . that is
much safer! please do this, whatever it
may say, my mind will be at rest . . .

all my love e

The writing was tiny and crowded into the middle of the page with white space all around. 'It was quiet,' Pattie recalls, 'yet bursting with passion.'

She had no idea who her correspondent was, beyond thinking it might possibly be some overspill from George's demented postbag. But that evening, Eric phoned and asked her, 'Did you get my letter?' She replied in all honesty that she'd had no idea it was from him and its contents had come as a total shock and the call ended in mutual embarrassment and confusion.

His solo album was being produced by Delaney Bramlett, the next step in what Delaney envisaged as a long and profitable collaboration with himself in the joint role of performing partner and mentor. During the sessions at LA's Village Recorder Studios, Eric and Alice Ormsby-Gore had stayed at the Bramlett family home in Sherman Oaks, hosted by Delaney's mother, a formidable matriarch known as Mamo who acted as a buffer against much of her son's violence against Bonnie.

Alice had not enjoyed the trip. Though she got on well with Delaney and the Bramlett family, she soon tired of hanging around the studio, watching Eric assemble tracks with his celebrity sidemen, Steven Stills and Leon Russell. He in turn had little time for Alice's aristocratic friends, who might share his fondness for dope but had none of his relentless work-ethic.

The tensions were worst back home at Hurtwood Edge, where Alice had been living with Eric since the previous autumn. Having grown up surrounded by domestic servants, she tended to treat his live-in couple, Arthur and Iris Eggby, in what they regarded as a 'hoity-toity' manner, even insisting on being addressed as 'Lady Alice', as she was entitled as the daughter of a lord. (In contrast, Eric's grandmother, Rose, did not find her a bit hoity-toity, and adored her.)

One day, after Alice had offended both Eggbys together, the normally placid Iris went to Eric and threatened to leave unless he took a hand. He and Alice had a tempestuous row which ended with her jumping into the Radford Mini George Harrison had given him and roaring off at supercharged speed. 'I think she meant to commit suicide,' Arthur Eggby says. 'She got as far as London, then crashed the car. It was a total write-off, though she wasn't hurt.' With Eric's customary luck, no mention of the incident appeared in the media.

Such was the domestic life he called 'a galloping farce' that had made him confess to Pattie how he'd felt about her for so long. And on trying again, he found her by no means unreceptive. For the fact was that Friar Park had not brought her and George closer together, as she had hoped. In planning refurbishments to the house and grounds, he preferred to consult with his Liverpudlian personal assistant, Terry Doran, and with specialist craftspeople, so she never felt it was really her home.

She and Eric began what she initially viewed as just a flirtation paying George back, mildly and in secret, for his own numerous infidelities and coldness towards her. Along with her unwillingness to endanger her marriage, and the unthinkability of cheating on George with his best friend, there was a powerful reason for keeping it on that level. Ever since Delaney & Bonnie's UK tour, Eric had been having an affair with her youngest sister, Paula, as a substitute for her, while also living with, and supposedly engaged to, Alice.

She now found herself talked into a series of random trysts with Eric, though she made sure they led to nothing further. One was in central London to see *Kes*, Ken Loach's poignant film about a boy's friendship with a kestrel. Walking down Oxford Street afterwards, Eric rather gauchely asked, 'Do you like me or are you just seeing me because I'm famous?'

'I thought you were seeing me because *I'm* famous,' she replied.

Friar Park was only ninety minutes by road from Ewhurst and Eric frequently dropped by there during George's many absences, albeit for no more than a chaste glass of wine or cup of tea. But Pattie was unable to visit him at Hurtwood Edge because, following the blow-up over the Eggbys and the totalling of his Mini, Alice had left and Paula might be staying there.

So the secret Surrey rendezvouses tended to be in Guildford, under the town clock like a platform-heeled, flare-trousered *Brief Encounter*. One cold day, Pattie tramped through Hurt Forest, below Eric's house, to meet him at a prearranged spot. 'He was wearing a wonderful wolf coat and looked very sexy,' she recalls. 'But I resisted.'

There was always a double feeling of guilt, both for straying from George and being indirectly responsible for her 'baby' sister being in a relationship with Eric, which she took far more seriously than he did and which was causing her family increasing concern. For in her impatience to grow up and follow Pattie and Jenny into the rock 'n' roll life, Paula had taken to drinking heavily and using drugs.

'My mother tried to get her away from Eric and both Jenny and I tried to guide her, but nothing we said had any effect,' Pattie reflects now with unquenched sadness. 'She was tremendous fun to be with and very funny, so easy to forgive for anything. And if someone is that determined to go out and play, there's nothing you can do about it.'

15

THE DOMINO EFFECT

Among Delaney & Bonnie's backing band, Eric's closest rapport had been with the keyboard-player Bobby Whitlock, a diminutive twenty-two-year-old whose impoverished and brutalised childhood in Arkansas had given him a boundless optimism and appetite for life that instantly drew the sheltered uptight Surrey boy to him.

Their friendship had deepened on the road in Europe, then in Los Angeles when the D&B band had joined the illustrious sidemen (including two of Buddy Holly's former Crickets) on Eric's debut solo album. Shortly afterwards, Whitlock left the Bramletts amid mutual reproaches and made his way back to Britain with almost no money but a promise from Eric of board and lodging at Hurtwood Edge whenever he might need it.

Whitlock soon settled into a household that had greatly diversified since Eric's initial camping-out period. In addition to his live-in couple, the Eggbys, there was now a Weimaraner dog named Jeep, a golden retriever named Sunshine (a reminder of the black Labrador that had been his boyhood companion) and a misanthropic green parrot named Maurice. It had formerly belonged to Rose, and, echoing her life's preoccupation, had only ever been taught to say, 'Where's Eric?'

The outdoor amenities of what Arthur and Iris Eggby always called 'the mansion' had been enlarged by a swimming-pool with a mosaic of a guitar on the floor of the deep end, and a

Native American totem pole like the one owned by Eric's old Ripley scoutmaster, Stu Paice. Whitlock had a practical bent possessed by few rock musicians, especially the master of the house, and earned Arthur's approval by professionally felling a diseased tree in the garden.

Soon there was a second long-term American house-guest, from somewhat deeper in Eric's past. This was Catherine James, the beautiful wanderer from California with whom he'd enjoyed a brief affair during Cream's first visit to New York. Since then, she had had a son by Denny Laine, formerly of the Moody Blues, later to join Stevie Winwood and Ginger Baker in the latter's next band, Ginger Baker's Air Force.

Meeting Catherine by chance at the Speakeasy and learning she was currently homeless, Eric invited her and her toddler son, Damian, to Hurtwood for as long as they wanted. 'Damian loved being there,' she remembers. 'He was allowed to ride his tricycle all through the house and scribble on the walls as much as he wanted.'

Whenever Pattie Harrison came by with George, both Catherine and Bobby Whitlock were acutely aware of Eric's feelings for her. And one evening, which did not necessarily end with a 'Goodnight' at the top of the stairs, he poured out the whole story to Catherine.

Whitlock provided uncomplicated male company that came as a relief from his ever more complicated love life. They enjoyed many blokey nights out, drinking at The Windmill, the pub at the end of Eric's front drive, roaming Surrey's wooded roads in his Ferrari, eating in the greasy spoon transport cafés he still preferred to expensive restaurants and seeing films at small-town cinemas little different from the Ripley 'Bughutch' of his boyhood.

The pair soon began to write songs together and talk about forming yet another band, in anticipation of which Eric made

Robert Stigwood put Whitlock on a generous weekly retainer. And one day, he disappeared off to London, returning at the wheel of an orange Porsche, which he presented to Whitlock, with the services of his own personal mechanic thrown in.

In March 1970, Delaney & Bonnie's *On Tour With Eric Clapton*, recorded live at the Fairfield Hall, Croydon, with L'Angelo Misterioso, aka George Harrison, became the Bramletts' most successful album ever. The couple had already heard that Eric might be starting a new band and each of them was independently phoning him, volunteering to join without their spouse, unaware that to him, individually or together, they were now history. 'I fielded the calls for a while,' Bobby Whitlock recalls, 'then we stopped answering the phones altogether.'

Meanwhile, the furtive visits to Pattie at Friar Park could have ended in headline-grabbing disaster, but for the seemingly infallible Clapton Luck. Driving home one night, euphoric after having won a first kiss from her, Eric took a corner too fast and flipped his lilac Ferrari onto its roof. Since he still didn't have a driving licence, he decided to abandon the car, make his way home on foot and report it stolen.

He jog-trotted for a couple of miles, then realised he was headed in the wrong direction and, after hiding out in a cemetery for a while, returned to the capsized car to a find crowd gathered around it and an ambulance already at the scene. He was taken to Guildford hospital for a check-up, pronounced unharmed, and collected by Bobby Whitlock, miraculously without the police ever becoming involved.

Eric was not the only one to have a debut solo album on the way. In March and April 1970, with the Beatles all but dissolved, George went into Abbey Road studios to record some of the large backlog of his songs that had been excluded from their albums by the irresistible Lennon–McCartney axis. The resulting triple-disc collection would be titled *All Things Must Pass*, a Hindu precept equally appropriate for what felt to George like recovering from acute constipation.

He produced the album jointly with the great Phil Spector, aided by an impressive cast of top musicians affirming the respect in which he was held outside the Beatles. Eric was his session-man-in-chief, not only playing but providing background vocals with Bobby Whitlock, credited as 'the O'Hara Smith Singers'. Whatever suspicions George had about Eric and Pattie and whatever guilt Eric felt were put on one side when there was music to be made.

News of the *All Things Must Pass* sessions travelled far and wide, and many American musicians came to London in the hope of participating. Among them were two more former members of Delaney & Bonnie's Friends, bass-player Carl Radle and drummer Jim Gordon, who had gone on to a temporary billet with Joe Cocker's Mad Dogs & Englishmen.

Thus, at a stroke, Eric could complete the band he'd been discussing with Whitlock. Radle and Gordon were hired for *All Things Must Pass* and in spare moments the four of them began playing together, using Abbey Road's facilities to cut two exploratory tracks under Phil Spector's supervision. When George's triple album wrapped, Radle and Gordon joined Whitlock at Hurtwood Edge to begin rehearsing in earnest. But with a new musical project to absorb him and the gorgeous Catherine James under his roof, thoughts of Pattie continued to gnaw at Eric.

After a few weeks of rehearsing at Hurtwood, he decided his new sidemen would be happier in London, where there was more to do of an evening than get stoned and listen to owls hooting in the trees outside. To help him find a flat there, he approached George's American PA, Chris O'Dell, whose hippy robes and corkscrew curls belied her formidable efficiency and seemingly infinite tolerance of British rock stars' little ways.

As one of the few females in George's orbit to repel his advances (despite which he later paid tribute to her in a song, 'Miss O'Dell'), she had become a close friend and confidante to Pattie. 'This was what we both look back on as George's bipolar period,' she recalls. 'Pattie used to ask me, "What's he got his hands in today, the prayer-beads or the cocaine?" If he was in his spiritual place, he was off on his own. But if he was doing coke, he'd want to drink and party.'

Now temporarily transferred to the Robert Stigwood payroll, she found Eric and his musicians a rented flat in South Kensington, opposite the Underground station. She knew how things stood between Pattie and Eric, but was unprepared for the intensity of his frustration, often at the flat's expense. 'He was obviously going through a lot of pain at that time. He was heavily into throwing glasses at the wall. 'One night, when we all went back to the flat after having Indian food, he picked up a glass ashtray and hurled it, then the other guys joined in. When all the glasses were smashed, the TV screen got it as well. The whole floor was covered with broken glass, but only in that one room. The rest of the flat was fine.

'When the renting agent next paid a visit, it still hadn't been cleared up. She went in there and then I heard her go, "Oh, my *God!*" "Don't worry," I said. "We'll pay."'

The new band made their live debut on 14 June, at a benefit concert for America's Civil Liberties Defense Fund at London's Lyceum ballroom.

Just for that one night they expanded to a five-piece with Dave Mason, formerly of Traffic and another ex-Friend of Delaney & Bonnie, on second guitar.

Not until they went onstage did they know for certain what they were to be called. Still backing away from the limelight, Eric had wanted to use a pseudonym incorporated into a pastiche of late-Fifties teen vocal groups like Dion and the Belmonts or Danny and the Juniors. He chose 'Derek' not as a tease on his own name but as the quintessence of un-rock-'n'-roll-ness. Whitlock, Radle and Gordon had agreed on Derek and the Dynamics but the evening's emcee, Tony Gardner, misheard and introduced them as Derek and the Dominos (always henceforward spelt without an 'e' like some Greek philosphical concept).

Rock 'n' roll pastiche went no deeper than the name, however. With months to go until they found their signature song, Derek and the Dominos were mainly about big, fat boogie, with Bobby Whitlock's voice shadowing Eric's as Eric's once had Jack Bruce's, but in this case energising and expanding it: not so much backing vocal as bicycle-pump.

Their repertoire was made up of the songs Eric had written with Whitlock at Hurtwood like 'Tell The Truth' and 'Roll It Over', advance previews of his forthcoming solo album and the odd Blind Faith remainder, like 'Presence Of The Lord'. There were also two blues covers unequally close to his heart. One was 'Nobody Knows You When You're Down And Out', a reminder of busking days at Kingston Art College. The other was Albert King's 'Have You Ever Loved A Woman?' which he used to do with John Mayall's Bluesbreakers, never dreaming what anguished relevance the words would one day acquire: 'Have you ever loved a woman/So-o-o much/That you tremble in pain . . .'

In the extremity of his obsession with Pattie Harrison, he even sought help from the supernatural. With Derek and the Dominos at the Lyceum benefit was the white blues singer/pianist known as Dr John, a sinister-looking figure who performed in the Mardi Gras costumes of his native New Orleans and was said to be endowed with the powers of Voodoo.

After the show, Eric went to Dr John, explained the Pattie situation and requested a 'love potion number 9', just like the one in the Coasters song, that would make her leave George for him.

The supposed witch doctor gave him a small box made of woven straw to carry in his pocket and written instructions for a secret ritual warranted to cast the necessary spell. Eric believed totally in the charm and 'did exactly as I was told'.

In fairness to the powers of darkness, they were not given much time to act. A couple of weeks later came the West End premiere of *Oh! Calcutta!*, a revue celebrating the end of British theatre censorship with frank depictions of sex and nudity, whose producer was Robert Stigwood. George and Pattie were invited but he had other, unspecified plans, so she was escorted by Peter Brown, a former key Beatles aide, now employed by Stigwood.

Unbeknown to her, Eric was also at the *Oh! Calcutta!* first night. When she returned to her seat after the interval, she found him in the adjacent one, having persuaded its occupant to exchange places.

Whatever George's suspicions by now, he had been indifferent to Pattie's absence that evening. But as it wore on, in a syndrome common among faithless husbands, a pang of possessiveness returned to him. He drove to Stigwood's house in Stanmore, where the after-show party was in progress, and found her in the garden with Eric. 'He asked what was going on,' she recalls, 'and, to my complete horror, Eric said, "I have to tell you, man, that I'm in love with your wife."'

George made no response – probably because it was no real surprise – but merely asked her which of them she would be ending the night with. Resisting whatever Voodoo power might be emanating from Dr John's straw box, Pattie replied, firmly, 'I'm coming home with you, George.'

However, back at Friar Park, among the Gothic towers and gargoyles, there was to be no rapprochement: George disappeared into his recording studio with the tapes of *All Things Must Pass* and Pattie went to her lonely bed.

*

Eric's first eponymous solo album was released in August 1970. The cover showed him in a fancy Western-style white suit, slumped in a chair with his Fender Stratocaster 'Brownie' beside him. He was back to being bearded yet again, and had a wary, reluctant look as if not totally convinced this was such a good idea.

It was not easy to change the deep-rooted perception of him as a brilliant contributor to albums rather than somebody able to carry a whole one on his own. And, although purchased in large quantities by his 'God' constituency, *Eric Clapton* failed to make either the British or US Top 10.

The music press, which had always been so kind to him, was almost unanimously dismissive: *Melody Maker* found 'depressing monotony' in 'a forced white version of soul and gospel as performed originally by Ike and Tina Turner and the Stax label artists', while *Fusion* magazine called it 'warmed-over Delaney and Bonnie with a little leftover Leon Russell'. A few tracks were singled out for praise, like 'Easy Now' and 'Let It Rain', a staple of his live shows ever afterwards.

Nor did it help that, at this moment of bidding for solo recognition, he was back in a band that didn't even mention his name and, instead of promoting himself on the international stage, was playing venues specially chosen for their smallness and obscurity. His way of launching Derek and the Dominos, that same month, was a club tour of the UK on which, at his insistence, all tickets cost only £1.

In London, rather than the Albert Hall or the Lyceum, they played the Speakeasy and his long-ago stomping-ground, the Marquee. If any club-owner slyly slipped his name onto a poster, he was furious.

To interviewers, he insisted that in Bobby Whitlock, Carl Radle and Jim Gordon he'd finally found his true soulmates, and that Derek and the Dominos could never go the way of Cream,

Blind Faith or Delaney & Bonnie. 'The only thing that might step in [our] way is that I'm English and they're American. They've come to my backyard and they might get homesick . . . But musically I think there's every reason for [us] to go on for ever.'

He continued to steal moments with Pattie Harrison while continuing his affair with her sister Paula, between a larger-scale UK tour immediately after his quixotic 'pound-a-nighter' and the band's departure to make their first and, it would prove, only album in Miami, Florida.

But, while more and more overtly attracted to him, Pattie still refused to give up on her marriage. All George's coldness and neglect had not killed off her love; she also shuddered to remember into what outer darkness another Beatle wife, Cynthia Lennon, had been cast after John's obsession with Yoko (not so dissimilar from Eric's with Pattie) drove Cynthia to seek a divorce.

Now, he had a visual aid to feed his obsession. In late August, Derek and the Dominos travelled to the South of France for a one-off engagement and found themselves billeted in a beautiful Provençal farmhouse belonging to the Franco-Danish painter Émile Théodore Frandsen de Schomberg. The artist himself was not in residence but his son, Émile junior, ministered to their visitors. Among the paintings on display was 'La Fille Au Bouquet' (Young Girl With Bouquet), a secretively-smiling face in a heart-shape of golden hair and white flowers that to Eric was the image of Pattie.

The gig was cancelled after 'revolutionaries' wrecked the stage and, in frustration, Eric started throwing eggs in the farmhouse kitchen, precipitating a battle in which only Carl Radle refused to join. Nonetheless, at check-out time, despite the trampled eggshells and yolk-smeared walls, the painter's son presented 'La Fille Au Bouquet' to him.

His pursuit of Pattie had become common knowledge among

Britain's rock elite and now brought forth a rival with little experience of losing such contests. Mick Jagger had recently broken
up with his long-term partner Marianne Faithfull, after her descent into heroin addiction, and had returned to playing a field
that for him stretched around the world. After some byplay with
Eric's house-guest, Catherine James, the insatiable Jagger eye fell
on Pattie.

In late September, the Rolling Stones' live album *Get Yer Ya-
Ya's Out!* was launched in Paris with a party at the Hotel George
V. Pattie happened to be visiting Paris and Jagger asked their
mutual confidante, Chris O'Dell, to invite her to the party. But
she declined: Eric was also in town, to jam with the Stones' two
guest stars Buddy Guy and Junior Wells, and they'd seized the
opportunity for another of their less and less secret trysts. 'I
think they showed up at the Stones' party together,' O'Dell says,
'which really annoyed Mick.'

Jagger was consoled by being introduced to the Nicaraguan
actress and political activist Bianca Pérez-Mora Macias, whom
he would marry the following year. It wasn't the last time that
he and Eric would compete for a beautiful woman's favours but
it was the only time Eric came out on top.

Since that excruciating scene in Robert Stigwood's garden,
George had remained strangely passive, never seeking any further explanation from Pattie (which she would have welcomed
as a sign that he still cared) nor forcing any confrontation with
Eric. The closest he came was a rock 'n' roll version of the 'pistols
at dawn' a wronged Victorian husband would have demanded –
in this case, guitars after dusk.

One evening, he asked Eric to come to Friar Park for what
Eric expected to be a cards-on-the-table discussion about Pattie.
Instead, he was waiting in the house's front hall, a cavernous
space doubling as a living-room where the cloistral fantasies of
its creator, Sir Frank Crisp, extended even to the light-switches.

These took the form of miniature friars' faces and were turned on and off by their noses.

However, the expected glum Liverpudlian tirade failed to materialise. Instead, George had two guitars and two amplifiers set up as if for a show, although the only audience consisted of his wife and the actor John Hurt, who happened to be staying with them.

Scarcely exchanging a word, Eric and he began to trade licks. It had the semblance of a jam but, on George's part at least, was clearly a duel – one which he had carefully weighted against his opponent. Even John Hurt's unpractised eye could see he'd given himself much the better of the two guitars and he kept plying Eric with brandy while himself drinking only tea.

Although no result could be declared, it was as plain as the nose on a friar light-switch's face. Even full of brandy, and almost as full of confusion, Slowhand still couldn't be beat.

Derek and the Dominos' debut album was his answering challenge to George as well as a last-ditch appeal to Pattie. What he never expected was for it to trigger a musical love affair which, in contrast with his problematic physical one, would find instant total fulfilment.

The sessions took place at Miami's Criteria Studios, a little-known facility whose most notable previous user had been 'the Godfather of Soul', James Brown. At the helm was Tom Dowd, the Atlantic Records producer who had done so much to develop Cream.

Unfortunately, Miami offered too many distractions in the form of swimming and sunbathing as well as those perforce enjoyed with the shades drawn. Drugs were more freely available than anywhere Eric had ever been. One simply placed an order with the motel gift shop and they were delivered in little brown paper packets. Consequently, after two days' work only three tracks were finished. The canny Dowd did not scream or sulk, as most producers would have done, but instead suggested that Eric and the others should go and see Florida's own Allman Brothers Band, who were giving an open-air show at the Coconut Grove convention centre.

Eric already knew of their leader, Duane 'Skydog' Allman, as a session musician who had contributed a brilliant solo to Wilson Pickett's cover of the Beatles' 'Hey Jude'. Allman and his younger brother, Gregg, had since formed a line-up, unusually employing both the terms 'brothers' and 'band', whose super-smooth country-rock most persuasively answered the burning question of where music in the Seventies could possibly go next.

When Eric's party reached the Coconut Grove, they found the only available car-parking space was about half a mile from the stage. Even at that distance, Duane Allman's slide guitar cut through the warm velvet night 'like a siren'. The Allman Brothers Band were all long, lean and bearded, but he was the longest, leanest and beardiest, with blond hair that somehow wrapped itself around his face like a Victorian motoring-veil.

'When he looked down and saw Eric,' Bobby Whitlock recalls, 'his mouth fell open and he just quit playin'.'

After the show, Eric, Whitlock, Radle and Gordon went backstage and the two bands got on so instantaneously well that they adjourned to Criteria Studios for a jam session. The result was that Duane Allman became an unofficial fifth Domino, giving the stalled album such a boost that its four sides took only ten further days to finish.

His rigidly structured guitar style could not have been more different from Eric's spontaneous, free-form one. 'Duane never went out of the box,' Bobby Whitlock says, 'and Eric never went into it.' Yet the blend of them created something verging on magic. Eleven of the fourteen tracks featured Allman as joint lead, playing a Gibson as a softer, warmer counterpoint to Eric's edgy, angular Fender. 'There had to be some sort of telepathy going on because I've never seen such inspiration on that level,' Tom Dowd remembered. 'It was like two hands in a glove.'

Between sessions, the two became inseparable. Eric envied Allman's solidarity with his brother Gregg, so different from the usual vicious rivalry of siblings in the same band, and the way he maintained his leadership without singing. As Eric later said, 'He was like the musical brother I never had, but wished I did.' Sadly, their partnership would have no chance to develop further: a year later, Allman was killed in a motorcycle accident a month before his twenty-fifth birthday.

In Miami, their empathy peaked with the song Eric had originally sketched out as a slow ballad loosely based on Albert King's, and Cream's, 'Born Under A Bad Sign'. Calling it 'Layla' after the heroine of the Persian love fable and recording it under the name Derek represented only token camouflage: it was plainly all about Pattie, his adoration of her and longing for her to dump his best friend for him.

Under Duane Allman's influence, its tempo upped and its tone changed from love letter to passion-loudhailer, Allman providing the famous bass riff like sexual tumescence made audible, followed by a right-angle key-change into Eric's now unrestrained confession. This most guitar-ridden track ever made then segued into an extended piano coda, contributed by the Dominos' drummer, Jim Gordon, a change of pace as complete as a post-coital drink and cigarette.

That autumn of 1970, two events intruded into Eric's preoccupation with Pattie and the album, to be entitled *Layla And Other Assorted Love Songs*, that would unveil it to the world.

While he was in America with Derek and the Dominos, Robert Stigwood phoned to tell him that his step-grandfather, Jack Clapp, had been diagnosed with a brain tumour. The taciturn working man had done much to steady Eric's destabilised child-hood as well as being the best of husbands to his beloved Rose. For the past two years, Jack had been partially paralysed by a stroke and bedridden and Eric was stricken with guilt at how little time he had spent with him.

Rushing home at once, he found Jack in hospital in Guild-ford, a pitiably shrunken figure, unrecognisable as the master craftsman who could once lay a row of bricks in immaculate symmetry or plaster an entire wall with a few deft broad-brush strokes. He died soon afterwards, aged only sixty. For years to come, Eric would be tormented by the thought that by moving Rose and him away from Ripley and into their luxurious cottage in Shamley Green, he had taken away Jack's dignity and so accel-erated his decline.

Then on 18 September, Jimi Hendrix was found dead in a London hotel-room, the first in a flurry of drug-related fatalities that would also add Janis Joplin and the Doors' vocalist Jim Mor-rison to the so-called '27 Club' founded by Robert Johnson. This extinction of the only rival who had ever seriously worried Eric was also the loss of a friend whose sweetness and modesty, so unlike his incendiary stage-presence, endeared him to everyone in the business.

It happened that while browsing through a West End guitar store not long before, Eric had come across a left-handed white Fender Stratocaster and bought it as a gift for Hendrix. On the night of 17 September, they had been due to meet up at the Lyceum to watch a performance by Sly and the Family Stone, when he intended to hand over the Strat. Hendrix failed to show and, a few hours later, was discovered, seemingly choked on his own vomit after an overdose of sleeping pills.

'When Jimi died, Eric was very deeply affected,' Chris O'Dell says. 'I remember him saying, "How could he leave me like that?"' By his own admission, when he heard the news, 'I went out in the garden and cried all day. Not because Jimi had gone but because he hadn't taken me with him.'

Another *Brief Encounter* tryst with Pattie took place under the clock in Guildford High Street, where Eric handed over a pair of the bell-bottomed jeans known as Landlubbers which she'd asked him to bring her from Miami. She thought he looked 'tanned and gorgeous' and felt an even stronger pull towards him, yet still fought against it.

When the album was mixed, he asked her to go to the Dominos' flat in South Kensington, where they'd also been wont to meet platonically. There he produced a cassette of 'Layla' and played it three times over, studying her face carefully for her reaction.

As she recalls, it was a mixture of awe that 'the most powerful, moving song I had ever heard' should have been written about her, and consternation that its lyric would be instantly decoded, not only by her husband, family and friends but by the tens of thousands of strangers who would buy the album:

> *I tried to give you consolation*
> *When your old man had let you down . . .*

Most discomfortingly of all, her sister Paula, she knew, had been with Eric in Miami. He must have played 'Layla' to her out there, and Paula must have realised at once that it wasn't about her, but Pattie. 'She really believed Eric was in love with her. She really believed it. And then finding out that he had written a song about me and not her and finally getting to understand how she'd been used . . . I think it broke her heart.'

As bad as she felt about Paula, 'the song got the better of me, with the realisation I had inspired such passion and such creativity. I could resist no longer.' But her surrender, she made clear, had been just a momentary lapse; after all that effort, 'Layla' seemed to have advanced him no further than its first three letters.

Not long afterwards he turned up unexpectedly at Friar Park while George was away and Pattie was alone in the house. He told her he couldn't live without her and she had to come away with him this very minute. When she refused, he took a small packet from his pocket and said it contained heroin, which he'd take if she didn't do as he asked. Horrified, she tried to grab the packet, but he held it in his clenched hand in his pocket.

Rejection had the same effect as always, however kindly or regretful. He said, 'Right, that's it, I'm off,' and left, presumably to plunge into a deadly habit for which Pattie would be to blame.

16

FANFARE FOR ERIC

The threat was emotional blackmail of a peculiarly shameless kind, since he'd already been taking heroin for months.

Before Derek and the Dominos, while indulging unrestrainedly in pot, LSD, cocaine and every kind of pill, he had always held back from smack, aka junk or Henry or H. As a film buff, he was all too familiar with Frank Sinatra's horrific portrayal of an addicted drummer in *The Man with the Golden Arm*. An equal deterrent was his mistaken belief that it could be taken only by shooting up – self-injection in the arm. Ever since his immunisation against diphtheria as a small boy, he'd had a horror of needles.

Playing in a band with Ginger Baker, one of British rock's pioneer smackheads, had revealed that it could also be snorted like cocaine or swallowed as a jack, or pill. Far from trying to turn him on to the habit, Baker had always warned in older-brotherly fashion that he'd 'have his balls' if he ever tried it. But Cream's drummer had been belligerent living proof that it didn't necessarily lead to writhing on the floor like Sinatra; that one could take it and still appear to function normally.

Eric himself explained how his initiation came about to Keith Richards' drug-dealer, 'Spanish Tony' Sanchez. 'The guy I was scoring coke from would only sell it to me if I bought smack as well. So I kept stashing it away in a drawer. I just didn't want to know about it. Then one day there was no coke around, so I thought I'd have a snort of smack, and it was quite nice. A lot of fuss about nothing, I thought.'

'Quite nice' is a pretty accurate description. For heroin does not carry out its deadly seduction with the mind-numbing of pot, the unpredictable thrill-ride of acid or the goggling hyper-energy of coke, but with a sensation of total calm, self-confidence and comfort inside one's own skin that Eric had never really felt in all his twenty-five years. 'Nothing bothers you whatsoever,' he discovered. 'Nothing will faze you out in any way.'

Bobby Whitlock remembers him taking it in the cafeteria at Abbey Road studios during the *All Things Must Pass* sessions – something the Beatles would never have dared. On that occasion, it was not its usual white but pale pink. 'He told me he felt warm all over as if there was a cotton wool cushion under his head and soft pink cotton wool all around him.'

The *Layla* album sessions in Miami had been saturated in drugs, including heroin, and repeated pleas from the producer, Tom Dowd, and even Atlantic Records' boss, Ahmet Ertegun, had been unable to check that brisk traffic via the motel gift shop. Ertegun, who had seen Ray Charles almost destroy himself with smack, actually wept as he begged Eric not to jeopardise his career in the same way. But, as many others had discovered, no ears could be more deaf when they chose.

For several months, he showed none of the instantly recognis-able symptoms his friend John Lennon had a few months earlier: the chalk-white face, the blurred speech, the tendency to vomit at inopportune moments like the middle of a TV interview. Quite the opposite: during Derek and the Dominos' American tour at the end of 1970, he looked the picture of health, clean-shaven once again, barbered in the new unisex layered style and deeply tanned by the Miami sun.

The American media pandered to his almost schizophrenic dual role of star frontman and just one of the guys. When the band appeared on Johnny Cash's television show, Cash introduced them one by one with Bobby Whitlock first and Eric last. Then, after a single ensemble number (Chuck Willis's 'It's Too Late'), he left the line-up to join Cash and the great Carl Perkins in an incandescent version of Perkins's 'Matchbox'.

Layla And Other Assorted Love Songs had been released in time for Christmas 1970. Its front cover image was Émile Théodore Frandsen de Schomberg's 'La Fille Au Bouquet', the sleepy heart-shaped face so much like Pattie's, which Eric now owned and insisted must be reproduced to art-gallery standard, unsullied by any title or artist credit. His name appeared in small type on the back cover, his picture was buried among a montage of band snapshots on the double-envelope gatefold.

The title track was not the only one aimed directly at Pattie. 'Bell Bottom Blues' pleaded, to the point of grovelling, for another rendezvous under the Guildford town clock where he'd handed over her Landlubber jeans from Miami. 'I Looked Away' declared that 'if it seems a sin to love another man's woman baby,/I guess I'll keep on sinning'. 'I Am Yours' adapted a poem by Nizami, the Persian author of the tale of Layla and Majnun: 'However distant you may be/There blows no wind but wafts your scent to me.' To say nothing of 'It's Too Late' and 'Have You Ever Loved A Woman' and 'Why Does Love Got To Be So Sad?' – heart-on-sleeve melancholia with guitars on fire.

Today, the album is generally recognised as Eric's greatest achievement but at the time it was seen as a commercial failure, reaching only number 16 in America and failing to chart in Britain. Most of the tracks were unsuitable for radio airplay, the seven-minute-long 'Layla' most of all, and so many people did not recognise the Dominos' leader that stickers reading 'Derek is Eric' had to be hurriedly pasted on thousands of copies. A single version of 'Layla', cut to three minutes, reached only the low fifties in *Billboard*'s Hot 100.

The critics were uniformly tepid. *Melody Maker*'s Roy Hollingworth complained that it veered 'from the magnificent to a few lengths of complete boredom . . . Eric spits and licks, bumps and grinds into seven-minute strutting boogies . . . then dawdles into love songs and . . . pretty atrocious vocal work . . .'

Consequently, when Derek and the Dominos reconvened to make a follow-up in April and May of 1971, they felt they had both too little and too much to follow up. Eric made no secret of thinking they would never again match 'Layla', for Duane Allman was not available to sit in with them this time. 'We didn't have the fire any more,' he would recall. 'We'd burnt out on one album.'

By now, too, there were beginning to be tensions within the band, mostly centred on their drummer, Jim Gordon, a curly-haired Californian with a touch of Ginger Baker ferocity in his playing. Unusually for a percussionist, Gordon was equally skilled on string instruments, as well as an aspiring songwriter, and his bandmates suspected him of plotting a solo career on the quiet.

Bobby Whitlock resented being usurped on keyboards by Gordon's extended piano coda to 'Layla', feeling it to be totally out of keeping with the first part (and claiming ever afterwards that it had been filched without acknowledgement from Gordon's then girlfriend, Rita Coolidge). Bass-player Carl Radle kept an uncomfortable low profile, much as Eric used to in Cream whenever Baker and Jack Bruce were scrapping.

Tempers became increasingly frayed until one day, according to their sound-mixer Ron Nevinson, 'Eric was taking forever to tune his guitar and Jim said something like "Why don't we do a song about tuning?" [Whitlock recalls it as "Do you want *me* to tune that damned thing?" – a far more serious piece of lèse-majesté.] With that, Eric put down his guitar and walked out. That was the end of Derek and the Dominos.'

★

Despite his dramatic exit from the last meeting with Pattie, he had not given up the pursuit. A couple of months after the incident with the heroin packet, she received a letter in instantly recognisable art-school handwriting posted from the tiny village of Llandewi Brefi in West Wales. He was staying there in a cottage belonging to his old Chelsea friend, the hoodlum-aesthete David Litvinoff.

Written on the torn-out title-page of a book (John Steinbeck's *Of Mice and Men*), the letter began 'dear layla' and was couched in the same apocalyptic style, with the same disdain for capital letters, as the first she'd had from him:

> *for nothing more than the pleasures*
> *past i would sacrifice my family, my*
> *god and my own existence, and still*
> *you will not move. i am at the end of*
> *my mind, I cannot go back and there*
> *is nothing in tomorrow (save you) that*
> *can attract me beyond today. i have*
> *listened to the wind, i have watched*
> *the dark, brooding clouds, i have felt*
> *the earth beneath me for a sign, a*
> *gesture, but there is only silence . . . if*
> *you want me, take me, i am yours . . .*

Pattie replied encouragingly ('Oh, I long to be with you there'), signing off 'Moons full of love L' and enclosing a poem by Charles Baudelaire which seemed to tell him just what he'd been wanting to hear for so long:

> *Cast bridle, spurs and reins away*
> *And let us race on steeds of wine*
> *To skies enchanting and divine*

251

As though two angels overcome
By fever's wild delirium.

Having sent it, she was overcome with embarrassment and wrote a hasty postcard:

Please forgive and forget my bold suggestion
Love L

Eric's reply came by return of post, on another torn-out fly-leaf, this time from a book of Scottish ballads, and was written in green ink. He had received both her letter and postcard by the same delivery, an experience, he said, 'like watching a boomerang in flight'. In a sudden but very typical fit of pessimism, not to say second sight, he continued: 'i don't think, even if we were the last ones left alive, that you could be happy with me, and as for me i think i am content to remain alone until someday i am free to be discovered. i love you even though you're chicken.'

That was the last she would hear of him for another eight months.

The collapse of Derek and the Dominos, allied to the continued impasse with Pattie, marked Eric's transition from occasional heroin-user to serious addict. At his habit's appalling height, he could very easily have gone the way of Robert Johnson, Jimi Hendrix, Janis Joplin, well before the fatal age of twenty-seven, but for the people who, as always, rushed to the aid of that 'wounded child'.

Like all great seducers, heroin bides its time, in his case for about a year. At first, he felt the need of its pink cotton wool swaddling only every couple of weeks, then it was twice or three times a week, then every day. 'It took over my life,' he would recall, 'without my really noticing.'

Throughout the experience he was to feel a perverse pride in emulating jazz legends such as Charlie Parker and Billie Holiday, who had always maintained that heroin enhanced their performance even as it was shredding their bodies and souls. There was a touch of his innate competitiveness in there, too: 'I wanted to prove I could do it and come out . . . alive.'

At a time when the physical effects were first starting to show, George happened to drop in at Hurtwood Edge, accompanied by Leon Russell. Seeing the state Eric was in, Russell became very angry – something few of his British friends would have dared – and asked what the hell he thought he was doing. He replied that he was 'on a journey into the darkness, and [had] to see it through and find out what was on the other side'.

His affair with Pattie's youngest sister, Paula, had ended after Paula realised she was not the inspiration for 'Layla', and she was now living with Bobby Whitlock. In March 1970, he'd picked up with Alice Ormsby-Gore again, although there was to be no further talk of their getting married (and he would later deny that they'd ever been engaged).

Alice, now eighteen, had developed theatrical aspirations and, during their separation, had won a part in an Israeli production of the 'tribal rock musical' *Hair* (which Robert Stigwood had originally brought from New York to London). Consequently, for most of that summer she was learning Hebrew for her role, then onstage in Tel Aviv and living in a fishing village beside the Sea of Galilee.

When the show's run ended, she returned to the very different milieu of Hurtwood Edge, where she was soon keeping Eric company in his heroin-habit. He frankly admits in his autobiography that 'it never crossed my mind it was wrong to bring her into my nightmare'.

He had always had people to do things for him, and keeping him in pink cotton wool was no exception. Alice took on the job of scoring their heroin, travelling up to London to rendezvous with their dealer, usually in Gerrard Street, Soho, at constant risk of arrest by the police and much else besides.

Snorting as they did – Eric with a gold spoon he wore around his neck – used up much more than injecting, so Alice's scoring-trips had to be very frequent. They always took care to overlap their supplies, so there was never any danger of running out.

Like most newcomers to heroin, Eric believed himself to be in complete control of his habit, able to stop whenever he chose and not in the slightest danger of becoming like those poor teeth-chattering junkies on the cinema screen. The first inkling of how seriously he was hooked came when he'd arranged to drive to Wales to see Alice at the Harlech family home, and suddenly realised he was in no condition to pilot a Ferrari 200 miles.

Postponing the visit for three days, he went cold turkey and experienced all the terrifying symptoms John Lennon had sung about on the record they'd made together. Sweat-soaked yet deathly cold, every muscle and nerve in his body in cramp, he could only curl into a foetal position, howling in agony.

No one knew about it at the time but his gardener/handyman, Arthur Eggby. 'Eric hadn't come downstairs so I knocked on the bedroom door and a strange voice told me to fuck off,' Eggby recalls. 'I wondered who it was, never thinking it could be Eric. I entered the room and there he was, all curled up, looking hor-rible and so pale.'

During 1971, he and Alice were still to be seen out and about together, an enviably cool-looking couple, charmingly spanning the class-divide. It was impossible to imagine them at home on the occasions when their heroin supplies simultaneously ran out and they'd literally go berserk, banging their heads against walls or burning themselves with cigarettes.

One such escape was the premiere of *Trouble in Molopolis*, the art film directed by Philippe Mora, which Eric had financed, with a cast including Germaine Greer and the editor of *Oz* magazine, Richard Neville. The premiere, at Chelsea's Paris Pullman cinema, was a fund-raiser for *Oz*'s defence against obscenity charges following its 'schoolkids issue' when Neville had turned the whole magazine over to a gang of predictably lewd-minded juveniles.

The evening reunited Eric with many old Pheasantry acquaintances, notably John Ivor Golding, the enigmatic tramp said to have inspired Harold Pinter's *The Caretaker* and now playing his one and only movie lead-role. True to past form, Golding fell asleep in his front-row seat, then defecated there in the cinema in front of everyone.

George Harrison's triple album *All Things Must Pass* had been a worldwide hit, momentarily overshadowing the solo careers of both John Lennon and Paul McCartney; its main single, 'My Sweet Lord', alchemised George's usually heavy-handed Hinduism into a sweetly unspecific hymn equally relevant to every religion. The Indian subcontinent had done much to bring about his transformation from underdog Beatle and in August 1971, he found a way to pay some of it back.

The former East Pakistan, now renamed Bangladesh, was stricken both by a terrible famine and genocide at the hands of the militaristic West Pakistan government from which it had seceded. Together with his sitar guru, Ravi Shankar, George put together a giant rock concert to aid Bangladesh's millions of starving refugees, staged at New York's Madison Square Garden and featuring fellow superstars like Bob Dylan and Leon Russell. Thinking it might bring some relief to the smaller disaster-area he still regarded as his best friend, he also asked Eric to participate.

Initially, Eric's addiction made the idea seem quite impracticable. He could not risk trying to smuggle heroin through US Customs, nor could he hope to do without it during the week of rehearsals before the Saturday show. 'I guess it was a dumb idea to put him on a plane when there was such a strong chance of him going into withdrawal and not being able to appear,' says Chris O'Dell, who was helping to organise the event. In the end, George had to promise to have a supply waiting for him in New York.

Even then, it was far from certain that he'd turn up. While he and Alice had briefly been absent from Hurtwood, a friend of the Eggbys' son, Kevin, had stolen several of his most cherished guitars including one he had built himself from vintage Fender Stratocasters, painted black and given the name Blackie. Although the thief had been caught and all the guitars recovered, they were being held as evidence by the Surrey police. 'But he knew how important this concert was,' O'Dell says. 'And he wanted to be there for George.'

Unfortunately, when he and Alice reached their New York hotel, the heroin supply laid on by George proved to be street-cut – i.e. mixed with talcum powder or baby-milk formula and only about a tenth of the strength his body now demanded. The next three days he spent in his hotel-room in sweating convulsions while George's people and Alice ran around town trying to find a dealer with merchandise of the proper purity.

Help eventually came from Allen Klein, the Beatles' last manager, who was still clinging to George as some consolation for their break-up. Klein gave Eric a medicine for stomach ulcers containing the heroin-substitute Methadone. That got him to rehearsals and by showtime, some of the real stuff had been found.

His condition was such that he barely noticed when Pattie arrived from London to join George just before the concert. Whenever she saw him, he was usually surrounded by people and she was unsure whether he even saw her. 'I think she regarded the thing with Eric as over,' Chris O'Dell says. 'He was back with Alice and she was really trying to make things work with George. In all the time we were together that week, I don't remember her ever mentioning him.'

Although not the first time leading musicians had donated their services to charity, the Concert for Bangladesh (actually, two concerts, in the afternoon and evening of 1 August) was a genuinely historic event in terms of its size and the attention it drew to its chosen cause, both in live performance and the album that followed. It was a personal triumph for George and the model for many future displays of collective conscience by what now recognisably became a rock 'community'.

Eric, moustached yet again (a rather bitty-looking Zapata), took the stage with George in a populous supergroup also containing Ringo Starr and Leon Russell, with a second lead guitarist, Jesse Ed Davis from Taj Mahal's band, very obviously shadowing him in case he should falter. 'I just wasn't there,' he would recall. 'I wasn't there at all.'

That isn't how it looks in the concert film footage when George gets to 'While My Guitar Gently Weeps' and the two of them play a single-string duet full of mutual esteem, unlike their former duel over Pattie in the great hall at Friar Park. Safely swaddled in pink cotton wool again, Eric gives a beatific smile, and millions of young men all over the world forget the human tragedy that has brought him there and simply yearn to have his life.

George's well-meaning attempt to coax him back to work seemed to have the opposite effect. When he walked offstage at Madison Square Garden, it was into a self-exile whose hellishness only the unfortunate Alice would be allowed to share.

The next three years of what should have been the best time in his life were not just ruled by heroin but lost to it. However much the drug may have sharpened Charlie Parker's or Billie Holiday's creativity, it obliterated Eric's – or, at least, took away the work ethic that had driven him from the first moment he picked up a guitar. He sought no new musical partners, wrote no new material and released no new records; just stayed holed up at Hurtwood Edge in the semi-comatose state between fixes that the Chinese call 'chasing the dragon'.

'What were you doing for all that time?' a journalist asked him later. 'Nothing,' he replied. 'Watching TV . . . building model cars and aircraft.' But hadn't he been bored? 'You don't get bored on smack. That is something you do not get.'

His appearance, in which he'd always taken such pride, rapidly went downhill, his face not only developing the heroin-user's chalky pallor but also crops of belated acne. Alice nominally did the cooking, but he lived mainly on junk food and the sweet things junkies tend to crave, with the result that his weight ballooned. He became chronically constipated and his libido, that once relentless engine, all but disappeared – though, paradoxically, despite almost never going out, he retained his obsession with clothes.

He deliberately cut himself off from all his friends, particularly those on whom he'd once relied for advice and guidance. As the front gates at Hurtwood were always left open, he would simply not answer their ring at the front door and wait for them to give up and go away like some lurking, alternately bearded and non-bearded Boo Radley.

The same treatment was even meted out to Ben Palmer, his old mentor and asylum-giver, who, worried by the rumours he'd heard, drove all the way from Wales to offer help. Though Eric was clearly visible through an upstairs window, Palmer received no reply to his repeated rings. He tried again on another day; that time, Alice opened the door but Eric made him feel 'like an intruder'.

As ever, his small store of consideration for others was spent on his grandmother, Rose, to whom he was guiltily aware he ought to be a support in her too-early widowhood. Rose knew nothing about heroin, or any other drug, and was told nothing of his problem. On his visits to her at Shamley Green, she thought he looked 'tired out' and, in her innocence, presumed he was just drunk.

Then his birth mother, Pat McDonald, happened to be visiting from West Germany, where she still lived with her Canadian army officer husband. She called at Hurtwood, but Eric was too self-conscious about his appearance to come downstairs and see her, so she spent several hours talking to Alice in the kitchen. It was from Pat, who otherwise knew so little about him, that Rose finally heard the awful news: 'He's on drugs, Mum.'

True to the relationship they'd had since he was a lost, spoilt little boy, she never spoke a word of reproach, nor even tried to discuss the matter with him. But 'I used to really pray,' she would recall. 'Get down on my hands and knees and say my prayers for Rick.'

Some of the heroin supply came via an addict Alice had got to know in London who received it on legal prescriptions in pill form. But the effect was nowhere near that of the snorting variety which came in soft brown nuggets like Demerara sugar and had to be ground to powder with a pestle and mortar. So institutionalised was the trade that its clear plastic packets had uniform red paper labels with Chinese characters and the logo of a white elephant.

By now Eric's craving had become so powerful that Alice had to give him almost all that she scored. She compensated with neat vodka, soon getting through two bottles per day.

The cost of the smack rose exponentially as the dealers discovered whom the aristocratic teenager was servicing and before long was running at £1,000 per week, equal to £10,000 today. Arthur Eggby became accustomed to the sight of Eric laying out four lines on the kitchen counter, as meticulously as his step-grandfather, Jack, used to lay bricks, and inhaling them through a tightly rolled £50 note that he would then toss into the waste-bin.

Since the notes had officially been thrown away, Eggby felt justified in covertly retrieving them, sponging off the heroin and hanging them up to dry in the kitchen for use on his and Iris's next holiday on the Isle of Wight.

Robert Stigwood had always been aware of what was going on with his biggest client next to the Bee Gees, and even occasionally dispatched an employee to score for him when Alice could not. Like Rose, Stigwood never uttered a word of protest or censure, although it was noticeable that in the whole three years of Eric's retreat, his manager never once set foot inside Hurtwood Edge.

Now, as his drug expenditure rocketed, with no new income being generated, a message came from Stigwood's office that the bank balance of whose size he had not the faintest idea was running low and he might soon have to consider selling off some of his possessions.

As news of his situation spread through the business, various plans to help him were mooted, some more serious than others. Ginger Baker wanted to transport him by Land Rover into the middle of the Sahara Desert, one place he (or, rather, Alice) would be guaranteed not to find a drug-pusher. In America, Bonnie Bramlett and Bobby Whitlock often discussed returning to Britain 'to kidnap his ass'. Ironically, the fellow musician who began the process of putting him back together was the one with an unrivalled reputation for smashing things up.

Eric had always admired the Who's Pete Townshend, British rock's most conspicuous art college alumnus, even if Townshend's ritual onstage trashing of guitars – in the name of auto-destructive performance art – struck him as gratuitous vandalism. Townshend had a similar regard for Eric and, hearing about the bad scene at Hurtwood Edge, with a sympathy not easily read in his long, contemptuous face, decided it was down to him to help.

Throughout 1972, he became almost the only visitor Eric allowed into Hurtwood. They reminisced at length about their shared history – Townshend with one band that, however explosive, had always managed to stay together as against Eric's five

260

– and made some tapes together in the small recording studio in the garage. Townshend was at no risk of being drawn into 'chasing the dragon', having given up drugs when he became a follower of the guru Meher Baba in 1967.

He was, however, drawn deeply into Eric's claustrophobic and tempestuous domestic life. He recalls getting almost nightly phone calls from Alice, begging him to come and mediate between them. 'It was an hour and a half's drive away, and always at awkward hours. Eric would be asleep somewhere and she would be running around hysterically . . . she was giving him all her heroin supply, most unselfishly, and then she was having to deal with Eric's extremely selfish outbursts, accusing her of doing the reverse.'

Townshend himself (an alcoholic, even though drug-free) was too opinionated and volatile to be a perfect therapist for Eric and there were sometimes blow-ups between them. In the aftermath of one, Arthur Eggby found a full bucket of water on a bedroom windowsill overlooking the front door. '"Leave that alone," Eric told me. "It's for Pete when he arrives." He emptied it over him, too.'

Otherwise, 1972 contained little but pink cotton wool clouds or the terrible hunger for them. At Townshend's invitation, Eric and Alice went to see the Who perform in Paris, taking enough heroin to last them through the day but obliged to get home by midnight, like two smackheaded Cinderellas, for their next snort. Alice briefly regained some life of her own when she went to New York for the fourth anniversary celebration of the *Hair* musical, in whose Israeli version she had appeared.

Atco in the US and Polydor in the UK put out a double compilation album entitled *The History of Eric Clapton*, as if his career was over, chronicling his appearances with the Yardbirds, Cream, Blind Faith and Derek and the Dominos, its cover a shot of him onstage and pink-cloudy at the Concert for Bangladesh. The tracks included 'Layla', which now finally charted as a single, reaching number 7 in Britain and 10 in the *Billboard* Hot 100.

Yet even at this nadir of self-degradation, the Clapton Luck still held. The father of the twenty-year-old whose life he seemed intent on ruining was a peer of the realm, a former government minister and ambassador and a public figure of unimpeachable respectability. Had the press discovered that Lord Harlech's daughter was not only a heroin addict but scoring the stuff on Soho streets, the scandal would have been tremendous and the severest penalties visited on the rock star responsible. But it never happened.

In addition, Harlech was a man of great kindness and sensitivity whom Eric, in his eternal quest for male role-models, had come to regard 'almost as a stepfather'. So now, rather than use the big stick at his disposal to protect Alice, he attempted to reform his erstwhile son-in-law through music.

He had met Pete Townshend at Hurtwood one day while pleading fruitlessly with Eric to try to kick the habit. Townshend recalls that when Alice was out of the room, Eric told Harlech he was afraid that giving up heroin might change his feelings for her.

Afterwards, the peer contacted the guitar-wrecker with a plan to bring Eric back into the public arena as a working musician and, hopefully, motivate him to get straight for good. This was for him to headline an all-star concert as part of the 'Fanfare For Britain' events marking the UK's entry into what was then known as the Common Market in early 1973.

Robert Stigwood gratefully embraced the idea and, Eric himself proving surprisingly unresistant, Townshend assembled a backing supergroup including Stevie Winwood, Rick Grech, Jim Capaldi and Ronnie Wood of the Faces, to be billed as the Palpitations. There was a week of rehearsals at Wood's house, The Wick, in Richmond, scene of so many Yardbird memories.

Eric turned up punctually for every one, looking in not too bad shape, and seemed to have lost none of his old touch.

His supposed comeback took place at the Rainbow Theatre – an all-rock venue recently conjured from the old Finsbury Park Astoria– on 13 January. Among those in the VIP seats were George and Pattie, Ringo, Jimmy Page, Elton John, Joe Cocker and Ahmet Ertegun. Never had so many top people in his profession united to support and encourage the 'wounded child'. But as the minutes ticked away to showtime, there was no sign of Eric.

Backstage, Pete Townshend encountered an agitated Stigwood, who suggested he should pray their headliner would turn up.

'You pray,' snapped Townshend. 'He's *your* artist.'

'Look, if I pray, He won't listen,' Stigwood replied. So Townshend went to a deserted stairwell and, three times over, said, 'Please God, make Eric come before the show.'

He did, very late and stoned, although that wasn't what had held him up. Thanks to his junk food diet, he'd been unable to get into the white suit he wanted to wear and Alice had to let out its waistband.

Wearing his recovered Fender 'Blackie', he received a tumultuous welcome and, shadowed by Townshend and Ronnie Wood, went straight into a ten-minute version of 'Layla' that made Pattie's blood run cold. 'He might have been wrecked for three years, but he hadn't forgotten how to tear at the heartstrings with his guitar,' she was to recall. 'All the emotion I had felt for him when he disappeared from my life welled up inside me.'

But this Fanfare for Eric portended nothing in the way of cleaning up or getting back to work or even trying afresh with Pattie. Afterwards, he and Alice returned to Hurtwood Edge and their private Purgatory for another seven months.

17

THE BLACK BOX

I t might have continued even longer but for the presence of the lord. In August 1973, Alice's father wrote to Eric with an ultimatum: if they didn't stop what they were doing to themselves and each other, Lord Harlech said, he'd have no hesitation in turning them over to the police.

But with the evidently serious threat came the offer of a lifeline couched in terms of extraordinary sympathy and affection, especially towards a young man Harlech had good reason to hate. 'For all that you can do and all that you can have in your lives, please let me help you . . . I will probably never know how much courage it will take, dear Eric, but for your own sake please do it.'

Through the violinist Yehudi Menuhin, Harlech had heard of Dr Meg Patterson, a Scottish neurosurgeon who claimed to be able to reduce heroin withdrawal symptoms by a treatment of her own invention called Neuroelectric Therapy. It was a form of acupuncture, widely used by the surgical profession to control post-operative pain but said to be equally effective in combating the horrors of cold turkey.

With his aversion to needles, Eric recoiled from the idea of acupuncture. Nonetheless, he agreed to meet Dr Patterson at the Harley Street clinic she ran in partnership with her husband, George. The couple had only recently returned to Britain after ten years in the Far East and had no idea who he was.

The consultation got off to a shaky start when Eric arrived with Alice half an hour late, both of them stoned. He announced that he didn't want to give up heroin and had come only because Lord Harlech thought the treatment might help Alice. However, he quickly warmed to 'Doctor Meg', a dynamic, smiley woman with lustrous coiled-up hair, and was fascinated by her stories of working among heroin addicts in China and Hong Kong, where she had developed her treatment. At the end of half an hour, he said, 'OK, I'll give it a try.'

The case-history that he and Alice related between them was as serious as any in her experience. Once, in an attempt at self-medication, Eric had swallowed enough of the illegal Mandrax sedative to kill most people. In his quest for stronger, quicker results, he'd even been ready to forget his needle-phobia and try shooting up, but Alice had managed to talk him out of it. By the time he found Dr Meg, her son Lorne recalls, 'it was a question of when, not if, he would die'.

Neuroelectric Therapy was administered by a small black box sprouting electrical leads attached to acupuncture needles, which were inserted around the contour of the patient's ear. These transmitted a mild electric current simulating the 'nod' or euphoric stupor of heroin. Withdrawal could thus take place without the body realising it was happening.

For both Eric and Alice, Dr Meg decreed, three or four one-hour sessions per day would be necessary over a period of at least a month. Since the treatment could be given only by its inventor, she and her husband and professional colleague, George, had to move into Hurtwood Edge accompanied by a full-time nurse, hired from an agency.

The Pattersons' therapy had a strong religious dimension: Dr Meg had combined her medical practice with missionary work in post-partition India (for which she'd been awarded an MBE in 1961) and George had pursued the same vocation in China and Tibet while variously employed as an engineer and journal-ist. The nurse they brought with them shared their beliefs to an even stronger degree and had to be dismissed after Eric com-plained she was too blatantly trying to convert him and Alice to Christianity.

He had expected to be weaned from heroin by slow degrees, but Dr Meg's first act was to order its total banishment from the house. Afterwards, she found him and Alice crawling around the floor, trying to snort up any last remnants from the carpet-pile.

To begin with, they received the treatment together in the small ground-floor room known as the Den. They were not the easiest of patients. A side-effect of their addiction was chronic insomnia, yet their bodies' tolerance of narcotics made them immune to the sleeping-tablets Dr Meg would have prescribed. And the mildness of the electric current flowing into his ear convinced Eric it couldn't possibly be having any effect.

After a week, the Pattersons realised that the cure had no chance of working unless he and Alice were separated, especially as she also needed treatment for alcoholism after the two bottles of vodka per day she'd been drinking to compensate for giving him all the heroin. Eric therefore moved into their Harley Street clinic while Alice went to a nursing home on the other side of Regent's Park. For the rest of their respective treatments, there was to be no communication between them.

The Pattersons did not normally accommodate patients and had only a tiny flat without even a spare bedroom. Like their two sons, fourteen-year-old Lorne and twelve-year-old Sean, Eric slept in the sitting-room while their ten-year-old daugh-ter, Myrrh, slept in the consulting-room. He was as model a house-guest as he'd been long ago with John and Ruth Mayall, though nowadays even more domestically incompetent. One day when Dr Meg was busy with other patients, she asked him to make some coffee. 'Meg, I don't know how to make coffee,' he confessed.

Away from his woodland mansion and his usual protective human screen, he opened up to them as never to anyone before, confessing his fear that heroin had robbed him of his talent as well as his friends, his career and most of his money. Yet he only had to strum the small acoustic guitar he'd brought with him to show how brightly that talent still burned.

Dr Meg believed that part of his trouble was 'deep spiritual trauma' and back in Harley Street, the question of faith was raised again, with rather more delicacy than it had been by the agency nurse. Like the vast majority of British children in the Fifties, Eric had received a Christian upbringing from which the Sixties had brought an immediate lapse. But he'd felt some renewed stirrings of faith thanks to a Scottish deejay he'd met on an American tour, though in no sense could he be considered born again.

Ever responsive to potential father-figures, he tended to talk more to the white-bearded George Patterson, usually while he prepared the evening meal. For the first time in any kind of therapeutic context, he spoke of his feelings about his 'illegitimate' birth, his abandonment by his mother as a toddler, the childhood-long pretence that Rose was his mother and Pat his big sister, and how far that might account for his drive to be the best blues guitarist in the world and have sex with almost every woman he met.

Patterson was no zealot, having struggled at length with his own faith, and he took care to avoid anything resembling missionary work on Eric. Rather, he focused on dispelling any romantic association of heroin with the likes of Charlie Parker and Billie Holiday, reiterating that talent comes from the spirit, not drugs. Only once, late at night, when Eric knocked on his bedroom door in the grip of 'a black scene' (i.e. mood), did he suggest they should pray together, which they did.

He was allowed the occasional visitor, like Lord Harlech, Robert Stigwood and the ever-solicitous Pete Townshend. Though the media was kept in total ignorance of his whereabouts, he gave one remarkably candid interview to the freelance journalist Steve Turner, admitting his former enslavement to what he coyly termed 'the naughty powder'. He said he hadn't touched a guitar for three years (an exaggeration), fearing he could never again reach the heights of the *Layla* album. Whatever he came up with, he said, would be 'an insult to music'.

Turner also received his confession that 'Layla' had been inspired by 'a woman I felt deeply about and that turned me down . . . It's the wife-of-my-best-friend scene . . . she was trying to attract his attention, trying to make him jealous and so she used me, you see, and I fell madly in love with her.' What had she thought of the song, Turner asked. 'She didn't give a damn [but] if she was to come in this room right now, I'd fall down at her feet.'

At another point, he volunteered: 'I have this death-wish. I don't like life. And I'm not going to live very long.'

He was occasionally allowed out alone, on his honour not to go near anyone who might lead him astray. Dr Meg's supervision extended to checking his room and after one such exeat she found he'd brought back some Vispetone, a Methadone-based syrup. In front of George and the children, she gave him a dressing-down such as he hadn't received since primary school, accusing him of betraying her, and then poured the Vispetone down the sink.

He seemed set to make the promised complete recovery when this instinct for self-sabotage kicked in again. He announced that he had to have some heroin and was already in touch with one of his former dealers about getting it delivered to him. But the dealer was a friend who knew all about the treatment he was receiving and refused to supply him without Dr Meg's permission.

She not only gave it, but allowed him to take the heroin on her premises rather than see him walk out and straight back into addiction. Anyway, by that time he'd passed the point of no return; the snort, he told her later, had been 'good but not as good as before'.

Hence, after less than a month, Dr Meg's black box could claim its first success from rock's top echelon. And in years to come, this pioneering example would be followed by Keith Richards, Keith Moon, Pete Townshend, when he fell back into drugs again, and Boy George.

Eric would always speak about the Pattersons in the warmest terms, despite a lingering resentment of that public dressing-down from Dr Meg. 'They gave me love, and I found that was the medicine I needed far more than the actual treatment.'

The day he left, he presented Dr Meg with the 24-carat gold snorting spoon he'd worn on a chain around his neck for the past three years. 'Thanks, Meg,' said the handwritten note that accompanied it, 'I won't be needing this.'

Many people who succeed in getting off heroin are soon undone when they return to their social circle of fellow addicts and dealers. Lord Harlech and the Pattersons had therefore formulated a second stage to Eric's rehabilitation that would remove him from all such temptation and provide an extended breathing-space in the healthiest possible surroundings.

The Harlech family's estate included a farm near Oswestry in Shropshire, close to the Welsh border, managed by Alice's younger brother, Francis, known as Frank. It was thither that his joint Harley Street and House of Lords support-team dispatched Eric early in 1974.

The idea had been that he should 'semi-work' on the farm, but mainly just soak up the fresh air, quiet and privacy. However, once there, he rediscovered the pleasure in manual labour that had almost turned him into a bricklayer like his step-grandfather, Jack Clapp. The rock star who seldom got up before afternoon took to rising at dawn and – the farm being virtually unauto-mated – putting in a full, strenuous day of mucking out animals, digging ditches and baling hay.

He had known and liked Frank Ormsby-Gore since Frank was a schoolboy – a reminder of how long he and Alice had been to-gether, on and off – and meshed in perfectly with the farm's two workers, Dai and Mike, neither of whom showed the slightest tendency to regard him as 'God.'

Indeed, it was therapy in itself to stop being Eric Clapton and become just one of a group of mates, working and playing to-gether with equal uncomplicatedness. After finishing the day's chores, they would go straight into Oswestry to make a round of the pubs, listen to jukeboxes and drink 'until we could hardly stand up'. Frank would cook dinner back at the farm, then they'd hit the pubs again until closing-time.

In this way, Eric would claim, he segued with hardly a beat from heroin addiction to the alcoholism that would rule his life just as powerfully but for much longer. Actually, it had always been there, lying dormant through eras when acid or coke seemed to deliver the biggest kicks.

As an art student, he used to drink himself insensible in the hope of impressing some girl or to drown his humiliation at being 'chucked' by one. A specially clear advance warning had been his bender at the Beaulieu Jazz Festival, aged sixteen, when he was abandoned by his friends, woke up in the woods with-out a penny in his pocket, slunk home dishevelled and unshaven with pissed-in and crapped-in pants – and couldn't wait to do it all again.

On the positive side, the farm made him fitter than he'd ever been since those long-ago bricklaying days with Jack. And mind-less physical labour in the fresh air broke his long creative block;

odd lines for songs would suddenly come as he humped sacks around or sat on the tractor, and he'd rush to find chords for them on a guitar which it was no longer a struggle to pick up.

At this point, fortuitously, he heard from Derek and the Dominos' bass-player, Carl Radle, the most thoughtful and least rowdy of their American personnel. Radle was now playing the clubs back in his native Tulsa, Oklahoma, and sent Eric some tapes he'd made with a keyboards-man named Dick Sims and a drummer named Jamie Oldaker.

The tapes were impressive, and with them came a simple message: 'We're waiting for you.' From then on, Eric began writing songs with the trio in mind and even imagining their possible running-order on an album.

He continued to have a faithful friend and tireless would-be benefactor in Pete Townshend. The Who were currently filming Townshend's ground-breaking rock opera *Tommy*, with Robert Stigwood as producer and the outrageous Ken Russell as director. Townshend asked Eric to join the several big names with cameo roles (the others included Tina Turner and Elton John) as a thank-you for organising his Rainbow comeback concert a year previously, when he'd so signally failed to come back.

Eric's cameo in *Tommy* was the weirdest postscript to the Christianity he'd lately absorbed with Dr Meg's Neuroelectric Therapy. It showed him robed as a priest, performing Sonny Boy Williamson's 'Eyesight To The Blind' from the pulpit of a church dedicated to Marilyn Monroe and filled with people in wheelchairs.

But that helpful gesture, too, backfired when Eric spent much of the day's filming getting smashed with Keith Moon. Even after all his recent training in the Oswestry pubs, Moon the Loon made him feel 'a lightweight'.

A surprise visit to the farm by George and Pattie Harrison did not promise to aid his recuperation. George knew by now that

'Layla' had been about Pattie and a direct criticism of himself, and might well have been monumentally offended. She in her turn might be under the illusion Eric had tried to feed her: that he'd taken to heroin when she rejected him.

However, the encounter brought no recrimination from any side; the three just had a drink in a local pub. Eric was touched by George's supportiveness, but couldn't help wishing Pattie had come on her own. Though they were evidently still a couple, Eric felt she was looking at him with more than mere friendly concern.

Towards the end of his time at the farm, Alice completed her treatment for alcoholism and came to join him. Dr Meg's instructions were that they should not share a bedroom or be intimately involved in any way lest they should pull each other back to where they'd been.

Alice might have started out by being posh-girl cool to Eric, but she'd ended by risking everything for love of him, including her life. Nonetheless, the third stage of the plan made by others for his survival was that he should break up with her. He didn't argue.

For the Ormsby-Gore family, who had been so instrumental in his succour, survival was to be more problematic. Later in the year Alice split from Eric, she found her twenty-two-year-old brother, Julian, dead from gunshot wounds apparently self-inflicted in a bout of depression aggravated by drugs and alcohol. In 1985, her father, the kindly and forbearing 5th Baron Harlech, was killed in a car crash, just as her mother had been twenty years earlier.

At the age of seventeen, Pattie had received an object lesson in how women ought to behave when their husbands were unfaithful under their very noses. Her tyrannical stepfather, Bobbie Gaymer-Jones, was openly carrying on with a family friend named Ingrid. But in those days of female subservience, her mother, Diana, resolutely turned a blind eye, even when Ingrid scrawled that erotic message on the windscreen of Bobbie's car with her diamond ring.

Now, history was repeating itself for Pattie in a Gothic mansion near Henley-on-Thames, whose light-switches were like the faces of miniature friars.

Since Eric's revelation of his obsession with her, George's swings from Hindu spirituality to coke-fuelled promiscuity had become more blatant and frequent. When he began sleeping with Ronnie Wood's wife, Krissie, they also began to involve women she'd previously looked on as friends.

Eric's obsession, in fact, had left a permanent scar on Pattie's family that would have justified recriminations in their brief pub encounter. Her youngest sister, Paula, whom George had originally planned to seduce, ended up with Eric apparently as a substitute for her, and had begun taking heroin in consequence.

Paula was now with the record producer Andy Johns and the mother of a baby son named William. But she still remained hooked, sometimes to the extent of not being able to remember whether or not she had fed William. On a trip to the Bahamas with Pattie, she'd carried smack in her bag (which she persuaded her sister to try at the airport) and miraculously got away with it.

At Friar Park, Pattie had come to feel increasingly isolated, even though the vast house was always full of people. Among them was an entire troupe of Hare Krishna singers, whom George had invited to move in with their spouses and numerous children. When one of the children fell into the lake, the Krishnas did not react, saying that God would rescue it, and George's PA, Terry Doran, had to turn lifeguard. After it happened a second time, the local doctor refused to answer any further calls for emergency resuscitations.

It was around the time of the visit to Eric that George broke the most sacred principle of the Beatles' once-indivisible brotherhood. He began an affair with Ringo's wife, Maureen.

None of his liaisons could have seemed less likely. A former Liverpool hairdresser, Maureen had been married to Ringo since 1965 and was always the least noticeable of the Beatle wives, small, mouse-like and publicly mute. To the other Beatles, she was like family; as George later acknowledged, seducing her had been 'incest'.

Pattie found out about it when she returned from visiting her mother in Devon and chanced on some photographs of Maureen taken at Friar Park in her absence. She further discovered that a necklace Maureen often wore in front of her had been a present from George. But, as always, he denied everything and accused her of paranoia.

Before long, he abandoned any attempt at secrecy. Late at night when Pattie was alone in the great hall with its friar-faced light-switches – rather like the newspaper tycoon's lonely wife in *Citizen Kane* – Maureen would arrive on the pretext of 'listening to George in the studio' and would still be there the next morning. 'Her attitude was very much that she had the right to spend the night with George if she felt like it.'

Pattie put up with it for a while, just as her mother had with her stepfather's mistress, still clinging to the hope that one day George might revert to the sweet, considerate person she'd met on the set of *A Hard Day's Night*. But then the affair moved to daytime; he disappeared with Maureen into one of Friar Park's many bedrooms while musicians were waiting for him in his studio. 'I thought, This is being deliberately rubbed in my face,' Pattie recalls. 'He and Maureen want me to know this is happening.'

Pushed beyond endurance at last, she sought out the guilty bedroom and hammered on the door. George opened it to reveal Maureen on a mattress on the floor, but still would not admit any guilt. 'Oh, she's a bit tired,' he explained. 'She's having a rest.'

A French or Italian wife at this point might have resorted to a loaded revolver. Pattie's milder English response was to attack Maureen with a brace of water pistols and then give two fingers to George's so very malleable Indian religiosity.

From the roof of Friar Park flew an OM flag, signifying that meditation was carried on there. She remembered that downstairs was another flag, left over from some fancy-dress party in happier times: a pirate skull-and-crossbones. With the help of two sympathetic studio engineers, she hauled down the OM and ran up the Jolly Roger.

In late April 1974, Robert Stigwood held a lavish press reception at Soho's China Garden restaurant to announce Eric's second comeback. The revenant was deeply tanned after his recent agricultural exertions and wore his hair cropped shorter than in any era since the Yardbirds. He was clean-shaven but, as *Melody Maker*'s indefatigable Clapton-watcher Chris Welch reported, had 'the beginnings of a beard and a moustache that were just enough to make redundant all photographs of [him] for the past 10 years'.

No explanation was given for his absence from public view since 1971 and none was demanded. Stuffed with Chinese food, then treated to an all-night booze-up at Stigwood's house, the press happily swallowed the line of a three-year, battery-recharging 'lay-off'.

Under Stigwood's after-care programme, the album he had begun mentally planning at the farm was already set up just as he'd pictured. It was to be made in Miami, where Derek and the Dominos had reached their brief apotheosis; the Carl Radle trio, whose tapes he had liked, would be his sidemen and the brilliant Tom Dowd once again his producer. He was to stay at a beach-fronted mansion whose address, 461 Ocean Boulevard, provided a ready-made title.

But the sessions back at Criteria Studios were no rest-cure.

Radle's two sidemen, keyboard-player Dick Sims and drummer Jamie Oldaker, were both young and as opinionated as they were talented. Eric had been out of the loop for three years and, moreover, was now pushing thirty, in those days still a milestone every rock star dreaded.

Working with Sims and Oldaker put him on his mettle, thereby doing him more good than all Stigwood's featherbedding, and resulted in a minimalist, almost austere sound at the opposite extreme from Derek and the Dominos' passionate superabundance.

The only reference to his recent ordeal was 'Give Me Strength' – words he had jotted down in the early stages of the Pattersons' treatment, when success seemed hopeless, now transmuted into a slide-guitar spiritual showing their Christianity had sunk in deeper than they could ever have imagined: 'Lord, I've done so much wrong/But please give me strength to carry on.'

The rest of the tracks were mostly cover versions chosen less to reflect what he'd been through than to help him forget it: Johnny Otis's 'Willie And The Hand-Jive', Robert Johnson's 'Steady Rollin' Man', Elmore James's 'I Can't Hold Out', 'Mainline Florida' (a reference to trains, not needles) by the local guitarist George Terry, one of his several auxiliaries in the studio.

Another was Yvonne Elliman, an actress and singer of part-Irish, part-Hawaiian descent who had played Mary Magdalen in Stigwood's Broadway and film versions of *Jesus Christ Superstar.* She was beautiful and flirtatious and, Eric's libido having returned with his other faculties, the two began a passionate affair that spilled over into the album. Their duet in the raunchy 'Get Ready', his first-ever vocal coupling with a woman, felt almost like eavesdropping outside the bedroom door.

During the sessions, George Terry suggested a last-minute addition, 'I Shot The Sheriff' from the Wailers' 1973 album *Burnin'.*

But there was little enthusiasm from Eric. Reggae was a form of black music with which he felt little affinity and the Wailers' moving spirit, Bob Marley, had not yet emerged as a genre-busting genius. He saw nothing for him in a Wild West song with a surreal dimension of Jamaican Rastafarianism. To please Terry, he recorded 'I Shot The Sheriff', but felt so uncomfortable with his version that he almost had it held off the album.

Released as a single in July 1974, it went to number 1 in the US – an achievement Eric was never to repeat – made the Top 10 in Britain and charted around the world. It played a major role in bringing reggae into the mainstream and propelling Bob Marley to the superstardom he would enjoy for the tragically brief remainder of his career.

The album from which it came, *461 Ocean Boulevard*, performed just as spectacularly, reaching number 1 in the US and the British Top 5 and, again, charting worldwide. The Miami Beach house it was named after became a tourist-attraction, creating such a traffic hazard that the street number had to be changed.

The crucial test of Eric's recovery was to be the first tour he'd ever made under his own name, which would keep him on the road until December, starting in Scandinavia, playing forty-eight cities across the US, circling back via Japan and sundry European capitals and ending in London at the Hammersmith Odeon. Before setting off, revitalised as he felt, he made another attempt to carry off Pattie Harrison.

He had heard about George's affair with Ringo's wife and the skull-and-crossbones episode, and hoped that Pattie might now find his blandishments irresistible. So one evening, after working with Pete Townshend on the *Tommy* album, he persuaded Townshend to drive him down to Friar Park. His plan was that Townshend would engage George's attention by talking about music in his studio, leaving the coast clear for the re-wooing of Pattie.

That day, as it happened, she had gone to Devon for her stepbrother Boo's wedding. She arrived back to find George, Eric, Townshend and fellow musician Graham Bell together in a weirdly charged atmosphere which, in her practical way, she tried to normalise by making soup for them all. Afterwards, Townshend talked music for two hours to George in his studio while Eric 'canoodled' with Pattie over the empty soup plates.

Even now, she wasn't ready to give up on her marriage – but they went back to brief-encountering. Not long afterwards, they joined Townshend and some mutual friends for dinner at a London restaurant, both arriving in gorilla masks in case any press photographers should be lurking. Townshend noticed that when Pattie took off her mask, she smiled more than he'd seen her do for years.

The tour rehearsals took place on Barbados, where Stigwood had hired a luxurious beach house with a full domestic staff. Eric's first evening there brought conclusive proof of his being back to his old self. The staff had prepared him and the band a welcome dinner of spaghetti Bolognese. As they took their seats, he picked up his heaped plate and threw it. His musicians followed his cue and the furnishings were soon covered in spaghetti and lumps of meatball.

Stigwood's increasing involvement in film and theatre projects was leaving him less and less time to be a pop manager, so to supervise Eric's comeback on the 1974 tour and afterwards, he turned him over to a senior member of his organisation named Roger Forrester.

Born in Grimsby, Lincolnshire, Forrester had worked variously as a butcher's deliveryman, for the Pontins holiday camp organisation and for London's poshest grocers, Fortnum & Mason, before drifting into pop-promotion, then being hired by

Stigwood as a booking agent for acts like Jimi Hendrix and the Bee Gees. With his combed-over hair and outsize 1970s glasses, he resembled an elongated, hyperactive Elton John. Eric was quite happy about the hand-over since Forrester, as well as being highly competent, possessed a laconic wit that had been known to crush even Ginger Baker.

He proved his worth a week into the tour's American leg. In daily touch with London, he heard that Pattie had finally left George and was currently in Los Angeles, staying with her sister Jenny, who had married Mick Fleetwood of Fleetwood Mac. Why didn't Eric give her a ring, Forrester suggested.

He did so, albeit without much hope, inviting her to meet him in Boston on 12 July when he was to appear at the Garden. But this time, she said yes.

18

E + P

Pattie's long resistance to Eric had melted into 'an intoxicating, overpowering passion', utterly different from the 'deep, gentle love' she'd felt for George. She realised the awesome extent of it that first night at the Boston Garden as she watched him perform 'Layla' to an audience of 15,000 whose flickering forests of candles and cigarette-lighters in the darkness seemed to wish them joy. For it had been achieved as much by a plectrum as by a man.

With Eric, the reverse happened: the obsession he had nurtured at a distance for five years began to ebb away the moment he won her. So it had been with his first acoustic guitar, in Bell's shop window in Surbiton, and anything he'd ever obsessed about; when he got it, he no longer wanted it.

Pattie had never been allowed to go on tour with George and at first life on the road with Eric seemed liberating after her mausoleum existence at Friar Park – the constant motion, the living out of suitcases, the freedom from responsibility, the juvenile jokes and pranks and non-stop partying.

Almost every city brought forth legendary names wanting to play with Eric or just hang out with him: Stevie Wonder, Freddie King, the Band. Nor was the ultimate one to be left out; in Memphis, an invitation arrived to 'watch a movie' with Elvis Presley.

Pattie had met Presley when she was with George and now was shocked by his bloated appearance just three years before his death aged only forty-two. The screening did not take place at his Graceland mansion but in a regular cinema specially hired for the evening, where instead of sitting with the King, she and Eric were firmly ushered to places five rows behind him.

When that film ended, he moved on to see another on a different screen and invited them to come along. 'It was a five-screen complex and we had visions of being there all night, five rows behind Elvis,' she recalls. 'So we made our excuses and left.'

The drinking to which Eric had turned after giving up heroin was already well on the way to an addiction equalling and, ultimately, surpassing it. The night Pattie joined him in Boston, he had been out on a boozy spree with some members of the Band before the show and took to the stage heavily under the influence. Also half-blind from conjunctivitis – caught from his backing singer Yvonne Elliman, with whom he'd gone on sleeping until the very last moment before Pattie's arrival – he collided with an outsize pot-plant that was part of the stage-décor.

Whereas heroin had kept him in a generally docile, biddable twilight, alcohol made him touchy and aggressive and prone to picking fights in public, often with the wrong people like airline officials, hotel concierges, even police officers.

He developed a mania for arm-wrestling, that hallmark of the pub braggart, enjoying a surprisingly high success-rate for one so unfit, provided he used his left arm. It was far stronger than his right one, as though galvanised by the power that flowed down it to his guitar fretboard.

Most seriously, alcohol made him break the first rule of performing: he rounded on audiences who expressed disapproval of the state he was so often in. After one shambolic duet with his great idol Freddie King on 'Hideaway', that easy-fingering old favourite from his R&B years, a disgruntled spectator wrote a letter of complaint to *Rolling Stone*: 'Eric Clapton stunk when he came to Buffalo . . . he walked out so drunk, he couldn't sing worth shit. He was constantly cursing the crowd. Many of the fans left before the show was over only to miss the Band lift Clapton up and carry his drunken corpse offstage . . .'

Swept away by adoration as she was, Pattie went along with everything; thrilled to be included in Eric's circle after being so long excluded from George's, she did her best to keep up with the drinking.

She stayed with the tour only until the end of its North America leg. After she'd gone, Eric continued to sleep with other women as if nothing had changed, true to the rock business's oldest axiom: 'It doesn't count on the road.'

Roger Forrester has a simple explanation for the success of his professional partnership with Eric over almost a quarter of a century. 'I did my job and he did his and neither of us ever tried to muscle in on the other.'

That is grossly selling himself short. For the man with the combed-over hair and Elton John glasses went far beyond the bounds of normal pop-star management as only Brian Epstein previously had with the Beatles – and Epstein had four demanding individuals to look after while Forrester had just one.

Just as Epstein called his doted-on charges 'the Boys', no matter how far into manhood they advanced, so to Forrester in conversation with third parties his sole client was always 'the Boy'. From the mid-1970s to late-'90s, he came closest to being the father Eric had never had.

Under Forrester's aegis, as under Stigwood's, the principal objective was to prevent him ever having to confront practical realities, such as money. Whenever he bought anything, be it a new shirt, a new Ferrari or a mansion in the Surrey woods, the bill was sent to Forrester's office and paid without demur.

In addition, Eric received £200 per week in cash from the Stigwood Organisation, even though the act of paying for something himself had long since become almost unknown to him. It came in a brown envelope, such as manual and office workers used to receive every Friday before the days of monthly bank-transfers and, if he was in the UK, would always be delivered personally by the Stigwood Organisation's bookkeeper, Gladys Bates.

He seldom spent any of the cash, yet it had huge significance for him as a connection with the world of 'real' working men like plasterers and bricklayers, embodied by his step-grandfather, Jack Clapp.

But while Stigwood had largely been content to leave him to his own devices (and look where *those* had got him), Forrester was at his beck and call around the clock, seven days a week, regardless of his own personal affairs, privacy or peace of mind.

On tours, his remit extended far beyond the thousand bureaucratic, logistical and hysterical human problems that every day – every hour – threw at him. 'I always drew up Eric's running-orders. He played brilliantly but he couldn't compile a programme for a two-hour concert to save his life.'

Forrester watched every performance from the side of the stage, his outsize spectacles irradiating enthusiasm and encouragement, willing Eric to get through everything on the list. 'He'd keep looking at me, like "I can't be bothered to do this." I got a couple of table-tennis bats which I'd use to signal to him how many songs he still had to go.'

A non-drinker himself, Forrester had instantly recognised the problem his charge was developing and devised a system to control it without confrontation. Eric's tipple of choice was Courvoisier brandy, one of the more expensive makes, so much diluted with 7Up that its flavour all but vanished. He would start on it soon after breakfast and continue all day, regardless of how it might impair his performance that night.

Forrester had calculated that if Eric stopped drinking by four p.m., it left enough time to sober up before going onstage at nine or ten. He therefore took charge of mixing the brandy and 7Up, like some medieval royal food-taster, but after four would substitute cold milkless tea, usually without Eric noticing any difference. The ruse sometimes failed and he'd go onstage blind drunk in weird mixtures of clothes, staggering around barely able to form a coherent sentence or chord, sometimes playing while lying flat on his back.

The non-boozing, even non-swearing Forrester nonetheless brought with him a flavour of the East End underworld that had made David Litvinoff such a fascinating companion to Eric at The Pheasantry. In his booking-agent days, he'd given employment to two members of the Kray gang and as a result had met, and even done some business with, their bosses Reggie and Ronnie before the twins were put on trial for murder and each sentenced to life imprisonment in 1969.

'Reggie [the non-gay, non-insane one] even ran a merchandising company for me. We used to have business meetings at Notcutts Garden Centre in Bagshot. He came into Stigwood's office once, and Stigwood rang me and said. "Have you got a *Kray* sitting in Reception?"

'People used to wonder why no one ever owed me any money. That was because the twins had their own notepaper, headed "The Kray Agency" with a picture of a bass drum, and I used it for letters saying "awaiting the favour of your remittance". The payment always came immediately.

'Eric didn't know them, but he knew they were around. He always liked the idea of there being gangsters in the picture.'

Eric had long been in need of a personal bodyguard and one of Forrester's first acts was to hire Marc Bolan's former chauffeur, Alphi O'Leary, whose brother, Laurie, had run various front establishments for the Krays prior to co-managing the Speakeasy. Six-foot-four in height, with a skullcap of curly hair, O'Leary was not the tough guy he looked and whenever called on to use muscle would suffer agonies of remorse for days afterwards.

Like many East Enders, he was outraged by the twins' incarceration, regarding them as local heroes who never harmed women or children and kept the streets safer than the regular police. 'When they went inside, Eric sent each of them something – an album, I think,' Pattie recalls. 'And he got the most beautiful thank-you letters back.'

Another bond with Forrester was created by his instant, unfeigned fondness for Eric's grandmother, Rose, and the royal treatment he extended to her whenever she came to a show. 'She was a wonderful character. I always had her sitting next to me at the side of the stage, and Eric told the audience she was there.

'One night at the Hammersmith Odeon, she suddenly took off, ran onstage, put her arms around his neck and started kissing him. I had to go out there and pull her off him. Afterwards, I asked her what had happened and she said, "Just overcome, dear."

'Rose liked a drink as well. She'd often ring me up and ask me to do things for her, like "Can you get someone to come and retune my piano?" The guy I sent to her said to me afterwards, "Do you know why her piano was out of tune? It was full of bottles of beer."'

After the huge success of 'I Shot The Sheriff', it seemed only sensible to pursue the reggae theme and, to gain maximum authenticity, Eric used an extended break in the 1974 tour to take the band to Jamaica to record at Kingston's Dynamic Sound Studios where his latest black role-models, Toots and the Maytals, often worked.

George Terry, who had steered him to 'I Shot The Sheriff', now a permanent band-member, had written a sequel to it entitled 'Don't Blame Me'. Among the local reggae legends brought in to help was Peter Tosh, aka Stepping Razor, a core member of Bob Marley's Wailers and, like Marley, destined for an early death (in his case tortured and murdered by a gang of house-breakers in 1987). Tosh and everyone else at Dynamic constantly smoked ganja in huge conical roll-ups known as trumpet spliffs. Eric needed little persuasion that joining them would not compromise his recent detoxification.

He was staying at the luxurious Ocho Rios resort, where Pattie joined him for what was supposed to be a real 'honeymoon'. In fact, after what she'd seen on the road, she was already having serious misgivings about what lay ahead. 'Even though I was madly in love with Eric, I realised what a wreck he was. I thought, What have I done, joining this group of mad people that he led? George had said I could go back [to him] whenever I wanted, and I was starting to feel I really wanted to.'

A visit by her friend Chris O'Dell, George's former PA, only stirred up thoughts of what she might have thrown away, and one day, with O'Dell's encouragement, she decided to phone him. Eric came into the hotel-room unexpectedly and caught her; there was a furious row which ended with Pattie locking herself in the bathroom and him kicking the door so violently that he broke a toe.

In any case, the honeymoon was cut short by news from Canada that Eric's half-brother, Brian, had been killed in a motorcycle accident, just as his guitar blood-brother, Greg Allman, had been, three years earlier.

He could not in any way be called close to this oldest of his birth-mother Pat's three children by her Canadian husband, Frank McDonald – the lucky ones allowed to call her 'Mommy' when he had to pretend she was his big sister. Nonetheless, he insisted on flying to Canada for Brian's funeral and that Pattie should accompany him. 'One of the things that alcohol does is heighten the emotions,' she says. 'I believe that if Eric hadn't been drinking so much, he never would have gone.'

Without a single conviction for his former massive drug-use, he was free to pop in and out of North America at will. But Pattie's small fine for possessing cannabis with George in 1969 was as repugnant to the Canadian immigration authorities as to the American and at first it seemed as if she wouldn't get in. 'I remember Eric screaming drunkenly at the immigration people while I was put in a special holding-area. Luckily, when we got on to Robert [Stigwood], he knew someone at the Canadian Embassy who managed to sort it out.'

Thanks to McDonald's senior army rank, Brian's funeral was conducted with full military honours. 'It was a big deal, with guns being fired and the Canadian flag folded up and placed on the coffin.'

Eric's mother was devastated by the loss of the son who'd filled his place. But, hardly knowing her as he did, he could offer only the most stilted sympathy. And even now, neither she nor he felt it was the moment for her to become Mum. 'He went on calling her Pat,' Pattie remembers.

In contrast, joining Eric at Hurtwood Edge meant a new identity for Pattie. He stopped using her first name, which for him was still too bound up with George – and reminiscent of the ever-unreachable Pat. Instead, he took to calling her Nellie, Nello or Nell, an odd choice for the former ravishing Layla with its comic/smutty echoes of Nellie Dean, Eskimo Nell and Nellie the Elephant. He would later rationalise it as a way of feeling less in awe of her.

Pattie didn't object, especially as he paired Nell with a rhyming nickname for himself like the signs on either side of a loving couple's car windscreen. In the Cockney style that shortens Derek to Del and Terry to Tel, Eric became El.

After the vastness of Friar Park, Hurtwood's mere six bedrooms and couple of acres of garden felt positively bijou. The many musicians who'd stayed there over the years had left their mark on the house's fabric and the carpets were spotted with dog faeces no one had bothered to clear up. Books and record albums out of their covers lay everywhere underfoot. Eric's live-in cleaner, Iris Eggby, made much of her position up at 'the mansion' but had little impact on its general chaos and grime.

He took just as little care of the clothes that were so important to him. The dozens of pairs of designer boots and shoes in his wardrobes were scuffed and dirty and all his shirts and sweaters lay in a tangled heap in the bath.

As Pattie explored the house, rather like Daphne du Maurier's Rebecca at Manderley, she came upon drawers and boxes full of mail Eric had never bothered to open even when it contained payments which had been sent directly to him rather than to Stigwood's office. She realised his naivety in money matters when she found a cheque for £5,000, but he refused to let it be paid into his bank account. 'Just having the cheque is enough,' he said.

In these first months, when touring was on hold for the present and his drinking was still under some kind of control, El's whole attention was focused on Nell. With the aid of his record collection, he gave her an intensive course on the history of the blues, with frequent spot-tests to see how much of the latest lesson she remembered. 'He'd sit me down and put on Robert Johnson or Ma Rainey and ask, "Who's this? And who's *this*?"

'And he could be so funny. When I was cooking, he'd make me put all the kitchen gadgets like the blender on at different speeds and then write music from the noise they made together. When he was too drunk to drive and I insisted on doing it, he'd simply move over and sit on my lap.'

For a long time, he remained fearful that at any moment she might decide to return to George or that he himself might be cuckolded as he had done to his best friend.' 'He was suspicious of every man I ever spoke to,' Pattie recalls. 'Even if it was only someone coming to the house with a delivery, Eric would say "Who was that? Do you know them?" and imagine I was secretly seeing this person. If I went in to Guildford to do some shopping, he'd follow me in his car and park and just watch me.'

With the only other woman in his life, Pattie never had any problem. Rose instantly adored her for her looks, warmth and charm, seeing her as a symbol of his return from the frightening, unspecified place where he'd been for so long.

His grandmother had little idea of what heroin addiction meant, even when Eric made a full confession to her during the family's 1974 Christmas party at Hurtwood. 'Naughty boy. Don't do it again,' she said, as if he was still her little Rick in trouble for kicking his football through a neighbour's window.

From Rose, Pattie heard the full story of how her daughter, Pat, had left the two-year-old Eric to marry her Canadian soldier, how Rose and her late husband, Jack, had brought him up to believe they were his parents and had tried to compensate by pampering him. 'When I met his old schoolfriends in Ripley, they said the same thing,' Pattie recalls. 'He had more toys than any other child in the village and he'd never let anyone else play with them.

'I got on fine with Rose. She was adorable, a sweet, sweet lady, but when Eric was growing up, she'd let him get away with anything. He didn't know how to behave because she didn't teach him. At meal-times, when he'd finished eating, even if we had guests, he'd just get up and go and watch TV or play his guitar. All that mattered was that *he'd* finished.'

Another legacy of Rose's laissez-faire approach was the discoloured teeth which contrasted so strangely with his fastidious personal grooming. 'She'd never made him clean his teeth and he still didn't, or hardly ever, so they were dreadful. He would have had halitosis if it hadn't been masked by the alcoholic breath and the smoking.'

Things were not so easy with Pattie's family, all of whom had experienced the most charming, considerate side of George. Her mother, Diana, never liked Eric, blaming him, rightly or wrongly, for her youngest daughter Paula's descent into heroin and alcoholism. The middle Boyd sister, Jenny, also had her reservations, having been like an elder sister to Alice Ormsby-Gore, but out of loyalty to Pattie, established a reasonable relationship with him.

Eric, on his side, viewed Diana as a rival for Pattie's attention and the whole genteelly-spoken family with a touch of working-class chippiness. 'He hated any of them phoning me,' Pattie recalls.

Hurtwood Edge was crying out for refurbishment, both house and garden, and after helping George with Friar Park, she was more than equal to superintending it. Only when she drew up a list of what was needed, including a modern kitchen to replace the old four-sink horror, did she fully realise Eric's disengagement from his own financial affairs and the power wielded by Roger Forrester over his private as well as professional life.

Anything Pattie wanted to buy for the house had to be approved by Forrester. 'Roger was like Eric's father,' she recalls. 'He even talked about him like a father. When he phoned the house and I answered, his first words were always "How's the boy today?"'

Despite Forrester's executive omnipotence, Robert Stigwood remained in overall charge of Eric's career – and Eric's money. He was also a favourite target of the elaborate, often wantonly destructive pranks that Eric so enjoyed. He never complained, not even when Eric and an accomplice methodically trashed a luxury villa on Barbados that he was renting, while he watched from a hammock, whimpering, 'I've never been so humiliated in my entire life', almost like some participant in a sado-masochistic sex game.

Scoring off each other turned into a kind of duel, increasingly heedless of expense or consequences. One Christmas, after Eric sent him a life-sized stuffed camel, Stigwood had three cattle delivered to Hurtwood. 'When we went to stay with him on his birthday, we took him a live piglet in a box,' Pattie says. 'And he always organised lots of silly games. I remember hiding behind a shower-curtain while he ran around the house firing a child's cap-pistol.'

Forrester proved a japester of the same no-holds-barred type, and the duel between Eric and him would continue throughout their twenty-four years together. 'Once when I was mixing him a drink, I put Sarson's vinegar with the Courvoisier instead of 7Up. He takes a big gulp, then starts spluttering and gagging . . .

'Another time, he tells me we're invited to dinner at Robert's with Pattie and my wife, Annette, and it's fancy dress. She and I go along in schoolboy and schoolgirl costumes, and when we get there, we're the only ones in fancy dress.'

The success of their working partnership owed much to Forrester's total unmusicality and ready acknowledgement of the fact. Unlike Stigwood, he never tried to get involved in Eric's recording-sessions or critique his performances. 'He used to tell me, "Don't tap your foot at the side of the stage because you're out of time." I could do a running-order all right, but as far as the actual songs went, I was tone deaf.

'We were once in Hong Kong at a soundcheck and I said, "This is easy, what you do, easy. I could do this." Eric went, "Go on then," and handed me a guitar. When I put it on, he said, "Can I give you one word of advice? The strings are supposed to face the audience."'

★

Outwardly, Pattie's defection seemed not to have left a mark on George. Within a couple of weeks, he started seeing Kathy Simmonds, a twenty-four-year-old model who'd previously been with Rod Stewart, and was reportedly happy and excited about the imminent launch of his own record label, self-referentially named Dark Horse (i.e. surprise winner in the ex-Beatles stakes).

His few public reactions were notably lacking in anger or resentment, as if the Hindu philosophies he'd absorbed for so long were coming to his aid. A track on his first album for Dark Horse, also entitled *Dark Horse*, delivered a kind of blessing to the miscreants in a pastiche of the Everly Brothers' 'Bye Bye Love': 'There goes our lady with you-know-who/I hope she's happy, Old Clapper too'. Later, he was to send Pattie a forgiving note showing some of the sweetness she'd thought he had lost: 'E+P God bless us all Love from G'.

But his first solo American tour, alongside his sitar-guru Ravi Shankar, at the end of 1974 told a rather different story. He described it as 'a kind of bender' after years of being married, as if he'd always been the soul of monogamy. Rather, his plunge into drinking and drugging suggested a need to forget something, and so damaged his voice that it became known as 'the Dark Hoarse Tour'.

Surprisingly, his setlist still included 'While My Guitar Gently Weeps', the White Album track on which Eric had played lead for him, and 'Something', the *Abbey Road* song inspired by Pattie. But in the first, he changed the words to 'while my guitar tries to smile' and in the second, 'something in the way she moves' became the more wistful 'something in the way she smiles'.

'Did you make a musical rebuttal to "Layla"?' he was asked at a press conference.

'That sounds nasty, doesn't it?' he replied. 'Eric Clapton's been a close friend for years and I'm very happy about it.'

'How can you be happy about it?'

'Because he's great and I'd rather she was with him than some dope.'

On Christmas Day, he turned up at Hurtwood while Eric and Pattie were at lunch. Seeing that Pattie was eating turkey, he scolded her for abandoning the vegetarianism they used to practise together. However, he accepted some wine and Christmas pudding and there was no trace of awkwardness between the three of them. Only later did she think it rather sad that he had nowhere else to go on Christmas Day.

'After that,' Pattie says, 'George and Eric went back to being as tight as they had been before. Tighter, in fact. And I played no part in their relationship. I was just caught in the middle, between these two incredibly manipulative men, feeling as if I'd become invisible.'

Nell's first taste of domesticity with El at Hurtwood lasted only a few months. The *461 Ocean Boulevard* album had earned him a huge sum in royalties and with the Labour government's current rate of 83 to 98 per cent, it no doubt became attractive to become non-resident in the UK for the year 1975–6. The choice of the Bahamas promised both another chance at a 'honeymoon' with Pattie and healthier climes which, hopefully, might bring about a reduction in his drinking.

The place of exile was Paradise Island, a few miles north-east of Nassau, where Stigwood had rented him a large beachfront estate adjacent to that of the actor Richard Harris. To remind him of home, and act as the gofer no rock star can be without, he took along Simon Holland, whose father, 'Dutch', ran The Windmill, the pub beside Hurtwood's front gate.

Paradise Island fully justified its name and, at first, life there was idyllic. Eric went clean-shaven again, sunbathed and swam away the last of his heroin-pallor, and limited himself to the 'few beers a day' that for him counted as near-abstinence.

Musician friends like Mick Jagger and Ronnie Wood came to stay, allowing Pattie to gratify her love of entertaining and dressing up with lunches where everyone had to wear a different kind of outrageous hat. Even being diagnosed with acute appendicitis and having to undergo surgery in Nassau could not spoil it for her. 'In the Bahamas, I was really, really happy.'

Much to Eric's disappointment, they never bumped into Richard Harris, but he instantly took to their other near neighbour, the Irish screenwriter Kevin McClory, who had scripted some of the earliest James Bond films and directed *Thunderball*. Himself no teetotaller, McClory would invite them to dinner, then screen a Bond film afterwards. 'Kevin would be so pissed when he worked the projector that we got used to watching them in all the wrong order,' Pattie says.

But after a while, Eric tired of the sea and sun and took to lurking indoors, where twilight and air-conditioning soon effected a changeover from his daily 'few beers' to brandy and vodka. 'We had glorious weather every day, a beautiful white sand beach right outside our door and lovely warm sea just a few feet away,' Pattie recalls. 'And Eric sat down and wrote a song called "Black Summer Rain".'

The album he'd made during their first abortive honeymoon in Jamaica had come out just as he left Britain. In a dig at the idolatry that still dogged him, he wanted to call it *E.C. Is God: There's One In Every Crowd*, but the record company didn't see the joke and insisted that the prefix be dropped.

Despite pressing all the same reggae and buttons as *461 Ocean Boulevard*, with a bit of gospel thrown in, it did not sell in anything like the same numbers; nor did 'Don't Blame Me' become another 'I Shot The Sheriff' notwithstanding Eric's faintly embarrassing mimicry of Bob Marley.

Far better for his profile in absentia was a live album, *E.C. Was*

Here, recorded on the previous year's American tour, its truth-telling cover a woman's bare back with the title written across it in lipstick.

If he missed the woods and pubs of Surrey, the Bahamas were a convenient jumping-off place for gigs all over the rest of the world, starting with a tour of Australasia and Japan when the honeymoon feeling was still strong enough for him to want Pattie with him.

Here, once again, the former gourmandiser of heroin, coke and acid could roam as he pleased while her sole drug conviction caused repeated problems. Eric could simply pick up his band in nearby America and fly direct to New Zealand but Pattie was still on the US Immigration Service's blacklist, so had to make a roundabout journey via London. In a thousand-to-one coincidence, their respective flights both touched down simultaneously en route at Anchorage, Alaska, but Eric was unable to get her transferred over to his.

Then when they reached New Zealand, Pattie was informed that her drug offence barred her from entry there also. Eric's rants against the immigration officials were of no avail and she had to fly on to Australia, where no such ban operated, and wait there on her own for three days until he could join her. Roger Forrester arranged for her to be looked after by some Australian disc jockeys who clearly thought she shared Eric's tastes. 'They wanted to take me pub-crawling around these terribly macho bars which held drinking-contests where the prize would be "a young aborigine girl".'

This time on the road with Eric was rather less wonderstruck than her first one. In Adelaide, their hotel was opposite a strip club and while Pattie was absent from their suite, Eric called to the club to send over a couple of strippers to give a private show for Forrester and him. 'We were lounging on the bed, waiting for the strippers to arrive, when Pattie came back unexpectedly,'

Forrester recalls. 'She laid into Eric, but he got out of it by saying it had all been my idea.'

Pattie's disillusionments didn't end there. 'After the shows, when the rest of the band were lining up their girls for the night, I could see how much he wanted to be joining in.'

Thereafter, Pattie's visa problems in America allowed him to go off there from the Bahamas on his own, leaving her in the charge of young Simon Holland. One trip was to play on Bob Dylan's new album, *Desire*, which once again proved not quite the honour it sounded. Eric arrived in the studio to find Dylan had hired almost the entire cast of his Rolling Thunder Revue tours the previous year, including four other lead guitarists. And when the album came out, none of them was on it.

He also appeared twice with the Rolling Stones on their current American tour. Jagger had made further approaches for him to join up permanently following the departure of Mick Taylor but, in the end, the vacancy had been filled by Ronnie Wood. It must count as one of Eric's luckier escapes: the Stones' internal politics made Cream look like the Three Musketeers, and with Keith Richards around, there's no telling how long his heroin cure would have lasted.

As a favour to his Tulsa sidemen Radle, Oldaker and Sims, he journeyed to their home city for an appearance at the famous Cain's Ballroom that resulted in the second brief incarceration of his career.

During the flight from Miami he became drunk and troublesome, and when it reached Tulsa, the police were waiting. A humble apology might have cleared up the difficulty but instead he threw two suitcases into a stairwell and was placed under arrest. With the drunk's characteristic overreaction to trifles, he took violent exception to being repeatedly asked 'Are you Eric Patrick Clapton?', storming that no one else had the right to use his middle name.

He was thrown into the drunk-tank and held for several hours, unable to convince anyone he was *the* Eric Clapton until a guitar was produced for him to prove it. He was then released at a cost of only $25, joining his band onstage at Cain's Ballroom at nine p.m. Next day, his picture appeared on the front page of the *Tulsa Tribune*, looking through prison bars with a guard beside him.

Yet the Clapton Luck still held: news of his ignominious twenty-four hours in Tulsa never leaked outside Oklahoma.

19

WONDERFUL TONIGHT?

He was just as lucky when punk rock stormed the mid-Seventies British charts like sans-culottes (in this case, with Mohawk crests and safety-pins through their cheeks) storming the Bastille to start the French Revolution.

The upsurge of punk in the UK in 1976, following on from an earlier, lower-key version in New York, supposedly negated all the expertise and finesse that pop had acquired over the previous fifteen years and turned every musician of Eric's generation, most of them like himself still barely past thirty, into 'dinosaurs'.

In reality, its annihilating screams of condemnation and mockery affected only pop's middle ranks, the bourgeoisie of glam-rockers, rock 'n' roll pasticheurs and creators of pretentious concept albums with titles like *Tales From Topographic Oceans*. The aristos of the topmost echelon – the Stones, Pink Floyd, Led Zeppelin, Dylan, Clapton – not only held but increased their followings.

Hence, the beginning of 1976 found Eric making a new album suitably called *No Reason To Cry* at Shangri-La Studios in Malibu, which had recently been purpose-built for Bob Dylan and the Band. Eight years earlier, transfigured by the Band's *Music From Big Pink* album, he'd visited their collective home in Woodstock to ask if he could join them, but then hadn't found the nerve. Even now, being outside that quintet of virtuosi who seemed like brothers felt like a hole in his life.

All five played on *No Reason To Cry*, infusing it with their special mix of laid-back blues, country, hillbilly and gospel. Eric shared the lead with the unreasonably pretty Robbie Robertson (who was amused to learn he'd once been after his job) and duetted with the shivery-voiced bass-player, Rick Danko, in a joint composition, 'All Our Past Times'. Dylan himself also happened to be on hand, living in a tent in the studio grounds for reasons that never became clear. In contrast with his former cavalier treatment of Eric in the studio, he offered two songs for the album, 'Seven Days' and 'Sign Language', and his services as vocal partner on the latter.

Despite a feeling that Eric's collaborators somewhat overshadowed him, and the increasing prevalence of punk, *No Reason To Cry* was a commercial success, reaching number 8 in the UK. Nor would it be the last time he got to realise his fantasy of playing with the Band. A few months later, when their brotherhood came to a rather abrupt end, he joined Dylan, Neil Young, Van Morrison, Muddy Waters, Joni Mitchell and others in the farewell concert filmed by Martin Scorsese as *The Last Waltz*.

Back home, the upheaval in music and youth culture might not have hit his pocket but – in a very rare instance – it did not leave him unscathed. The year 1976 brought the most damaging incident of his professional career and the most serious warning of the self-destructiveness to which alcohol could lead him.

Britain by now had come a long way from the 'love and peace' its young had pursued so ardently in the Sixties. The far-right, racist National Front, whose members were predominantly skinhead rock fans, waged a campaign of intimidation and mob violence against the country's unexceptionably peaceful, hard-working immigrant communities for which it was rewarded with a surge of success in local government elections. The punks' ceaseless quest to shock and offend had turned the Nazi swastika, symbol of concentration camps and genocide, into a fashion statement. No less a stylistic taste-maker than David Bowie announced that Britain was 'ready for a fascist leadership' and described Adolf Hitler as 'one of the first rock stars'.

In this highly-charged atmosphere, in August 1976, Eric walked onstage at Birmingham's Odeon theatre, very clearly under the influence, and, before playing a note, launched into a barely coherent rant as bad as any to be heard at a National Front rally. Allegedly sparked by 'some fucking Arab who grabbed my wife's [sic] bum', it lumped all immigrants together as 'wogs' or 'coons' and urged them to leave the theatre, and Britain, forthwith.

It was made all the worse because Birmingham had a particularly large Asian community and just a few streets away, in 1968, the Conservative politician Enoch Powell had made his notorious 'rivers of blood' speech, prophesying that uncontrolled immigration would lead to Armageddon. Eric repeatedly invoked Powell's name as the only man who could 'send 'em all back' and stop 'my country' from becoming 'a black colony'.

The outburst was not filmed or recorded but the writer Caryl Phillips, one of the few black spectators, recalls that Eric seemed unable to drop the subject. 'He'd stop and play a couple of numbers, then start again.'

The general amazement and revulsion were matched by incredulity that someone could hold such views who'd built a career on the work of black musicians from the bluesmen to Bob Marley. A humble apology might have defused the outcry, especially as he'd never before been guilty of such a gaffe. But at a press conference at the Albany Hotel, Eric did not seem overly repentant and stuck doggedly to his support of Enoch Powell, maintaining that Powell's philosophy was not racist but humanitarian.

'I don't think he cares about colour of any kind. His whole idea is to stop being unfair to immigrants because it's getting out of hand ... The government is being incredibly unfair to people abroad to lure them to the promised land, where there is actually no work . . . Racial aggravation starts when white guys see immigrants getting jobs and they're not . . .'

Not for years would he admit to having spoken 'through a drunken haze' and feeling regret, 'because unless you know what you're talking about, you should keep your mouth shut'.

The episode had one positive outcome. Two weeks afterwards, the *New Musical Express* published a letter from the leftist actor and photographer Red Saunders, stingingly denouncing what he called 'rock's greatest colonist'. 'Come on, Eric, own up. Half your music is black . . . You're a good musician but where would you be without the blues and R&B? . . . Who shot the sheriff, Eric? It sure as hell wasn't you.'

Saunders' letter ended with a call for 'a rank-and-file movement against the racist poison in music'. It received an instant, overwhelming response from performers and fans who abhorred the rise of organisations like the National Front but had previously felt powerless against them. So the highly articulate and effective Rock Against Racism movement was born.

In June 1977, Pattie's divorce from George was made absolute by their having lived apart for two years. Her settlement was £120,000, a laughable sum in comparison with later celebrity divorces, even then grossly inadequate for her contributions to his career and the sacrifices it had necessitated (steering him to the Maharishi, inspiring 'Something', being smuggled around in laundry-baskets and acquiring a drugs-record to name but a few).

She was also allowed to keep the red Mercedes he'd bought her, but Eric couldn't stand the thought of her continuing to drive it and bought her a black one instead.

Her future had seemingly been settled when she first left George and the three of them were sitting together in the hall at Hurtwood Edge – although, such was the men's blokey bond, she might as well not have been there.

'I suppose I'd better divorce her,' George said.

'Well, if you do divorce her,' Eric replied, 'I suppose that means I've got to marry her.' However, after one failed marriage, she was in no hurry to try again, and he seemed not to be either.

All the punks' studied ineptitude on guitar had not reduced the demand for Eric Clapton albums and in 1977 came *Slowhand*, utilising the so-flattering nickname which in his Yardbird days had been anything but. The producer was Glyn Johns, whose distinguished pedigree included both the Beatles and Stones (and whose brother, Andy, had lived with Pattie's troubled youngest sister, Paula).

As with *There's One In Every Crowd*, Eric and Pattie chose images for the collage in the gatefold cover, credited as 'El and Nell Ink'. Among them was a photograph of a wrecked Ferrari 365 GT4 BB whose significance was lost on most purchasers.

A year earlier, returning from his Australasian tour in his usual state of inebriation, Eric had insisted on driving himself back to Ewhurst in the Ferrari. A couple of miles from London-Heathrow he'd collided with a stationary drycleaning van, crushing the car so badly that firemen had to cut him out of the wreckage, yet suffering only a perforated eardrum, cuts and bruises.

Rushed to hospital nonetheless, he ended up in the next bed to the van-driver, Dave Birch, who'd also suffered only minor injuries and was thrilled to discover who had caused them. Despite Birch's allegation that Eric had driven straight at him at around 90mph, no police action resulted; Stigwood quietly paid off the drycleaning company and not a word about it got into the papers.

Slowhand contained 'Wonderful Tonight', his most famous song after 'Layla', similarly inspired by Pattie – and destined to create as much misconception as his nickname. Its genesis was an evening when they were to drive up from Ewhurst to London to a launch party for Paul McCartney's annual Buddy Holly memorial week. Pattie couldn't decide which dress to wear and kept trying different ones on while Eric waited downstairs.

His lyric, the best he'd yet written, recreated this moment in terms of glowing spousal adoration and contentment: the domesticated rock star watching his wife put on her makeup and brush her instantly identifiable 'long blonde hair', proudly leading 'this beautiful lady' around a starry late-night party, then being driven home by her in a gently sozzled state and helped by her into his so-enviable bed.

To all her tender enquiries as to his well-being, his reply was a conjugation of 'wonderful tonight' ('You look . . .'; 'I feel . . .'; 'You were . . .'). The riff that went with it echoed the feeling of a safe haven after all the turmoil and insecurity of 'Layla'; as slow-handedly warm and comfortable as the best marital sex.

In reality, the time Pattie took to get ready had put him in a bad mood; at the party, he had got rather more than gently sozzled and little of the night had turned out wonderful, either for him or his second-time muse.

The reality was that she was living with an alcoholic, albeit a still-undeclared one, and having to deal with the unpredictability and distorted emotions and reactions that go with it.

All the classic symptoms were there, to keep her in a constant state of tension and confusion. The sudden mood swings, as when he'd say he was hungry, then refuse to touch the Indian food she spent hours preparing for him. The bursts of rage, as when she could not immediately locate whichever of his 200 shirts he wanted to wear and tried to fob him off with a similar one. The deafness to reason and common sense, as when he insisted on driving a Ferrari to the Windmill pub at the top of his drive, only to crash it on the 300-yard return journey (it was on private land, so no police needed to be involved). The unpredictable seesawing between barely-sensate TV-watching and promiscuous conviviality when he'd return from other pubs with a crowd of strangers or derelicts he'd picked up en route – 'men of the road', he romantically called them – and expect her to cook for them.

Yet at other times epic selfishness could give way to surprising intuition and sensitivity where she was concerned. In September 1978, George married a young secretary working at his Dark Horse record company named Olivia Arias, who had already borne him a son named Dhani. Although greatly upset by the wedding, Pattie didn't mention it to Eric, uncertain as ever how he'd react. 'I thought I was giving nothing away, but I must have been showing shock or unhappiness because he picked up on it.'

A couple of days later, he played her a new song he'd written, 'Golden Ring', which clearly suggested they follow George's example: 'If I gave to you a golden ring/Would it make you happy, would it make you sing?' She didn't take him up on it, but was deeply touched as well as flattered to have inspired him yet again. 'I'd never realised before how perceptive he could be.'

Life at Hurtwood Edge might seem less and less wonderful for Pattie by night or day, but there were still interludes of fun and fascination when Eric's drinking became merely a part – if not a prerequisite – of rock 'n' roll craziness.

In his stadium-filling superstardom, he still felt the old lure of anonymity, half-wishing to be back at the side of the stage with John Mayall's Bluesbreakers or Delaney & Bonnie's Friends. So it came about on 14 February 1977 that the village hall in Cranleigh, a few miles from Ewhurst, held a St Valentine's dance to the music of 'Eddie the Earthquake and the Tremors'. It was Eric with his band, ahead of another massive world tour, playing old numbers like 'Goodnight Irene' and 'Alberta' and encouraging his stunned audience to dance and join in the choruses.

The worst part of touring for him had always been the

wearying short-haul flights between concerts, so on one European tour, when he was supported by Ronnie Lane's band Slim Chance, Roger Forrester arranged for part of the journey to be by train. Pattie went, too, as did Forrester's wife, Annette, and Lane's wife, Kate. The women had a spot in the show, performing a can-can routine as an opener.

Eric's party occupied three sumptuous Art Deco carriages, once owned by Hitler's deputy, Hermann Goering, which were attached to a succession of modern expresses. One carriage was for eating, one for sleeping, one for hanging out; Cordon Bleu cooks staffed the kitchen and the passengers were awoken each morning with a glass of champagne. A film crew were on board too, shooting a documentary to be entitled *Eric Clapton's Rolling Hotel*.

Also in the retinue was his old friend Ben Palmer, fully recovered from the trauma of being Cream's tour manager and entrusted with receiving and personally guarding the proceeds of each night's show. But Palmer, so often a steadying influence on Eric in the past, could do little to rein him in now.

The train's claustrophobic atmosphere and long periods of inactivity between stops – plus the unlimited champagne – created ideal conditions for the pranks he so enjoyed and in which, as always, he found plenty of willing accomplices. The main victim was a Danish promoter friend of Robert Stigwood's named Erik Thomsen whose attempts to retaliate only spurred his tormentors to greater extremes. Finally, he was thrown off the train in a Hamburg goods-yard at dead of night with his head forcibly shaved and painted blue, the bottoms cut off his trousers, his wallet emptied and his passport defaced.

When Eric grew tired of being interviewed by earnest continental journalists, one of the road crew who resembled him slightly would do them in his place without a single interviewer ever noticing the difference.

After Goering's train came a sea voyage from Cannes to Ibiza, where Eric was to play in the bullring, though in transport of much lesser luxury. Pattie recalls it as 'two tugboats without stabilisers'; during the crossing, a storm of such ferocity blew up that she seriously thought they'd all drown, and threw an SOS message in a bottle over the side. But the Clapton Luck was on watch as usual.

Pattie would also occasionally be included when he met or re-encountered one of the legendary bluesmen he'd worshipped as a boy. 'We once went to Muddy Waters' house and he was sweet. He had an adult-size tricycle that he let me ride.' The best thing about such occasions for her was that Eric, his reverence undiminished, always took care not to be too drunk.

One side-activity of his that she relished, despite its alcoholic element, was a legacy of his year in the Bahamas and friendship with the Irish film producer and screenwriter Kevin McClory. In that era, McClory had staged a 'charity celebrity circus' at his home in County Kildare, featuring some of the major movie names he'd got to know through his James Bond projects. The great director John Huston played ringmaster and Eric appeared as a red-nosed clown – alongside Shirley MacLaine and the first and best Bond, Sean Connery – slamming custard pies into people's faces to his heart's content.

McClory's guest artistes were put up at the Barberstown Castle Hotel in the nearby village of Straffan. It had been converted from a genuine thirteenth-century castle but what most captivated Eric was that on his first visit to the bar, he was not asked to pay for anything during an entire evening.

When the hotel subsequently came up for sale, Roger Forrester decided to buy it. 'Then Eric said to me, "You've got half my racehorses so I want half of the hotel."'

Thus the Barberstown Castle became that dream of every

drunk, his own private pub. He would regularly take groups of his British cronies there for weekends, the hotel reserving all twelve of its bedrooms for their use while keeping the – very good – restaurant open to the public. For Pattie, the only foodie (and only woman) among the drinkers, it was a chance to eat Irish soda bread and learn dishes like devilled kidneys from the chef.

Despite his inclusion of J. J. Cale's 'Cocaine' on *Slowhand* – a live-concert crowd-pleaser ever afterwards – Eric had managed to stay off hard drugs for four years. But the supreme test came when his old Cream bandmates Jack Bruce and Ginger Baker, both of them still habitual users, visited him at Hurtwood at the same time.

'Ginger came and stayed the night and Jack arrived the next day,' Pattie recalls. 'Eric had told me about all their fighting in the band and I dreaded what might happen with the two of them in the house at once. But Eric was the mediator, just like he'd always been.

'Jack soon left – he just struck me as an angry little Scot – but Ginger stayed on. I took a photograph of him playing dice with Eric, looking completely mad. And though he was scary, he was very sweet. I'd got into a terrible muddle with my sewing-machine and all the reels of cotton, so he made me a special board with hooks on it so that I'd know exactly where to find each one.

'The three of us were sitting round, drawing, and Ginger said he thought I ought to try a little bit of heroin. After I did, I needed to throw up and went into the loo, where I fell asleep. I woke up, still sitting there, and thought, "Well, *that's* a boring drug."'

Throughout the Seventies, Robert Stigwood had become increasingly involved in his film and theatre projects and so removed from regular contact with Eric. In 1977, he scored a massive hit with his film *Saturday Night Fever* with a soundtrack by the Bee Gees that transformed the all-too-easily mockable Gibb brothers into supersmooth stars of the new disco era.

Although Eric was perfectly content in Roger Forrester's charge, he still resented the loss of Stigwood's attention and began to harbour dark suspicions about his business dealings. The (never-to-be-shown) *Rolling Hotel* documentary contained an uncomfortable scene in Paris when he'd drunkenly accused Stigwood of using his money to finance *Saturday Night Fever* and so put the Bee Gees in the record-charts above him.

'Robert would go months without seeing Eric or even talking to him,' Forrester recalls. 'Whenever they did have a meeting, he'd have to come to me first and say, "What have you been doing?" I'd say, "Well, we've been in America . . . Australia . . . Japan . . ."'

Forrester, as it happened, was also unhappy in Stigwood's employment, shouldering the huge pressures and responsibilities of running Eric without commensurate financial reward. 'I had a meeting with Eric – it was at Ripley Cricket Club – and told him I wanted to start up on my own. He immediately said, "I'll come with you. Where's your office going to be?" I said, "Guildford." He said, "You can't move from Mayfair to *Guildford*."'

Eric's current contract with the Robert Stigwood Organisation was about to expire, and Stigwood felt sufficient concern to turn up personally at Hurtwood with a new one for his signature. 'Don't leave me alone with him or I'll sign it,' Eric told Nigel Carroll, the newest recruit to his entourage. Stigwood was fobbed off by a pub-crawl around Ripley, then departed without a signature but with a tangible mark of Eric's disfavour.

As farewells were being said in the front drive, the chauffeur of Stigwood's Rolls-Royce Corniche made a slighting remark about Eric's Ferrari collection. 'He said, "Still got those old bangers in the garage?"' Nigel Carroll recalls. 'Eric said, "I'll show you an old banger", and kicked the door of the Corniche so hard, it made a dent.'

So Forrester became an independent manager with just one client. It was agreed that his commission would be 15 per cent, but of Eric's net earnings rather than the usual gross. 'There was no contract between us. He could walk away at any time and so could I. 'Robert was upset with me at the time, but he never bore me any grudge. Anyway, he was so big by that point that losing Eric was just an incidental detail.'

Only when invested with the full powers of Eric's manager did Forrester discover his total lack of interest in his own financial affairs. 'He refused to ever meet with his accountants. At the end of tours, I used to say to him, "Can I tell you how much you've netted?" But it was always "No. Not interested." For thirty, forty years, he never knew how much he'd got. He called it "excess baggage".'

As before, the bills for everything he bought were sent directly to 'the office'. The only money with any reality for him was the weekly £200 in a brown envelope, delivered to him by Gladys Bates, now no longer Stigwood's bookkeeper but Forrester's.

'He did once ask Gladys for a raise,' Forrester recalls. 'She said, "No, Mrs Thatcher won't allow it."'

Cycling apart, sport never seemed to have had much appeal for Eric, but in his late twenties he became interested in both cricket and football. As always with him, interest meant instant, overwhelming obsession.

It was first manifest in cricket, a game at which (unlike fellow rockers such as Mick Jagger and Elton John) he had never possessed the slightest aptitude. Yet before sitting down to watch the Test match on television, he would don immaculate cricketer's 'whites' as if expecting to be called out onto the pitch at any moment.

Even tiny Ewhurst had its own team and he became a regular spectator at home matches. One Saturday when they were playing Ripley, he spotted a familiar face among the enemy fielders. It was his closest childhood friend, Guy Pullen.

They had been born a few houses apart, sat next to each other at primary and secondary school, and Guy had been his first audience out on Ripley Green as he struggled through Big Bill Broonzy songs on his £2 acoustic guitar. Then in the early Sixties they'd lost touch when Eric went to Kingston Art College and Guy began work for Ripley's lord of the manor, Charles Hughesdon, ending up as a broker in Hughesdon's insurance company, Stewart Smith.

'I suddenly heard this voice shout out, "Good God, it's Pullen!"' he recalls. 'We picked up our friendship again as though we'd last seen each other yesterday. And we both still had the same silly sense of humour.' After that came reintroductions to other childhood cronies from around The Green like Stuart Shoesmith and Gordon 'Scratcher' Perrin, and yet more long sessions in pubs. Guy became a regular on drinking weekends at Eric's personal Irish hostelry, the Barberstown Castle Hotel, somehow staggering back to work at Stewart Smith on Monday mornings.

In football, at which he possessed no more skill than at cricket – as Pullen well remembered from their boyhood games – he became a fanatical supporter of West Bromwich Albion, the Birmingham side better known as West Brom, WBA or 'the Baggies'.

He claimed it was because his grandparents, Rose and Jack, had always been West Brom fans; even so, there could hardly have been a more diplomatic gesture to Birmingham after his drunken outburst there in 1976. When not abroad on tour, he seldom missed a home game, wore his blue-and-white supporter's scarf on every possible occasion and had his guitar-picks engraved 'Up the Baggies'.

In November 1978, Nigel Carroll joined the inner Clapton circle of Roger Forrester, bodyguard Alphi O'Leary and Ben Palmer.

Thirty-year-old Carroll had previously worked in real estate and for Terence Conran's Habitat stores; his sole, indirect experience of the music business had been dating Pattie's sister Paula.

The downward spiral for Paula that began when Eric threw her over for Pattie had led to her becoming such 'a raging alcoholic' and heroin-user that Carroll had no choice but to end their relationship. Feeling sorry for him – and because Forrester as a chauffeur lacked almost all sense of direction – Eric offered employment as his driver. 'Roger told me my job was to get him onstage, on time and as sober as possible,' Carroll recalls. 'I managed the first two, but not always the third.'

To be sure, there was now barely a moment in the day when he wasn't drinking. In the limo in which Carroll took him to concerts there was a black box with WBA (for West Bromwich Albion) on its lid, containing a bottle of Courvoisier, a bottle of 7Up and a single cocktail glass. The box was also taken on plane journeys so that he wouldn't have to stop between take-off and the start of drinks service from the trolley.

Carroll's job soon came to include spending weekends at Hurtwood Edge and driving Eric from pub to pub, never letting a drop of alcohol pass his own lips but without seeming a spoilsport. 'I made a deal with the landlord of The Ship in Ripley. "Whenever he orders me a brandy," I said, "just serve me a ginger ale. You can still charge the price of a brandy for it."

'When I stayed at Hurtwood, I always had the same room, above the kitchen. I'd get up at about eight; Eric would be in the study, reading the papers with his brandy and 7Up, and he'd keep topping it up through the day.'

Although Carroll generally found his passenger 'a happy drunk' and 'a lovely fellow', there were occasional disagreements if, say, Eric suggested stopping at a pub when they had a concert deadline to meet or wanted to drive the car himself when manifestly under the influence. 'Then I'd have to say no.

Roger would ring me up afterwards and say, "Don't contact him for a couple of days – he's just fired you." Then the next Friday, Eric would ring and say, "Are you coming for the weekend?"'

Carroll also served as an escort to West Bromwich Albion matches where Eric proudly flaunted his blue-and-white 'Baggies' scarf even though this was an infamous era of violence between rival British soccer fans.

'We once went up by train to see them play Manchester City at home, when they won 1–0. Afterwards as we were leaving, we stopped to buy a hot pie at a stall and the guy who served us said, "You were lucky to get this far." Eric thought he meant in the league and said, "Well, we're number three, man." "No," the guy said, "I meant you were lucky to get so far down this road" [i.e., without being set upon by aggrieved Manchester supporters].

'On the way to the station, we passed a model shop and Eric went in and bought a replica handgun. We're sitting on the train when a Manchester supporter comes through the first-class section and says, "You had a lucky win today." Eric takes out the replica gun, puts it on the table and goes, "*This* says it wasn't."'

Even in those less security-conscious times it was an appallingly silly trick which could have led to bad publicity at the level of his Birmingham rant. But it didn't.

Pattie was no longer invited to go on the road with Eric and had given up hoping to be. She accepted his excuse that he couldn't have any distractions on tour (as if it were all some stern physical and intellectual test, requiring an almost monk-like dedication and solitude), and shut out all thoughts of what he must surely be getting up to, wherever he was.

On these 'stag' tours, there were times when his love of drunken pranks resulted in scenes she was lucky not to have witnessed. Like the night in Honolulu when hotel staff spotted him climbing from his thirtieth-floor room into an adjoining

Hurtwood Edge, Eric's main home since the late 60s:
'like a Tuscan palazzo set down in the Surrey woods'.

(Rex/Shutterstock)

With Alice Ormsby-Gore, 'the frizzy-haired sprite who seemed to
fly into his life from the pages of Lewis Carroll'.

With Delaney & Bonnie and Friends (including George Harrison) onstage in Liverpool, 1969, where George suggested Eric should sleep with Pattie while he himself seduced her younger sister, Paula.

(Camera Press)

Eric and Bobby Whitlock, who lived with him at Hurtwood during the formation of Derek and the Dominos – and to whom he gave an orange Porsche.

(Getty Images)

Pattie gets to grips with the rock 'n' roll life.
Eric would give her quizzes about blues singers.

(Pattie Boyd)

Eric with Roger Forrester, the manager who came closest to being
a surrogate father. Forrester always referred to him as 'the boy'.

Hanging out at Hurtwood:
after Eric had lured away Pattie,
he and George became even
closer – leaving her feeling
excluded.

(Camera Press)

Eric and Pattie's wedding in Tucson, Arizona, 1979:
the result of a bet with his manager over a game of pool.

(Alpha Press)

With Lory Del Santo
at Conor's funeral in
Ripley, when the village
closed ranks to protect
him from the paparazzi.

(AP/Shutterstock)

With Bruce and Baker at Cream's 2005 reunion: 'three sexagenarians with shirts untucked around thickening waists summon back the era of Flower Power'.

(PA Images)

Eric onstage in 2015

(Linda Wnek)

one, clad only in pyjama-bottoms and carrying a Japanese Samurai sword at horrific risk to his genitalia. The idea was to give a passion-killing surprise to his drummer, Jamie Oldaker, who was in bed with a girl picked up after that night's show. Thinking the stealthy figure with the sword was a murderer, she began to scream hysterically and two security guards instantly materialised, pointing handguns at him in the crouch position.

Pattie, meanwhile, resigned herself to the role of stay-at-home 'little woman', consoling herself with their two dogs and Matthew, the donkey she'd bought for Eric. She also began keeping chickens, baffled at first when she kept finding broken eggshells on the ground outside their run. As Hurtwood's gardener/ handyman Arthur Eggby explained, it was a sign of rats cleverly working in pairs: one lay on its back, clutching a stolen egg, while its partner scooped a hole under the chicken-wire and pulled it through by its tail.

During these lengthy periods of rock-widowhood, she was no longer totally isolated. The middle Boyd sister, Jenny, had by now split from Mick Fleetwood – whom she would divorce, remarry, then divorce again – and had settled with their two young daughters in a cottage at Farley Green, only a few minutes away by car.

Despite the sisters' closeness, Jenny hesitated to weigh in too strongly on Pattie's side against Eric for fear of causing additional problems. Her relationship with her brother-in-law had, anyway, never been easy. 'He liked to find your weakness and then play on it,' she recalls. 'Then, when he'd got you in tears, he'd put his arm around you. And you never knew what was going to upset him. I once said that shaking Bob Dylan's hand had felt like a wet fish and he got *so* cross about that.'

He had begun keeping a diary; not just a record of appointments but a large-format journal in which he made entries of three or four hundred words of closely packed italic script without capital letters, each one signed with an elaborate 'EC' and decorated with little line-drawings. They had a spontaneity of which he was seldom capable in real life, veering between anguished soul-searching, attacks of guilt concerning Pattie and anorak chitchat about West Bromwich Albion:

> nelly saw me pouring myself a double brandy and lemonade about mid-morning (while she was talking to her mother on the phone) and gave me the evil eye at which point i promptly slipped over and spilt my drink on friday's page . . .

> my guitars are staring at me and screaming 'play me, play me'. i may be going mad i dream about health and death all the time . . . southampton won against leeds last night, knocking them out of the league cup come on you baggies! . . .

> dear nell whatever you may think of my love, it is there, all the time, and sometimes it makes me do very foolish things pardon me . . .

Pattie was under no illusions about what he got up to on the road, for the evidence had a way of turning up at Hurtwood. One winter day, she answered the door to a young Spanish woman in torn jeans, to whom he'd given his address after some Iberian liaison, then forgotten about. That was almost funny, especially when he suggested insouciantly Pattie might lend the ragged-kneed visitor, Conchita by name, something from her own wardrobe. But it wasn't so funny when the same thing started happening off-road. 'I couldn't bring any of my girlfriends home because Eric would automatically pounce on them.'

She still kept in contact with the couture world she had left to marry George, and took a keen interest in the very different generation of fashion models that had followed hers. During the winter of 1978–9 she got to know the newest sensation on

London's catwalks, a pair of stunning twin sisters named Susie and Jenny McLean. One fateful March day when Eric was home, Jenny came down from London to visit her and stayed so late that she invited her to stay the night.

Next morning when she came downstairs, neither Jenny nor Eric was in the house: they had gone shopping together and then to the pub. Pattie decided to pay a visit to the other Jenny, her sister.

She returned that afternoon to find Jenny McLean and a very drunk Eric sitting close together on a sofa, he smitten by another of his instant, apocalyptic infatuations. When Pattie tried to speak to Jenny, he rounded on her furiously for intruding. 'Can't you see I'm in love with this girl and I'm courting her? Go away and leave us alone.'

Pattie fled upstairs and sat on her bed, in shock. One-night stands with nameless groupies in faraway places were one thing. But this exactly recreated the humiliation George had visited on her with a supposed friend of hers in her own home – indeed, George's dalliance with Ringo's wife now seemed almost discreet by comparison. 'Eric thought there was nothing wrong in it because we weren't married.'

She phoned her sister Jenny, who at once drove over from Farley Green to pick her up but, ever wary of Eric, did not come to the house or even approach too near. Without any further words with him, Pattie ran out into pouring rain and got into Jenny's car at the end of the drive.

Eric's diary-entry the next day gave his version of the scene after describing having got up at noon and been 'freaked out' by the strong wind blowing through the Hurtwood forests:

> i lost nell i asked her to go away and she left without a word i
> tried to find her but i don't think she wants to be found . . . i do
> love jen and now i realise how much i worry about nell . . .

The following day's entry was headlined by its most important event in his eyes: 'wba v red star [Belgrade] uefa cup away':

> *no word from nell yet and I'm shaking so hard that I can hardly hold the pen . . . jen called me and said she was going mad roger called to tell me that wba lost one-nil*

He made little attempt to find out where Pattie was; by the time she felt equal to phoning him, a week later, he'd recovered from his attack of remorse and simply said they could both do with 'a bit of a break'. He admitted that Jenny McLean was still there.

Pattie had gone to Los Angeles to stay with a record producer friend, Rob Fraboni, and his wife, Myel. On the journey, she'd cried so much that a flight attendant asked her to move to the back of the first-class cabin because she was upsetting the other passengers.

Meanwhile, Eric's affair continued with the fashion-model twin his diary now called 'sweet jen'. He travelled to Ireland for some concerts and on 17 March – Pattie's birthday – recorded that

> *the gig was great and sweet jen flew in to make the day perfect we talked and talked about our respective wounds . . . i am a bad man and i think the world better roll on without me for a while anyway all in love is fair.*

Pattie herself was convinced their relationship had ended and resigned herself to never seeing him again, maybe even staying in America for good. Then on 23 March, she awoke to find that Eric had telephoned her host, Rob Fraboni, in the middle of the night and asked Fraboni to give her a message. It was that he wanted to marry her and needed an immediate answer, otherwise she could 'get on her bike'.

This most unromantic of proposals sprang from no great resurgence of love on Eric's part but from a pool game between

Roger Forrester and him a couple of days earlier. Forrester had warned that if he were not more circumspect about the affair with Jenny McLean, his long immunity from the paparazzi might come to an end. Eric, in humble mode, had denied being that newsworthy and the argument had somehow ended with him drunkenly betting £10,000 that Forrester couldn't get his name into a national paper the following day.

Forrester had immediately contacted the *Daily Mail*'s gossip columnist, Nigel Dempster, with the pure fiction that Eric was to marry Pattie in Tucson, Arizona, at the start of his next American tour the following week. Next morning, the story featured prominently on Dempster's page.

When Eric saw it, he drove to Forrester's office in a fury, his mood not helped by two *Daily Mail* readers, a petrol-pump attendant and a pub landlord congratulating him on his imminent nuptials en route.' 'He came storming in when I was having a meeting, picked up a phone and whacked it down on my head,' Forrester recalls. 'Split it open actually.'

Staunching a bloody comb-over, Forrester not only managed to pacify him but to convince him it was time matters with Pattie were resolved one way or another and he might as well go ahead with the wedding as advertised and get his proposal in to Pattie before she saw the *Mail* story.

Pattie herself was understandably dumbfounded by his change of tone since she'd last seen him and far from enchanted by the 'get on your bike' line. But when he repeated the proposal to her directly over the phone, phrased a little more alluringly, and swore that the thing with Jenny McLean was now over, she accepted.

'Why did I go for it? I was still so mad about him that I deluded myself into thinking he'd realised I was the only woman he wanted to be with. It wasn't until later that I found out it had all come from a game of pool between Roger and him.'

Eric's diary-entry for 23 March contained a drastically edited account of the episode:

proposed to nell . . . and she said yes even when i told her that always id be a bad boy

20

'GOD BLESS OUR WEDLOCK'

Eric and Pattie were married on 27 March 1979, in Tucson, Arizona, as Roger Forrester had pre-ordained. To reduce the risk of intrusive media, Forrester had booked several churches for the ceremony, only at the last minute choosing the modest redbrick Apostolic Assembly of Faith in Jesus Christ. A Mexican cleric, Pastor Daniel Sanchez, officiated, assisted by a black organist bearing an uncanny resemblance to Billy Preston.

Traditionally, bridegrooms are not allowed to see their brides on the wedding-eve, but when Pattie arrived from Los Angeles she found herself firmly kept apart from Eric. They had separate rooms at the equally no-frills Sheraton Pueblo Hotel and his driver/PA, Nigel Carroll, acted as go-between.

As usual, everything had been arranged to spare him the smallest effort. Arizona law required that he take a blood test for venereal diseases, rubella or genetic disorders. Because he was so terrified of needles, his vaguely lookalike assistant who'd impersonated him for interviews on the 1977 European tour took the blood test for him, once again with nobody noticing any difference. The wedding-rings, two plain gold bands, were purchased by Carroll from a local mall.

Pattie went to the altar in a cream silk-satin dress with a lace jacket, while Eric wore a black-braided white suit, cowboy boots and a $200 Stetson. Roger Forrester gave the bride away, Rob Fraboni was best man, Pattie's sister Jenny was matron of honour and Carroll and Eric's bodyguard, Alphi O'Leary, were ushers. His band and road crew all attended, wearing hired tuxedos in a variety of garish colours set off by scruffy trainers as they'd forgotten to hire matching shoes.

Afterwards, there was a small reception at the Sheraton Pueblo and the newlyweds posed for a local photographer in front of their multi-tiered wedding cake. Bored by this over-lengthy ritual, Eric threw a piece of cake at the photographer, spattering the camera with white icing. It was the signal for one of the food fights so dear to his heart.

His diary-entry that night was headed WE ARE WED and accompanied by a little sketch of Pattie and himself:

> i married nell today, hurrah . . . it was a beautiful wedding . . .
> the bash was unbelievable – what more can i say – god bless our
> wedlock

As he was starting a tour the next day, Pattie accepted there could be no honeymoon. Far more important than that, he wanted her with him on the road again.

At the opening show in Albuquerque she watched from the wings, his guitar not only flooding her with desire, as of old, but smoothing away the pain and humiliation of his blatant affair with Jenny McLean. Halfway through, he called her onstage and sang 'Wonderful Tonight' to her like a confirmatory wedding vow as the audience sent up waves of envious felicitation. It was the same the next night in El Paso and the next in Dallas.

Then as they headed for New Orleans, he suddenly announced that he wanted her to fly back to Los Angeles, pick up the luggage she'd left at Rob Fraboni's and return to England. He gave no reason but, anxious not to spoil the new loving atmosphere, she didn't argue.

The reason was that, after only a couple of days of married life, he'd contacted Jenny McLean and asked her to come out and join him. The changeover was tight, his wife's flight taking off and his twin-model lover's touching down within minutes of one another. 'I took Pattie to the airport and brought Jenny back to the hotel in the same trip,' Nigel Carroll recalls.

Even on a travelling rock show where considerateness towards women was seldom a high priority, Eric's treatment of Pattie caused outrage. 'There was a total rebellion,' Carroll recalls. 'The band, the road crew, everyone said, "This is not right . . . this is not fair," and Roger was really upset.'

It was a severe shock for someone so long accustomed to doing whatsoever he pleased without incurring so much as a raised eyebrow – all his life, in fact – but for the good of the tour he capitulated. Jenny stayed just one night, then went home.

Back in Britain, Pattie threw her energies into organising a proper wedding party, which took place at Hurtwood Edge during a break in the tour, on 19 May. All the greatest names in British rock attended, along with Eric's family and Ripley cronies; there were two marquees, an outdoor stage and dance floor and quantities of food and alcohol that would have amazed Jay Gatsby.

The party was Roger Forrester's gift to Eric, with security provided by the many contacts Forrester still had in the old Kray organisation. As Eric walked down the drive, a man with a sawn-off shotgun popped out of a bush and demanded that he identify himself.

The sole exception to the celebratory mood was Cream's bass-player, Jack Bruce, who still felt resentful about his treatment in the band and took it out even on the guiltless Pattie. 'As he came in, he hissed at me, "You know what's the matter with you? You're not nearly as good as your sister [Paula]." He meant that because Paula was on heroin, she was in the cool club and I wasn't.'

The highlight of the afternoon was an orchestra-size jam session including Mick Jagger, Bill Wyman, Ronnie Wood, Robert

Plant, Jeff Beck, and George Harrison, Paul McCartney and Ringo Starr, playing live together in public for the first time since the Beatles' break-up. Earlier, John Lennon had phoned from New York to wish the newlyweds luck, and said he too would have come to the party if he'd known about it, possibly creating the Beatles' only full onstage reunion. However, the star of the show was Lonnie Donegan, whose skiffle music had first ignited British boys' love affair with the guitar. 'They wouldn't let him off the stage,' Guy Pullen recalls.

Sitting with Eric's closest family, Rose, his uncle Adrian and aunt Sylvia, was an unfamiliar woman with auburn hair and a slightly hawk-like face to whom he seemed to be paying particular attention. It was his mother.

After thirty-five years of seeming contentment in her marriage Pat had left her Canadian husband, Frank McDonald, and returned from Canada to the son she'd left behind when he was two. This time, it was not the customary visit of a few weeks: she was back for good, accompanied by Heather, the younger of her two daughters with McDonald, now aged twenty-six.

The geographical distance between her and Eric may have been greatly reduced but the emotional one scarcely was. Having given birth to him at sixteen, Pat was still not yet fifty and hardly looked capable of having a son in his mid-thirties. Although Eric introduced her as 'my mum', he went on calling her Pat and she still behaved more like his older sister. That lie on which he'd been brought up remained inescapable.

The trait that mother and son most definitely shared was partiality to alcohol, and this became the lubricant of their relationship. Pat joined what Pattie called Eric's 'drinking team', along with Guy Pullen, 'Scratcher' Perrin and whichever band-members happened to be around, revelling in the company of so many good-looking younger men and flirting shamelessly with them all. This persona made her very little like a mother-in-law to Pattie, and certainly no kind of competitor. 'She was great fun and could be very witty in a rather sharp-tongued way. I always thought she liked me, but perhaps that was just a way for her to be accepted by Eric. She needed me on her side.'

Pattie had hoped that now, at long last, Eric and Pat would would be able to sit down and talk about her desertion of him as a two-year-old and the reasons behind it, thereby finding the intimacy that had always eluded them. 'There was a certain closeness through alcohol, but they never had a proper talk – a *sober* talk.' Once or twice, Pattie herself tried to broach the subject, but was firmly rebuffed. 'She'd never go there.'

Numerous colour snapshots, mostly taken in pubs, show Eric arm-in-arm with Pat, seemingly the picture of filial pride. But, as Pattie recalls, he never really lost that wounded child's stored-up hurt and anger. 'There was always a moment when he put the brakes on. He never allowed her into his heart.'

Still, he was generous to her and his half-sister Heather, as they adjusted to their new life. 'He bought Pat a car, a VW Beetle,' Guy Pullen recalls. 'He had it parked in the drive at Hurtwood, ready to give her, but he left the handbrake off and it rolled down the slope and hit a wall. So he was "Here's your present but I'm afraid one wing's dented."'

Pat was never likely to lack male admirers and, before long, moved in with Scratcher Perrin's bachelor uncle Sid whom she'd gone out with when they were in their teens, before she became a teenage unmarried mother. Since Sid Perrin was one of Ripley's best-known figures, that meant a homecoming almost back to the place she'd started out from in 1947. His cottage in Newark Lane was just behind the little house on Ripley Green where she'd given birth to Eric.

Sid had been Eric's boyhood hero before any bluesman with his legendary capacity for booze, his fund of hilarious stories,

above all his impassioned vocal performances for the delecta-
tion of his fellow drinkers. Even now, he symbolised everything
about Ripley that the international megastar remembered most
fondly: a beamingly tipsy man getting up on Saturday night in a
smoke-filled British Legion club and launching into Mario Lanza's 'Cara Mia' while Rick and his gang listened outside with
their bottles of Stansfields pop and bags of crisps.

Eric's British tours always included an extra, unadvertised
show at Guildford's Civic Hall for which the Ripley crowd
turned out en bloc. 'At one of them, he got Sid up onstage to
sing,' Guy Pullen recalls. 'It was "In A Monastery Garden", complete with all the bird noises. While Sid was doing it, Eric and the
band gradually backed away, leaving him alone in the spotlight.'

Eric was therefore delighted when Pat got together with Sid
– though at times he himself seemed less so. 'She had a sharp
tongue and was very unpredictable. Any little thing you said
could upset her,' Eric's aunt Sylvia recalls. 'And she and Sid used
to have terrible rows. He'd sometimes come round to our house,
saying, *"Please*, tell her to go home" [i.e. to Canada].'

She took a part-time job at Ripley's Ye Olde Sweet Shop – still
run by Miss Bush, as it had been during Eric's boyhood – where
she revealed a love of practical jokes similar to her son's. 'A group
of us went up to watch the cricket at Lord's one time and took a
packed lunch,' Pullen says. 'When Sid opened the sandwiches Pat
had made him, they were Cheddar cheese and red jelly babies.'

Eric entered the 1980s with his business affairs in excellent shape,
ironically thanks to his old bugbears, the Bee Gees.

Despite his perennial gripe about Robert Stigwood giving
them preferential treatment, the Gibb brothers and he were
signed to Stigwood's publishing company by similar agreements
under which they gave up their song-copyrights and received
only minimal royalties. This used to be known as 'standard

industry practice', although a more accurate term might have been theft.

At the end of the 1970s, the Bee Gees had begun litigation to recover their copyrights – now hugely enriched by the *Saturday Night Fever* film soundtrack – on the grounds that Stigwood's dual role as a manager and publisher represented a conflict of interest. Thanks to an astute British lawyer named Michael Eaton, their entire back-catalogue had reverted to them without the necessity of a hugely expensive and risky court case.

By the time Roger Forrester took over as Eric's manager, Stigwood had all but quit the pop business, having sold his management and recording interests to PolyGram and his publishing business to Chappell. Now retained by Forrester, Michael Eaton repeated his Bee Gees strategy, notifying Chappell that Eric's publishing agreement with Stigwood had also amounted to a conflict of interest and threatening legal action unless his songbook was made over to him, too. There was a measure of bluff involved as Eaton already knew Eric well enough to suspect he would shy away from the expense and uncertainty of actually going to court.

However, Chappell's president, Nick Firth, took the view that more would be gained by keeping Eric with the company. An out-of-court settlement was reached, giving him the rights to all his past songs, as well as those of future ones at an increased royalty, in return for supplying Chappell with twenty new works over the next five years.

British pop's two greatest songwriting partnerships, Lennon–McCartney and Jagger–Richards, had both suffered a decade of vast legal fees and drawn-out court hearings in vain pursuit of the same objective. Yet Eric's people had pulled it off for him without so much as a writ being served.

Live performances, sadly, were another story, for by 1980 his drink-problem was well known in every country where he appeared and his audience braced for disappointment in many languages. ERIC CLAPTON TOO DRUNK TO PLAY said a headline in a Munich newspaper after his performance there was cancelled – unjustly, for once, as the problem had been purely technical.

He usually walked onstage with a glass in his hand and kept drinking throughout the show, growing more and more bellig-erent towards the dissatisfied shouts his playing provoked. One heckler who told him with wounding accuracy 'You just keep relying on your past, mate' was invited to step up onstage and get filled in.

At another UK show, he had to leave the stage after forty-five minutes for fear of falling off it. Pete Townshend – so often his conscience in the past – happened to be guesting with his band that night and furiously berated him for unprofessionalism. Chastened, he went back on again and got through the rest of the show by miming to Townshend's singing and playing.

Pattie could only look on with dismay each far-from-wonderful night when he came to bed with a pint glass of Courvoisier and 7Up, drank himself to sleep and started sipping whatever was left the moment he awoke. He was getting through two bottles a day in addition to all the beer he downed with his drinking team.

As she had discovered, getting him away from Ewhurst and into seemingly healthier climes made little difference. Wherever they went, there were always people who enjoyed seeing him get drunk or saw some advantage or profit in it.

When they first got together, they'd spent what promised to be an idyllic holiday in Jamaica, staying at 'Goldeneye', the former home of James Bond's creator, Ian Fleming. 'Every morning, the gardener would arrive with a huge spliff for Eric, then take him off to a so-called tea room which sold rum by the mugful. By evening, he would have passed out and the butler would say to me, "Dinner for one again?"'

She suspected the house was being cased for a break-in and would lie awake each night with a harpoon-gun for protection while Eric snored, oblivious, beside her.

What worried her most was the rate at which alcohol was using up his seeming nine lives. During a holiday in the Greek Islands, they'd had dinner on Robert Stigwood's yacht, then a more than usually plastered Eric insisted on driving the tender boat back to shore. Thanks to the Clapton Luck, they collided with no other craft, but then back in harbour, stepping from one boat to another, he fell into the water and sank like a stone. Pattie managed to grab one of his arms and hold on until help arrived.

At other times, booze could literally be a life-saver. Whenever his mind turned to suicide, as it often did, what held him back was the thought that if he were dead, he'd no longer be able to drink.

Yet he still fiercely rejected any suggestion that he was any more than someone who 'liked a drink', like Ripley's saloon-bar Colossus, Sid Perrin. 'I couldn't see the end of it,' Pattie recalls. 'I kept thinking and believing and hoping that one day he'd stop drinking and be sober and life would be as it should be.'

In desperation, she turned to the drinking team's leading members, Guy Pullen and Eric's mother, for help in somehow cutting down his intake. 'We used to have meetings about it,' Pullen recalls. Eric's oldest friend recognised the problem and agreed to do what he could. 'Pat wasn't so passionate about the idea,' Pattie says, 'because drinking was the basis of her relationship with Eric.'

Lately, another local pub had come into his ken with a pull stronger than The Windmill at his front gate or even Ripley's Ship. This was The Parrot at Forest Green, owned by Gary Brooker, keyboard-player for Procol Harum and the lead voice on their Bach-inflected, gloriously nonsensical greatest hit 'A Whiter Shade Of Pale'.

Under Brooker's proprietorship, the pub put on regular music nights with an informal Parrot Band featuring musician friends like Ronnie Lane, Andy Fairweather-Low and Dave Mattacks, at £1 per head including food. Between tours, Eric often sat in with them, relishing the anonymity almost as much as the free beer he received.

Although born in London's East End, Brooker had turned himself into a thoroughgoing countryman, establishing a small farm alongside The Parrot and becoming one of the most expert dry-fly fishermen in Surrey. When he talked about fishing, Eric pictured the kind the Ripley Green boys used to do with bent pins in the River Wey. Brooker then explained how fly-fishing for trout or salmon was not mere angling but a battle of wits with canny creatures that only the most skilfully-cast artificial flies could deceive.

Eric decided to give it a try, although for him that still meant ordering a full set of rods and creels from London's most famous dealer, Hardy's of Pall Mall. His first outings were to the lake behind Hurtwood Edge, whose inhabitants, while neither salmon nor trout, proved canny enough. 'At first, he kept complaining that he didn't catch anything,' Nigel Carroll recalls. 'He told me he'd buy a fish from a shop in Cranleigh, take it home and tell Pattie he'd caught it.'

He was instantly hooked, nonetheless, by the peace and solitude, the male camaraderie, timeless etiquette and subtle, cut-throat competitiveness of the riverbank. Gary Brooker showed him how to cast a fly on the pub lawn and he practised it as obsessively as he once had Muddy Waters licks.

Casting of a different sort became an issue when George Terry left his backing band after four years as back-up guitarist and vocalist. Terry's successor, Albert Lee, was no mere sideman but a virtuoso soloist, albeit in the country-picking mode of Chet

Atkins and Jerry Reed, who had always been seen as one of Eric's main British rivals.

Amiable though the tiny, tangly-haired Albert was, he proved a disruptive influence, for he shared Eric's love of zany English humour, the Goons and Monty Python, like nobody since Cream's Pete Brown. Unfortunately, it was lost on the remaining Americans, the so-called Tulsa guys, Carl Radle, Dick Sims and Jamie Oldaker. The band became increasingly divided along laughter-lines until Eric ordered the firing of the Tulsa guys by telegram while he himself 'looked the other way'.

To replace them, he hired three top London session musicians, keyboard-player Chris Stainton, bassist Dave Markee and drummer Henry Spinetti (brother of the actor Victor), so creating the first all-British line-up he'd played in since Blind Faith. Gary Brooker took a sabbatical from pub-keeping to join up as well, which meant the band now had two vocalists and two keyboard men as well as two lead guitarists; it was a supergroup in fact, although no one mentioned the word.

The new line-up was broken in on a mammoth world tour starting in November 1979 at Cranleigh Village Hall and going on to Eastern Europe, Israel, Thailand, Hong Kong and Japan. As ready as ever to share applause, Eric allowed both of his distinguished recruits their own spot in the show: Gary Brooker performed 'A Whiter Shade Of Pale' and Albert Lee gave a dazzling display of fasthandedness alone in the spotlight.

Unusually for him, he felt lingering guilt over dropping Carl Radle, who'd offered him his first way back into music from heroin-addiction. In May 1980, Radle died of kidney-failure brought on by drug- and alcohol-abuse, aged thirty-seven. It sent Eric into a black mood, both self-reproaching and self-pitying, which he sought to palliate in the usual way.

Then on 9 December at Hurtwood, his gardener/handyman, Arthur Eggby, had to answer an early-morning phone call since no one else was up yet. 'There was a voice saying, "I'm a state policeman calling from New York with a message for Eric Clapton,"' Eggby recalls. '"I regret to tell you that John Lennon has been shot." I said is he OK and the policeman said, "He's dead, shot five times!"'

Eggby delayed breaking the news to Eric until he woke in the early afternoon – he and Pattie had slept in separate rooms after a row – and emerged stark naked, as was his wont, for his first cigarette of the day.

'I had prepared two glasses of brandy, one for him and one for me, and I said, "Take a sip of this. You're going to need it!" He didn't take it in at first, then he shouted, "Arthur, I don't want to see you again today. You've brought me bad news . . . You've brought me very bad news." Then he went back inside and slammed the door and that was the last anyone saw of him for hours.'

In March 1981, he took the new band on a fifty-eight-date American tour to promote their first album, *Another Ticket*, little dreaming how quickly it would lead to a return one.

For some time he had been suffering from severe back pain – the result, so he thought, of a too-hearty thump between the shoulderblades from one of his Irish drinking buddies at the Barberstown Castle Hotel – and was taking a codeine-based analgesic called Veganin. Nigel Carroll carried what was intended to be the tour's whole supply, along with the usual five bottles of Courvoisier and 3,000 Rothmans cigarettes. By the end of the first week, Eric had run through almost all of it and the effect was rapidly diminishing.

In Madison, Wisconsin, a doctor had to be called to give him an injection to get him through that night's performance. When he came offstage, he collapsed in agony and was taken to hospital in the nearest large city, Minneapolis. He was released after

X-rays appeared to show a shadow on his lung; then the hospital revised its diagnosis to five bleeding ulcers, one 'the size of a small orange'.

Roger Forrester wanted to fly him straight back to Britain, but doctors warned that one of the ulcers was pressing on his pancreas and could burst at any moment. He was rushed back to hospital in Minneapolis and put on an IV machine 'forty-five minutes from death' according to one of the resuscitation team. 'A doctor was looking down his throat with a camera on a tube,' Forrester recalls. 'Then he handed another one to me and said, "Here, you have a look." I was looking right into Eric's stomach. I could actually see the ulcers, all red-raw.'

Forrester had no choice but to cancel all the tour's remaining forty-seven sold-out dates, causing such insurance losses that Lloyd's of London rang the famous Lutine bell that normally signals major disasters at sea. Pattie was sent for and Nigel Carroll and Alphi O'Leary kept a round-the-clock watch over Eric, taking turns to sleep in a room next to his.

He stayed in hospital for six weeks, being treated with the ulcer-healing drug Tagamet. Hundreds of get-well cards poured in, local radio stations broadcast regular bulletins on his condition and the now-valueless tour-merchandise was given away. As he recovered, he was allowed supervised forays around Minneapolis, where his first act was to look for a fishing-tackle store. He found one, bought twenty-five rods and practised casting in the hospital corridors.

To complete his recovery, his doctors recommended a fishing-trip, so Forrester and Pattie returned to Britain and Carroll drove him to Seattle in a Winnebago stocked with fishing tackle, a tent and a canoe. The results were hardly recuperative. In Seattle, Eric went out to dinner with friends, but he walked out in a huff, cadging a lift from a young woman who'd been at their table. Chauffeuring Eric Clapton made her so nervous that she ran a red light and was broadsided by a taxi. He suffered bruised ribs and ended up back in hospital in Minneapolis, additionally diagnosed with pleurisy.

From there he wrote to Pattie, begging her to come back in terms that melted her heart all over again:

> *you are the only one i can truly rely*
> *on for strength and cheer and you*
> *can spend as much money as you like*
> *while you wait for me to mend*

During his numerous medical consultations, the subject of his drinking inevitably came up. But because medication had temporarily killed his desire for alcohol, none of his American doctors realised the scale of the problem. When he returned home, he made a stab at moderation, to placate Pattie, but was soon back to his old level. One thing he'd been told categorically in Minneapolis was that he mustn't drink two bottles of brandy per day. So he switched to two bottles of whisky or vodka.

The rest of 1981 brought several further grave warnings about what he was doing to himself, all of them similarly not taken to heart.

First, Sid Perrin, his exemplar of bar-room glamour since boyhood – now his mother's partner, so his unofficial stepfather – died aged only sixty. Though the cause was bowel cancer, which Sid's lifetime of drinking had left him ill-equipped to fight the disease. His protracted decline, which included undergoing a colostomy, wiped out all the ebullience that once seemed so magical to a fatherless small boy; when Eric last saw him, with Pat, he was hallucinating and talking to pub companions who weren't there. But, rather than take warning, Eric made a point of getting smashed at the wake with his uncle

Adrian because, he told himself, 'Sid would have wanted it.'

Then, on a visit to Japan, he returned to his hotel-room to find a well-wisher had sent him a bottle of sake with flakes of pure gold floating in it. Downing the whole bottle by himself at one sitting, he came out in a horrendous rash that made his skin flake off like a leper's.

Pattie's efforts to keep temptation out of his way could have even more frightening consequences. That autumn, they spent a weekend with friends in Rutland whom she had forewarned to make every meal alcohol-free. Eric passed out at the dinner table and woke up in an ambulance, having suffered a 'grand mal' caused by a sudden cessation of drinking while not under medical supervision. Admitted to the Wellington hospital in north London, he was found to have a late-occurring form of epilepsy.

The film footage of him in this era is harrowing. At one moment, he's seen sitting on the ground in a cowboy hat, clutching a bottle: the archetypal down-and-out amid all his millions and minions. His eyes meet the camera, so full of quiet desperation that one almost forgets it is wholly self-inflicted.

Pop music history is littered with stories of stars drinking or drugging themselves to death, surrounded by highly paid entourages who don't lift a finger to help them. But the care Eric received from Roger Forrester now became literally parental. During stays in hotels – the location of choice for such 'deaths by misadventure' – a baby alarm was put beside his bed so that during the night Forrester or Alphi O'Leary or Nigel Carroll could check that he was still breathing.

Rather than this holding operation, Pattie wanted him to have a course of treatment for alcoholism, an idea she thought Forrester resisted because of the disruption to business. She discovered differently at a Genesis concert that December, when they both tried but failed to box Eric in to prevent him getting to the bar. During these few minutes' privacy, Forrester said he'd booked him on such a course in the New Year but didn't want to break the news until after Christmas.

Many guests had been invited to Hurtwood Edge that holiday season but midnight on Christmas Eve found him alone and drunk beside the tree Pattie had decorated with her usual splendour. Loath as ever to wait for anything or anyone, he began opening his share of the presents beneath it. Among these was the one thing lacking in his store of fishermen's requisites, a set of thermal underwear, which he decided to try on then and there.

On Christmas morning, Pattie awoke to find his side of the bed empty. As lunchtime approached and still there was no sign of him, enlightenment came from Arthur Eggby: 'We started on the brandy a bit early . . . you'll find him on the logs.'

She went to the cellar and found Eric sprawled on the log-pile, still wearing his new thermals and alternately laughing and weeping. Taking a firm line that was never more overdue, she banned him from the festivities and locked him in the bedroom, bringing him food and just enough drink to keep him sedated.

The next day, having absorbed another skinful, he went to the River Wey in the new thermals to fish for pike. On the opposite bank were two hardcore anglers with a tent who'd clearly been there all Christmas. He set out to impress them but, unfortunately, did the opposite, drunkenly stumbling onto one of his delicate Hardy rods and breaking it in two at the handle.

True to the riverbank's taciturn code, the other fishermen's only reaction was an exchange of embarrassed looks. Yet for Eric it was a humiliation worse than any he'd ever brought on himself in front of larger audiences. In that moment, he finally recognised that he didn't just 'like a drink', but was a full-blown alcoholic in desperate need of help.

21

MADE IN MONTSERRAT

On 7 January 1982, he and Roger Forrester took a Northwest Airlines flight back to Minneapolis, where bleeding ulcers had almost killed him a year earlier. He'd been given only a day's notice of departure and, at the outset, had no idea where he was going. In a final fling before the bar closed for ever, he drank the plane almost dry.

His destination was the Hazelden Foundation, a non-profit treatment centre a few miles outside Minneapolis. It proved to be a Gothic-looking mansion surrounded by drab grey concrete blocks reminiscent of a low-security prison, looking all the bleaker under a thick covering of snow. When Elvis Presley had been brought here in the 1970s, he'd taken one look and refused to get out of his limo.

Eric was booked in as a resident patient for an initial six-week period following which, if insufficiently responsive to treatment, he would be moved to the clinic's psychiatric unit. Forrester's plan had been simply to drop him there, then return to London. But during the registration process – when Eric gave his manager's rather than his wife's name as the person to contact in an emergency – it transpired that Forrester's reliance on Valium, mostly to allow him to sleep on plane journeys, put him, too, into the addict class.

'So they booked me in as well,' he recalls, 'even though I only had the clothes I stood up in. There were different units for different kinds of addiction. Eric went into the booze unit and I went into the pills unit. For the whole six weeks, they kept us completely segregated. We could say "Hello" if we passed each other in the corridor but we weren't allowed to socialise.'

Since, as Eric already knew, sudden total withdrawal from alcohol could have dire physical consequences, he spent his first forty-eight hours in the hospital wing receiving heavy doses of librium. He'd been asked for a list of everything he was already taking, but hadn't liked to admit to sharing Forrester's Valium habit, regarding it as 'a woman's drug'. This macho conceit so unbalanced his medication that he suffered another frightening 'grand mal' seizure.

Hazelden operated Alcoholics Anonymous's Twelve-Step Programme, which is as much psychological and spiritual as medical, demanding total frankness on the sufferer's part – as in the obligatory self-introduction 'Hi, I'm so-and-so and I'm an alcoholic' – and recognition of a 'higher power' as an indispensable part of overcoming it.

The inmates were divided into single-sex units of twenty-eight, each a self-contained, mutually supportive community named after a pioneer of the Twelve-Step Programme. Eric was not allowed to take a guitar into his Silkworth unit and found that here his celebrity meant nothing; they were all simply fellow victims, characterised only by the histories of their addictions.

Not the least shock was having to share a room, something he hadn't done – at least, not with a man – since Yardbird days. But his room-mate, a New York fireman known only as Tommy, didn't know who he was and didn't care. '[Tommy] was only concerned with the way we connected on a personal level and I had no idea how to do that because I was either above or below everybody,' he would recall in hindsight. 'I was either towering above as Clapton the guitar virtuoso or cringing on the floor because if you took away my guitar and my musical career, then I was nothing.'

To begin with, his fellow patients looked after him; then he had to do his share of the chores, cleaning up and making his own bed for the very first time in his life. Any neglect of these duties brought a severe reprimand (another 'first' for him) from a group leader known as 'the Pig Master'.

So packed with lectures and activities was each day that he went to bed exhausted and so, for the first time in years, could drop off to sleep without a beaker of brandy or vodka. Yet, like an amputee who can still feel a vanished limb, he continued to wake in the morning feeling drunk.

The most difficult part for him were the group therapy sessions, where one was encouraged to spare no detail of the ruin one had suffered – and caused. 'I had never learned to look honestly at myself – in fact, to protect my drinking it was important not to do that,' he would recall. 'Lying and deflection had become second nature to me.'

To help patients face the truth about themselves, questionnaires had been sent to their wives or partners. Pattie had completed one and part of Eric's therapy was to read it aloud, which reduced him to tears. 'That broke my heart. I was made to understand that I'd behaved like an animal.'

Such moments apart, he began to enjoy what was in effect a complete rest from all the pampered agonies of being Eric Clapton. The dormant student in him lapped up the lectures, often given by highly distinguished doctors or scientists, and he had many fascinating conversations with fellow inmates, some of them far worse cases than himself on their fourth or fifth spell at Hazelden. He saw how many drugs were smuggled into the anti-booze citadel on its weekly family-visitation days, but felt no pull in that direction and, anyway, had nobody to supply him.

Elsewhere, too, Hazelden's vigilance proved fallible. Male and

female patients were totally segregated with even social inter-
course between them strictly forbidden. However, Eric managed
to convince the management that he needed a private room and
subsequently found several nocturnal companions more rewarding than a drying-out fireman.

Pattie, who was enrolled in AA's Al-Anon organisation for the
wives and partners of alcoholics, flew out to spend five days on
the course with him. In group discussions, she found it far easier
than he had to share experiences that had previously been bot-
tled up, and the clinic's atmosphere so calmed and reassured her
that she didn't want to return home.

After alternating fits of despair and rebellion, Eric was by now
determined to finish his treatment in the allotted time and so
avoid the disgrace of the psychiatric unit. His innate competitiveness kicking in, he refused to join those many who gave up
and discharged themselves prematurely. One wealthy inmate
had his wife land a helicopter in an adjacent field and disappeared
overnight.

He applied his newly clear head to strategic thinking, working out just what responses his counsellors most wanted from
him and supplying them. In group discussions, he became adept
at turning the counsellor's attention away from his problems to
other people's, so adding to the image of steady progress. As a
result, he received his discharge bang on time, with a certificate
and medallion warranting him to be clean. But not permanently,
as it would prove.

On his return home, Pattie found him quiet, introverted and 'a
bit too clean, like he'd been through the drycleaners a few too
many times'. Ironically, one of the first things that happened to
him back in Surrey was being stopped by the police and breathalysed, which he'd avoided for all those years of drink-driving.

Hazelden had arranged aftercare in the form of a 'sponsor'

named David who lived in Dorking. (Under AA rules, two people constitute a quorum for a meeting.) But David's was a lone voice in a world seemingly united in a beckoning, winking, rib-nudging campaign to lure him back to the bottle.

Pattie had cleared all hard liquor from the house, but no one at Hazelden had told her she should stop drinking, too, and a size-able stock of wine, which he didn't normally care for, remained in the cellar. Hardest of all to resist was the rosy embrace of the pub. His 'drinking team', Guy Pullen, Scratcher Perrin and the rest, had all been solidly behind his quest for sobriety, but could hardly be expected to turn teetotal in sympathy. Rather than have to sip orange juice while they sank pints, he cut himself off from them completely. 'I didn't see him for the next couple of months,' Pullen recalls. 'But l realised it was the only way.'

Not everyone was so understanding. The first Saturday after his return, a regular drinking buddy stopped by to collect him for the time-honoured morning session. When Eric explained the situation, his visitor shouted, 'Fuck you then', and drove off.

His driver/PA, Nigel Carroll, who hadn't been with him in Minnesota, was amazed at the transformation. 'Whenever I went to Hurtwood, he'd always open the front door with a brandy in his hand. When I caught hepatitis and had to stop drinking, it would be a large port and brandy – that was his idea of a joke. Now when I arrived, he said, "Do you fancy a cup of tea?"'

Carroll realised that the clinic partly blamed Eric's manage-ment team for his addiction when in fact they'd been largely responsible for keeping him alive through its worst excesses. 'We'd been cast as the enablers and he was a bit wary of us as if he thought we *wanted* him to fall off the wagon. But I was more than happy not to have to carry brandy in the car all the time.'

Though the craving for alcohol might have gone, he mourned it like a lost loved one and hugely resented the fact that Pattie could continue drinking, which she now did rather heavily, albeit on nowhere near his former scale. He tried to compensate by smoking even more and buying huge quantities of clothes. 'He'd go to Armani and find a nice suit,' she recalls, 'and then want it in every colour.'

His main solace, that convalescent summer of 1982, was fly-fishing, the one activity outside guitar-playing at which he'd ever shown any skill, on the nearby Clandon Estate or in the lakes at Willinghurst and Whitley Farm near Dunsford. Sometimes Pattie would accompany him and spend the time photographing wild flowers, but mostly he went alone, leaving home at 7.30 a.m. and not returning until late afternoon with a creel full of trout for her to clean, which she'd learned to do at express speed. Though the fish had literally lost their innards, he was the one whose booze-free life left him feeling gutted.

The El–Nell sexual chemistry, which once sold millions of records and cuckolded a Beatle, had already dwindled to almost nothing in his drinking days when Pattie would deliberately go to bed first, hoping that by the time he followed he'd be too out of it to try anything. Yet she remained totally in love with and in thrall to him – an addiction, she now admits, as real as any of his.

'I absolutely adored him. He would adore me, but then be cruel and hurt me, and my only desire would be to get that adoration back. It was a treadmill. I often wanted to leave because I knew it would be healthier for me, but there was always such a strong pull to stay with him and hope things would be better tomorrow.'

The booze might have gone but the moods still came out of nowhere. Once, while he was out of the country, a new addition to his Ferrari collection was delivered, this one sky-blue with cream upholstery. When he returned, Pattie thought it would be a nice surprise for her to be waiting at the airport with the new car. Instead, he was furious because someone else had driven it before him, saying that it was spoilt now and he'd have to sell it.

*

Four months after leaving rehab, he returned to work with an American tour. It was so long since he'd gone onstage completely sober that he barely recognised the sound of his own playing without its habitual 'veil of alcohol and drug-distortion'.

Touring offered the greatest temptations of all to get drunk, but now at least there was powerful additional therapy to hand. At every stop in the vicinity of rivers or lakes, he and his co-star keyboard-player, Gary Brooker, would go fishing. He also kept a conscientious look-out for AA meetings and attended a few that didn't conflict with gigs.

At the final show, in Pembroke Pines, Florida, on 30 June, Muddy Waters made a guest appearance and he and Eric duetted on 'Blow Wind Blow'. It would be their last: ten months later, the father of the Chicago blues and secret tricycle-rider died in his sleep, aged seventy.

Time was also running out for the all-British band Eric had so patriotically formed in 1980. After the tour, they were to make their second album at Compass Point Studios in the Bahamas with producer Tom Dowd. But the beery bonhomie that had launched them seemed to be evaporating: not only was Eric off beer but Dave Markee, the bass-player, had become a devout Christian and was antagonising his colleagues by trying to convert them.

Dowd had been quite happy with their performance on *Another Ticket* the previous year, but this time around he told Eric that all of them – except the guitar wizard Albert Lee – were 'substandard'. In their place, he wanted to use three brilliant Americans, bassist Donald 'Duck' Dunn from the Stax studios in Memphis to replace Markee, keyboard-player Roger Hawkins from the Muscle Shoals studios in Alabama to replace Chris Stainton, and the singer, producer and matchless slide-guitarist Ry Cooder.

Offered such stellar support, Eric felt no compunction about firing his whole line-up, excluding Lee but including the very *un*-substandard Gary Brooker. With the new self-reliance instilled by Hazelden, he didn't look the other way as usual while Roger Forrester did the dirty work, but took them all out to dinner and broke it to them personally. He later reprieved Stainton who, as an undischarged bankrupt, needed money badly and was popular with the Ripley crowd for playing piano for singsongs at the cricket club.

Recording with the new American sidemen, especially the prodigious Ry Cooder, was a stressful experience that could no longer be relieved by drinking. During the sessions, he suffered 'a mini-breakdown', at one point bursting into tears in front of Tom Dowd.

The album contained two more songs about Pattie with a mood-swing like those she so dreaded in real life. 'Pretty Girl' was in his old worshipping 'Wonderful Tonight' mode ('My love will always guide me home, my pretty girl') but 'The Shape You're In' bitchily bemoaned her freedom to drink when he couldn't ('I could tell by the smell that she'd had a few'). Grieving for alcohol was in the album's very title. He called it *Money And Cigarettes*, that seeming to be all he had left, albeit both in very large quantities.

He was more inclined to count his blessings when his friend and occasional songwriting and jamming partner Ronnie Lane was diagnosed with multiple sclerosis at the age of thirty-three. Lane coped bravely with the cruel disease and, in September 1983, was the motivator for an event in aid of the charity Action into Research for Multiple Sclerosis (ARMS) at London's Royal Albert Hall. Eric headed a large cast that also mustered Jimmy Page, Steve Winwood, Jeff Beck, Bill Wyman and Charlie Watts, and afterwards led them on a short American tour.

Later that month, he was back at the same familiar venue

with a similarly large company in a show for Prince Charles's personal charity, the Prince's Trust. The new blonde, beautiful Princess of Wales had introduced rock-fandom into the British Royal Family, along with a great deal else, and he was one of her favourites.

Most alcoholics emerge from treatment resolved never to touch another drop. But Eric's aim was merely to change from a drunk into a moderate drinker, using alcohol as a lubricant for pleasant conversation and good fellowship. He fantasised about standing in a pub on a sunny evening, savouring a tall glass of ice-cold lager with a dash of lime juice. Banished from his memory were the nights unimaginable at that glamorous royal gala – nights alone with a bottle of vodka, a gram of coke and a shotgun, seriously wondering whether to blow his brains out.

'He thought he could have a couple of beers and there'd be no harm done,' Nigel Carroll recalls. 'But the beers were always Carlsberg Special Brew, which is incredibly strong stuff – and it never stopped there.'

Money And Cigarettes had neither coined it nor set the world alight, so as a follow-up Roger Forrester suggested an overtly commercial move such as would have disgusted the purist Yardbird Eric of ten years earlier.

The newest sensation in British pop was Phil Collins, the drummer in Genesis and latest incarnation of the British white blues voice, now to be heard in massively successful hit singles like 'Something In The Air Tonight' and 'You Can't Hurry Love'. Forrester's idea was an album with Collins in the dual role of producer and co-instrumentalist.

Eric had no love for the synthesiser symphonies pioneered by Genesis which had pushed the guitar to the sidelines. But Collins was a Surrey neighbour and had become a frequent visitor to Hurtwood, especially during his traumatic divorce from his first wife, Andrea, so at least the sell-out would have a friendly face.

The pairing had the desired effect of putting Eric on his mettle: to write new songs for the album, he had Nigel Carroll rent him a cottage in the wild Welsh region known as the Brecon Beacons where he lived alone in Hazelden self-help style, chopping his own logs for the open fire and visiting the village pub only to sip an anonymous lemonade.

Recording began in March 1984 at George Martin's AIR Studios on the West Indies island of Montserrat. Collins proved to be an inspirational producer who, far from swamping Eric's guitar with synthesisers, coaxed it to a form it had not reached in many half-blotto years past. He wrote euphorically in his diary:

> between now [midnight] and yesterday we've got five great
> tracks phil is so great to work with you get so much done but it
> doesn't feel like hard work at all . . . I hope it never stops

He hadn't checked out what AA support was available on Montserrat, but at first seemed able to do without it, doggedly sticking to soft drinks while his fellow musicians gargled the local rum and did 'blow'. The management of his hotel had not been forewarned and on first arriving in his suite, he'd found the welcome-gift of a bottle of rum on the sideboard. Rather than overreact by pouring it down the sink, he put it away in a cupboard where he couldn't see it.

Then one evening, out to dinner with the band, he tried his social drinking formula of 'a couple of beers'. It was enough to reopen the flood-gates that operated only inwardly and later, alone in his hotel suite, he downed the bottle of rum at a sitting. The next day, he followed this dive off the wagon by seducing AIR's studio manager, a beautiful young (married) woman of mixed Yorkshire and Montserratian parentage named Yvonne Kelly.

Now beyond any help from his AA sponsor, David in Dorking, he went straight into another tour, this time as sideman to

Roger Waters promoting first solo album, *The Pros and Cons of Hitch Hiking*. The staging had all Floyd's trademark grandiosity with its backdrop of Gerald Scarfe animations directed by Nicolas Roeg, but Waters insisted there should be no mention of the band in the advertising. 'That had to change because they were playing 120,000-seat arenas with only about a few hundred people turning up,' Nigel Carroll recalls. 'And there were quite a few shouts for "Layla!"'

Eric's section of the itinerary, covering Europe and North America, brought him, in his own words, 'some pretty crazy sexual liaisons, ménages-à-trois and the like' ('I knew nothing about that,' Carroll says, 'I was never one of the trois').

Back to drinking as heavily as ever, he suffered a couple of 'mini-seizures' not bad enough to require medical help, but a serious warning nonetheless, and another in the realm of the spiritual rather than physical. In Toronto to play the Maple Leaf Gardens, he polished off two six-packs of beers and 'hit a wall of desperation . . . when I saw the absolute squalidness of my life'. It inspired a song called 'Holy Mother', an appeal to a divine entity whose name assuredly was not Pat, full of longing for the moment 'when my hands no longer play/My voice is still, I fade away . . .'

His new record company, Warner Brothers, to which Forrester had signed him, had by now listened to the tapes made with Phil Collins, and such sober enthusiasm, on Montserrat. But the verdict on what was supposed to have been a commercial no-brainer was crushing. WB felt that his songs as they stood were not strong enough and wanted much of the album to be re-recorded in Los Angeles with different studio musicians under two in-house producers. They also sent Eric some demos by a young Texan singer-songwriter named Jerry Lynn Williams with instructions to make his own versions and add them to the Montserrat material.

There had been a time when such interference would have made him threaten to quit the record label and brought an instant, contrite backdown from said label. But these were different days: he was no longer a boy prodigy but a well-worn thirty-nine, and record companies were no longer fawningly indulgent like Ahmet Ertegun's Atlantic; as Van Morrison had recently shown, no artiste was too big to be dropped if he or she proved recalcitrant.

Eric therefore passed over Warner Brothers' huge slight to Collins and bowed to their wishes. It was made easier by discovering that Jerry Lynn Williams, the songwriter they'd forced on him, not only 'looked like Jack Nicholson and sang like Stevie Wonder' but was a willing companion on his fast-accelerating backward journey. He took to hanging out with Williams at the Band's Shangri-La Studios and 'before I knew it I was up and running again with blow and prescription drugs as well as alcohol'.

Montserrat had come back to haunt him in another way, too. On returning from the Roger Waters tour, he found a letter from Yvonne Kelly at AIR Studios telling him that she was pregnant and he was unquestionably responsible. Yet even as his private hell plumbed new depths, the Clapton Luck that had carried him through 1,000 one-night stands without comebacks still held.

Kelly did not go public with the story and her husband, Malcolm, agreed to accept the child as his, both of them seeing it as a way of strengthening a marriage in difficulties. Apart from making some financial provision, Eric did not have to be involved.

The sad irony was that Pattie had wanted a baby since she and Eric first began living together but even in the days of their fieriest passion had never been able to conceive. She put all the blame on herself despite the possibility that his drug-taking, drinking and smoking had reduced his sperm-count. He would never moderate his lifestyle in the cause of fatherhood and regarded any querying of his sperm-count as a slight on his masculinity. Now, unbeknown to her, it had proved serviceable.

Towards the end of 1983, she decided to try IVF, the fertilisation of eggs outside the womb pioneered by British doctors six years earlier. Eric thought it unnatural but agreed to go along with it, although he refused to talk through the procedure with her specialist, Professor Ian Craft.

Her initial high hopes began to fade as one after another ovary-implant failed. In addition, she now lived with a drinker not secret so much as schizophrenic, attending AA meetings but at the same time hiding liquor all over the house or in his cars – half-bottles of vodka, for example, fitted snugly under drivers' foot-mats.

In the years of being left on her own, Pattie never so much as looked at another man. That she did so now was due to Pink Floyd's Roger Waters who had done what Eric once could have and married an aristocrat. Her name was Lady Carolyne Christie and her Old Etonian brother, Willie, was a photographer and video-director. Pattie met him at a mutual friend's wedding while Eric was away on tour, then again by chance at a party at the Natural History Museum where the paparazzo Richard Young snapped them together. The picture got into Nigel Dempster's *Daily Mail* gossip column with a story saying no more than that Christie was helping her with her photography.

When Eric saw it, he was outraged (impeccably faithful spouse that he'd always been) and refused to believe Christie was merely an acquaintance. After that, the addiction that had tolerated everything he threw at her finally began to weaken.

More than ever, her main strength was her sister Jenny, who had also been experiencing tough times following the collapse of both her marriages to Mick Fleetwood and problems with alcohol and cocaine. One day, the sisters went together to Vidal Sassoon and had their long blonde hair – Pattie's stamp on 'Wonderful Tonight' – shorn to almost nothing. That evening, Jenny showed her a photograph of herself which shockingly revealed how bloated and unkempt all the drinking with and without Eric had made her.

In September 1984, with her IVF treatment still ongoing, she walked out on him, choosing a moment while he was comatose on the sitting-room couch. Her mother Diana happened to be living in nearby Haslemere a few miles away, where her youngest sister Paula, now separated from a second husband, rug-dealer David Philpot, and with three children – but as much prey to drug-addiction and alcoholism as ever – had been placed in local authority accommodation. Pattie moved in with Diana and resumed her habitual efforts to help Paula while she tried to decide on her next move.

Eric soon tracked her there and every day for the next four weeks sent her a dozen red roses. Finally, he turned up in person, looking pale and haggard – never less welcome to Diana – and begged her to return, but she refused. Subsequent entreaties proving equally useless, he agreed to a trial separation.

She moved into a small house in Devonshire Mews, west London, paid for by Roger Forrester, and began dating Willie Christie, a sympathetic, restful man who did help her with her photography. Jenny was currently seeing a psychotherapist who'd proved so beneficial that Pattie did the same, much to the puzzlement of her mother, who thought she'd do better to consult the local vicar.

But sessions with a female therapist, who was also an astrologer and dream analyst, did not bring the same comfort or insight Jenny had found. 'We were just exchanging information. Mine was learnt by experience, hers was mostly read in books.'

Eric had also begun seeing a therapist, recommended by

Roger Waters. His main emotional outlet, however, continued to be his diary, where he recorded feeling 'lost' and 'desperate' after learning of Pattie's involvement with Willie Christie. He had even driven up to London intending to bring her back to Hurtwood 'caveman-style' but she was out, presumably seeing Christie.

As a result, he'd suffered 'a complete relapse with all the fears and guilt of the drinking days [and] the coke was the worst part of it'. He spent a whole day 'getting more and more suicidal' until a phone call from Roger Forrester pulled him back from the brink and he threw away the coke and neutralised its effects by drinking glass after glass of water.

Despite having been so rudely displaced as its producer, Phil Collins continued to work on the Montserrat album, now called *Behind The Sun* after a line from one of Eric's favourite Muddy Waters songs, 'Louisiana Blues'. He recorded the title track at Collins's house with a simple guitar-synthesiser arrangement, then took it straight to Pattie, hoping to weaken her resolve as 'Layla' once had, with a vocal palpably on the edge of tears: 'My love has gone behind the sun/since she's gone the darkness has begun'.

In November, before leaving on an Australian tour, he wrote in his diary:

> *i walked and talked with nell this afternoon she is lovelier*
> *than ever and I believe she wants to be left alone with her*
> *new man and her new life . . . but i still believe that she*
> *loves me and that i can net her with patience i have hope and*
> *persistence on my side and i will never give in*

As he went on to tell himself, there was no inconsistency in sleeping with an occasional girlfriend named Valentina the day he arrived in Sydney:

*it felt so good to be cared for again ive been hungry for so long
. . . but it doesn't stop the deeper yearning which i keep for my
wife . . .*

A week into the tour, he heard from Forrester that his marital
troubles were headlines in Nigel Dempster's *Daily Mail* column.
Mortified by this first-ever invasion of his privacy, he had a
phone conversation with Pattie that went far beyond anything
he'd intended. 'Well its over,' he wrote afterwards. 'i spoke to
nell about divorce and she agrees to it i have gone back into shock
god help me . . .' He hastily phoned back, asking her to spend a
week with him in Florence, where they had a rented apartment,
to talk things over.

Meantime, returning home 'confused and depressed', he
did himself no favours with Pattie by writing to Willie Christie, wondering whether Christie appreciated the seriousness of
usurping the love of someone's life. Equally counterproductive
was his view that behind Pattie was a 'blonde Mafia', dedicated to turning her against him. (Roger Waters' wife, Carolyne,
was certainly a staunch supporter, but she had precious few
others.)

One night, he received a phone call from Alice Ormsby-Gore,
whom he hadn't seen since throwing her over for Pattie but who,
despite all else that she'd lost, had never lost hope of getting back
with him. She kept the conversation light – joking that she'd
always known Pattie would end up with 'a toff' like Christie –
but suggested Eric should come and see her in Paris, where she
now lived. Fortunately for them both, he didn't.

Florence is a city that should be able to replenish any love
affair, especially backed up by the heart-shaped ruby set with
diamonds which he'd bought for Pattie in Australia. But he was
over-eager to restore the 'Layla' passion and she refused to be
pushed. 'the most memorable part,' he told his diary, 'was the

fact that she has proved or established that she finds me sexually repulsive.'

In the run-up to Christmas 1984, he decided he could no longer endure Hurtwood on his own and wanted to be near her in London, however useless it might be. Nigel Carroll booked him temporarily into the ultra-traditional Connaught Hotel (re-assuring a nervous management that there'd be no screaming fans and he'd be using an alias, 'Mr W. B. Albion'), then found him a flat in Davies Street just off Berkeley Square. He stayed there over Christmas, even though Pattie was on holiday with a female friend in Sri Lanka. 'I had to go out and buy a tree,' Carroll recalls.

When Pattie returned from Sri Lanka, she found another of the letters with which Eric had been bombarding her. But in-stead of the usual apocalyptic emotion, it was full of news about their dogs and Rose and Pat, guaranteed to get to her. It ended:

> *i ask you please please don't take up*
> *with will again the moment you get*
> *back i think it would be the end of*
> *me . . . please come home where you*
> *belong i promise i won't let you down*
> *again . . .*

She agreed to go away with him again and try to sort things out, this time to Eilat in Israel. On a drive into the desert, Eric gave her a tablet of something called Ecstasy which, he said, had been developed by therapists to help couples regain lost intimacies. Later, they bathed in the Dead Sea, its high salt con-tent allowing them to float weightlessly like astronauts on the Moon. Buoyed-up and ecstatic as she felt, Pattie could hold out no longer.

22

CAPTAIN SMIRNOFF

The honeymoon was short-lived; two weeks after their return from Israel, Eric left on a tour of the UK and Europe. Meanwhile, his first child had just been born to Yvonne Kelly, the AIR studio manager he'd seduced on Montserrat the previous summer. Kelly had returned to her hometown of Doncaster in Yorkshire to have the baby, a girl named Ruth. Thanks to her refusal to exploit her situation, not a word of it had got out, either to the media or Pattie.

To celebrate Eric's fortieth birthday on 30 March 1985, Pattie threw an extravagant party for him at Hurtwood Edge. The throng of musicians who attended made the house come alive again and seemed to set the seal on El and Nell's reconciliation. Immediately afterwards, he was back on the road for fifteen more weeks in the US and Canada.

He took a break on 13 July to join Live Aid, the simultaneous marathon concerts on two continents instigated by Bob Geldof for victims of the horrific famine in Ethiopia. His recurrent conscience, Pete Townshend, got him involved and his new collaborator, Phil Collins, linked the two shows, first performing at London's Wembley Stadium, then crossing the Atlantic on Concorde to play drums for Eric before his own set at the John F. Kennedy Stadium in Philadelphia.

Eric's contributions were the Cream classic 'White Room', taking Jack Bruce's vocal as he once would never have dared,

'She's Waiting' from the *Behind The Sun* album and, inevitably, 'Layla'. The acts with whom he was competing (among them Bob Dylan, Paul McCartney, Mick Jagger, David Bowie, Elton John, Tina Turner, Madonna and Queen) brought on a near-paralysing fit of nerves, his microphone was giving off electric shocks, and both he and his bass-player, Donald 'Duck' Dunn, almost fainted in the heat.

Pattie was with him in Philadelphia to hear herself hymned to a worldwide TV audience of almost two billion – for, as part of his pledge to reform, Eric had revoked the 'no wives on tour' rule. However, she had too many bad memories of joining him on the road, when he'd be all over her at first, but soon start to feel the magnetic pull of stag drinking and groupies. 'I went to the odd concert – and wouldn't have missed Live Aid for the world – but I didn't want to trail around, watching women throw themselves at him.'

She therefore wasn't around late that October when Eric played two concerts at the Teatro Tendo in Milan. Otherwise, he might not have mentioned to the local promoter that, despite his love of all things Italian, from Ferraris to Armani suits, he'd somehow never dated an Italian woman. The promoter took the broad hint and at the after-show dinner introduced him to an exquisite representative of the species with a heart-shaped face, an unruly mass of black curls and a slightly wicked smile. Her name was Loredana – aka Lory – Del Santo.

Twenty-seven-year-old Lory was a sizeable celebrity in her homeland as the star of several films and a regular on *Drive In*, a TV comedy show modelled on America's *Saturday Night Live*. She was just as considerable a socialite whose successive rich and powerful men friends had once included the billionaire Saudi Arabian arms dealer Adnan Khashoggi.

On first meeting Eric, she claimed not to know who he was: a virtually guaranteed way for an attractive woman to entice a rock bigwig. Along with her physical charms, he would recall, she had a playfulness that instantly broke through what he still liked to regard as his innate shyness with the opposite sex. Lory on her side would maintain that he'd 'snared' her.

At any event, barely ten months after reuniting with Pattie, he was smitten yet again. Back at Hurtwood a few weeks later, he asked her to make a dinner reservation at a local Italian restaurant – a seeming treat as they seldom went out by themselves. Instead, amid painfully appropriate breadsticks and Chianti flasks, he announced that he thought he was in love with Lory Del Santo and was going back to Milan to be with her.

Lory showed typically Italian pragmatism when he reappeared at her apartment without any prior warning. 'Her attitude was one of "Come and live here and let's see where it takes us,"' he would recall. He needed no second invitation to give up everything and become a troubadour again on the threshold of middle age. 'I thought, "I'm going to start my life from scratch here in Italy without any idea at all of where it's going to go."'

Lory was developing an additional career in fashion photography and for menswear assignments began using him as a model – something few British photographers beyond the Queen's brother-in-law had ever done – and taking him to shows by labels like Armani, Valentino and Versace of which he'd never been able to get enough.

She would later claim not to have really noticed his drinking (for serious alcoholics seldom appear drunk). But as a typically voluble, forthright, passionate member of her race, she was baffled by his sudden dark moods and silences that could sometimes go on for days. 'He was so difficult to be with,' she would reflect. 'But then he'd say one beautiful line to me and I knew I had to stay.'

Very soon, their respective accounts agree, they began to discuss having a baby together. Possibly in the looseness of pillow-talk, Eric said he'd always wanted children and represented Pattie's inability to conceive as a sorrow rather than the escape he might have considered it. At twenty-seven, especially in matriarchal Italy, Lory felt her biological clock ticking. 'I said I wanted a baby [and] he said, "Oh, me too,"' she would recall. '"If you're really, really serious, let's do it."'

They moved on to Rome, where Lory had a second apartment. One day while she was out, he found some albums of photographs of herself with the many other famous men she'd dated, footballers, actors, politicians and musicians. In every shot, he would recall, 'she struck the same pose, wearing the sort of smile that wasn't really a smile at all'. For an actress, it was hardly an unusual foible but, together with the backlog of old boyfriends, it traumatised Eric. 'I felt like someone had punched me in the stomach. I went ice-cold and my hair stood on end. In that moment, I knew we were doomed.'

Nonetheless, he brought her to London to live with him at the flat in Davies Street, Mayfair, which he'd acquired when Pattie left him. It did not go well. He found the street-noise oppressive (although neither Milan nor Rome had been exactly quiet) and filled the flat with recording-equipment to make demos for his next album. When he began writing a song called 'Tearing Us Apart', about the 'Blonde Mafia' he blamed for turning Pattie against him, it was clear in whose direction his thoughts were returning.

After two or three weeks, he told Lory their relationship wasn't working and he was going back to his wife. She would recall that, once she was 'snared', he seemed to lose interest in her, a syndrome which other women – to say nothing of guitars – had already experienced.

He drove down to Hurtwood, expecting to walk back in with a 'Hi, I'm home'. But during his absence, Pattie had again begun seeing the restfully uncomplicated Will Christie. Looking in at the kitchen window, Eric saw the two of them and Christie's small daughter cooking together like the happiest of families. Pattie refused to let him in, deaf to his aggrieved protests of 'It's *my* house.'

With a mistress he no longer wanted and a wife who no longer wanted him, feeling that 'my world was absolutely in tatters', he attempted suicide by swallowing a whole bottle of Valium. But the Clapton Luck refused to let go : ten hours later, he awoke with no after-effects except feeling stone-cold sober.

Unable to wrest any future commitment from him, the independent-minded Lory returned to Milan. When he renewed his pleas to Pattie, she agreed to have him back yet again, believing that, like Jenny McLean after their wedding, the threat had now gone away.

One day while she was arranging flowers in a vase, Eric came in and told her Lory was pregnant. That he should easily have achieved with someone else what they had so long failed to do together – and she was still pursuing with round after round of IVF treatment, each time reducing her chances of conceiving naturally – made her feel 'like my heart was about to disintegrate'.

For rock stars in such situations there was normally a ready remedy but because Lory was a Catholic, an abortion was out of the question. Twisting the knife in the womb, Eric went on to extol her talent and success in the field of photography, where Pattie was struggling to get started.

She did not instantly start divorce proceedings, believing with her usual optimism that they'd somehow get through all this. But she refused to go on sleeping with him and insisted he move into a separate bedroom, above the kitchen.

The two principals in Eric's family, his grandmother Rose and his mother Pat, both loved Pattie, but neither one ever breathed a word of criticism of him and they weren't about to start now.

'I did try talking to Pat about things. She'd just say, "That's awful, dear" and never go any further,' Pattie recalls. But with Rose, it was clearly useless to raise the subject. 'To her, Eric could do no wrong – he was her king. It wasn't a conversation she'd ever want to have.'

Much the same happened with George, to whom Pattie still felt a connection all these years after their divorce and his remarriage. 'I went to see him and told him everything. He seemed sympathetic, but didn't really engage with what I was saying. Keeping his friendship with Eric was obviously the most important thing to him.'

That friendship was reaffirmed when the two appeared together, with Ringo and Johnny Cash's daughter, Roseanne, on a Channel 4 tribute to Carl Perkins. It was George's first public performance since his disastrous America solo tour in the aftermath of losing Pattie to Eric a decade earlier. Now came their first television appearance together, picking Perkins classics like 'Matchbox' and 'Blue Suede Shoes' as reverential sidemen to a country-rock legend they both adored. What woman could possibly be more important than that?

To add to Pattie's anguish, the British press – still as unaware of this Clapton pregnancy as of the earlier one – stuck doggedly to her so-recent reunion with Eric and obediently printed every story they were fed that it was going fine. In February 1986, he won a BAFTA award for his soundtrack to the hit TV thriller *Edge of Darkness*. Pattie was beside him at the awards-ceremony as he told reporters they were back together 'for good'.

In the spring, he was away again, making an album in Los Angeles, co-produced by Phil Collins and Tom Dowd, in an undiminished vodka haze. He and Nigel Carroll shared a house, where at intervals Carroll would discreetly collect and dispose of the empty bottles. 'I rented a Mercedes for him and a Volkswagen Polo for me. In California, you can have anything you like on a car's front registration-plate, so I had one made for Eric saying Captain Smirnoff and one for Phil saying Little Elvis. Eric had been driving around for days before he noticed his.'

Despite the current chaos of his home life, the album turned out to be full of good things. 'It's In The Way That You Use It', co-written with the Band's Robbie Robertson, would be used in the Tom Cruise film *The Color of Money*. 'Tearing Us Apart', his fulmination against Pattie's alleged Blonde Mafia, became a storming duet with Tina Turner. 'Holy Mother' made no reference to the mothers of his children, born and unborn, but was dedicated to the Band's keyboard-player Richard Manuel, who had hanged himself in March.

The friendship with Phil Collins was to cool when, in an interview with *Q* magazine, Collins questioned how Eric could play the blues with any conviction in a £5,000 Armani or Versace suit.

'Well, the point is, Phil,' he bristled back, 'that the blues is a state of mind. It's got nothing to do with acquisition . . . It's an inside job. Once you find out that money and fame and success don't do it, where do you go? When I was at the height of my drinking I had a beautiful wife, cars, home, money, friends, all the things you think a man could need and . . . I was depressed. I was suicidal.' The only inaccuracy there was the past tense.

Lory spent most of her pregnancy believing that Eric didn't want the baby. In her third month, she later said, she received a phone call from someone in his management pressuring her in 'painful' terms to have an abortion. This was unthinkable, not only on religious grounds: her mother had raised her and her sister single-handedly after their father's premature death, and she was determined to follow that example come what may.

The signals from Eric himself were at best contradictory, at worst deeply disquieting. At one point, Lory alleges, he telephoned to tell her he'd made a second suicide attempt, this time by hanging himself, but had fainted and then awoken to find himself still alive. Always at his most eloquent on paper, he sent her a letter, couched in such loving terms that she kept it under her pillow. It was his only written acknowledgement of paternity and during one of his visits, so she claimed, it mysteriously vanished.

But as the birthdate in late August neared, he'd finally recognised 'the one thing in my life that good could come out of'. When the LA album wrapped, he went to see Lory in Milan and from then on gave her every attention. Because the baby's father was English, she insisted, it must be born in London. Eric therefore had Roger Forrester book her into the private Lindo maternity wing at St Mary's hospital, Paddington, and rent her a mews house in Chelsea for the pre- and post-natal periods.

On 21 August, she gave birth to a boy by Caesarean section. Putting a lifetime of squeamishness and evading life's unpleasantnesses behind him, Eric chose to be present at the delivery. To the very last, he remained his old self, asking how long all this would take as he was exhausted and needed to get away on holiday. But, as for every parent, the baby's first piercing cry was a command to start growing up. When his son, to be named Conor, was put into his arms, 'it felt as if it were the first real thing that had ever happened to me'.

Pattie at the time was staying in the South of France with the Genesis guitarist Mike Rutherford. Rutherford's wife, Angie, was pregnant, as was Pattie's fellow guest, Chris O'Dell. 'Everyone was pregnant,' she recalls, 'except me.'

One evening as she sat with the Rutherfords in their garden, Eric rang to tell her of Conor's arrival. He seemed to have no awareness that for the wife who had so long yearned to bear his child, it might be less than welcome news. He described every detail of the birth and how it had thrilled and moved him, all as if he were talking 'to his sister or a friend, not his jilted wife', Pattie recalls. For months, she had managed to hide her feelings in the proper English way, but that made her finally break down.

The responsibilities of fatherhood this second time were to be little more onerous than with Yvonne Kelly. Lory accepted that she and Eric would separate after Conor's birth and she would assume custody of him and take him back to Italy while allowing his father regular visitation rights. So, after going on holiday, as he had planned, Eric could return to Hurtwood with another 'Hi, I'm home'.

For Pattie, that sensation of a heart disintegrating had barely got started. The album he'd made earlier in the year was named *August*, in honour of Conor's birth-month, and reached number 3 in Britain. (Actually, he'd made an attempt to spare her feelings by withholding a track called 'Lady Of Verona', inspired by Lory.) His first idea was that Conor should live with them at Hurtwood for extended periods until he reached school age. Lory vetoed that, however, and instead he began paying monthly visits to Milan, assuring Pattie they were for no other purpose than spending time with his son.

At the beginning of 1987, she began a new course of IVF, clinging to the hope that his newly awakened paternal feelings might yet be invested in a baby she had given him – but was disappointed yet again. And after every visit to Milan he would return full of heart-shredding stories of Conor's adorability, leaving her wondering what might have gone on with Lory while the baby was asleep.

The strain of commuting between two homes in different countries began to tell on him, too, and was alleviated in the usual way. Only for about four hours per day would he be coherent and then often verbally abusive, railing against his banishment to a separate bedroom and accusing Pattie of using the house 'like a hotel'. 'I thought he was going to go mad with the drink or kill himself and I eventually knew I had to get out for his sake as well as mine.'

After seeing various divorce lawyers (one of whom observed that if Eric fished, he couldn't be such a bad chap, while another seemed to favour putting out a contract on him), she went with the venerable firm of Theodore Goddard, whose eponymous founder played a leading role in the abdication of King Edward VIII. Goddard's advised that she should on no account leave the marital home, so Eric reluctantly moved back into his Davies Street flat.

He hated being there, but all Roger Forrester's pleas on his behalf couldn't persuade Pattie to vacate Hurtwood. She did, however, yield to Forrester's sympathetic-sounding diagnosis that she needed a complete rest and allow him to send her skiing in France with Nicole Winwood, the similarly estranged wife of Eric's Blind Faith bandmate, Stevie. As if a broken heart were not enough, she broke a wrist while ice-skating and had to have her arm put into a cast.

Returning to Hurtwood, she found Eric back in possession. Early in the morning of 17 March, her forty-third birthday, he burst drunkenly into the marital bedroom from which he was now banned, accused her of not being 'a proper wife', ordered her out of the house and began hurling her possessions through the window – 'a cruel and vicious thing to do', as he himself would later admit. With no one – certainly no 'Blonde Mafia' – to shield her, she had no choice but to go.

During Eric's first months of fatherhood, he did not allow it to alter his lifestyle. He never drank while he was with Conor but spent the whole time in a state of what he called 'white-knuckle sobriety', waiting for Lory to take the baby away to be fed or changed so that he could pour himself a vodka, then another and another.

Occasionally he thought of drying out again, but the social bonds of alcohol were too strong. He now headed a drinking team in the literal sense, having formed his own cricket eleven in partnership with the Robert Stigwood Organisation's former chairman, David English. His incompetence at the game was such as to confound even the Clapton Luck: on his first appearance as a fielder, he sustained a broken finger; then, as he walked back to the pavilion, a bumble bee stung him on his other hand.

To him, cricket was mainly another excuse for 'a good piss-up', whether in the company of fellow musicians like Rolling Stone Bill Wyman – who kept a cigarette in his mouth while fielding and even bowling – or the current stars of England's national team, David Gower and Ian 'Beefy' Botham.

Touring Australia in the summer of 1987, he began suffering uncontrollable shaking fits. These prompted the sudden awful thought that he might somehow pass on alcoholism to Conor; that the flawless baby in his cot might one day go through the exact same cycles of delusion and humiliation. 'I realised I had to break the chain and give him what I never really had – a father.' In November, he asked Roger Forrester to book him back into the Hazelden clinic.

This time around, the treatment was dominated by a counsellor named Phil, whose disrespectfully caustic humour was a tonic in itself to someone so steeped in deference. Nonetheless, Eric once again found himself ticking off the days until his sentence ended and he could return to the bottle. As time ran out, the prospect so overwhelmed him with panic and despair that his legs gave way beneath him. Finding himself on his knees – as so many times metaphorically in 'Layla' – he began to pray for real.

He had in his time worshipped many deities, from Robert Johnson to Muddy Waters, and been worshipped as one himself. Despite that double idolatry, Heaven proved as ready to let him off as everyone down below. This time when he left Hazelden, he would never touch alcohol again.

*

After being evicted from her home on her birthday morning, Pattie decided she would still go to the celebratory lunch she had arranged with some girlfriends at San Lorenzo in Knightsbridge. She looked so grief-stricken that the restaurant's motherly Italian owner, Mara Berni, slipped her a small statuette of the Madonna.

She spent that first night at an hotel and stayed with Eric's guitar 'tech', Alan Rogan, then Nicole Winwood until Roger Forrester provided her with a small rented flat in Queen's Gate Place, Kensington. She had left Hurtwood with little more than the clothes she stood up in, but put off returning to collect her possessions until a day when she knew Eric wouldn't be there.

Her friend Chris O'Dell had promised to accompany her but Chris, too, was having marital problems and couldn't get away so she had to ask her mother, Diana, 'the last person I wanted to see'. Walking from room to room in a trance of grief, she had no idea what to take and in the end came away with little more than some photographs and her passport. The worst part was leaving her beloved Airedale terrier, Trouper, in the care of the Eggbys.

Eric bombarded her with letters, some angry, some reproachful but most pleading with her to return in the tone of mingled adoration and self-condemnation he seemed to reserve for his italic nib. One was addressed to 'the Adorable Butterfly' and signed 'majnun, el, slowhand, rick, ALL OF ME xxx'.

In April 1988, she began divorce proceedings on the grounds of his adultery with Lory Del Santo and 'unreasonable behaviour'. He had kept on trying to talk her out of it, if not for his sake then because of the distress it would cause Rose. When the process finally got underway, her lawyers received two defendant affiadavits. 'One was signed by Eric, the other by Roger Forrester,' she recalls. 'I was divorcing both of them.'

Therapy had shown Pattie how, since the age of twenty-one, she'd had no real existence of her own, but lived entirely for and through two hugely powerful, charismatic rock stars. It also made her regret how easily she had segued from one to the other – despite an inner warning voice that things with Eric would not turn out well – and wish she had fought for her first marriage harder than with a pair of water pistols.

She recognised she was grieving as much for the loss of George as of Eric, and realised which loss cut deeper. 'Eric and I were playmates but George and I were soulmates.'

Even so, she couldn't bear to go near Hurtwood Edge again or even drive the tree-tunnelled Surrey roads around it. Once, when she had to go to nearby Cranleigh, she was pulled over for careless driving and burst into tears so far beyond what the circumstances warranted that the kindly local copper let her go with a warning.

She wasn't so lucky after attending a charity lunch when she got stopped on Hammersmith Bridge, breathalysed and charged with drink-driving. With no Roger Forrester or Brian Epstein any more to smooth things over, she was fined and banned from driving for a year.

London provided little relief, for the Underground she now had to use was full of posters for Eric's four current albums, shops and department stores pumped out his music in uniform disregard for her feelings and, a few streets away from her not-very-nice flat, the Royal Albert Hall would be hosting him yet again for a run of nine concerts with an extra sideman, guaranteeing – if that were needed – that they'd all be sell-outs.

Despite the dehumanised machine-made sounds that dominated Eighties pop, Britain's biggest band was built around a single free-range lead guitar. They were called Dire Straits and their part-Hungarian frontman, Mark Knopfler, could solo and sing simultaneously just like Jimi Hendrix used to do. Like so many younger players, Knopfler's passion for the guitar dated from hearing Eric's Gibson Les Paul on the *Blues Breakers* album in 1966.

Eric had seen Knopfler in action at Live Aid and recognised the most distinctive talent to appear since Hendrix's death. So admiring was he that when Dire Straits toured their *Brothers In Arms* album at the end of that year, he volunteered himself as a special guest for seven nights at the Hammersmith Odeon.

Although his and Knopfler's techniques could not have been more different, the one visceral, the other lyrical, their temperaments were remarkably similar. Knopfler had never aspired to be a frontman, any more than Eric had, and after several years' huge success with Dire Straits – swelled by the accolade of being Princess Diana's favourite band – was longing for some anonymity as someone else's sideman, as Eric had been for Delaney & Bonnie.

He was also just as unassuming. When he heard of Eric's nine-night London season in January of 1988, he contacted Forrester's office, asking if he could 'come to the Albert Hall'. At first, this was interpreted as simply a request for tickets.

His and Eric's approaches to performance were as different as their playing styles. 'Mark was so meticulous that at rehearsals he wrote out all his songs on a blackboard,' Dire Straits' then manager, Ed Bicknell, recalls. 'Eric's set changed so little from year to year that he'd just call out the next one to his band.' But on stage, they proved natural brothers in arms. 'I loved the feeling of just helping Eric to keep things going, sometimes slipping a little extra bit into "Lay Down Sally" where I thought it would help,' Knopfler recalls. 'And I felt strangely protective of him.'

Dire Straits were first to sign up to a Live Aid-style concert on 11 June marking Nelson Mandela's seventieth birthday and adding to worldwide pressure for Mandela's release from life imprisonment by South Africa's apartheid regime. The band's second guitarist, Jack Sonni, had to drop out as his wife was about to have twins, so Eric was invited to deputise. The organisers initially objected, citing the charges of racism levelled at him in 1976. Dire Straits replied that if he didn't appear, neither would they, and there was no further attempt to edit their line-up.

Eric was still not long out of Hazelden, and Knopfler and the others showed great sensitivity to his fragile condition. 'Whenever any of them ordered a drink in a bar, they always asked him if he minded,' Ed Bicknell recalls.

Subsequently, Knopfler took a sabbatical from Dire Straits to join Eric's next US tour as an (unpaid) alternate lead guitar, in each two-hour show playing only one song of his own, the aptly titled 'Money For Nothing'.

Rehearsals took place on a sound-stage at Las Colinas, just outside Dallas. 'We had to get used to Eric's little japes,' Bicknell says, 'like locking a roadie in a cupboard for a couple of hours.

'He was still a very naughty boy. One night, the whole band, except the girl back-up singers, went to this lapdancing club called the Pink Pussy or something. And Eric ended up with one of the dancers. Everyone else was saying, "Is he really *serious*?"'

Eric and Pattie's divorce action was settled out of court in 1989. She received a settlement of £600,000 – allowing for inflation, not a great deal more than the £120,000 from George in 1976 – plus a small two-bedroom flat at Thames Reach in Richmond. Some years later, Eric bought a £360,000 cottage in West Sussex where she lived as a tenant until he eventually gave it to her.

A few years later, she would have had an automatic claim on half his assets, bolstered by the extent to which she'd advanced his career by inspiring his two most famous songs. At the very least, she could have sought a share of the royalties from 'Layla' and 'Wonderful Tonight'.

She tried to improve the sum on offer, which was £100,000 less than Nicole Winwood had received from Stevie, a nowhere-near-comparable name. 'But my lawyers were old-fashioned English gentlemen. They were no match for Roger, and he said Eric couldn't afford any more.' (The previous year, he'd had four albums out, including *Crossroads*, the first double-platinum-selling box set.)

Rose was, indeed, greatly upset by the divorce but, aside from Pattie herself, the one most hurt by it was probably her nephew, Will, the son of her sister Paula. Hurtwood had been Will's refuge from his unstable life with a mother who'd never shaken off the drug- and alcohol-addictions she'd picked up when she was Eric's eighteen-year-old girlfriend. Pattie had given Will his own room, paid some of his school fees, even considered fostering him, and Eric had been good to him, buying him guitars and taking him fishing, thereby indirectly making some amends to Paula.

All attempts to help Paula by her mother, sisters and three children were doomed to end in failure and she would die in 2007, aged fifty-six. Though there were no suspicious circumstances, Pattie believes she committed suicide, knowing she'd never get clean and wanting to spare her family any further trouble or shame.

'I once asked Paula why she needed heroin so much,' Pattie recalls. 'But all she said was, "It's the pain."'

'When I asked Eric what he thought she meant, he just said, "Don't you *know?*"'

23

'PLEASE, JUST DON'T CRY'

I n Eric's first shaky years of sobriety, fatherhood should have been a Heaven-sent replacement for alcohol. His son, Conor, was a spectacularly beautiful child with the same golden hair he himself had had as a toddler, and a joyful, loving nature that made itself felt even from the cradle. The word used by everyone who knew Conor, in the later sad past tense, would be 'magical'.

As a rule, his father visited him in Milan but from time to time Lory brought him to stay at Hurtwood Edge, sometimes accompanied by both her mother and sister. The house that had always looked like a stray bit of Tuscany now echoed to the sound of Italian, for Lory's mother, Clorinda, didn't speak a word of English. There, too, he found a doting great-grandmother in Rose and a more guarded grandma in Pat.

Lory handled all the childcare, proving herself an efficient and loving mother; even so, Eric found it hard to cope with the mess of baby-maintenance and with no longer being the centre of all female attention.

Things became easier as Conor started metamorphosing into a boy and they could kick footballs around Hurtwood's tiled verandah together. He soon discovered his father's occupation and demanded a little plastic guitar of his own, which he would thumb proudly, albeit left-handedly. But it was inevitable that he should always turn first to his mother – and such innocent snubs wound Eric out of all proportion.

Trapped as he felt with Lory, he began casting wistful backward glances at his ex-wife, now happily involved with a property developer named Rod Weston. *Journeyman*, his first completely sober album since going solo, included 'Old Love', co-written with Robert Cray, its inspiration as plain as 'Layla' or 'Wonderful Tonight' ('old love, leave me alone . . .'). There were also wistful letters in which his italic pen could still sink a hook in Pattie's heart. 'Sometimes', one of them ended, 'it's enough just to know that you're somewhere in the world smiling.'

Ever magnanimous, her divorce settlement notwithstanding, she would occasionally meet him for lunch at San Lorenzo, hardly recognising the precise, well-organised individual he'd become since his cure. She even visited Hurtwood during one of Conor's stays, smiling bravely while father and son played together. Eric later wrote to her, with a practicality equally new for him, that Conor was suffering from traumatic asthma caused by emotional stress and he would have to leave him in Italy for a while.

Once Conor had learned to walk, Lory began talking about having another child. That seemed to decide Eric to back out of their relationship. Towards the end of his marriage, he'd had a brief affair with the freelance stylist currently doing his hair, an elfin young Englishwoman named Vivien Gibson, later Griffin. Their casual, no-strings liaison turned into friendship and early in 1988, immediately after parting from Lory, he invited Vivien to go on holiday with him to Antigua. 'He'd recently come out of rehab,' she recalls. 'He was a bit shaky and I went along as a non-drinking friend.'

At the outset, Eric made an attempt to restart their affair, even though in the interim Vivien had become seriously interested in another man. 'As always with him, he wanted whatever he couldn't have. It was the more or less reflex action of people who find themselves together in a tropical island paradise. It wasn't significant, it wasn't very serious and it wasn't acted on.'

The constant dread of all recovering alcoholics is encountering some old boozing buddy who will irresistibly tempt them back to their old ways. It could well have happened to Eric on this Antigua holiday when he bumped into Keith Richards on the beach and Keith invited him to a party at his villa that night. However, with Vivien to lend moral support, he managed an immaculately dry half-hour there before making a graceful exit.

Immediately after their return to Britain, Vivien was astonished to hear that he'd not only returned to Lory but become engaged to her. 'God knows how he let himself be talked into it. She did genuinely love him, but he just wasn't there.' Vivien was quietly amused 'that he could make a pass at one woman [as he had to her in Antigua] then propose marriage to another within days'.

Assured that 'the sex and the drink were both out of the way', Vivien became his secretary – another sign of the new, organised Eric – for one day a week. Being organised felt so good that he asked her to join his 1990–91 world tour promoting the *Journeyman* album. She agreed despite Roger Forrester's well-known hostility towards anyone who might come between him and 'the Boy'.

The tour's American leg saw Eric give himself his stiffest-ever onstage competition, with guest appearances by Robert Cray, his greatest living blues idol, Buddy Guy, and the Texan guitarist Stevie Ray Vaughan, a tousled force of nature whose drinking and hell-raising he could at least enjoy vicariously.

On 26 August, the troupe appeared at a Wisconsin ski resort named Alpine Valley. The show was a specially good one, ending with Eric, Cray, Guy, Stevie Ray and his brother, Jimmie, together in a fifteen-minute version of Robert Johnson's 'Sweet Home Chicago'. Eric was keenly looking forward to further appearances with Stevie Ray, at the Royal Albert Hall or at a tribute to Jimi Hendrix in Paris the following month.

By the time the audience let them go, it was well past midnight and a thick fog had descended on the fleet of helicopters chartered to ferry them back to their Chicago base. Stevie Ray had intended to drive but, at the last minute, decided to join the fliers instead.

As Eric boarded his helicopter, he noticed the pilot using a concert-souvenir T-shirt to wipe condensation off its perspex dome. Ever since Buddy Holly's fatal plane-ride in this same part of the Midwest, fear of crashing had haunted every performer and come true for many: Jim Reeves, Patsy Cline, Otis Redding, Ricky Nelson, Jim Croce and two members of Lynyrd Skynyrd. But the new calm, rational Eric said nothing for fear of causing unnecessary alarm.

As the rotors began to turn, there was a flurry of seat-switching. Vivien Griffin expected to ride with Eric but instead Peter Jackson, the tour manager, put her on the helicopter assigned to Stevie Ray, booking agent Bobby Brooks and road-crewman Colin 'Colie' Smythe. Roger Forrester then told Eric's bodyguard, Nigel Browne, to travel with Vivien, overruling Browne's protests that he shouldn't leave his boss. Browne boarded Stevie Ray's helicopter but at the last minute Vivien found an alternative aboard the smallest of the fleet with the tour's female backing singers.

When the choppers lifted off, it seemed to Forrester that the one carrying Stevie Ray's party abruptly vanished. However, as the fog almost immediately gave way to clear night sky, he thought no more about it.

At two o'clock the next morning, Vivien was woken by a call from Forrester and summoned to his hotel-room with such urgency that at first she thought it was one of his habitual pranks. 'Roger was there with Peter Jackson. They'd been told that one of the helicopters was missing. Peter was on the phone and some information was just coming through. "What?" I heard him say. "*All* of them?"

The chopper carrying Stevie Ray Vaughan, Bobby Brooks, Nigel Browne and Colin Smythe had banked the wrong way on take-off and flown straight into an artificial ski-slope. There were no survivors. When Eric was woken with the terrible news, his first thought was that Vivien had also been lost. He'd seen her board the missing aircraft and not realised she'd switched to another at the last moment.

The names of the dead couldn't be given out until their families had been informed, so the first newspaper headlines said ERIC CLAPTON AND MANAGER KILLED IN HELICOPTER CRASH.

The old Eric would have left Forrester and Jackson to deal with the crash's grim aftermath. But the new one involved himself totally in it. 'Someone had to break the news to Stevie Ray's brother, Jimmie,' Vivien recalls. '"I'll do that," Eric said at once.'

He also volunteered to accompany Forrester and Jimmie Vaughan to the Chicago mortuary where the bodies had been taken. 'He was ready to go in and identify them,' Forrester says. 'But I told him there was no need for both of us to do it. "How do you deal with something like that?" he said to me afterwards.'

Alas, he would find out for himself soon enough.

It was decided to finish the tour, with a nightly dedication to Stevie Ray Vaughan. 'Everyone voted to carry on, but without Eric it probably would have fallen apart,' Vivien recalls. 'He kept the whole show together.'

By early 1991, he had managed to end the engagement to Lory and detach himself from her without endangering his access to Conor. She had taken up with a wealthy Milanese businessman named Silvio Sardi who lived part of the time in New York.

Eric had been smitten yet again. A friend of Lory's, in fact, introduced him to a combination of almond eyes, sculpted cheeks and perfect frame that pulverised his heart as never before. She was a twenty-three-year-old supermodel, half-Italian and half-French, who also happened to be heiress to the CEAT car-tyre fortune. Her name was Carla Bruni. 'I absolutely loved Carla,' Vivien Griffin recalls. 'She wasn't only the most beautiful woman I'd ever seen but was so charming and had such good manners. For once, I didn't blame Eric for thinking she was the love of his life.'

Though Carla, in fairness, never made any kind of commitment to him, everything seemed to go well until they chanced to be in New York together when the Rolling Stones' *Steel Wheels* tour came to town. Carla asked Eric if she could meet the Stones, by which – like every other woman who wanted to meet the Stones – she meant Mick Jagger. Eric could not refuse, despite knowing it would be like introducing a wolfhound to a Tournedos Rossini. 'Please, Mick,' he actually said as he did so, 'not this one. I think I'm in love.'

It may be too much to suggest Jagger had been out for revenge since Pattie had passed him over for Eric two decades earlier in Paris. More likely he was simply exercising his automatic *droit de seigneur* over any beautiful female who crossed his prancing path.

Whatever the explanation, Carla was soon deep in an affair with Jagger. Eric made an attempt to win her back at her family home in St Tropez but received a frigid reception. Around town later, he met a couple of her ex-boyfriends who told him commiseratingly how quickly she tended to go through men.

'He was absolutely devastated,' Vivien Griffin recalls, 'and very angry with Mick.' It still didn't stop him guesting with the Stones later in their tour, often with Carla present backstage.

For all his chagrin at the time, he would come to realise that he'd got off lightly. The four-year romance that followed fatally undermined Jagger's (sort of) marriage to Jerry Hall and gave the world's number-one heartbreaker his first-ever taste of the runaround, while for Carla it was but a stop on the road to meeting Nicolas Sarkozy and utilising her immaculate manners as France's First Lady.

Indeed, the episode was of positive value to the Twelve-Step recovery programme Eric was following through AA. Its most important psychological step weans alcoholics away from the belief that they're helpless victims and makes them acknowledge how their behaviour for years or decades past may have led inexorably to their predicament. In his case, he realised how much it was bound up with a compulsion to pursue women that almost amounted to an obligation, with never a thought for the resulting havoc.

'Bad choices were my speciality,' he would reflect in his autobiography. 'I thought I wasn't worthy of anything decent, so I could only choose partners who would ultimately abandon me, as I was convinced my mother had done all those years ago ... If anything honest and decent came along, I would shun it and run the other way.' But now something had come along answering that description in excelsis and he was neither shunning nor running.

In February and March 1991, he wound up the *Journeyman* tour with a run of twenty-four shows at the Royal Albert Hall, breaking his own, and the house's, record of eighteen the previous year. For the first six nights, he fronted a small band with Phil Collins, for the next six, a larger band including percussionist Ray Cooper, for the next six, a pure blues band with Robert Cray and Buddy Guy, and for the final six, the National Philharmonic Orchestra conducted by Michael Kamen.

*

On 19 March, Lory handed Conor over to him at Silvio Sardi's luxurious New York apartment on the fifty-third floor of the Galleria building on West 57th Street. It was the first time he'd ever taken the four-year-old out anywhere by himself and, rather old-fashionedly, he'd bought tickets for the circus at Nassau Coliseum on Long Island.

That sawdust-scented afternoon showed him what he'd been missing. When they returned, with Conor chattering excitedly about the clowns and elephants, Eric told Lory that from now on he intended to be a proper father and look after him unaided on his visits to Hurtwood.

The next day, they were to visit the Bronx Zoo, followed by lunch at an Italian restaurant. In the morning, before Eric's scheduled return, a janitor arrived at the Sardi apartment to clean the windows. Lory was in the bathroom and Conor in the care of a nanny but careering around excitedly, impatient to see his 'Papa' again.

The janitor had been working on the ceiling-high cantilevered windows in the living-room, one of which still hung open. Most New York high-rises were required by law to fit such windows with protective guards, but not condominiums like the Galleria. He called out to the nanny to watch the child but before she could react, Conor dashed past her, jumped up onto the low window-ledge where he'd normally press his nose against the glass, and disappeared.

Eric was preparing to set off from his hotel, the Mayfair Regent at Park Avenue and West 64th Street, when Lory came on the phone, screaming that Conor was dead. The idea was so beyond monstrous, all he could find to say was 'Are you sure?' She managed to convey that she was: their little boy had fallen from the living-room window on the fifty-third floor.

Eric was in such a daze that he chose to walk the seven blocks to the Galleria, amid the normality of yellow cabs and uniformed doormen, still thinking there must be some mistake. As he neared his destination, he saw an ambulance, a police line and crowds outside the entrance and, at first, continued down the street as though it was no concern of his. Realising later that Conor might have been in that ambulance, he was engulfed in shame that would stay with him for the rest of his life.

Roger Forrester was at home, near Brookwood in Surrey, when Eric telephoned. 'He said, "You're not going to believe this . . . Conor's dead,"' Forrester recalls. 'In my shock, I said the stupidest thing – "Are you sure?"'

Forrester persuaded British Airways to hold their supersonic Concorde until he could get to Heathrow Airport and so was able to reach New York in only four hours. 'As I'm on my way to Eric's hotel suite, I see a copy of the *New York Post* and on its front page is a picture of Conor, dead, lying on the concrete. Some woman who lived in the same building had photographed him from forty floors up.'

Forrester accompanied Eric to the formal identification process at Lenox Hill Hospital's mortuary, where light-bulbs of only 15 watts did their best to minimise the ordeal. 'Whatever physical damage Conor suffered in the fall, by the time I saw him they had restored his body to some normality,' Eric would recall. 'I remember looking at his beautiful face in repose and thinking, This isn't my son. It looks a bit like him, but he's gone. I went to see him again at the funeral home to say goodbye and apologise for not being a better father.' In Eric's mind, despite the rival claims of Italy and Catholicism, there was nowhere his son could be laid to rest but in the churchyard of St Mary Magdalen in Ripley, a few hundred yards from where he'd been born and grown up and next door to his first school. Accordingly, he and Lory flew back to Britain with Conor's body, into the first real media storm of his career.

In Surrey, before burial could be carried out, he had to formally identify his son all over again. 'The American mortuary had only had 15-watt bulbs,' Roger Forrester recalls. 'But in Britain, they were 100-watt.'

The Rev. Chris Elson had been vicar of Ripley for only three years and had never met Eric until he asked him to officiate at Conor's funeral. Elson was relatively young, so knowledgeable about pop music and fully aware of his parishioner's celebrity (unlike a Ewhurst cleric who'd once got Eric to play in the church there with no idea who he was).

'I think it helped the situation that when I was growing up, I hadn't followed Cream but the Beatles,' Elson recalls. 'If it had been George I was talking to, I would have found it harder to retain my professional composure.'

Theoretically, St Mary Magdalen's tiny churchyard was open to any member of Elson's flock, but over the years had become so crowded that interments took place in the adjacent parish burial ground. However, a place was found for Conor in the protecting lee of the church, below a stained-glass window which, in another life, his father might have constructed.

When the news reached Vivien Griffin she'd gone straight to Hurtwood Edge to offer whatever practical help she could. 'Eric was in the kitchen,' she recalls. 'The first thing he said to me was, "Please, just don't cry." The house was full of Italians – Lory, her mother and sister and, I think, her new boyfriend. They were all at one end of the house, wailing, and the stiff-upper-lip English were at the other, having cups of tea.'

The funeral took place on 28 March, designated in the Anglican calendar as Maundy Thursday, the start of the Easter festival, and two days before Eric's forty-sixth birthday. Everyone connected with it had been sworn to secrecy, but the pact was broken – by one of the florists who supplied wreaths, it was thought – and a brief official statement had to be issued by Chris Elson.

However, the media who descended on Ripley in a ravening

pack found the whole village united in protecting Eric. Reporters who toured the pubs, trying to pick up gossip about him, met only blank stares and turned backs. Residents with windows overlooking St Mary's refused all offers to rent them out as vantage-points. Cameramen who'd chained stepladders to the church railings overnight found the chains sawn through the next morning. One photographer hid in a tree in the churchyard but was betrayed by the noise of his camera's motor-drive and shaken down like a bad apple.

The mourners included George, Phil Collins and so many other faces from Chris Elson's teenage record collection that he almost pinched himself in the pulpit. Pattie, characteristically, was there too. At the graveside, there was an awful moment when Conor's Italian grandmother, Clorinda, tried to throw herself on the ornate, vastly oversized American coffin. But Eric, recalls Elson, 'behaved with enormous dignity and maturity throughout'.

Conor's English grandmother was not one for such displays of emotion. In her spasmodic reunions with Eric during his childhood and throughout the fame and torments of his adulthood, Pat had stayed the same rather remote, wary and sharp-tongued presence, seemingly incapable of giving him the affection he'd craved, in the second phase hardly less than the first.

But now, as the funeral congregation dispersed and the limos rolled up, she and Eric's aunt Sylvia went back into the churchyard and stood wordlessly by the newly covered grave. 'She was very destroyed,' Sylvia recalls.

Hundreds of letters and messages of condolence had poured in from all over the world, including one from Prince Charles. After the Italians had gone and the house was empty, Eric began to open them. The hardest moment of all was finding a sheet of green paper, posted when he still had a circus outing in New

York to look forward to. It read: 'I LOVE YOU I WANT TO SEE YOU AGAIN A KISS LOVE CONOR CLAPTON.'

In the 'waking nightmare' of the next few months – literally, since he barely slept – even music seemed to lose its power to comfort and heal. But at last his current producer, Russ Titelman, persuaded him to listen to the tapes of his Royal Albert Hall shows the previous March that were to be used for his live album, *24 Nights*.

There were plenty of blues masterpieces there to ease the pain, but the track he found himself playing over and over was 'Wonderful Tonight'. For it brought back a seemingly idyllic time in his now bleak and mourning house when upsets came no bigger than Pattie taking too long to dress for a party. And the sound of his own slow, somnolent riff sent him to sleep like a lullaby.

As perspective returned, he saw how his loss could be turned to positive effect in highlighting the dangers to all children living in high buildings. That summer, he filmed a message on behalf of the New York State Health Department that could not fail to strike any parent to the heart: 'Fit guards on windows and safety-gates on stairs. It's easy and it could prevent a terrible tragedy. Believe me, I know.'

When he could bear to pick up a guitar, it was only a small Spanish model, not much more assertive than Conor's toy one, and, before he knew it, chords began arranging themselves around the golden-haired vision in his head. Their source was not the blues this time, but reggae star Jimmy Cliff's 'Many Rivers To Cross' and black spirituals back into history on the theme of sorrows patiently endured. Such was the genesis of 'Tears In Heaven'.

However, it stayed at the back of his mind until the American director Lili Fini Zanuck offered him the diversion of co-writing a song for an already-completed action movie called

Rush. Although not enamoured of film work, he responded to its theme, that of an undercover female narcotics agent, and would have a distinguished collaborator in Will Jennings, whose credits included several of Stevie Winwood's solo albums.

They had already completed a ballad entitled 'Help Me Up' when Lili Zanuck heard 'Tears In Heaven' and insisted on using it in the film. Eric had written only its first verse and left Will Jennings to write further ones and a bridge, despite Jennings's reluctance to take over something so profoundly personal.

The marvel was that he ever got through it in the recording-studio, not just once but in take after take until producer Russ Titelman was satisfied. Whatever the internal cost, he gave a performance that would cause tears on earth for many years to come. Unfathomable, indescribable grief pushed his voice into a new register, stripped of its usual bluesy roughness; a near-falsetto that might have come straight from the bewildered child who had always lived inside him.

Yet 'Tears In Heaven' had none of the mawkishness and melo-drama of most 'death songs'. Nor did it express any of the despair or rage or self-reproach for which it might have acted as cathar-sis. It did not describe Conor or even mention his name. He was an invisible celestial presence, to whom his father reached out rather shyly, as if still uncertain of having won him over in life: 'Would you hold my hand/If I saw you in Heaven?' There has never been a better example of what Carlos Santana called 'Holy Ghost Music'.

Not until December of 1991 did he feel equal to touring again and then only in a brief, twelve-concert visit to Japan. George and Olivia Harrison had been among the most supportive of his friends in the aftermath of Conor's death, and now he invited George to co-headline with him in Japan.

Like the Delaney & Bonnie tour in far-off 1969, it showed a concern for his Beatle buddy that could always override his own troubles. George hadn't been on the road since his disastrous American tour of 1974 just after Pattie had left him. As in the Beatle break-up time of '69, Eric's idea was to ease him back to the concert stage with which he'd always had such a troubled relationship.

'Eric said, "Look, Japan is the easiest place to tour and you can have my band and my whole set-up,"' Vivien Griffin recalls. 'Even so, George took a long time to make up his mind; first it was on, then it was off, then it was on again, and he didn't want Roger Forrester there, though Roger did go in the end.'

The six-piece band had been chosen for their sensitivity to Eric's fragile emotional state and continuing determined sobriety as much as for their musicianship, considerable though it was. They included Elton John's long-time percussion wizard Ray Cooper and, on third guitar, Andy Fairweather-Low from the Sixties band Amen Corner (who clearly could not expect to feature with his biggest solo hit, 'Wide-Eyed And Legless').

However, the two headliners' musical empathy was no longer quite what it used to be. Latterly, George had developed an enthusiasm for the ukulele and a fixation on George Formby, the toothy north-country comedian who'd played that midget great-nephew to the guitar in numerous British films of the 1930s and '40s. 'He brought along a couple of ukuleles,' Andy Fairweather-Low recalls. 'But Eric took no interest in them at all.'

The shadow of tragedy overhung the whole tour, onstage as well as off. George's section of the programme included 'While My Guitar Gently Weeps', in which Eric's riffs seemed to take on a new, searing intensity. 'And you had to be careful not to say the wrong thing,' Fairweather-Low recalls. 'Like complaining because the windows in our high-rise hotels were always sealed shut.'

Far from being a good companion to Eric, George relapsed into the same 'minxiness' (to use Pattie's term) as on the Delaney

& Bonnie tour all those years ago. 'Eric didn't hang out with the band, but George was always inviting them to his room to drink and listen to him play the ukulele,' Vivien Griffin says. 'He kind of seduced the band and split the camp.'

The minxiness did not stop there. When the troupe reached Hiroshima, Lory turned up at their hotel, the Sun Plaza, having come specially from Milan to see Eric. Since Conor's funeral, she had had a child with Silvio Sardi – another son, Devin by name. Sardi, with whom Eric got on well, had sent him a fax warning that she was on her way. 'He talked to her, saying it was completely inappropriate and he didn't want her there,' Vivien Griffin recalls. 'But George was very sweet to her and she ended up staying a few days.'

In 2007, Lory would claim they'd had a three-day affair, which on her part had been 'sweet revenge' on Eric for leaving her, and on George's, for his wooing away of Pattie. Vivien recalls much gossip about it, especially among the tour's female back-up singers, which somehow never seemed to reach Eric.

Ten months after Conor's death, the inquest took place, not in New York but Guildford, Surrey, where it had been registered. Again, no stand-in was possible: he relived the terrible morning of 20 March calmly and clearly, refusing to place any blame on Jose Pastrana, the janitor who had left the window open.

He had kept up his attendance at AA throughout the Japanese tour and by now had become so involved in the movement that he was sometimes asked to chair meetings about the Third Step, in which one hands oneself over to a 'higher power'. Then he'd describe that turning-point at the Hazelden clinic when, in the words of 'Layla', he'd gone down on his knees, 'beggin' of you, please'.

The very fact of his still being in AA after what he'd been through proved a motivation in itself. After one meeting, a woman told him he'd taken away an excuse for going back to drunkenness she'd always kept in reserve – that it would be pardonable if something terrible ever happened to one of her children. 'But you've just shown me that's not true.'

'Eric turned out to have huge strength of character,' Vivien Griffin says. 'The kind of tragedy he'd suffered would have sent most people back to the bottle. What kept him going, he always said, was the thought that it would be a betrayal of Conor.'

24

A PLACE TO STAND

Ever since Eric learned the blues, he'd been haunted by the legend of Robert Johnson's soul-bartering rendezvous with the Devil at a midnight crossroads. Now he discovered for himself at what terrible a price success could come.

'Tears In Heaven', released as a single in January 1992, went to number 2 in the *Billboard* Hot 100 and by the year's end had sold almost three million in the US alone. It would become one of the best-selling singles of the 1990s and his biggest apart from 'I Shot The Sheriff', which would stand as his only American number 1.

It was premiered in the restrained ambience of an *MTV Unplugged* concert, where purveyors of high-voltage rock could be heard in softer acoustic mood. Seated before a small British studio audience – the first ever to see him wearing glasses – Eric seemed at once a figure of infinite sadness and heroic resilience who still didn't neglect his tailoring. Also in his set was an unamplified version of 'Layla' played at a gentle lope rather than thunderous gallop, its frantic importuning now the mildest of suggestions. The show won MTV more viewers than any other in the series and Eric's *Unplugged* would set a new record for live albums, selling 26 million worldwide.

At the same time, retrospective honour was being done to two of the bands he'd left behind in his ascent. In 1992, twenty-four years after breaking up, the Yardbirds were inducted into the Rock 'n' Roll Hall of Fame by U2's lead guitarist, nouned rather than named the Edge.

Two of the band's other guitar-hero graduates, Jimmy Page and Jeff Beck, were present, but not Eric. There was, in fact, a slight edge to the occasion, as if memories of his disruptiveness still lingered. The only 'absent friend' to receive a mention was vocalist Keith Relf, who had died in 1976 (ironically, not from his awful respiratory problems but from accidentally electrocuting himself with his own guitar).

The following year, Cream also took their place in the Hall of Fame, inducted by ZZ Top, a latter-day trio whose long-bearded lead guitarist and bass-player resembled twin Old Testament prophets in sunglasses.

All three ex-Creamers attended, with hatchets firmly buried. Jack Bruce, that sadly undervalued talent, thanked Ginger Baker for 'showing me some mad African rhythms that I can't get over' (omitting other things such as knives) and paid tribute to Eric 'for clearing my mind and teaching me the purity of the blues and the honesty of it'.

Baker, whose later career had taken him to Africa, raising horses and, somewhat implausibly, playing polo, contented himself with a simple, wolfish 'Thank you'. Eric said that rehearsing the inductees' traditional performance had been the first time they had played together in twenty-five years. 'And it was pretty amazing. It was wonderful.'

'Sunshine Of Your Love' followed in a necessarily chamber version, Eric alternating lead vocal with Bruce as they never had in the old days. But enough of the old passion and precision was there to make Cream mourned all over again.

A month later at the Grammy awards in Los Angeles, his heartbreak took him to the summit of his career. 'Tears In Heaven' won in three categories, Record of the Year, Song of the Year and Best Male Pop Vocal; *Unplugged* won Album of the Year and Best Male Rock Vocal, and the unplugged 'Layla' won Best Rock Song.

'I have received a very great honour, but I've also lost the one thing I truly loved,' he told an audience of 5,000 at the Shrine Auditorium. 'I would like to thank a lot of people but the one person I would like to thank is my son for the love he gave me and the song he gave me.'

Then, as the reality of the six little gilt gramophones sank in: 'I just feel so incredibly guilty. I don't know why I feel so guilty about taking so many of these . . .'

Recovering alcoholics can be as difficult as drunks, or even more so, and Vivien Griffin wisely spent some time on the Al-Anon programme for spouses and relatives to help equip her for her twelve-year stint as Eric's personal assistant.

In some respects, sobriety only magnified old traits like his impatience and whim of iron. 'He'd say to me that he wanted a certain jacket. I'd tell him, "It's in transit by road, Eric. It means finding out where the truck is, stopping it and then searching through the back for the right wardrobe trunk . . ." He'd smile and say, "Yes, and I'd still quite like that jacket."'

In other ways, his personality seemed to have changed completely. 'He could get angry very suddenly about the smallest things and I had to learn it usually had nothing to do with me and not get upset by it. When he was drinking, he'd been a typical lackadaisical rock star who never cared what time it was. Now he got annoyed if anyone was even a minute late for a meeting.'

The first, pressing requirement of this new Eric was new surroundings. He could not face living on alone at Hurtwood Edge, with its echoes of a golden-haired tot kicking footballs around the terrace. The house's very name and that of the Hurt Forest below it seemed to conspire to rub in the pain.

After years of cherished rural isolation, he felt drawn back to the distracting noise and bustle of London, specifically to Chelsea, where he'd had such great times with the *Oz* crowd and artists and criminals and philosophers at The Pheasantry. On the first day of viewing potential properties with Vivien, he fell in love with the third they saw, a three-storey town house in Old Church Street. Roger Forrester arranged the purchase without demur and the interior designer David 'Monster' Mlinaric was hired to effect a complete refurbishment.

There was also a ready-made refuge in Antigua, for many years past the one place where he'd felt able to relax. He bought a plot of land in the south of the island, near English Harbour, intending to have a house built on it. At one point, he wanted to sell Hurtwood and buy a new country retreat near Oxford, but Forrester decreed that the property-splurge had gone on long enough.

Conor's death did have one positive outcome, thanks to a woman who must be reckoned a major occurrence of Clapton Luck. For six years, the recording studio manager Yvonne Kelly, now Robinson, had been quietly raising her child by Eric in Montserrat without seeking any recognition of the child from him. While he'd always been fully aware of his daughter, Ruth, and never shirked financial responsibility for her, the distance between them had prevented any meaningful contact.

Latterly, Yvonne had moved back to her home town, Doncaster in Yorkshire, for the sake of Ruth's education. When she heard of Eric's loss, she wrote to him, offering as much access to his daughter as might bring him comfort.

Moved by this 'incredibly generous act' he invited Yvonne to bring Ruth on a cruise round Antigua with Roger and Annette Forrester in the summer of 1991. The beautiful, bubbly six-year-old offered him 'a lifeline in the sea of bewilderment and confusion' and back in Britain he began seeing her regularly and trying to be a 'real' dad.

He was by now attending AA meetings twice a week and

proselytising for AA and the Twelve-Step Programme at every opportunity. For example, 1992 saw his inauguration of an annual booze-free New Year's party at Guildford Leisure Centre. Even in his never-slackening love life, he looked for women in recovery like himself. But the tendency to be 'smitten' regardless of common sense or consequences remained as strong in the new Eric as in the old, and soon led him into trouble yet again.

Francesca Amfitheatrof was a part-Italian, part Russian-American jewellery designer who supplied major fashion houses like Lagerfeld and Chanel (and would eventually become creative director of the Tiffany company). Eric met her because her mother, a fashion PR, worked for his favourite suitmaker, and now friend, Giorgio Armani. She combined the gamine look of Lory Del Santo with the killer cheekbones of Carla Bruni and within a few months, he would recall, in yet another echo of 'Layla', 'I was on my knees.'

The trouble was that Francesca was only in her mid-twenties while he was now pushing fifty and increasingly conscious of a generation gap between his dates and himself. He was, for instance, unaware of younger people's hostility to nicotine until she forbade him to smoke in her New York apartment. People did not normally say 'no' to Eric. It sent him off to take a hypnotherapy course, which ended the forty-a-day habit he'd begun on his twenty-first birthday.

Francesca meted out the kind of treatment he'd escaped when Carla chose Mick Jagger, refusing to live with him or make any kind of commitment. Their relationship had a volatility he might have found exciting at twenty-four but which, at nearly fifty, was merely nerve-racking. 'As far as he was concerned, she was a total nightmare,' Vivien Griffin recalls. 'But the more she led him round the houses, the more he pursued her. As usual with Eric, it was the attraction of the unavailable.'

★

In the Queen's New Year's Honours list for 1994, he received the OBE (Officer of the Most Excellent Order of the British Empire) for his 'contribution to British life'. 'He went off to the Palace on his own to collect it,' Vivien recalls. 'Then in the evening, he had to pick up another award, from *GQ* magazine. Later, I found him sitting at the kitchen table with both of them in front of him, looking absolutely miserable because he'd had to come home to an empty house and there was no one to share his honours with.'

A few months later, Rose Clapp died from cancer, aged eighty-seven. She had been the most important person in Eric's life, both as a mother and grandmother, offering him unfailing unconditional love, and it would be harder than ever to face the world without her.

As Rose had grown frailer, he'd brought her back from Shamley Green to Ripley, buying her one of the new houses on the site of his old primary school, next door to the church, and installing his mother, Pat, in a similar dwelling just across the High Street. He had thought that living barely fifty yards apart would be more companionable for them both, but instead it created a rivalry where he was concerned that had never existed before, and he could never go to see one without feeling guilty that he wasn't with the other.

Rose's funeral service at St Mary Magdalen was conducted by the Rev. Chris Elson, as Conor's had been, and the eulogy was given by Guy Pullen (whose mother, Peg, her old neighbour from The Green, would pass away at the same age not long afterwards). Eric arranged for a local florist to place fresh flowers on her grave every week.

After Rose's death, he bought Pat a new house on the outskirts of the village, with a bigger garden in which she delighted to work. She was by now in poor health herself, suffering from emphysema as a result of a lifetime's heavy smoking and dependent on oxygen and prescription drugs that her formerly heroin-addicted son viewed with concern.

For all the years she'd been back in his life, they seemed never to have found any real intimacy or trust. He had hoped that someday they'd finally be able to talk about her abandonment of him as a two-year-old, when Rose had assumed the title as well as duties of his mother, but she still always refused to go there.

Once, when Pat was receiving in-patient treatment at London's Lister Hospital, Vivien Griffin spent a whole morning running errands for her and so committed the new sin of being late for lunch with Eric at San Lorenzo. However, he was more concerned that in the process of buying her soap and toiletries, Pat might somehow have turned Vivien against him.

Not long after Rose's death, Pat decided to return to Canada, whither she had originally decamped in 1947. Her two daughters with her ex-husband, Frank McDonald, were still there and wanted her near them for whatever time she had left. Although the circumstances were vastly different this time, she was rejecting and abandoning Eric all over again.

His brief time with Conor had inevitably stirred thoughts of his own father, the Canadian soldier Edward Fryer, who'd had a wartime one-night stand with fifteen-year-old Pat, then abandoned her the moment she fell pregnant with him. Rock stars' long-lost fathers had a tendency to resurface when their offspring became famous and wealthy – John Lennon's the best-known case in point – but throughout Eric's decades in the spotlight, nothing had ever been heard from Fryer.

Those wonderings about the man who'd rejected him pre-natally refused to subside, and eventually went into a song as atypically personal as 'Tears In Heaven'. 'My Father's Eyes' juxtaposed the adoring gaze Conor had received from him with the one he never had from Edward Fryer, to his ultimate, irreparable cost: 'I'm like a bridge that was washed away/My foundations are made of clay.'

When 'My Father's Eyes' was released, three years later, it would bring some answers about Edward Fryer at long last. The song's Grammy-winning success prompted a Canadian journalist, Michael Woloschuk of the *Ottawa Star*, to investigate Fryer's history after he returned to his homeland with a dishonourable discharge from his regiment some time around 1945.

It turned out to have paralleled his discarded son's in all sorts of ways, minus the celebrity. He had resumed his pre-war occupation of playing piano in clubs and bars, travelling extensively through the United States, once even visiting the Mississippi Delta, and earning extra money, though never very much, from his talent as an artist. Highly attractive to women, he had married several times and had numerous affairs. One ex-wife portrayed him as selfish, charming, feckless and prone to apocalyptic emotion, recounting how he'd once tried to commit suicide by driving a hired car into Niagara Falls.

He had died from leukaemia in 1985, apparently without ever having identified himself as Eric Clapton's father, leaving, so far as could be computed, two daughters and a son, also named Edward, who'd grown up to be a rock musician with a drug-problem.

Eric was chary about making contact with these possible reincarnations of his father's eyes. Although the alleged photograph of Fryer in the *Ottawa Star* certainly resembled him, he felt that conclusive identification could come only from Pat – something impossible to ask of her. 'He was in two minds about the whole thing,' Vivien Griffin recalls. 'At the start, he wanted to follow up on it, but then things all started to get a bit muddy and murky, with more and more people claiming to be related to him. He was only really interested in his father, not partners or children.'

He remained locked in the tumultuous on-off affair with Francesca Amfitheatrof, despite its withering effect on his self-esteem. There seemed no way out until two married friends from the therapy world, Richard and Chris Steele, came to stay at his new house on Antigua's Galleon Beach. Richard had been his staunchest supporter in the battle for sobriety while Chris headed the alcoholic and addiction unit at The Priory psychiatric hospital in Roehampton.

One evening, he confessed his troubles with Francesca to the Steeles and showed them a letter he proposed to send her. Chris's immediate response was: 'Why are you giving all your power to this woman?'

Aside from her executive duties at The Priory, she agreed to give him one-to-one counselling there. Her first question, 'Who are you?', was one that he'd never been able to answer without a guitar in his hands. The sessions that followed were in effect a mental sobering-up, showing him that his problems really had nothing to do with Francesca but reached right back into a childhood that he'd never managed to let go; that for all his formidably adult achievement in slaying his addictions, he was emotionally still only about ten years old.

There followed a major step in the evolution of the new Eric: realising that other people had problems, too. He volunteered for peer-support work at The Priory, taking a short training course that allowed him to sit in on the group-therapy sessions at the start of each day. 'Going outside himself and trying to help other people made him feel like a real, substantial person,' Vivien Griffin says. 'I remember him telling me, "I've finally found a place to stand."'

His semi-official status at The Priory brought a visitant from the darkest of the old days. Towards the end of 1994, Alice Ormsby-Gore's family contacted him with the news that she had left Paris, where she'd lived for some years, and was seriously ill in a hospital in Shrewsbury. Eric got Richard and Chris Steele to visit her and persuade her to check into The Priory.

After decades of drug-addiction and alcoholism Alice was

unrecognisable as the frizzy-haired sprite who'd seemed to fly into his life straight from the pages of Lewis Carroll; although still barely into her forties, she looked like an infirm, mal-nourished woman twenty years older. Yet, despite a later life of increasing financial hardship, she'd made no attempt to sell the story of their five years together to tabloid newspapers that would have paid her a fortune.

It did not quite come about that the man for whom she had scored heroin as a teenager turned into her drug-counsellor. Because of their past association, Eric was excluded from the group-therapy sessions in which she participated. However, Chris Steele told him that she still felt a lot of anger towards him and suggested he speak to her in private.

The half-hour encounter was a kind of shock therapy in itself as Alice furiously spelt out all that she'd done for love of him and the consequences she had suffered in his heedless wake. 'It was terrifying', he would recall, 'to realise the damage I had done to this poor girl.'

The Priory seemed to be making that good at long last. When-ever Eric bumped into her later around the clinic, they could talk in a friendly way and Alice said her treatment was 'going great'. She did, indeed, complete the course, then went on to a half-way house in Bournemouth where he had once spent some time, seemingly on track to full recovery. The next, and last, time he saw her was at Rose's funeral – a tribute, as Lory Del Santo's presence also was, to his grandmother's sweetness.

In April 1995, a few days before her forty-third birthday, Alice was found dead in a Bournemouth bedsitting-room after shooting up six times the fatal dose of heroin. It had happened some time before but nobody had missed her. Everything she possessed was in two plastic bin-liners and the syringe was still stuck in her arm.

A post-mortem found that she'd also been drinking heavily.

Back at The Priory, she'd told Chris Steele what Eric had felt for so many years – that she couldn't stand the pain of being sober.

On the evening of 25 March 1996, Eric returned to his house in Old Church Street, Chelsea, after a day out. When he opened the front door, black smoke billowed into his face. Unnoticeably as yet from the street, the whole top floor was on fire.

He had been lucky, like always. The fire had started in a light-fitting in the corridor outside his bedroom; no one else was in the house and had he been in bed asleep, he could have suffo-cated. As it was, he had time to rescue all the guitars he had on the premises before the fire brigade arrived from nearby King's Road and ordered him to safety in a nearby mews. The flames had not reached the other three floors and most of the damage was from the smoke.

For Eric, the event symbolised the recent collapse of his com-bustible affair with Francesca Amfitheatrof into ashes and his determination not to get burned like that again. 'He started from scratch with the house,' Vivien Griffin says. 'He got rid of his art collection and all the antiques David Mlinaric had put in. He had the whole interior painted white, with just a double bed, a sofa and a TV set.

'When he started refurnishing it, he didn't go back to Mli-naric or any other interior designer, but went out and chose everything for himself. I thought that was a really important moment for Eric, when he had the confidence to take control of his own surroundings.'

Taking control of fabrics and furnishings proved to be only the beginning. Latterly, his stays at his house on Antigua had been marred by the number of drug-addicts and drunks always to be found around nearby English Harbour – so much so that, as he told his friends Richard and Chris Steele, he was thinking of selling up and leaving. Rather than that, Richard suggested, he should provide the island with its first treatment centre, as payback for the refuge it had given him and in thanksgiving for his own recovery.

The new altruistic, socially aware Eric seized on the notion of a clinic that would serve the whole Caribbean area, using its income from wealthy American and European clients to fund free treatment for local people – 'taking from the rich to feed the poor', as he saw it, just like Robin Hood.

The plan was for him to put up a third of the cost and assume an advisory role based on his own hard-won experience. The remaining capital and professional know-how would come from the American company that owned The Priory, Community Psychiatric Centers Inc., and construction would be carried out by a local subsidiary of the McAlpine company.

The new Eric showed a patience, concentration and attention-span unknown in the old one as he attended meetings and briefings, studied reports and financial forecasts and made personal submissions to the Antiguan government whose approval and co-operation were vital. In the Caribbean, drug-addiction and alcoholism still meant social ostracism and many officials to whom the project was outlined simply did not get the point of it. One asked if he'd be able to stay at the clinic if he needed to lose some weight.

Nonetheless, the government threw its weight behind the project, virtually donating a ten-acre site for the new clinic on a peninsula jutting into Willoughby Bay. Its name expressed its aim to be a turning-point in its future patients' lives while also harking back to the location of Robert Johnson's diabolic midnight tryst, since referenced innumerable times onstage by his heir-apparent. It would be the Crossroads Centre.

Construction was about one-third complete when boardroom machinations back in the US threatened to bring the whole hopeful edifice crashing down. Without any prior warning to

Eric from its executives, his alleged partners, Community Psychiatric Centers, were taken over and renamed the Transitional Hospitals Corporation. This new entity felt no sense of mission towards rehabilitating addicts on Antigua and immediately announced its withdrawal from the partnership; at this late stage, if he wanted Crossroads to open, his only recourse was to buy out THC's two-thirds interest.

The unequivocal view of his manager, Roger Forrester, was that the project had become a bottomless pit and he should cut and run. But, for the first time ever, Eric flatly rejected Forrester's advice. He repaid the Transitional Hospitals Corporation their entire investment (save for around $2 million that they wrote off) and henceforth would effectively shoulder Crossroads' costs on his own.

Long before this, he and Forrester had been inevitably approaching their own crossroads. In Forrester's eyes, he was still 'the Boy', a helpless man-infant who needed protecting from himself even to the extent of a baby-alarm in his bedroom at night. 'Roger had done a great job of looking after Eric the boy and Eric the drunk,' says Vivien Griffin. 'But after he got sober, he stopped being a boy. He wanted more of a say in the running of his career, but Roger couldn't move with him. Roger didn't want anything to change.

'He loved Eric, but he didn't love him enough to help him grow up and turn into a normal human being. He still wanted to keep the same control as before.'

As so often in such situations, a build-up of small grievances on both sides led to the final showdown. When Eric received a personal invitation from Luciano Pavarotti to appear in the great tenor's Modena festival, he said 'yes' on the spot, a breach of managerial protocol that made the telephone-line practically ice up when he informed Forrester.

During this period, Eric and the Scottish musician Simon Climie, with whom he had co-produced 'My Father's Eyes', were working on an album seasoning traditional R&B with contemporary music styles like trip-hop, ambient and club. They called their studio band TDF (standing for Totally Dysfunctional Family) and, in a throwback to Derek and the Dominos, Eric was credited only as 'x-sample'. TDF's bills at Olympic Studios made Forrester blanch, but again he managed to bite his lip.

Though Forrester had worked as hard as anyone to help Eric achieve sobriety, he now felt he'd been 'brainwashed by his AA people'. 'When Eric was drinking, his friends had always been music people that Roger could keep an eye on,' Vivien says. 'Now they came from a completely different environment and weren't subject to Roger in any way. That was another bit of control that he'd lost.'

By 1998 – when the Crossroads Centre opened its doors and 'My Father's Eyes' won the Grammy for Best Male Pop Vocal Performance – the two were barely communicating. 'I went to see Eric in Portland, Oregon, and he refused to even speak to me,' Forrester recalls.

Finally, he sent his errant 'boy' a long, reproachful letter, reminding him of all the great deals he'd made for him and listing the mistakes which, in Forrester's view, he was now making on his own. The result was his 'Boy's' ultimate feat of self-reliance.

'The greatest courage I ever saw him show was when he sacked Roger,' Vivien Griffin recalls. 'He said, "I'm going to do it myself and I'm going to his office to do it."' Expecting he knew not what kind of verbal onslaught from the famously acid-tongued Forrester, he took the precaution of wearing a necklace of sacred Tibetan Dzi beads under his T-shirt.

The meeting took barely ten minutes, and the expected storm never broke. Sad rather than angry, Forrester behaved with dignity and restraint, even offering to find Eric a new manager to replace him. It rubbed several bushels of salt into an already grievous wound to discover that he'd already unwittingly done so.

His successor was to be his lawyer, Michael Eaton, who had negotiated the recovery of Eric's song copyrights from Chappell in 1983 – and who was already playing an active part in the Crossroads project. Eaton, however, would have the lesser title of business manager, not dictating to Eric as Forrester had in so many areas, but implementing whatever he decided. Forrester would always suspect his lawyer of having plotted against him, but Eaton says his elevation came as a complete surprise. 'I knew Roger and Eric were going to have a row but I had no idea Roger was going to get fired.'

Although there had never been a formal management contract between them, Forrester could have created huge problems over his summary dismissal, perhaps even dragging Eric into court for the very first time. But he says it didn't cross his mind. 'In all the years we'd worked together, I'd never sued anyone and I wasn't going to start now. I was holding all his money – he still didn't really know how much – but I just arranged for it to be transferred to him.'

Less compliant was Forrester's bookkeeper, Gladys Bates, who for years had handed Eric his weekly 'workman's' pay envelope containing £200. 'Afterwards, he sent Gladys a guitar and some other things. But she sent them back to him with a letter saying she thought he'd behaved disgracefully.'

'I think that at first Roger didn't think Eric was serious and that after about a week he'd be reinstated,' Vivien Griffin recalls. 'But then Eric wrote him a letter, thanking him for everything he'd done, and he saw it was really over. After all the laughs they'd had together, Eric still wanted there to be some relationship between them, but Roger cut himself off completely, even from people in the team that he'd always got on with, like Peter

Jackson and Nigel Carroll. We'd had a bit of a chequered history, but even I felt terribly sorry for him.'

The severance terms eventually agreed were generous, Eaton recalls. Forrester would continue receiving his full commission for five years and half of it for a further five, plus some further money from tours he'd set up which Eric had yet to make.

But the emotional impact of losing Eric was greater than anyone who knew the lean, hyperactive man with the outsize specs and careful comb-over would have imagined. 'Roger was gutted. Absolutely gutted,' his fellow manager Ed Bicknell recalls. 'He'd been Eric's crutch for years. He'd done good, brilliant deals for him and got him out of one after another impossible situation.'

Bicknell realised the stress-level of Forrester's job one night during Eric's Japanese tour with Mark Knopfler when they were joined onstage by Elton John at the 60,000-capacity Tokyo Dome. 'The set started with Eric playing "Crossroads" in the wings. As soon as Roger heard the opening chords, he went white and gripped the arms of his seat. Because, for all those years when Eric was drinking, there was never any telling what he'd do when he came on. Roger had once had to sit and watch him play a whole show at the Tokyo Budokan lying flat on his back.'

Eric had always known that, in addition to his investment of around $6 million, his name would be a huge promotional asset to the Crossroads Centre. But, with his new sensitivity to patient care, he found it hard to reconcile giving out commercials from the concert stage with the privacy and discretion its clientele were guaranteed.

After barely a year, Crossroads' need for some further boost from him was becoming urgent. Its overseas clients, paying $9,000 per twenty-nine-day course, did not nearly cover the free treatment to Antiguans known as 'scholarships', yet he wouldn't hear of expanding one to the detriment of the other. Early in 1999, he admitted the centre was 'struggling' and warned that he 'couldn't go on bankrolling it for ever'.

He had lately bought himself another new home, this one in Venice, California, and struck up a friendship with the Oscar-winning Hollywood producer/director Lili Fini Zanuck. It was she who came up with the answer to his dilemma over Cross-roads – a charity auction of his guitar collection, followed by a benefit concert and live album of it in the mode of his old friend George.

While he was involved in preparations for both events, his half-sisters Cheryl and Heather telephoned from Canada to say that their mother was gravely ill with cancer. He immediately flew to see Pat in hospital in Toronto, where he was informed that her condition was inoperable and she had only a little time left.

Even in such circumstances, mother and son found communication little easier. Having benefited so much from counselling, Eric felt it might help Pat, too, but she refused to entertain any thought that she might not get better. Only after she slipped into a coma did he discover she had told her doctors she didn't wish to be resuscitated.

At all events, the unerasable wound he had received from her was not repaid in kind. She had left him at the beginning of his life, but he stayed by her as if she were the best of mothers until the end of hers.

Since returning to Canada, she had spoken to Eric's old friend Guy Pullen on the telephone and expressed a wish to be buried in her home village. Accordingly, she was cremated and her ashes were brought back to Ripley for a funeral service at St Mary Magdalen. The Rev. Chris Elson officiated, as he had done for her mother and grandson, and to general surprise, the mourners included Lory Del Santo.

At Eric's request, Pullen gave the eulogy, skirting around the controversial aspects of Pat's life and accentuating her positive qualities, like her vivacity and sense of humour. 'I said to Rick afterwards, "You owe me for that,"' Pullen recalls. 'He said, "Well, I'll do yours."'

On 24 June, the auction of a hundred of his guitars for Crossroads Centre took place at Christie's, New York, ahead of the benefit concert at Madison Square Garden featuring Bob Dylan, Andy Fairweather-Low, Mary J. Blige and Sheryl Crow.

Previously, the record price paid for a guitar hero's 'axe' had been £320,000 for one that had belonged to Jimi Hendrix. Eric's 1957 tobacco Stratocaster (Brownie), which he'd played on 'Layla', received an opening bid of $200,000 and finally went to an anonymous buyer for $497,000. The actor Michael J. Fox paid $36,800 for a 1949 Gibson ES 125, similar to one used by B. B. King in the 1950s, and $42,500 for a 1930s National Duolian. The net proceeds for Crossroads after deductions were just short of $4.5 million.

Eric was rehearsing for the concert in Los Angeles, so could only watch on a live internet feed as so many old, true friends went under the hammer. But he had attended a preview of forty lots a few days earlier at Quixote Studios in West Hollywood. The event included music from Jimmie Vaughan, the unlucky Stevie Ray's brother, with whom – naturally – he got up and jammed.

During the evening, one of the young women showing guests to their tables asked him if they could have a picture taken together. To the love-wearied yet still love-seeking superstar, her smile seemed 'totally open and genuine'. Her name was Melia McEnery.

25

'THE HEM OF GOD'S GARMENT'

Having already made the Rock 'n' Roll Hall of Fame twice, as
a member of the Yardbirds and Cream, Eric received an unprecedented – and still unmatched – third induction, this time as
a solo performer, in March 2000, just before his fifty-fifth birthday. His friend Robbie Robertson delivered the citation, recalling
with amusement how in 1968 he'd turned up at the Band's Woodstock headquarters, overtly coveting Robertson's lead guitar
spot.

Also in 2000, his uncle Adrian, whom Rose always called
'Son', died after a long illness. Adrian had been an indelible
part of Eric's childhood with his record collection, extravagant
jitterbugging and habit of sprinkling vinegar over all his food,
puddings included. He had never strayed far from Ripley, working for years in the office of a local Ford Motors dealership. Yet
his celebrity nephew had always rather envied his innate joie-de-
vivre and how early, in the vivacious Sylvia, he had found the
love of his life.

With Billy Preston on keyboards and the Impressions on
backing vocals, Eric's 2001 album *Reptile* might have seemed like
a homage to black soul music. But white working-class Ripley in
the 1950s was curled around its heart. 'Reptile' was the childhood
nickname given to him by Charlie Cumberland, the village pub
celebrity ('Still playin' that ol'banjo, boy?'). The cover artwork
included a snapshot gallery of family and Ripley friends, while

a gentle instrumental track, 'Son & Sylvia', celebrated his uncle and aunt's long, happy marriage.

The same nostalgia carried over into his 2002 live album, *One More Car, One More Rider*, a memory of the funfair on Ripley Green and the bumper cars sparking on their poles, when he would await that command to jump into an empty car from the owner's formidable wife, Mrs Benson.

Since his rather uncomfortable Japanese tour with George in 1991, there had been no further musical interaction between them. Indeed, his best friend's life had taken a turn unimaginable back in the days when being a Beatle was equated, however misguidedly, with unadulterated happiness.

In 1997, George was diagnosed with throat cancer, the result of a lifetime's heavy smoking, but had seemingly made a full recovery after surgery and radiation treatment. Then on 30 December 1999, a deranged Beatles fan named Michael Abram broke into Friar Park and stabbed him repeatedly with a carving knife. He suffered a punctured lung and lacerations to the head and was resigned to dying, there in his own bizarre baronial hall, when his wife Olivia courageously fought off his assailant, wielding a poker and a lamp.

Eric had last seen him early in 2000, when they'd sat in Friar Park's kitchen with a mutual friend, the rock-book publisher Brian Roylance, and George had relived the episode, as drolly Liverpudlian as ever but still plainly shaken to the core.

Since then, Eric had been living with Melia McEnery at his house in Los Angeles, heavily preoccupied with matters of a non-musical sort. In June 2001, Melia gave birth to their first daughter, Julie. There was an initial period of anxiety when the baby refused breast-milk and her skull was found to have insufficiently decompressed after delivery, making it difficult for her to swallow without gagging. The problem was corrected by a sacro-cranial therapist, but for some months she suffered badly from colic and her father had to get used to carrying her around while she was screaming with pain. Not much chance of keeping a low profile there.

Meanwhile, George's cancer had returned with a vengeance. That May, he had a malignant growth removed from one of his lungs; in July, he received treatment for a brain tumour, first in Switzerland, then in Staten Island, New York, where, in November, they told him there was no further hope.

Coincidentally, Eric was back touring Japan when George died on 29 November in a Los Angeles house rented, and later owned, by Paul McCartney. On front pages and TV news throughout the world, it was the only story capable of displacing the fall-out from 9/11, and it brought the same chill thought to Fab Four-lovers, now of every age and nationality. Only two of them left.

His first wife, at least, knew he'd felt no more bitterness about losing her to Eric. A few months before his death, he'd phoned Pattie out of the blue at her West Sussex cottage. 'He said, "I'm in the area visiting Ringo and Barbara [Bach, Ringo's second wife] and if you're home, I'll drop in and see you,"' she recalls. 'He brought me flowers and little presents, like a figure of the Indian monkey god, Hanuman. We walked in the field behind the cottage; he looked very fragile and I somehow knew he knew it was the last time we'd ever see each other.'

On New Year's Day, 2002, Eric returned to the church of St Mary Magdalen in Ripley in infinitely happier, more secluded circumstances than in March 1991. The Rev. Chris Elson conducted the double christening of a now healthy six-month-old Julie and Eric's first daughter, Ruth, now rising seventeen, just a few feet from where their little brother lay beyond the stained-glass window.

The baptisms then segued into a wedding ceremony for Eric and Melia which to the entire congregation, her parents included, came as a complete surprise. So well had the secret been kept that not a single paparazzo was lurking. 'I said to Rick, "I'll bet you're the only bridegroom who's ever been pleased to find no one outside the church,"' Guy Pullen recalls.

On the first anniversary of George's death, a memorial concert of his songs performed by his closest friends took place at the Royal Albert Hall, organised by Olivia Harrison, their son Dhani, and Brian Roylance, with Eric as musical director. The cast included Ravi Shankar; Paul McCartney and Ringo Starr from his first, not altogether happy band; Jeff Lynne and Tom Petty from his later, much happier one, the Traveling Wilburys; and members of the Monty Python team whose film *Life of Brian* would have been stillborn if he hadn't mortgaged Friar Park to finance it.

The new Eric was everywhere, ruling the backstage corridors where the old Eric used to lounge passively before showtime with a drink and a cigarette. He was especially nice to twenty-four-year-old Dhani Harrison, an almost uncanny facsimile of George and a talented guitarist and songwriter in his own right. With George-like shyness, Dhani expected to make only a brief appearance, but Eric insisted on his being a full member of the illustrious outsize band.

The only slight backstage argument was over 'Something', George's one-time love letter to Pattie and the most covered of his songs. Olivia asked Eric to sing it, but Paul McCartney had long been doing it in his own concerts, plucking a ukulele George had given him. Eric wanted Paul's main contribution to be 'All Things Must Pass', which he considered the show's key moment, so they compromised by doing 'Something' as a duet. But even with McCartney and a ukulele added, the echoes of rock's strangest love-triangle remained inescapable.

With Eric, as always, the most poignant memory of his touchy, vulnerable, spiritual, sweet-and-sour friend was 'While My

Guitar Gently Weeps' and being brought in to Abbey Road studios to play on it for George after the other Beatles could scarcely be bothered. Now he was singing for George, too, backed – yes, *backed* – by Paul, and there was extra meaning in the line 'with every mistake we must surely be learning'.

After the birth of his second daughter, Ella, in January 2003, he ticked the final box in a country squire's recreations after cricket, fly-fishing and racehorse-owning by taking up shooting. The two events were not wholly unconnected: pigeons roosting in the eaves at Hurtwood had been waking his little girls with their burbling at ungodly hours of the morning.

From his teenage days as a humble beater for pheasant-shoots around Ripley, he knew several people involved with the sport. One of them was Ivor Powell, a fellow primary-school pupil who'd given him an early taste of fishing. 'I arranged for him to join a shoot over at Cranleigh,' Powell recalled. 'When he turned up, he had a gun worth about £100,000 which the makers had just let him borrow. The next time I saw him, he'd bought a pair worth about £150,000.'

True to form, he began collecting guns as obsessively as he once had guitars, cherishing them for their comparable craftsmanship in metal and wood rather than their power to knock inoffensive birds out of the sky. All were tailor-made for him by the finest English gunsmiths, Purdey or Holland & Holland, with the initials EPC in gold under their stocks, and soon there were so many that a special room had to be built at Hurtwood to display them.

Shotguns became his special passion and, in a way, another symbol of the new Eric since there now was no risk whatsoever of his plunging into an alcoholic depression and turning one on himself. The most lavishly customised were a pair of Wm. Evans twelve-bores engraved with vignettes of him playing a guitar and playing a trout on a line. But the streak of working-man puritanism he'd acquired from his step-grandfather, Jack Clapp, drew the line at that; however beautiful, he said, a gun should remain primarily a tool.

Fellow musicians like Gary Brooker, Roger Waters and Mark Knopfler had also caught the shooting bug, so there was always a chance of a kindred ribald spirit among the Gulf States princes and City financiers who made up the most desirable shoots. His hardiness in the field would have amazed Pattie, who used to plead in vain with him to take more physical exercise. 'I walk onstage and I walk off,' he would reply. 'That's enough.'

In 2004, the Queen's New Year's Honours, whose ancient, anachronistic titles nowadays descend on rock celebrities as freely as on politicians or captains of industry, upgraded him to CBE (Commander of the Most Excellent Order of the British Empire) from the OBE (Most Excellent Order of the British Empire) he received in 1994. The award was seen as a near-miss of the knighthood already bestowed on Paul McCartney, Elton John, Mick Jagger and Tom Jones – although Rod Stewart would have to sweat out nine years as a CBE before his eventual elevation to 'Sir Rod'.

The album he set out to make in 2004 with an elite studio band including Billy Preston and Andy Fairweather-Low was intended to be a reflection of his new-found domestic contentment. But contentment, unlike its opposite, is a tricky thing to convey in music and, despite the talent on hand, the project stubbornly refused to come together. Whenever work stalled, rather than let his sidemen mope around in frustration, Eric made them play a Robert Johnson song. These mounted up and eventually made an album of their own entitled *Me And Mr Johnson*.

In fact, he'd always subconsciously wanted to offer such a tribute to the long-lost, little-known genius of the Delta blues, Hendrix twenty years too early, who'd been his ultimate

exemplar since he was an art student. The album cover under-
lined that closeness with Eric seated on a bentwood chair, guitar
on knee in traditional sepia pose, respectfully clean-shaven and
besuited, beside the only two extant photographs of Johnson.
Through all his chameleon changes, that soul-shivering voice
recorded in a 1930s hotel-room had remained 'the landmark I
navigate by whenever I feel myself going adrift . . . I have always
trusted its purity, and always will.'

That same year, he organised his first Crossroads guitar festival in Dallas, Texas, featuring B. B. King, Buddy Guy, J. J. Cale
and Carlos Santana, all of whom were asked to donate an instrument to another Christie's auction in aid of the Crossroads
Centre. He himself parted with his Stratocaster, Blackie, and the
cherry-red Gibson ES 335 he'd had since he was with the Yardbirds. He visited them privately to say goodbye before they went
for $959,500 and $847,500 respectively.

In 2005, his sixtieth year, the arrival of a third daughter, Sophie,
came as some relief, for he'd grown used to little girls and had
mixed feelings about starting afresh with another boy. Melia
organised a sixtieth birthday bash for him at the Banqueting
House in Whitehall, a huge gathering of past musical colleagues
even including some of the Glands, with whom he'd made that
bizarre road-trip to Greece in 1966.

Since Cream's performance for the Rock 'n' Roll Hall of Fame
in 1993, he had often been asked if they might ever reunite in
earnest. It was a time when many other historic bands who had
dissolved in acrimony were coming back together, setting aside
their mutual hatred for the sake of the huge money on offer. The
initiative could come only from Eric, since he was the one who'd
broken up the trio in the first place. And in 2005, he decided the
moment had come.

On paper, logic seemed to be on his side. Almost forty years on, the trio were still considered the most influential British band of the Sixties after the Beatles and Stones and the model for every generation of heavy metal since. Although Jack Bruce and Ginger Baker had kept working in the interim, neither had any current pressing commitment to another band or project. There was just the question of whether sufficient amnesia could be found to blot out fist-fights, flying knives and one member getting so fed up that he walked offstage in mid-performance and went home without the other two even noticing.

Bruce, whom Eric approached first – and who might have been expected to harbour most ill-feeling from the old days– was immediately in favour. The latterly Africa-dwelling, polo-playing Baker initially refused point-blank, but was talked round. A week of concerts was booked for May at the Royal Albert Hall, where they'd made their farewell appearance in 1968, and sold out within hours.

Rehearsals took up most of the preceding month. Bruce had recently undergone major surgery and was not yet fully recovered, and Baker was suffering from back problems, so both had to build up gradually to the almost two hours onstage which for Eric had remained second nature.

Yet, apart from one 'minor skirmish' at the outset, they again seemed to hit it off well enough. Baker had mellowed sufficiently to credit the other two with the 'perfect time' he used to claim as his alone. Bruce said that hearing Baker's Sixties-whimsical monologue 'Pressed Rat And Warthog' played live almost brought a tear to his eye. Eric said how good it felt to be back with two 'perfectionists and devoted musicians'. Just before opening-night, he developed a flu virus, but insisted the show must go on.

They walked onstage to a standing ovation that continued for three minutes. The advances in sound-technology since they'd last played together meant that for the first time they could hear themselves as a balanced ensemble rather than just their own individual, combative uproar. And the chemistry was still there, if now with a faint whiff of liniment; three sexagenarians with shirts untucked around thickened waists, summoning back a whole pot-smoky world of kaftans and headbands and joss-sticks and light-shows and nudity and male dominance and Flower Power.

Eric thanked the audience for 'waiting all these years' and blamed Cream's too-brief life on 'the slings and arrows of outrageous misfortune that cut us down in our prime'.

'What do you mean?' Baker roared from behind him. '*This* is our prime!'

The reviews were mostly ecstatic ('focused power and undiminished strength', *Rolling Stone*; 'Cream are just getting re-ignited', *New York Times*; 'massive, glorious', *Daily Telegraph*) and so, despite Baker's misgivings about returning to America, it seemed only sensible to go on to a three-night engagement at Madison Square Garden, like 'the Albert' a scene of many former triumphs, the following October.

In preparation, rather like a boxer between rounds, Eric took his family and parents-in-law to his new house in Provence; then, joined by Brian Roylance, they spent a month cruising round Corsica and Sardinia in a rented luxury motor yacht named the *Va Bene*. Learning that the 150-foot craft was for sale, Eric decided to buy that, too, even though it would put him in the novel and uncomfortable position of needing to borrow money. Ripley values remained as strong as ever.

But the three Madison Square Garden concerts, for which tickets changed hands for as much as $4,000, brought an end to Cream's second honeymoon. After their cohesion at the Albert Hall, individual egos began to materialise like dinosaurs conjured from long-dormant DNA and two of them recommenced roaring at each other as Ginger Baker renewed his old complaint that Jack Bruce's over-loud bass-playing had permanently damaged his hearing. Eric was no longer willing to be piggy-in-the-middle and, besides, thought that in the Garden's huge spaces they sounded 'small and tinny'.

'I was pretty sure we'd gone as far as we could without some-one getting killed,' he would recall. And 'I [didn't] want to be part of some tragic confrontation'.

So for them there were to be no return trips to what someone had called 'the biggest ATM in the Universe'. Bruce would die in 2014, still grossly undervalued for his musicianship and one of the most individual singing voices in rock history. Baker would be recognised in a 2012 film documentary about his life, the opening scene of which showed him breaking the film-maker Jay Bulger's nose with a cane. Its all-too-appropriate title was *Beware of Mr Baker*.

What keeps them going so long after normal retirement-age, those former longhairs who were once told with such certain-ty that they'd be forgotten by the age of thirty? It's money, of course, even though they already have more than they could ever spend. It's mass adulation, a drug more potent and harder to kick than any they ever smoked or snorted. It's still being able to mesmerise an audience in the same way one did half a century ago, and the insatiable need to do so, regardless of the increasing physical toll. In 2016, Eric revealed that he now suffers from per-ipheral neuropathy, a chronic tingling sensation in the legs and hands to which guitarists are especially prone. 'It's hard work to play,' he admitted, 'and I've had to come to terms with the fact that it will not improve.'

He has the precedent of his greatest blues idols, the Muddy Wa-terses and B. B. Kings, on whom age set no limits of virtuosity, vitality – or cool. With him, too, there is a spiritual dimension, albeit never one overtly professed. Carlos Santana was not alone in thinking him capable of 'Holy Ghost Music'. His former sister-in-law, Jenny Boyd, likewise instances moments in performance when he seemed to 'touch the hem of God's garment'.

From being the nonpareil Beatles insider, Jenny went on to become a psychologist and co-author of *It's Not Only Rock 'n' Roll*, a collection of revealing interviews with major rock figures about the roots of their creativity. Eric described the moment of perfect communion with his audience which normally happened only once in every show and which for him, unlike many of his peers, was not just about rampant personal ego:

'It's not something I could experience on my own. It has to be in the company of other musicians onstage and of course with an audience. Everyone in that building or place seems to unify at one point. It's not necessarily me that's doing it; it may be another musician. But it's when you get that completely harmonic experience, when everyone is hearing exactly the same thing . . . You could call it a unity, which is a very spiritual word for me . . . the defeating aspect is that the minute you become aware of that, it's gone.'

He continues to live largely out of the headlines, seldom if ever seen on television talk shows or red carpets, more likely to figure in his local Surrey press for philanthropic gestures – like helping his old primary school in Ripley build a four-classroom extension – than in any tabloid or trade paper. Such interviews as he gives tend to be about his shooting or fishing. *Men's Journal*, for instance, received generous access when, for the second year running, he caught the biggest salmon of the summer season in Iceland.

Other than onstage, his main appearances have been by proxy in plush auction-rooms on both sides of the Atlantic. Kingston Art College proved not to have been such a waste of time when, in 2001, he paid $3.4 million for three outsize canvases by the German abstract painter Gerhard Richter, which he sold piecemeal over the next decade for a profit of around $74 million. In

2012, his Patek Philippe platinum watch, said to be one of the rarest in the world, fetched $3.6 million.

Recent years have brought the deaths of almost every important figure in his career, surrogate fathers all: Ahmet Ertegun after a fall backstage at a Rolling Stones concert in 2006, aged eighty-three; B. B. King in 2015 at the prodigious (for a bluesman) age of eighty-nine; his first two managers, Giorgio Gomelsky and Robert Stigwood, both in 2016 aged eighty-one. Among collaborators and friends, he has lost Billy Preston, publisher Brian Roylance and his former bodyguard, the reluctant heavy Alphi O'Leary. The greatest blow was Ben Palmer's death from motor neurone disease in 2017. He owed an incalculable debt to the gentle woodcarver-turned-blues pianist, not least for talking him out of quitting the music business when he left the Yardbirds.

His entourage is a tiny one for a rock star of such magnitude and its central figures have barely changed over three decades. Vivien Griffin spent fifteen years first as his secretary then his PA, only leaving with the greatest regret in 2005 when she and her husband went to live in Normandy. Nigel Carroll, his man in America, and Peter Jackson, his tour manager, have been with him since his drinking days, a distinction both wear with the pride of military campaign ribbons. 'Peter was always like Daddy to everyone on the tours,' Vivien says. 'He's very big and always completely calm. I've seen him literally enfold Eric in his arms when he had a cold and various aches and pains but still had to do a two-hour show. He put his head on Peter's shoulder and said, "I just can't face it." "Don't worry," Peter told him. "When you get out there and in front of the mike, you'll be fine."'

In 2016, Eric followed the example of other historic rock names, notably Mick Jagger and the Stones, by financing, and thereby controlling, a definitive film documentary on himself. Unusually in such circumstances, the aim was not to sanitise his life but come absolutely clean about it.

The producer/director was Lili Fini Zanuck, for whose film *Rush* he had co-written 'Tears In Heaven'. Zanuck's two-hour *Eric Clapton: Life in 12 Bars*, was premiered in 2017, a depressing, sometimes harrowing watch for its subject, but 'proof that from all of that mess I could end up as a reasonably behaved human being with a sense of responsibility'. It was dedicated to 'my friend and mentor Robin Benwell Palmer'.

In a TV interview after its premiere in Toronto, the question of his retirement came up yet again. 'Four more shows and it's over,' he replied. 'And I've been saying that since I was seventeen.'

It's appropriate to end on a sartorial note. Back before he enjoyed even a glimmer of fame, he used to travel up from Ripley to London for the Marquee club's weekly blues nights even though they ended too late for him to catch the last train home and, unable to afford even the cheapest hotel, he would have to walk the West End streets until dawn.

Often his wanderings would take him along Piccadilly to a shop named J. C. Cording & Co., purveyors of country clothing since Victorian times, in whose window a boot stood submerged in a tank of water to demonstrate its utter impermeability. So famous was this hardy boot that it became one of the London landmarks which taxi drivers had to know before receiving their licences.

Even when Eric's taste inclined more to kaftans and beads, he fantasised about a particular Cording's suit, three-piece in green herringbone with enough give in the shoulders to let a gun-user take aim in comfort. When at last he could afford to cross the shop's threshold, it felt like entering some exclusive gentleman's club.

Cording's had been struggling for years under successive corporate owners and in 2004 he became part of a management buyout, purchasing just under 50 per cent of the business and assuming the role of design director. His influence was immediately felt in a new décor of unashamed traditionalism, with sporting prints, fishing-rods and stuffed pike in glass cases.

One tradition was not included: after more years than anyone could remember, the eternally resilient boot in its water-tank disappeared from the shop window. But another great survivor had taken its place.

ACKNOWLEDGEMENTS

This book should not be regarded as an exhaustive guide to Eric's albums, tours and fluctuating band-personnel, which – other than for a few hardcore fans – would have been as boring to read as it would be to write, and would probably have filled almost as many more pages again. Those seeking the pure statistics and logistics of his career should consult his fan website, Where's Eric?, whose meticulous American custodian, Linda Wnek, I was fortunate to have among the fourteen people who fact-checked my manuscript wholly or in part. However, no non-fiction book can hope to be 100 per cent error-free and for any slips that got through, the responsibility must be mine alone.

As with my biographies of John Lennon, Paul McCartney and Mick Jagger, I must acknowledge the help of a brilliant, indefatigable research assistant in Peter Trollope. I am hugely grateful to Pattie Boyd for sharing memories of Eric – and George – that are harrowing and hilarious in equal measure, and allowing me the use of her photographs; to Eric's lifelong friend Guy Pullen, for vividly evoking his childhood in Ripley and the village's lasting hold over him; to his adorable Aunt Sylvia for memories of his mother, Pat, his grandparents, Rose and Jack Clapp, and his idiosyncratic Uncle Adrian; and to his former manager, Roger Forrester, for the first-ever detailed interview about their long business and personal relationship. My sincere thanks to Eric himself for permission to reproduce the poem he wrote as a

Hollyfield student and to quote from his letters and diaries.

For interviews and guidance, my gratitude also to Bob Adcock, Keith Best, Jenny Boyd, Ed Bicknell, Bonnie Bramlett, Pete Brown, Janet Bruce, Nigel Carroll, Alan Clayson, Jennie Cliff, Chris Dreja, Sue Cullen, Michael Eaton, Arthur Eggby, the Rev. Chris Elson, Andy Fairweather-Low, Hugh Flint, Vivien Griffin, Mike Harper, David Holt, Catherine James, Lesley-Ann Jones, Mark Knopfler, John Mayall, Ruth Mayall, Jim McCarty, Tom McGuinness, Charlotte Martin, Dutch Mills, Philippe Mora, Lorne Patterson, Gordon Perrin, the late Ivor Powell, Paul Samwell-Smith, Chris Stainton, Top Topham, Steve Turner, Chris Welch and Ray Williams.

In addition to Eric Clapton's and Pattie Boyd's autobiographies, my main printed sources have been: *Conversations with Clapton* by Steve Turner (Abacus, 1976), *Survivor* by Ray Coleman (Sidgwick & Jackson, 1985), *Yardbirds: the Ultimate Rave-Up* by Greg Russo (Crossfire Publications, 1997), *Cream* by Chris Welch (Backbeat Books, 1994), *A Rock 'n' Roll Autobiography* by Bobby Whitlock (McFarland & Co., 2010), and the Rock's Backpages site, where the best British music journalism from the past fifty years is archived. In common with all non-fiction writers, my research has been made immeasurably easier by the vast store of old TV footage instantly available on YouTube, which I cannot believe will be there, free of charge, for ever.

My main film documentary sources were: *Cream Farewell Concert* (BBC 1969); *Cream: Strange Brew* (dir. Paul Justman, 1991); *The Yardbirds* (BBC documentary, 1996); *Jack Bruce: the Man Behind the Bass* (BBC Scotland); *Beware of Mr Baker* (dir. Jay Bulger, 2012); *Legend: the Eric Clapton Story* (multi-part US documentary, 1990s); and *Eric Clapton: A Life in 12 Bars* (dir. Lili Fini Zanuck, 2017).

My warmest appreciation, as ever, to my agents and dear friends Michael Sissons in London and Peter Matson in New York, to Fiona Petheram and Alexandra Cliff at PFD, Alan

Samson and Lucinda McNeile at Orion, and Philip Marino at Little Brown. A special thank you to Miki and Lili Miller for affording me a workspace with brilliant natural light during a house-move which would otherwise have had catastrophic effects on my concentration.

This book is dedicated to Sue and Jessica, my reasons for working and living.

Philip Norman,
London 2018

INDEX